Hiking Montana

Hiking Montana

A Guide to the State's Greatest Hikes

Tenth Edition

Bill Schneider and Russ Schneider

FALCONGUIDES

GUILFORD, CONNECTICUT
HELENA, MONTANA

AN IMPRINT OF GLOBE PEQUOT PRESS

FALCONGUIDES®

FalconGuides is an imprint of Globe Pequot Press.
Falcon, FalconGuides, and Outfit Your Mind are registered trademarks of Morris Book Publishing, LLC.

Front cover photo: Two of the author's grandchildren, Josie and Casey, enjoying Stanton Lake with the Great Northern looming in the background.
Back cover photo: Hiking into the Martin Lake Basin in the Absaroka-Beartooth Wildnerness.

Project editor: Lynn Zelem
Layout: Sue Murray
Maps redesigned by Josh Comen; updated by Sue Murray © Morris Book Publishing, LLC

ISSN 1547-8947
ISBN 978-0-7627-8498-1

Printed in the United States of America
10 9 8 7 6 5 4 3 2 1

Contents

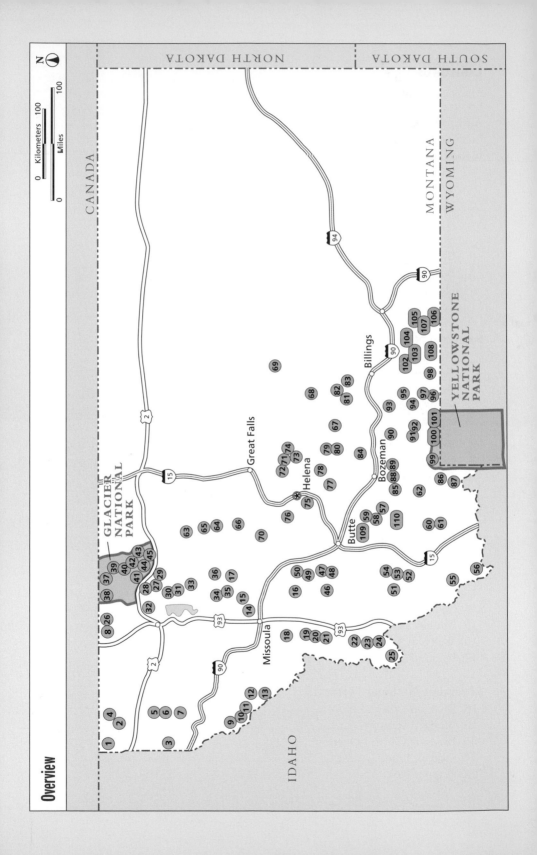

Overview

N

0 Kilometers 100
0 Miles 100

CANADA

NORTH DAKOTA

SOUTH DAKOTA

MONTANA

WYOMING

IDAHO

GLACIER NATIONAL PARK

YELLOWSTONE NATIONAL PARK

Great Falls

Helena

Billings

Bozeman

Butte

Missoula

2

15

94

90

90

93

90

15

ACKNOWLEDGMENTS

I truly wish I could adequately thank all the people who have worked throughout the past thirty-five years and ten revisions to make *Hiking Montana* a success, but I'll have to settle for listing as many as I can remember. My sincere apologizes to anybody I missed.

First and foremost, of course, are my longest-term hiking partners, my family, Marnie, Russ, Greg, and Heidi, who made hiking all those miles so enjoyable. I'm not sure it could've happened without them.

I didn't write all the hikes in the first edition of *Hiking Montana,* which came out in 1979. Several friends helped me get the book out by providing route descriptions of hikes they'd done, and I then edited them into the final manuscript. So, way back in the late 1970s, the following people were invaluable in making *Hiking Montana* possible: Wayne Avants, Don Berg, Bill Brown, Pat Caffrey, Bruce Chesler, Mike Comola, Frank Culver, Bill Cunningham, Art Foran, Herb Gloege, Linda and Tom Hurlock, Loren Kreck, Joe Mussulman, Dave Orndoff, Bob Oset, Mike Sample, Douglas Schnitzspahn, Elaine and Art Sedlack, Elaine Snyder, Fred Swanson, and John Westenberg. The late Larry Thompson provided original art for the first edition, and the late Gary Wolf did the original maps that have since been replaced by more modern cartography. I've lost track of most of these people, and sadly some are no longer with us, but it sure would be interesting to have a reunion someday with the survivors of the original *Hiking Montana.*

In later editions, the following people contributed more hikes and photos: Ted Anderson, Susan Bryan, Tom Elpel, Harry Engels, John Gatchall, Jack Johns, Kirk Koepsel, Ed Madej and Rosemary Rowe, Doug O'Looney, Don Reed, Karen Renne, Richard Terra, Mark Tokarski, Fay Valois, Bob Wagenknecht, and Kim Wilson.

In addition, I want to thank the following USDA Forest Service employees who were particularly helpful in checking facts and reviewing hike descriptions during the first nine editions: Marty Almquistt, Babete Anderson, Jaine Arnold, Crystal Avey, Elizabeth Brann, Ken Britton, Beth Burren, Marcy Butts, Allen Byrd, Jodie Canfield, Dave Cary, Marc Childress, Frank Cifala, Bob Coats, Nancy Denning, John Ericson, William Fortune, Errol Hammond, Eric Heyn, Bruce Hoflich, Daniel Hogan, Jon Jeresek, Carole Johnson, Jonathan Klein, Kraig Lang, Ernie Lundberg, Charlie Mabbot, Mark Mason, Kay McCoy, Steven Penner, Mark Petroni, Remy Pochelon, Ron Roginske, Bill Sansler, Mary Skordinsky, Bill Sprauer, Diane Teliaferro, Eric Tolf, Dan Tyers, Mike Wilson, and Ron Wiseman.

In this, the tenth edition, additional Forest Service recreation specialists and trails coordinators went over route descriptions and helped update them. They are Carl

Always expect great scenery, like this snapshot of the Clarks Fork of the Yellowstone in the Beartooths. BILL SCHNEIDER

Anderson, Gordon Ash, Ian Bardwell, Roy Barkley, Jenny Blake, Jocelyn Dodge, Alex Dunn, Nate Gassmann, Bob Gliko, Bill Goslin, Sonja Hartman, Kathryn Hickman, Colter Pence, Joy Sather, Mark Smith, Todd Stiles, Wendi Urie, Allie Wood, and Jeremy Zimmer.

As far as photography, a special thanks to Jackie Corday for her professional-quality scenic and wildflower photos. Also, thanks to Kim Schneider, Laura Schneider, Mike Harrelson, Pat Besting, and Marnie Schneider.

And, of course, I'd like to thank the 100,000 or so hikers who have purchased the book over the past thirty-five years. Without them, there obviously wouldn't be a tenth edition.

Collectively, all of the above have helped make this book something similar to a Montana tradition.

Silver Run Basin, filled with small lakes.

PREFACE

This Book Has a History

In 1979 Mike Sample, a Billings photographer who still publishes *The Montana Calendar,* and I started a book publishing company called Falcon Press. That same year we published our first book, this book, originally titled *The Hiker's Guide to Montana.*

Now, thirty-five years later, this book is still alive and well, which in the world of book publishing is unusual, if not mildly amazing. Most books have a much shorter life, starting strong and tailing off in sales until they go out of print in a few years. *Hiking Montana* has done the opposite. Sales have been fairly steady through the decades, and now, a third of a century later, it seems as popular as ever. Roughly 100,000 hikers have purchased this book through the years.

Bill and grandson Alex in the Beartooths. MARNIE SCHNEIDER

Bill's primary hiking partner, Marnie, at Lion Lake in the East Pioneers. BILL SCHNEIDER

Now, it's just one of many FalconGuides—more than 800 titles and going up every year—together making Falcon the most recognizable brand in the outdoor recreation guidebook marketplace. I'm proud to say it all started with this book.

I'm getting a little long in the tooth now, so sometime in the future, I won't be able to do those 2,000-foot grinds or 20-mile days. Hopefully, though, the family will carry on with *Hiking Montana* for a few more decades.

A family affair. *Hiking Montana* has always been a family affair. Our family has enjoyed many, many wonderful days on Montana's trails. If you look carefully at the photos in past editions and this new revision, the book takes on the image of a family album.

Of special note was the cover of the first nine editions of this book. If you have one, check out that little guy leading the pack on the front cover—my son Russ on his first big backpacking trip at age six. Now Russ is forty-something and the co-author of the last three editions of this book—although in reality the byline should read "Marnie, Bill, Heidi, Greg, and Russ Schneider."

Normally the publisher likes to change the photo on the cover of guidebooks with each new edition, but as each edition of *Hiking Montana* came around, I appealed successfully to keep this photo for personal reasons. This time, I decided it was time for a new photo to go with the new generation, especially since I could use the cover photo we did, a stunning shot of Stanton Lake with mighty Great Northern looming in the background—and Casey and Josie, Russ's children and two of my grandchildren. So, *Hiking Montana* is still a family affair, including the cover, but now you could also call it the "Grandfather's Edition."

How fortunate can a man be, watching all his children and now all his grandchildren grow up to love wilderness and hiking and be part of *Hiking Montana*?

Favorites. Through the years, the number one question I am asked when talking about hiking in Montana is, "What are your favorite hikes?" I've avoided answering

Bill, son Greg, and grandsons Alex (left) and Ryan in the Pintlers. Marnie Schneider

Russ and Casey on the summit of Great Northern. BILL SCHNEIDER

it for two reasons. First, it's a tough question with no easy answer—I like them all! Second, I didn't want to "hot spot" and create overuse, but in recent years I have become less concerned about this problem. Hikers seem to really take care of the wilderness nowadays.

So, here we go. For various personal reasons, these are my favorite hikes in this book: Northwest Peak, Valley of the Ancients, Great Northern, Three Passes, Boulder Pass, Crow Creek Falls, Crazy Mountains Crossing, Hilgard Basin, Snowcrest, Martin Lake Basin, Sky Rim, and Silver Run Plateau.

Constantly changing. This, the tenth edition, has 110 hikes, plus options and side trips for most routes. The first edition, back in 1979, had only 80 hikes. With each edition we've added new routes and for various reasons removed others, but the size of the book has gradually grown. Hikes have been removed for two reasons:

by request from land management agencies that thought having them in the book might cause some resource overuse, and, regrettably, because the hiking trails had been taken over by ATVs and turned into "troads."

Focus unchanged. Even though the book's content changed with each edition, the guiding focus has remained the same. Montana has thousands of hiking trails, of course, and many world-famous hiking areas such as Glacier and Yellowstone National Parks, the Bob Marshall and the Absaroka-Beartooth Wildernesses, and others. *Hiking Montana* includes a few hikes in these famous areas, but the main focus is lesser-known, usually more-threatened wild areas such as the Pioneers, the Gallatin Range, Snowcrest, Crazies, Swan Range, Italian Peaks, Purcells, Big Belts, and many others.

We have never attempted to comprehensively cover the trail system in any area. Instead, we have tried to introduce hikers to a new wild area with one or two choice hikes. If they like it, and they usually do, they can get a map and explore the rest of the area—and hopefully, when the time comes, support its protection.

Granddaughter Josie enjoying a hike in Glacier National Park. BILL SCHNEIDER

More than hiking. Since 1998 we've re-hiked almost all the routes in the book to check for accuracy and changing conditions. During this process it became clear that the book does not only offer a wilderness experience, it also allows hikers to experience Montana's back roads, hidden valleys, and little communities far away from any freeway—places like Pony, where they have microbrew on tap and a sculpture of a woolly mammoth across the street; or Sula, where they sell handguns at gas stations; or Roscoe, home of the mighty Grizzly Burger; or York, the Cribbage Capital of the World; or Dell, Checkerboard, Mammoth, Yaak, Moore, Glendale, Melrose, Martin City, Polaris, McLeod, Savage Lake, Pray, Fishtail, Judith Gap, Wise River, and all the rest of Montana's special, out-of-the-way communities. While researching this book, we enjoyed seeing this hidden Montana as much as the hiking. You might too.

But you might need a new vehicle. In the old days we accessed most trailheads with a small, two-wheel-drive, low-clearance vehicle, but later upgraded to my trusty Toyota Tacoma—the second one, in fact. After driving to a lot of remote trailheads during the

Backpacking with Superman, aka Bill's grandson Casey. RUSS SCHNEIDER

last decade, I'm not sure I could have made it in that little compact. It could be my imagination, but the roads seem to be getting worse in many cases, perhaps a result of steadily reducing agency budgets. So, read the "Finding the trailhead" sections carefully. We try to include information on road conditions because some vehicles probably can no longer make it to some trailheads.

The soft sell. Through the years this book has helped me prove something to myself—and hopefully, to a few of my critics. Anybody who has read my books or commentaries knows I'm a staunch advocate of preserving our remaining wildlands, but through the years I've learned that the most effective way to convince people to support the protection of our last wilderness is to introduce them to it. And this book has helped introduce many thousands of people to the wildest places in Montana, most still unprotected, and I have no doubt that most of these people now vote for more wilderness whenever they get a chance.

I've seen it happen many times. People who might not be so convinced we need any more wilderness take a hike into a remote wild area away from noise, lights, electronic gadgets, and the stress that plagues us all, and without even realizing it, the essence of wildness sneaks into that person's psyche and takes root. Anybody who spends a night or two camped at a wilderness lake, watching trout dimple the surface as the moon rises and seeing

Bill and daughter Heidi on Triple Divide Pass in Glacier National Park. BILL SCHNEIDER

the first rays of sun melting away the morning mist with loons serenading the event in the background, does not need any more convincing.

No doubt in my mind, the soft sell works better than advocacy.

Some people have criticized me for revealing some of Montana's hidden treasures and then, the theory goes, ruining them. I've written an entire commentary about this issue later in this book, but for here, let's just say that I'm proud to have helped send many thousands of people into Montana's wilderness, helping them understand that it is one of our most precious and most threatened resources.

Ahead of its time. Nowadays hikers diligently accept and practice zero-impact ethics. Now it's actually rare to find even a gum wrapper or tissue along a wilderness trail. But such was not the case thirty-five years ago. Not hardly. In the early years I personally carried many backpacks full of trash out of the wilderness, everything from frying pans to discarded tents to worn-out hiking boots, and at least a ton of aluminum foil, but no more.

This is one battle that has been won: Hikers now take care of the wilderness. And I believe *Hiking Montana* played a small, early part in winning that battle. From the first edition on, the book has advocated treating wilderness like a masterpiece of a great artist. We first called it "Touch the Land Lightly"; later it became "Zero Impact." But the message didn't change.

The big reward. I remember clearly the day about twenty years ago when my son Greg and I hiked into a remote lake in the Beartooths and came across another group of backpackers camped there, one of them sitting on a log reading *Hiking Montana*. I didn't introduce myself, but I asked him what he thought of the book, and he described how he had made it his lifelong vacation planner and was in the process of hiking every hike in the book. Through the years I've heard the same from other people—all enjoying a lifetime of adventure because of this book. They could

Bill hiking up the Columbia Mountain Trail, which would've seemed flat back in 1978 when he wrote the first edition of Hiking Montana. BILL SCHNEIDER

do it without the book, of course, but it made it easier somehow. From a guidebook author's perspective, that's the ultimate reward. Thank you to everybody who has used this book to enjoy Montana's wild country.

Something else happened. I do believe some trails became overused because they were featured in the original book, and through the years we removed a few of them from revised editions to lessen damage. But something else happened, and it was a big surprise to me. While re-hiking the trails in the book, we noticed a trend. During the past thirty-five years, timber cutting and road building have claimed many thousands of acres of roadless Montana, but without exception, the routes described in the original book have been spared.

I sincerely hope that this guidebook helped bring more and more hikers into these unprotected areas, collectively creating a constituency for preserving the area and prompting the land-managing agencies to avoid developing it. If it's true, well, on second thought, that would be my ultimate reward.

Bill Schneider

INTRODUCTION

Although we still hear claims that only the young and the rich use wilderness, quite the reverse is true. Anybody who believes such claims hasn't been out on the trails much, where everybody enjoys hiking and backpacking—all genders, ages, sizes, races, political persuasions, with no restriction on net worth. All that is needed is a small amount of physical conditioning and equipment—a minimal investment compared to almost any other form of outdoor recreation.

Like any other sport, hiking can be expensive if you choose to make it so, but it doesn't have to be. Day hiking requires little more than a pair of hiking shoes and minimal safety gear. You can even use spent running shoes and clothes you have in the closet. How many sports can you take up without at least one trip to the store to buy gear?

Overnight trips cost more, but even this expense would qualify as a small investment. The price of a two-week vacation with motel stays and restaurant meals would be sufficient to outfit an entire family for backpacking with all the gear they need for decades. After that initial investment, you can see millions of acres of spectacular, roadless country without spending another penny on equipment. You would only need to spend a few dollars for food and for transportation to the trailheads, almost always less than one night in a motel.

Not only is hiking almost free in the economic sense, but it's also almost free of the stress of modern America. Once on the trail, you can forget the tension of work, bills, noise, and the computer that doesn't work. It's all behind you for a few hours or days—especially if you do the right thing and leave all your electronic gadgets at home. You can't even hear the bad news on the radio. Hiking gives you an escape— a chance to smell the fragrance of wildflowers, to hear the wind whistling through mature pines, to see the sunset reflected in a mountain lake, to taste the waters of a clear mountain stream, to feel the tug of a native trout at the end of your fly line.

All this and more is there for the taking, and in Montana it's available in abundance. After using *Hiking Montana* to get an introduction to a hiking area, you can find nearby trails on your own, or you can go from hike to hike in this book and get a taste of all major hiking areas in the state. But be forewarned: It could mean a lifetime of backcountry adventure.

In this book we have included at least one hike in almost every roadless portion of Montana. We describe trails through well-known areas, such as Glacier and Yellowstone National Parks and the Absaroka-Beartooth and Bob Marshall Wildernesses. Yet we have been careful not to forget the many splendid areas that aren't as famous but are just as beautiful. We have included hikes for all kinds of hikers—beginners, families, and seniors, as well as experienced backpackers. There is bound to be a hike just right for you and a trailhead nearby to begin your adventure.

The route to Davis Mountain from Northwest Peak. BILL SCHNEIDER

Hikes Near Your Town

Libby: Northwest Peak, Valley of the Ancients, Fish Lakes Canyon, Baree and Bear Lakes, Cedar Lakes, Leigh Lake

Eureka: Boulder Lakes, Ten Lakes

Thompson Falls: Valley of the Ancients

Whitefish/Kalispell/Columbia Falls/Bigfork: Jewel Basin, Crater Lake, Stanton Lake, Marion Lake, Great Northern, Granite Park, The Nyack Loop, Swan Crest, Akokala Lake, Thoma Lookout

Seeley/Swan: Palisade Lake, Sapphire Lakes, Crescent Lake, Cold Lakes, Pyramid Lake

Missoula: Stuart Peak, Welcome Creek, Peterson Lake, Boulder Lake

Superior: Bonanza Lakes, Hub Lake, Heart Lake, Illinois Peak, The Great Burn

Hamilton: Stony Lake, Canyon Lake, Blodgett Canyon, Blodgett Canyon Overlook
Darby/Sula: Tin Cup Lake, Trapper Peak, Overwhich Falls, Blue Joint
Deer Lodge: Trask Lakes, Dolus Lakes, Little Blackfoot Meadows
Phillipsburg: Tamarack Lake, Heart of the Pintlers
Anaconda/Butte: Humbug Spires, Hollow Top Lake, Curly Lake, Louise Lake
Dillon: Snowcrest, Antone Peak, Grayling Lake, Torrey Lake, Sawtooth Lake, Bobcat Lakes, Selway Mountain, Italian Peaks
Ennis: Helmet and Sphinx
White Sulphur Springs: Castle Mountains
West Yellowstone: Hilgard Basin, Coffin Lakes, Sky Rim
Bozeman/Belgrade: Hyalite Lake, Emerald and Heather Lakes, Spanish Peaks, Sacajawea Peak
Livingston: Pine Creek Lake, Cottonwood Lake
Gardiner: Passage Falls, Elbow Lake, Black Canyon of the Yellowstone
Cooke City: Lady of the Lake, Aero Lakes, Rock Island Lake, Pebble Creek
Big Timber: Blue Lake, Crazy Mountains Crossing, West Boulder Meadows, Lake Plateau, Bridge Lake
Townsend: Edith-Baldy Basin, Boulder Basin, Crow Creek Falls
Three Forks: Bear Trap Canyon
Lewistown: Big Snowies Crest, Sand Point
Great Falls/Choteau/Augusta: Mount Wright, Our Lake, Devils Glen, Gateway Gorge
Browning: Three Passes, Lake Isabel, Upper Two Medicine Lake, Triple Divide Pass, Iceberg Lake, Boulder Pass
Lincoln: Heart Lake
Helena: Mann Gulch, Hanging Valley, Trout Creek Canyon, Mount Helena Ridge, Bear Prairie
Boulder: Elkhorn and Crow Peaks
Billings/Red Lodge/Columbus: Sylvan Lake, Silver Run Plateau, Island Lake, Sundance Pass, Glacier Lake, Granite Peak, Martin Lake Basin

Trail Finder

The following section attempts to help hikers find special types of trips, but please keep in mind that no hike automatically falls into any category. A long backpacking trip could be a moderate day hike or an overnighter for some hikers, just as a moderate day hike could be an extended backpacking trip for others. Nonetheless, the following trail finder should help you choose your next adventure.

Best Easy Day Hikes: Northwest Peak, Valley of the Ancients, Bonanza Lakes, Mann Gulch, Trout Creek Canyon, Blodgett Canyon Overlook, Upper Two Medicine Lake, Passage Falls, Devils Glen, Crow Creek Falls, Lady of the Lake.

Long, Hard Day Hikes for the Fit and Experienced: Tin Cup Lake, Torrey Lake, Palisade Lake, Three Passes, Bear Prairie, Stuart Peak, Edith-Baldy Basin (loop

Clarks Fork River at the trailhead. BILL SCHNEIDER

option), Great Northern, Mount Wright, Silver Run Plateau, Sky Rim, Helmet and
Sphinx, Snowcrest, Bridge Lake, Overwhich Falls.

For That First Backpacking Trip: Fish Lakes Canyon, Ten Lakes, Hub Lake,
Bonanza Lakes, Jewel Basin, Upper Two Medicine Lake, Devils Glen, Lady of the Lake.

Moderate Overnighters: Cedar Lakes, Baree and Bear Lakes, Hub Lake, Peter-
son Lake, Bobcat Lakes, Grayling Lake, Louise Lake, Curly Lake, Hollow Top Lake,
Bear Trap Canyon, Little Blackfoot Meadows, Our Lake, Granite Park, Crater Lake,
Blue Lake, Pebble Creek, Sylvan Lake, Rock Island Lake, West Boulder Meadows.

Extended Backpacking Trips: Boulder Pass, The Great Burn, Heart of the
Pintlers, The Nyack Loop, Spanish Peaks, Hilgard Basin, Black Canyon of the Yel-
lowstone, Lake Plateau, Aero Lakes, Martin Lake Basin, Crazy Mountains Crossing,
Blue Joint.

Good Base Camp Hikes: Island Lake, Martin Lake Basin, Hilgard Basin, Blue Lake, Sapphire Lakes, Jewel Basin, Edith-Baldy Basin.

For Trail Runners: Illinois Peak, Stuart Peak, Blodgett Canyon, Curly Lake, Trout Creek Canyon, Hanging Valley, Mount Helena Ridge, Pine Creek Lake, Sacajawea Peak, Castle Mountains, Sylvan Lake, Sundance Pass, Blue Joint (Divide Trail section only).

For Peak Baggers: Northwest Peak, Illinois Peak, Trapper Peak, Hollow Top Lake, Antone Peak, Snowcrest, Elkhorn and Crow Peaks, Mount Wright, Great Northern, Thoma Lookout, Sacajawea Peak, Sky Rim, Granite Peak.

For Hikers Who Want a Real Adventure: Valley of the Ancients (Sawtooth Mountain option), Boulder Pass, Lake Isabel, Snowcrest, Aero Lakes, Granite Peak, The Nyack Loop, Blue Joint.

Hikes to Waterfalls: Fish Lakes Canyon, Crow Creek Falls, Overwhich Falls, Our Lake, Hyalite Lake, Passage Falls, Iceberg Lake, Upper Two Medicine Lake, Sapphire Lakes, Blue Lake, Crazy Mountains Crossing.

Hikes You Can Do in May or June: Valley of the Ancients, Black Canyon of the Yellowstone, Bear Trap Canyon, Crow Creek Falls, Trout Creek Canyon, Bear Prairie, Mann Gulch.

Hikes Where You're Most Likely to See a Grizzly Bear: Boulder Pass, Iceberg Lake, Granite Park, Lake Isabel, The Nyack Loop, Triple Divide Pass, Three Passes, Sky Rim, Black Canyon of the Yellowstone, Pebble Creek.

Using This Guidebook

This guidebook won't answer every question you have about your planned hike, but then most people don't want to know everything before they go, lest they give up the thrill of making their own discoveries while exploring Montana's wild country. This book does provide the basic information needed to plan a successful trip, and what follows here are some tips on better using this book to help you have a more pleasant trip.

Types of Trips

Suggested hikes have been split into the following categories:

Out-and-back: Traveling to a specific destination, then retracing your steps back to the trailhead.

Loop: Starts and finishes at the same trailhead, with no (or very little) retracing of your steps. Sometimes the definition of loop is stretched to include "lollipops" and trips that involve a short walk on a road at the end of the hike to get back to your vehicle.

Shuttle: A point-to-point trip that requires two vehicles (one left at the other end of the trail) or a prearranged pickup at a designated time and place. One good way to manage the logistical problems of shuttles is to arrange for another party to start at the other end of the trail. The two parties meet at a predetermined point and trade keys. When finished with the hike, they drive each other's vehicles home.

Base camp: A point-to-point hike where you spend several nights at the same campsite, using the extra days for fishing, relaxing, or day hiking.

Difficulty Ratings

The original edition of this book listed a vast difference in the difficulty ratings from hike to hike. The good folks who helped put this book together had different levels of physical fitness and tolerance for hill climbing. We tried to standardize these ratings as much as possible for this edition.

Easy trails are suitable for any hiker, including children and seniors. They feature little or no elevation gain, no serious trail hazards, and no off-trail or faint trail route-finding.

Moderate trails are suitable for most hikers who have some experience and at least an average fitness level. These hikes may be suitable for children or seniors with above-average fitness levels. The hikes may have some short sections where the trail is difficult to follow and may include up to 1,500 feet in elevation gain.

Strenuous trails are suitable for experienced hikers with above-average fitness levels. These trails may be difficult to follow or feature off-trail routes requiring serious map and compass skills. These hikes almost all have serious elevation gain and possibly dangerous river fords or other hazards.

Distances

It's almost impossible to get precisely accurate distances for most trails. The distances used in this guidebook are based on a combination of actual experience hiking the trails, distances stated on trail signs, databases provided by agencies, and estimates from topographic maps and GPS tracks. Keep in mind that distance is often less important than difficulty—a rough, 2-mile cross-country trek can take longer than 5 or 6 miles on a good trail. Also, keep mileage estimates in perspective because they're almost always slightly off. Almost all trail signs, for example, use estimates in whole miles. You've probably seen a sign saying it's 5 miles to a lake, but what's the chance that it's exactly 5 miles? Have you ever seen a sign saying it's 5.34 miles to the lake? Should we fret about it?

Trail Running

Many hikes are rated according to suitability for trail running. In reality there is no real difference between a trail-running guidebook and a hiking guidebook, but the two criteria we used to recommend some routes for trail running were trail surface and bear awareness. If a trail was not too rocky and rough and went through country where the likelihood of surprising a bear was minimal, we recommended it for trail running—keeping in mind, of course, that you could run into a bear on any route in this book and that all trails have some rough sections.

Special Regulations and Permits

Land-managing agencies have special regulations for hikers and backcountry trail riders on many trails. In some cases the regulations apply throughout a large area, but

Hiking down into Martin Lake Basin in the Beartooths. BILL SCHNEIDER

in other cases they apply to ranger districts, specific trails, or even sections of trails. Check with the appropriate agency before you leave on your trip, and be sure to read and follow any special regulations posted on the information board at the trailhead. Agencies don't come up with regulations to inconvenience backcountry visitors. Instead, the regulations are designed to promote sharing and preservation of the wilderness and make your trip as safe as possible.

In Montana we're lucky enough to not need permits in most areas. In this book, only hikes in Glacier and Yellowstone National Parks require you to get a permit, and then only for overnight trips. You can take a day hike in the parks without a permit.

Best Time to Hike

The best months to hike in Montana are usually July, August, and September. Snow lingers in the high country in most places until at least June and often into mid-July. The snow gives up some routes earlier in the year, however. Check the Trail Finder for these routes. Montana weather being what it is, however, you should be prepared for winter weather every day of the year and especially when hiking before and after the traditional July through September season.

Maps

USGS topographic quadrangles have contour lines of the landscape and identify landmarks and landscape features such as lakes, streams, and peaks. Most quadrangles usually have contour intervals of 40 feet, cover an area of approximately 9 miles by 7 miles, and are on a scale of 1:24,000—that is, 1 inch on the map is equivalent to 24,000 inches on the ground. Although they're getting harder and harder to find with the advent of electronic mapping programs, you can still purchase topographic maps at some sporting goods stores, and you can order directly from the USGS.

US Geological Survey
Denver Federal Center
Box 25286
Denver, CO 80225
(303) 202-4700
www.usgs.gov

Most hikers have switched over to electronic mapping programs or online mapping services, which offer extra services and are usually cheaper. Keep in mind, though, that most of these programs and websites still use the same USGS topographic data as a basis for their maps, and the USGS hasn't updated many of these maps for fifty or more years.

Some newer Forest Service maps have contour lines, but older maps do not and instead focus on roads, lakes, peaks, rivers, trails, and other major landmarks. They have trail and road numbers for all current Forest Service roads and trailheads, which are especially helpful in reaching the trailhead. (Beyond finding the trailhead, however, a topo map is better.) Forest Service maps are also the most up-to-date maps for hiking in Montana. They're available at district offices, ranger stations, and most regional sporting goods stores.

Also, check your local library for a collection of topographic and Forest Service maps. Photocopies of these maps are just as good as the originals if kept dry—and much easier on your budget.

The maps in this guidebook were designed to assist in planning your hike, finding trailheads, and giving you a general idea of the route. They aren't intended to be your only map, so before you head for the trailhead, make sure you have a topographic or other detailed map.

Getting to the Trailhead

Make sure your vehicle is in good condition and appropriate for the roads to the trailhead; check the "Finding the trailhead" section of each hike for vehicle

Fireweed always follows a forest fire. BILL SCHNEIDER

recommendations. Have a full tank of gas and carry basic emergency equipment, such as a shovel, an ax, a saw, extra water, emergency food, and warm clothing. If you're unsure about road conditions, check with the appropriate agency in advance.

Elevation Profiles

The hike descriptions in this book include elevation profiles. These charts represent the changes in elevation over the distance of the hike. The vertical axis shows the elevation in feet; the horizontal axis shows the distance in miles. Because these scales don't vary from hike to hike, some profiles may show gradual hills to be steep and steep hills to be gradual. Instead of simply glancing at the profile and forming an opinion on how strenuous a hike might be, pay close attention to the vertical and horizontal scales, which give you a better understanding of the true difficulty of the hike. You can also compare the grade and distance to routes you've already hiked. Hikes without elevation charts have little or no elevation gain.

Rating the Hills

In the process of publishing dozens of hiking guides, FalconGuides has been trying to come up with a consistent rating system to help hikers determine how difficult those "big hills" really are. Such a system would help hikers decide how far they wanted to hike that day or even whether they wanted to take that trail at all. In the past, guidebook authors have described hills to the best of their ability, but subjectively. What is a big hill to one hiker might be a slight upgrade to the next.

Also, it isn't only going up that matters. Some hikers hate going down steep hills and the knee problems that go along with descending with a big pack. These "weak-kneed" hikers might want to avoid Category 1 and Category H hills.

This new hill rating system combines the elevation gain and the length of that section of trail with a complicated mathematical formula to come up with a numerical hill rating similar to the system used by cyclists. The system only works for climbs of a half mile or longer, not short, steep hills.

Here is a rough description of the categories, listed from easiest to hardest:

Category 5: A slight upgrade. Hardly worth mention, and we usually don't.

Category 4: Usually within the capabilities of any hiker.

Category 3: A well-conditioned hiker might describe a Category 3 climb as "gradual," but a poorly conditioned hiker might complain about the steepness. It's definitely not steep enough to deter you from hiking the trail, but these climbs will slow you down.

Category 2: Most hikers would consider these "big hills," steep enough, in some cases, to make hikers choose an alternative trail, but not the real lung-busting, calf-stretching hills.

Category 1: These are among the steepest hills. If you have heart or breathing problems, or you simply dislike climbing big hills, you might look for an alternative trail.

Category H: These are hills that make you wonder if the person who laid out the trail was on drugs. Any trail with a Category H hill is steeper than any trail should be. (Incidentally, *H* roughly translates as "Horrible.")

The hills in this book are rated according to the following chart. Some climbs are rated in the hike descriptions of this book, but if not included (or to use this formula in other hiking areas), get the mileage and elevation gain off the topo map and look them up on this chart.

Following Faint Trails

Trails that receive infrequent use often fade away in grassy meadows, on ridges, or through rocky sections. If the trail fades away before you, don't panic. These sections are usually short, and you can often look ahead to see where the trail goes. Focus on the trail ahead and don't worry about being off the trail for a short distance. Also watch for other indicators that you're indeed on the right route, even if the trail isn't clearly visible. Watch for cairns, blazes, downfall cut with saws, paths cleared through thick timber, and trees with the branches whacked off on one side. Nowadays land managers discourage

FALCON HILL RATING CHART

ELEVATION GAIN (in feet)	DISTANCE (in miles)	0.5	1.0	1.5	2.0	2.5	3.0	3.5	4.0	4.5	5.0	5.5	6.0
	200	4.2	5.0	5.4	5.5	5.6	5.6	5.7	5.7	5.7	5.7	5.7	5.7
	300	3.3	4.5	4.9	5.2	5.3	5.4	5.5	5.5	5.5	5.5	5.6	5.6
	400	1.8	4.0	4.5	4.8	5.1	5.2	5.3	5.3	5.4	5.4	5.4	5.4
	500	1.0	3.5	4.2	4.5	4.7	5.0	5.1	5.2	5.2	5.2	5.3	5.3
	600	H	3.0	3.8	4.2	4.4	4.6	4.9	4.9	5.0	5.1	5.1	5.1
	700	H	2.5	3.4	3.9	4.2	4.3	4.5	4.8	4.9	4.9	4.9	5.0
	800	H	1.4	3.1	3.6	3.9	4.1	4.2	4.3	4.7	4.7	4.8	4.9
	900	H	H	2.7	3.3	3.6	3.9	4.0	4.1	4.2	4.6	4.7	4.7
	1,000	H	H	2.3	2.9	3.4	3.6	3.8	3.9	4.0	4.1	4.5	4.6
	1,100	H	H	1.9	2.7	3.1	3.4	3.6	3.7	3.8	3.9	3.9	4.5
	1,200	H	H	H	2.4	2.8	3.1	3.4	3.5	3.6	3.7	3.8	3.9
	1,300	H	H	H	2.1	2.6	2.9	3.2	3.3	3.5	3.5	3.6	3.7
	1,400	H	H	H	1.8	2.3	2.7	2.9	3.1	3.3	3.4	3.5	3.5
	1,500	H	H	H	1.6	2.1	2.4	2.7	2.9	3.1	3.2	3.3	3.3
	1,600	H	H	H	H	1.9	2.2	2.3	2.7	2.9	2.9	3.1	3.2
	1,700	H	H	H	H	1.7	1.9	2.3	2.5	2.7	2.8	2.9	3.0
	1,800	H	H	H	H	1.5	1.8	2.0	2.3	2.5	2.6	2.7	2.8
	1,900	H	H	H	H	1.3	1.7	1.9	2.1	2.3	2.4	2.6	2.6
	2,000	H	H	H	H	H	1.5	1.7	1.9	2.1	2.2	2.4	2.5
	2,100	H	H	H	H	H	1.3	1.6	1.8	1.9	2.0	2.2	2.3
	2,200	H	H	H	H	H	1.2	1.4	1.6	1.8	1.9	1.9	2.1
	2,300	H	H	H	H	H	1.0	1.3	1.5	1.7	1.8	1.9	1.9
	2,400	H	H	H	H	H	H	1.2	1.4	1.5	1.6	1.8	1.8
	2,500	H	H	H	H	H	H	1.0	1.2	1.4	1.5	1.6	1.7
	2,600	H	H	H	H	H	H	H	1.1	1.3	1.4	1.5	1.6
	2,700	H	H	H	H	H	H	H	H	1.1	1.3	1.4	1.5
	2,800	H	H	H	H	H	H	H	H	H	1.1	1.3	1.4
	2,900	H	H	H	H	H	H	H	H	H	1.0	1.2	1.3
	3,000	H	H	H	H	H	H	H	H	H	H	1.0	1.1

the use of blazes, and rangers use small metal reflective markers instead. However, you can still see old blazes along many trails in Montana. If you rely on blazes to follow a faint trail, make sure you follow only official blazes, which are shaped like an upside-down exclamation point, instead of blazes made by hunters, outfitters, or other hikers.

Sharing

We all prefer our own wilderness area all to ourselves, but that happens only in our dreams. Lots of people use Montana's trails, and to make everyone's experience better, we all must work at politely sharing the wilderness. For example, hikers must share trails with trail riders. Both groups have every right to be on the trail, so please do not let it become a confrontation.

Keep in mind that horses and mules are much less maneuverable than hikers, so it becomes the hiker's responsibility to yield the right-of-way. All hikers should stand on the downhill side of the trail, well off-trail for safety's sake, and quietly let the stock pass. Stand on the downside of the trail so if the horses spook, they'll go uphill, which is safer for them, as opposed to taking the chance of spooking them downhill and perhaps tumbling down a steep grade.

Another example of politely sharing the wilderness is choosing your campsite. If you get to a popular lake late in the day and all the good campsites are occupied, don't crowd in on another camper. Doing so is aggravating to others, as these sites right-fully go on a first-come, first-served basis. If you're late, you have the responsibility to move on or take a less desirable site a respectable distance away from other campers.

Zero Impact

Going into a national park or wilderness area is like visiting a famous museum. You wouldn't leave your mark on an art treasure in the museum. If everybody going through the museum left one little mark, the piece of art would be quickly destroyed—and of what value is a big building full of trashed art? The same goes for a pristine wilderness, which is as magnificent as any masterpiece. If we all left just one little mark on the landscape, the wilderness would soon be despoiled.

A wilderness can accommodate a lot of human use as long as everybody behaves. But a few thoughtless or uninformed visitors can ruin it for everybody who follows. All wilderness users have a responsibility to know and follow the rules of zero-impact camping. You can find these guidelines and more, including the most updated research, in the FalconGuide called *Leave No Trace*. Another great source is www.lnt.org.

Nowadays most wilderness users want to walk softly, but some aren't aware that they have poor manners. Often their actions are dictated by the outdated habits of a past generation of campers who cut green boughs for evening shelters, built campfires with fire rings, and dug trenches around tents. In the 1950s these "camping rules" may have been acceptable. But they leave long-lasting scars, and today such behavior is unacceptable. The wilderness is shrinking, and the number of users is mushrooming. More and more camping areas show unsightly signs of heavy use.

Always set up a zero-impact camp. BILL SCHNEIDER

Consequently, a new code of ethics is growing out of the necessity of coping with the unending waves of people who want a perfect wilderness experience. Today we all must leave no clues that we have gone before. Canoeists can look behind the canoe and see no sign of their passing. Hikers—and all other outdoor recreationists for that matter—should have the same goal. Enjoy the wilderness, but make it a zero-impact visit.

FalconGuides' Zero-Impact Principles

- Leave with everything you brought in.
- Leave no sign of your visit.
- Leave the landscape as you found it.

Most of us know better than to litter—in or out of the wilderness. Be sure you leave nothing, regardless of how small it is, along the trail or at the campsite. In addition to

The campfire, always a bonus for the backpacker, but usually precluded by either regulations or zero-impact ethics. BILL SCHNEIDER

packing out everything you carried in, pick up any trash left by others.
In addition, please follow this advice:

- Follow the main trail. Avoid cutting switchbacks and walking on vegetation beside the trail.
- Don't pick up "souvenirs" such as rocks, antlers, or wildflowers. The next person wants to see them too, and collecting such souvenirs violates national park regulations.
- Avoid making loud noises that may disturb others. Remember, sound travels easily to the other side of a lake. Be courteous.
- Carry a lightweight trowel to bury human waste 6 to 8 inches deep and pack out used toilet paper. Keep human waste at least 300 feet from any water source.

- Finally, and perhaps most important, strictly follow the pack-in/pack-out rule. If you carry something into the backcountry, consume it or carry it out.

Leave no trace of your passing—then put your ear to the ground in the wilderness and listen carefully. Thousands of people coming behind you are thanking you for your courtesy and good sense.

Make It a Safe Trip

Perhaps the best single piece of safety advice I can offer you is this: Be prepared! For starters, that means carrying survival and first-aid materials, proper clothing, a compass or GPS unit, and topographic maps—and knowing how to use them.

Perhaps the second-best piece of safety advice is to tell somebody where you're going and when you plan to return. Pilots file flight plans before every trip, and anybody venturing into a blank spot on a map should do the same. File your "flight plan" with a friend or relative before taking off.

Close behind your flight plan and being prepared with proper equipment is physical conditioning. Being fit not only makes wilderness travel more fun, it also makes it safer.

Here are a few more safety tips:

- Check the weather forecast. Be careful not to get caught at high altitude by a bad storm or along a stream in a flash flood. Watch cloud formations closely so that you don't get stranded on a ridgeline during a lightning storm. Avoid traveling during prolonged periods of cold weather.
- Avoid traveling alone in the wilderness.
- Keep your party together.
- Study basic survival and first-aid skills before leaving home.
- Don't eat wild plants unless you have positively identified them and know they are safe to consume.
- Before you leave for the trailhead, find out as much as you can about the route, especially any potential hazards.
- Don't exhaust yourself or other members of your party by traveling too far or too fast. Let the slowest person set the pace.
- Don't wait until you're confused to look at your maps. Follow them as you go along, from the moment you start moving up the trail, so you have a continual fix on your location, especially when hiking off-trail.
- If you get lost, don't panic. Sit down and relax for a few minutes while you carefully check your topo map and take a reading with your compass or GPS unit. Confidently plan your next move. It's often smart to retrace your steps until you find familiar ground, even if you think it might lengthen your trip. Lots of people get temporarily lost in the wilderness and survive—usually by calmly and rationally dealing with the situation.

- .Stay clear of all wild animals.
- Always carry both a first-aid kit and survival kit.

Last but not least, don't forget that the best defense against unexpected hazards is knowledge. Read up on the latest in wilderness safety information.

Lightning: You Might Never Know What Hit You

The high-altitude topography of the Northern Rockies is prone to sudden thunderstorms, especially in July and August. If a lightning storm catches you in the open, remember:

- Lightning can travel far ahead of a storm, so be sure to take cover before the storm hits.
- Don't try to make it back to your vehicle ahead of the storm. It isn't worth the risk. Instead, seek shelter even if it's only a short distance back to the trailhead. Lightning storms usually don't last long, and from a safe vantage point, you might enjoy the sights and sounds.
- Be especially careful not to get caught on a mountaintop or exposed ridge, under large solitary trees, in the open, or near standing water.
- Seek shelter in a low-lying area, ideally in a dense stand of small, uniformly sized trees.
- Stay away from anything that might attract lightning, such as metal tent poles, graphite fishing rods or trekking poles, or pack frames.
- Get in a crouch position and place both feet firmly on the ground.
- If you have a pack (without a metal frame) or a sleeping pad with you, put your feet on it for extra insulation against an electrical shock.
- When hiking with a group, don't walk or huddle together. Instead, stay 50 feet or more from each other, so if somebody gets hit by lightning, others in your party can give first aid.
- If you're in a tent, stay there, in your sleeping bag with your feet on your sleeping pad.

Hypothermia: The Silent Killer

Be aware of the danger of hypothermia—a condition in which the body's internal temperature drops below normal. It can lead to mental and physical collapse and death.

Hypothermia is caused by exposure to cold and is aggravated by wetness, wind, dehydration, and exhaustion. The moment you begin to lose heat faster than your body produces it, you're suffering from exposure. Your body starts involuntary exercise, such as shivering, to stay warm and makes involuntary adjustments to preserve normal temperature in vital organs, restricting blood flow in the extremities. Both responses drain your energy reserves. The only way to stop the drain is to reduce the degree of exposure.

Hiking in the high-altitude Beartooths and watching the storm on the horizon. BILL SCHNEIDER

Be wary of trendy "ultralight" backpacking ideas and equipment. To guard against hypothermia, you need a good tent (double-walled), rain gear, a sleeping bag, and a set of always-dry clothes.

With full-blown hypothermia, as energy reserves are exhausted, cold reaches the brain, depriving you of good judgment and reasoning power. And you aren't aware of what's happening. You lose control of your hands. Your internal temperature slides downward. Without treatment this slide leads to stupor, collapse, and death.

To defend against hypothermia, stay dry. When clothes get wet, they lose most of their insulating value. Wool loses relatively less heat; cotton, down, and some synthetics lose more. Choose rain clothes that cover the head, neck, body, and legs and provide good protection against wind-driven rain. Most hypothermia cases develop in air temperatures between 30 and 50 degrees Fahrenheit, but hypothermia can also develop in warmer temperatures, especially if you become exhausted or dehydrated, or both.

If your party is exposed to wind, cold, and wet, automatically start thinking hypo-thermia. Watch yourself and others for these symptoms: uncontrollable fits of shivering; vague, slow, slurred speech; memory lapses; incoherence; immobile, fumbling hands; frequent stumbling or a lurching gait; drowsiness (to sleep is to die); apparent exhaustion; and inability to get up after a rest. When a member of your party has hypothermia, he or she may deny any problem. Believe the symptoms, not the victim. Even mild symptoms demand treatment, as follows:

- Get the victim out of the wind and rain.
- If the victim is only mildly impaired, give him or her warm drinks. Get the victim into warm clothes and a warm sleeping bag. Place well-wrapped water bottles filled with heated water close to the victim.
- If the victim is badly impaired, attempt to keep him or her awake. Put the victim in a sleeping bag with another person, trying for as much skin-to-skin contact as possible, especially in the torso area. If you have a double bag, put two warm people in with the victim.

Fording Large Streams

When done correctly and carefully, crossing a big stream or river can be safe, but you must know your limits. So be smart and cautious. There are cases where you simply should turn back. Even if only one member of your party (such as a child) might not be able to follow taller, stronger members, you still might not want to try a risky ford. Never be embarrassed about being overly cautious and turning back.

One key to fording rivers safely is confidence. If you aren't a strong swimmer, you should become one. Not only does being a strong swimmer allow you to safely get across a river that's a little deeper and stronger than you thought, but it also gives you the confidence to avoid panic. Like getting lost, panic can easily make a bad situation worse.

Another way to build confidence is to practice. Find a river near your home and carefully practice crossing it both with a pack and without one. You can also start with a smaller stream and work up to a major river. After you've become a strong swimmer, get used to swimming in the current.

Here is some sound advice for safely fording rivers in the Northern Rockies:

- When you reach the ford, carefully assess the situation. Don't automatically cross at the point where the trail comes to the stream and head on a straight line for the marker on the other side. A mountain river can reform itself every spring during high runoff, so a ford that was safe last year might be too deep this year. Study upstream and downstream and look for a place where the stream widens in a riffle and the water is not more than waist deep on the shortest member of your party. The inside of a meander sometimes makes a safe ford, but a long shallow section can be followed by a short deep section next to the outside of the bend where the current picks up speed and carves out a deep channel.

- Before starting any serious ford, make sure your matches, camera, billfold, clothes, sleeping bag, and other items you must keep dry are in watertight bags.
- In the Northern Rockies most streams are cold, so have dry clothes ready for when you reach the other bank to minimize the risk of hypothermia, especially on a cold, rainy day.
- Minimize the amount of time you spend in the water, but don't rush. Go slowly and deliberately, taking one step at a time, being careful to get each foot securely planted before lifting the other foot.
- Take a 45-degree angle instead of going straight across, following a riffle line if possible.
- Don't try a ford with bare feet. Wear hiking boots without socks, sneakers, or tightly strapped sandals.
- Stay sideways with the current. Turning upstream or downstream greatly increases the force of the current.
- In some cases two or three people can cross together, locking forearms, with the strongest person on the upstream side and the weakest on the downstream side.
- If you have a choice, ford in the early morning when the stream isn't as deep. In the mountains, cool evening temperatures slow snowmelt and reduce the water flow into the rivers.
- On small streams a sturdy walking stick or trekking pole used on the upstream side for balance helps prevent a fall, but in a major river with a fast current, a stick or pole offers little help. If you use one, make sure you have both the stick and one foot firmly planted before lifting the other foot.
- Loosen the belt and straps on your pack. If you fall or get washed downstream, a waterlogged pack can lead to drowning by anchoring you to the bottom, so you must be able to easily get out of your pack. For a short period your pack might actually help you become buoyant and float across a deep channel, but in a minute or two, it could become an anchor.
- If you're 6 feet 4 inches tall and a strong swimmer, you might feel secure crossing a big river, but you might have children or vertically challenged hikers in your party. In this case the strongest person can cross first and string a line across the river to aid those who follow. This line (with the help of a carabiner) can also be used to float packs across instead of taking a chance of a waterlogged pack dragging somebody under. (If you know about the ford in advance, you can pack along a lightweight rubber raft or inner tube for this purpose.) Depending on the size and strength of the stream, you might also want to carry children.
- Be prepared for the worst. Sometimes circumstances can arise where you simply must cross instead of going back, even though the ford looks dangerous. Also, you can underestimate the depth of the channel or the strength of the current,

especially after a thunderstorm when a muddy river hides its true depth. In these cases, whether you like it or not, you might be swimming. It's certainly recommended to avoid these situations, but if it happens, be prepared. Don't panic. Try not to swim directly across. Instead, pick a long angle and gradually cross or swim to the other side, taking 100 yards or more to finally cross. If your pack starts to drag you down, get out of it immediately, even if you have to abandon it. If you lose control and get washed downstream, go feet first so that you don't hit your head on rocks or logs.

- And finally, be sure to report any dangerous ford as soon as you finish your trip.

Be Bear Aware

They're everywhere! Every hike in this book passes through bear country, and with the expansion of the grizzly population in recent years, that usually means both black bears and grizzlies, so always, on every hike, be bear aware.

Here are some of the basics, excerpted from my book *Bear Aware*. If you want even more information, buy a copy of this little, "packable" guide to bear country behavior—it's small enough to take with you.

Hiking in Bear Country

Nobody likes surprises, and bears dislike them too. The majority of bear maulings occur when a hiker surprises a bear, now called "defensive encounters." Therefore it's vital to do everything possible to avoid these surprise meetings. Perhaps the best way is to know the six-part system. If you follow these six rules, the chance of encountering a bear on the trail sinks to the slimmest possible margin.

- Be alert at all times.
- Watch the wind.
- Go with a group and stay together.
- Stay on the trail.
- Hike in the middle of the day.
- Make noise.

No substitute for alertness. As you hike, watch ahead and to the sides. Don't fall into the all-too-common and particularly nasty habit of fixating on the trail 10 feet ahead. It's especially easy to do when dragging a heavy pack up a long hill or when carefully watching your step on a rocky or heavily eroded trail.

Using your knowledge of bear habitat and habits, be especially alert in areas most likely to be frequented by bears, such as avalanche chutes, berry patches, streambeds, and stands of whitebark pine.

Watch carefully for bear signs and be especially watchful (and noisy) if you see any. If you see a track or a scat but it doesn't look fresh, pretend it's fresh. Bears obviously frequent this area.

A sign at the Welcome Creek Trailhead, but it could be anywhere in western Montana, so always assume you're in bear country. Bill Schneider

Watch the wind. The wind can be a friend or a foe. The strength and direction of the wind can make a significant difference in your chances of an encounter with a bear. When the wind is blowing at your back, your smell travels ahead of you, alerting any bear that might be on or near the trail ahead. Conversely, when the wind blows in your face, your chances of a surprise meeting with a bear increase, so make more noise and be more alert.

A strong wind can also be noisy and limit a bear's ability to hear you coming. If a bear can't smell or hear you, the chances of an encounter greatly increase, so watch the wind and take extra precautions.

Safety in numbers. There have been very few instances where a large group has had an encounter with a bear. On the other hand, a large percentage of hikers mauled by bears were hiking alone. Large groups naturally make more noise and put out more smell and probably appear more threatening to bears. In addition, if you're hiking alone and get injured, there is nobody to go for help. For these reasons rangers often recommend parties of four or more hikers when going into bear country.

If the large party splits up, the advantage goes away, so stay together. If you're on a family hike, keep the kids from running ahead. If you're in a large group, keep the stronger members from going ahead or weaker members from lagging behind. The best way to prevent this natural separation is to ask one of the slowest members of the group to lead. This tactic keeps everybody together.

Stay on the trail. Although bears use trails, they don't often travel on them during midday when hikers commonly use them. Through generations of associating trails with people, bears probably expect to find hikers on trails, especially during midday.

On the other hand, bears probably don't expect to find hikers off trails. Bears rarely settle down in a day bed right along a heavily used trail. However, if you wander around in thickets off the trail, you're more likely to stumble into an occupied day bed or cross paths with a traveling bear.

Sleep late. Bears—and most other wildlife—usually aren't active during midday, especially on a hot summer day. Wild animals are most active around dawn and dusk. Therefore, hiking early in the morning or late in the afternoon increases your chances of seeing wildlife, including bears. Likewise, hiking during the middle of a hot August day greatly reduces the chance of an encounter.

Be noisy. Perhaps the best way to avoid a surprise meeting with a bear is to make sure the bear knows you're coming, so make lots of noise. Some experts think metallic noise is superior to human voices, which can be muffled by natural conditions, but the important point is to make lots of noise, regardless of what kind. One research project found snapping twigs scared bears more than any other sound; clapping or smacking a stick against trailside trees and rocks roughly resembles the sound of branches breaking.

In addition to the aforementioned six rules, there are other precautions you can take to avoid an encounter.

Running. Many avid runners like to get off paved roads and running tracks and onto backcountry trails. But running on trails in bear country can be seriously hazardous to your health. Bears can't hear you coming and you approach them faster than expected, and, of course, it's nearly impossible to be fully alert when you have to watch the trail closely to keep from falling.

Leave the night to the bears. Like running on trails, hiking at night also can be very risky. Bears are more active after dark, and you can't see them until it's too late. If you're caught out at night, be sure to make lots and lots of noise, and remember that bears commonly travel on hiking trails at night.

You can be dead meat too. If you see or smell a carcass of a dead animal when hiking, immediately vacate the area. Don't let your curiosity keep you near the carcass a second longer than necessary. Bears commonly hang around a carcass, guarding it and feeding on it for days until it's completely consumed. A bear can easily interpret your presence as a threat to its food supply, which can result in an attack.

If you see a carcass ahead of you on the trail, don't go any closer. Instead, abandon your hike and return to the trailhead. If the carcass is between you and the trailhead, take a very long detour around it, upwind from the carcass, making lots of noise. Be sure to report the carcass to the local ranger. Doing so might prompt a temporary trail

Recently recycled huckleberries, a sure sign you're in bear country. BILL SCHNEIDER

closure or special warnings and prevent injury to other hikers. Rangers will, in some cases, go in and drag the carcass away from the trail.

Cute, cuddly, and lethal. If you see a bear cub, don't go even one inch closer to it. It might seem abandoned, but it isn't. Mother bear is close by, and female bears fiercely defend their young.

Bear pepper spray doesn't do you any good in your pack. Always carry bear pepper spray and know how to use it, but don't bury it in your pack. Such protection won't do you any good if you can't have it ready to fire in one or two seconds. Keep it as accessible as possible. Most bear spray comes in a holster or conveniently attaches to your belt or pack. Before hitting the trail, read the directions carefully and test fire the spray.

"But I didn't see any bears." You know how to be safe: Walk up the trail constantly clanging two metal pans together, and you almost certainly won't see any bears. But you probably won't enjoy your "wilderness experience" either. Didn't you leave the city to get away from noise and stress? Yes, you can be very safe, but how safe do you want to be and still be able to enjoy your trip? It's a balancing act. First, be knowledgeable, and then decide how far you want to go. Everybody has to make his or her own personal choice.

Here's another conflict. If you do everything listed here, you most likely will not see any bears—or any deer, moose, eagles, or any other wildlife. Again, you make the choice. If you want to be as safe as possible, follow the rules of bear awareness reli giously. If you want to see wildlife, including bears, take all of this advice in reverse, but then you're increasing your chances of an encounter instead of decreasing it.

Camping in Bear Country

Staying overnight in bear country is not dangerous, but it adds a slight additional risk to your trip. The main difference is the presence of more food, cooking, and garbage. Plus, you're in bear country at night when bears are usually most active. Once again, however, following a few basic rules greatly minimizes this risk.

Storing food and garbage. If the campsite doesn't have a bearproof storage box or bear pole, be sure to set one up or at least locate one before it gets dark. It's not only difficult to store food at night, but also easier to overlook a juicy morsel on the ground. Store food in airtight, waterproof bags to prevent food odors from circulating throughout the forest. For double protection, put food and garbage in securely closed ziplock bags and then seal tightly in a larger plastic bag.

The illustrations in this chapter depict three popular methods for hanging food and garbage. In all cases, try to get food and garbage at least 10 feet off the ground.

Hanging food and garbage between two trees.

Hanging food and garbage over a tree branch.

Hanging food and garbage over a leaning tree.

FOOD STORAGE ORDER

The national forests in Montana have issued a legally binding "Food Storage Order," which is posted at most trailheads.

A Food Storage Order requires that:

- Food must be actively attended while transporting, preparing, and eating it.
- All attractants must be stored in a locked bear-resistant container or a closed vehicle constructed of solid, non-pliable material *or*
- Suspended at least 10 feet clear of the ground at all points and 4 feet horizontally from supporting tree or pole.

The Food Storage Order prohibits:

- Camping within 0.5 mile of any animal carcass or within 100 yards of any acceptably stored animal carcass.
- Leaving an animal carcass unless it is (a) at least 0.5 mile from any sleeping area, trail, or recreation site or (b) at least 100 yards from any sleeping area, trail, or recreation area and acceptably stored or (c) being eaten, being prepared for eating, or being transported.

For questions and clarification, call your local Forest Service office. To learn more about bear-resistant containers or the Interagency Grizzly Bear Committee, visit www.igbconline.org.

Special equipment. It's not really that special, but one piece of equipment you definitely need is a good supply of zip-locked bags. This handy invention is perfect for keeping food smell to a minimum and helps keep food from spilling on your pack, clothing, or other gear.

Take a special bag for storing food. The bag must be sturdy and waterproof. You can get "dry" bags at most outdoor specialty stores, but you can get by with a trash compactor bag. Regular garbage bags can break and leave your food spread on the ground.

You also need 50 feet of nylon cord to hang food and garbage. Go light; parachute cord will usually suffice unless you plan to hang large quantities of food and gear (which might be the case on a long backpacking excursion with a large group).

You can also buy a small pulley system to make hoisting a heavy load easier, but it's only necessary if you have a massive load to hang.

What to hang. To be as safe as possible, store everything that has any food smell. This includes cooking gear, eating utensils, bags used to keep food in your pack, all garbage, toiletries, even clothes with food smells on them. If you spilled something on your clothes, change into other clothes for sleeping and hang clothes with food smells with the food and garbage. If you take these items into the tent, you aren't separating

Many campsites now have food storage facilities; be sure to use them. COURTESY OF NPS

your sleeping area from food smells. Try to keep food odors off your pack, but if you can't, put the food bag inside and hang the pack.

What to keep in your tent. You can't be too careful in keeping food smells out of the tent. In rare cases where a bear has become accustomed to coming into a campsite looking for food, it's vital to keep all food smells out of the tent. This often includes your pack, which is hard to keep odor-free. Usually only take valuables (like cameras and binoculars), clothing, flashlight, bear pepper spray, and sleeping gear into the tent.

The campfire. In many areas, regulations prohibit campfires, but if you're in an area where fires are allowed, treat yourself. Besides adding nightly entertainment, the fire might make your camp safer from bears.

A campfire provides the best possible way to get rid of food smells. Build a small but hot fire and thoroughly burn everything that smells of food—garbage, leftovers,

Many Montana trails are a paradise for wildflower lovers. BILL SCHNEIDER

fish entrails, everything. If you brought food in cans or other incombustible containers, burn those too. You can even dump extra water from cooking or dishwater on the edge of the fire to erase the smell.

Be very sure you have the fire hot enough to completely burn everything. If you leave partially burned food scraps in the fire, you are setting up a dangerous situation for the next camper who uses this site.

Before leaving camp the next morning, dig out the fire pit and pack out anything that has not completely burned, even if you believe it no longer carries food smells. For example, many foods like dried soup or hot chocolate come in foil packages that might seem like they burn, but they really don't. Pack out the scorched foil and cans (now with very minor food smells). Also pack out foil and cans left by other campers.

Types of food. Perhaps the safest option is freeze-dried food. It carries very little smell, and it comes in convenient envelopes that allow you to "cook it" by merely adding boiled water. This means you don't have cooking pans to wash or store. Freeze-dried food is expensive, however. Many backpackers don't use it, but they still safely enjoy bear country.

Dry, pre-packed meals (often pasta- or rice-based) offer an affordable compromise to freeze-dried foods. Also, take your favorite high-energy snack. Avoid fresh fruit and canned meats and fish.

The key point is this: What food you have along is much less critical than how you handle it, cook it, and store it. An open can of tuna has a strong smell, but if you eat all of it in one meal, don't spill it on the ground or on your clothes, and burn the can later, it can be quite safe.

Hanging food at night is not the only storage issue. Make sure you place food correctly in your pack. Use airtight packages as much as possible. Store food in the containers it came in or, when opened, in zip-locked bags. Doing so helps keep food smells out of your pack and off your camping gear and clothes.

How to cook. The overriding philosophy of cooking in bear country is to create as little odor as possible. Keep it simple. Use as few pans and dishes as you can.

Unless it's a weather emergency, don't cook in the tent. If you like winter backpacking, you might cook in the tent, but you should have a different tent for summer backpacking.

If you can have a campfire and decide to cook fish, try cooking it in aluminum foil envelopes instead of frying. Then, after removing the cooked fish, quickly and completely burn the fish scraps off the foil. Using foil means you don't have to wash a pan.

Be careful not to spill on yourself while cooking. If you do, change clothes and hang the clothes with food odor with the food and garbage. Wash your hands thoroughly before retiring to the tent.

Don't cook too much food, so then you don't have to deal with leftovers. If you do end up with extra food, however, you have only two choices: carry it out or burn it. Don't bury it or throw it in a lake or leave it anywhere in bear country. A bear will find and dig up any buried food or garbage.

Taking out the garbage. In bear country, you have only two choices: burn garbage or carry it out. Prepare for garbage problems before you leave home. Bring along airtight zip-locked bags to store garbage. Be sure to hang your garbage at night along with your food. Also, carry in as little garbage as possible by discarding excess packaging while packing.

Washing dishes. This can be a problem, but there is one easy solution: If you don't dirty dishes, you don't have to wash them. So try to minimize food smells by using as few dishes and pans as possible. If you follow the principles of zero-impact camping, you're probably doing as much as you can to reduce food smells from dishes.

If you brought paper towels, use one to carefully remove food scraps from pans and dishes before washing them. Then, when you wash dishes, you have much less food smell. Burn the dirty towels or store them in zip-locked bags with other garbage. Put pans and dishes in zip-locked bags before putting them back in your pack.

The mostly off-trail side trip to Kerlee Lake. JACQUELYN CORDAY

If you end up with lots of food scraps in the dishwater, drain out the scraps and store them in zip-locked bags with other garbage or burn them. You can bring a lightweight screen to filter out food scraps from dishwater, but be sure to store the screen with the food and garbage. If you have a campfire, pour the dishwater around the edge of the fire. If you don't have a fire, take the dishwater at least 200 feet downwind and downhill from camp and pour it on the ground or in a small hole. Don't put dishwater or food scraps in a lake or stream.

Although possibly counter to accepted rules of cleanliness for many people, you can skip washing dishes altogether on the last night of your trip. Instead, simply use the paper towels to clean the dirty dishes as much as possible. You can wash them when you get home. Pack dirty dishes in zip-locked bags before putting them back in your pack.

Finally, don't put it off. Do dishes immediately after eating so that a minimum of food smell lingers in the area.

Selecting a campsite. Bears and people often like the same places, which makes selecting a campsite a key decision. Sometimes you have little choice about where you camp. If you're backpacking in a national park, regulations probably require that you stay in a designated campsite reserved in advance.

When you get to your campsite, immediately think bears. Look for bear sign. If you see fresh sign, move on to another site with no signs of bear activity. If you see a bear in or near the campsite, don't camp there—even if you're in a national park and you have reserved this campsite. If you have time before nightfall, return to the trailhead and report the incident to a ranger. If it's getting late, you have little choice but to camp at an undesignated site and report it to the ranger after you finish the hike. Safety always prevails over regulations.

THE BEAR ESSENTIALS OF HIKING AND CAMPING IN BEAR COUNTRY

- Knowledge is the best defense.
- There is no substitute for alertness.
- Hike with a large group and stay together.
- Don't hike alone.
- Stay on the trail.
- Hike in the middle of the day.
- Make lots of noise while hiking.
- Never approach a bear.
- Females with cubs are very dangerous.
- Stay away from carcasses.
- Carry bear pepper spray and know how to use it.
- Choose a safe campsite.
- Camp below timberline.
- Separate sleeping and cooking areas.
- Sleep in a tent.
- Cook just the right amount of food and eat it all.
- Store food and garbage out of reach of bears.
- Never feed bears.
- Keep food odor out of the tent.
- Leave the campsite cleaner than you found it.
- Leave no food rewards for bears.

Great Northern reflecting in Stanton Lake. MARNIE SCHNEIDER

Don't get yourself in a situation where you have to hike or set up camp in the dark. Plan your hike so you aren't setting up camp a half hour before nightfall, because this won't leave enough time to move to another campsite if necessary. If you set up camp in the dark, you have little chance to check around for bear sign or signs of previous campers who might have left food and garbage around.

Key features of a good campsite. One key feature of a good campsite in bear country is a place to store food. Most designated sites in national parks and in some national forests have a food-storage device like a metal box or "bear pole." However, in most national forests and in some national parks, you're on your own, so scout the campsite for trees that can serve as a food-storage device. You need a tree at least 100 yards from your tent with a large branch, or two trees close enough to suspend your food between them on a rope. You can also use a tree that has partially fallen but is still leaning securely on other trees. In any case, however, the trees must be tall enough to get the food at least 10 feet off the ground and 4 feet from the tree trunk.

Avoid camping along trails, streams, or lakeshores, which often serve as travel corridors for bears. Camping above timberline or north of the treeline makes food storage difficult, so avoid this when possible.

Choosing a tent site. Try to keep your tent site at least 100 yards from your cooking area. Store food at least 100 yards from the tent. You can store it near the cooking area to concentrate food smells.

Not under the stars. Some people prefer to sleep out under the stars instead of using a tent. This might be okay in areas not frequented by bears, but it's not a good idea in bear country. The thin fabric of a tent certainly isn't any real physical protection from a bear, but it does present a psychological barrier to a bear that wants to come closer.

Do somebody a big favor. Report all bear sightings to the ranger after your trip. It might not help you, but it could save another camper's life. If rangers get enough reports to spot a pattern, they will manage the area to prevent potentially hazardous situations.

Be Aware of Mountain Lions Too

The most important advice for safely hiking in mountain lion country is recognizing the habitat. Mountain lions feed primarily on deer, so where you have a high deer population, you can expect to find mountain lions. Fish and wildlife agencies usually have good information about deer distribution from population surveys and hunting results.

Safety Guidelines for Traveling in Mountain Lion Country

To stay as safe as possible when hiking in mountain lion country:

- Travel with a friend or group. There's safety in numbers, so stay together.
- Don't let small children wander away by themselves.
- Don't let pets run unleashed.
- Avoid hiking at dawn or dusk—the times mountain lions are most active.
- Know how to behave if you encounter a mountain lion.

How to Get Really Bear and Mountain Lion Aware

For all the essential information you need to safely hike in bear and mountain lion country, get copies of *Bear Aware* and *Lion Sense,* both handy, inexpensive Falcon-Guides. These small, "packable" books contain the basic advice for reducing the risk of being injured by a bear or mountain lion to the slimmest possible margin, and they're written for both beginners and experts. In addition to covering the all-important subject of how to prevent an encounter, these books include advice on what to do if you're involved in an encounter.

Map Legend

Transportation

≡≡(15)≡≡ Interstate Highway

≡(2)≡ U.S. Highway

≡(56)≡ State Highway

≡[7468]≡ Forest/Local Road

= = =: Gravel Road

= = =: Unimproved Road

Trails

------ Featured Trail

------ Trail

·········· Primitive Trail

Water Features

Body of Water

River/Creek

Marsh

Spring

Waterfall

Symbols

≍ Bridge

▲ Campground

▲ Campsite (back country)

✕ Mine

▲ Mountain Peak/Summit

🅿 Parking

≍ Pass/Gap

🛆 Picnic Area

■ Point of Interest/Structure

🛈 Ranger Station

o Town

① Trailhead

🗺 Viewpoint/Overlook

❓ Visitor/Information Center

Land Management

— · — · — State Line

— — — Continental Divide

National Forest

Wilderness/Scenic Area

Kootenai National Forest

1 Northwest Peak

A short uphill hike to a mountain summit with an old lookout cabin, vast views of the Northwest Peak Scenic Area and, on a clear day, the Canadian Rockies

Start: 40 miles northwest of Libby
Distance: 5.0-mile out-and-back
Difficulty: Moderate

Maps: USGS Northwest Peak; Kootenai National Forest Map

Finding the trailhead: Drive west of Libby on US 2 for 29 miles (through Troy) and turn right, heading north on Yaak River Road. After a beautiful 27-mile drive up the Yaak River Valley, turn left just before mile marker 27 and head northwest on Pete Creek Road (FR 338). If you reach the tiny town of Yaak, you have gone too far. At 6.5 miles, the road forks; go straight. At 11 miles, it forks again; go left. After 13 miles on the narrow, partially paved Pete Creek Road (Forest Road 338) and turn left (west) onto West Fork Road, continuing to follow FR 338. Finally, turn right onto Winkum Creek Road (still FR 338) for the last few miles to the trailhead. At 18 miles you'll see a parking area and sign that says NORTHWEST PEAK SCENIC AREA, but this is not the trailhead, which is another mile up the road. After 19 miles from Yaak River Road, at 6,100 feet, you'll find the trailhead on the left (south) side of the road. Limited parking; no toilet; only undeveloped camping in the area. GPS: N48 57.950' / W115 56.217'

The Hike

Northwest Peak (elevation 7,705 feet) is the central attraction of a high mountain ridge, the most striking portions of which are included in the Northwest Peak Scenic Area, an official designation of the Forest Service that recognizes and protects the unique qualities of the area. The trailhead is a long drive from almost everywhere except Yaak. Hence not many people make the effort to hike to the summit of Northwest Peak.

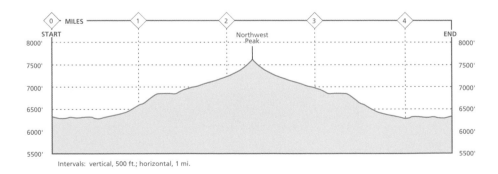

Intervals: vertical, 500 ft.; horizontal, 1 mi.

Last pull to the summit of Northwest Peak. BILL SCHNEIDER

Tank up on water before hitting the trail; you won't find any along the trail. This area usually receives more than its share of snow, however, so wait until July to conquer Northwest Peak.

Trail 169 is well marked and easy to follow. It climbs steadily for 2 miles through mature, unburned forest (mostly spruce and tamarack) until you break out into the open. The last half mile or so goes through an open alpine area sprinkled with a few alpine larch and whitebark pines, and then through a long rock field at the top, 1,600 feet above the trailhead, a nice Category 2 climb.

At the summit you'll find an old lookout cabin, complete with rusty pans and other nostalgic artifacts, that the Forest Service is in the process of restoring, and, surprisingly, probably the highest-elevation outhouse in Montana. The terrain drops down to alpine lakes on three sides of the peak. The views are extensive, with the Cabinet Mountains to the south and the Canadian Rockies far to the north.

This is a great hike for a hot summer day. Most of the first 2 miles is shaded, and the air-conditioning is always on up at the summit.

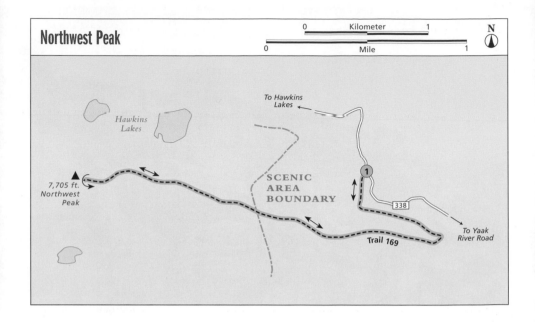

Northwest Peak

Miles and Directions

0.0 Trailhead.
2.5 Northwest Peak.
5.0 Trailhead.

Side Trips: If you didn't get enough exercise on the way up and if you have time, consider continuing south along the ridge toward 7,583-foot Davis Mountain. (Originally contributed by Pat Caffrey, re-hiked by the authors.)

Montana's highest outhouse on the summit of Northwest Peak. BILL SCHNEIDER

2 Fish Lakes Canyon

A day hike or overnighter to a 50-foot waterfall and a chain of five lakes in a rugged, low-elevation canyon

Start: Vinal Creek/Fish Lakes Trailhead, 30 miles north of Libby
Distance: 12.0-mile out-and-back

Difficulty: Moderate
Maps: USGS Lost Horse Mountain, Mount Henry, and Yaak; Kootenai National Forest Map

Finding the trailhead: Drive north of Libby on the paved Pipe Creek Road (FR 68) for 32 miles and turn right onto Vinal Creek Road (FR 746). Drive 6.1 miles north on Vinal Creek Road past the Vinal Lake turnoff and look for the Vinal Creek/Fish Lakes Trailhead on your right, just after crossing Vinal Creek. Limited parking; no toilet; only undeveloped camping. GPS: N48 51.633' / W115 38.650'

The Hike

To some people Fish Lakes Canyon is an overnight trip. To others it's a full day's hike. For every hiker, however, it's one of the most scenic and diverse trips he or she will ever take.

The trail is well maintained and gets rocky only along a few talus slopes, and there's plenty of drinking water along the way. Elevation gain is a mere 600 feet to the northernmost lake. Fish Lakes Canyon and its chain of five lakes are suitable for almost any hiker, from families with children to veteran backpackers.

The area feels remote if you start at the Vinal Lake Road trailhead, but logging roads to the north and to the south parallel the trail. When I visited the area in 1998, I was able to drive to within a mile of Lower Fish Lake, but since then the Forest Service has closed those roads to motorized use. Much of the surrounding area has been logged, and along a few short sections of this trail there is some evidence of a large fire

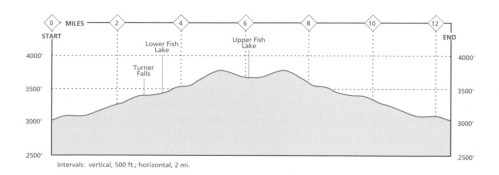

Fish Lakes Canyon. BILL SCHNEIDER

that burned in the area in 2000, but you don't really notice that when hiking down in the canyon, which has been maintained in a fairly pristine condition.

The trail goes through some fabulous old growth, especially some massive tamaracks. It crosses Vinal Creek six times, all on sturdy bridges.

Wildlife and wildflowers abound and are characteristic of northwestern Montana—moose, deer, black bears (and a few grizzlies), wake-robin, Canada dogwood, and clematis, to name a few. Wild roses and perhaps every species of berry in Montana line Vinal Creek in great abundance. Mosquitoes can be dangerously abundant in June and July; waiting until August gives you a good chance of avoiding them.

From the trailhead, follow Vinal Creek Trail 9 along Vinal Creek for the first 3 miles to Turner Falls. About a quarter mile past the falls, the trail splits. Turn left (north) onto Trail 397 where Vinal Creek Trail 9 goes right (east) toward Mount Henry. Then, after about a quarter mile, turn right at the junction where Trail 51 goes left to Hoskins Lake. After the second junction, you head into Fish Lakes Canyon and its string of lakes. After enjoying them, perhaps spending a night or two, turn around and retrace your steps back to the trailhead.

Perhaps the most outstanding feature of the hike is Turner Falls. Even without the falls, however, this would be one of the most beautiful hikes in Montana—five

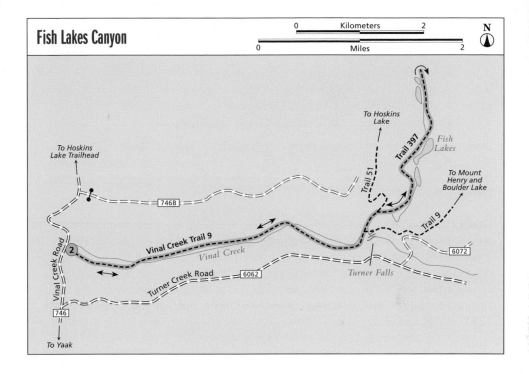

Fish Lakes Canyon

0 — Kilometers — 2

0 — Miles — 2

N

To Hoskins Lake

To Hoskins Lake Trailhead

Trail 397

Fish Lakes

Trail 51

To Mount Henry and Boulder Lake

746B

Trail 9

Vinal Creek Trail 9

Vinal Creek

6072

2

Vinal Creek Road

Turner Creek Road

6062

Turner Falls

746

To Yaak

trout-filled mountain lakes strung through a narrow, rugged canyon lined with a quiet forest of large cedar and larch trees. The lakes have several outstanding campsites and lots of fat cutthroats to keep anglers happy. The Forest Service has designated the Fish Lakes/Vinal Creek Trail as a National Recreation Trail and given the route semi-primitive, nonmotorized recreation status. (Originally contributed by Linda and Tom Hurlock, re-hiked by the authors.)

Miles and Directions

0.0 Vinal Creek/Fish Lakes Trailhead.

3.0 Turner Falls.

3.2 Junction with Mount Henry Trail 397; turn left.

3.5 Junction with Trail 51; turn right.

4.0 Lower Fish Lake.

6.0 Upper Fish Lake.

12.0 Vinal Creek/Fish Lakes Trailhead.

3 Valley of the Ancients

A special day hike through an old-growth western red cedar forest and an optional trip up Sawtooth Peak or across Pillick Ridge, with superb views of the Cabinet Mountains and the Bull and Clark Fork Valleys

Start: Ross Creek Trailhead, 35 miles south-west of Libby
Distance: 4.0-mile out-and-back
Difficulty: Moderate

Maps: USGS Sawtooth Mountain, Smeads Bench, and Heron (Smeads Bench and Heron needed only for Pillick Ridge option); Kootenai National Forest Map

Finding the trailhead: Drive 15 miles west of Libby on US 2 to the junction with MT 56 and turn left, heading south for 17.7 miles. Turn right onto Ross Creek Road 398, heading west for 4 miles to Ross Creek Cedar Grove Scenic Area. After 0.9 mile, stay left at a junction. The road is paved and dead-ends at Ross Creek Trailhead at the far end of the picnic area loop. Ample parking, a short self-guided nature trail, picnic area, and toilet. No developed camping at the trailhead, but the Bad Medicine Campground is nearby at the south end of Bull Lake. GPS: N48 12.517' / W115 54.833'

The Hike

This route in the Ross Creek Cedar Grove Scenic Area definitely qualifies as a must-do hike for any hiker. Some of the ancient western red cedars are 500 years old, and we aren't talking about a few trees. We're talking about hundreds of giants all along the 2-mile trek to Ross Creek and even a few after that, if you decide to go farther—and not just cedars, but also some massive western white pines and grand firs, probably the best remnant of the real old-growth forest that survived the chain saw in Montana.

Along with the spectacular trees, you'll find lots of fauna and flora such as pine martens, flying squirrels, fishers, and more, and some rare wildflowers poking through the fern carpet, such as wild ginger, queen's cup bead lily with its striking single

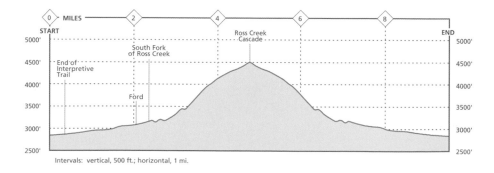

Hiking among the ancient cedars of Ross Creek. BILL SCHNEIDER

upright berry, and the always elegant trillium. You'll want photos, of course, but getting them can be frustrating. The mighty trees throw out some serious shade, so you'll need your flash, and even then, it isn't easy to take a picture of a 200-foot tree when you're standing beside it.

The Forest Service has lined a short loop at the beginning of the hike with informative interpretive displays. The only question the interpretation doesn't answer is what miracle occurred to keep this truly spectacular forest from being cut down for cedar shake roofing.

The trail leaves the west side of the parking lot and follows the Ross Creek Cedars Interpretive Trail, passing through probably the most beautiful forest in the state, mostly ancient western red cedars hundreds of years old, some 8 feet in diameter and 200 feet in height. Stay right along the interpretive trail loop, and after about a half mile leave the loop, continuing on Ross Creek Trail 142.

As you climb up the valley on a gentle grade, you'll notice the burned cores of gargantuan ancient stumps. Wildfire burned up this valley around the turn of the last century and killed some of the ancient trees. You'll also see several changes in the makeup of the forest.

At 2 miles, the trail reaches a ford of Ross Creek, which would be a good place to take a break, enjoy the gorgeous stream, and then turn around unless you want to add a little adventure to your trip by taking some of the optional extensions.

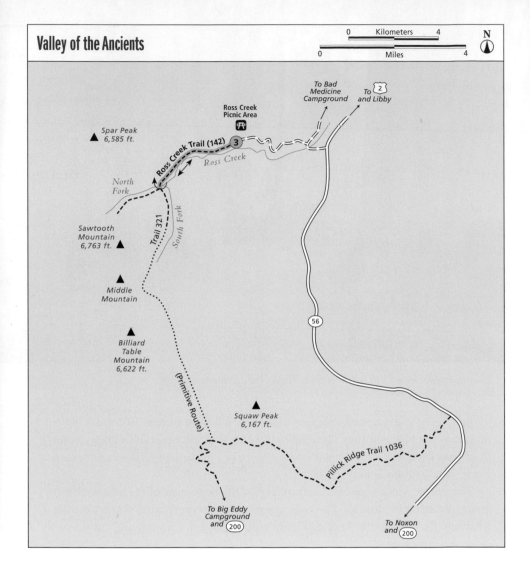

Ross Creek Picnic Area

Spar Peak 6,585 ft.

Ross Creek Trail (142)

Ross Creek

To Bad Medicine Campground

To 2 and Libby

North Fork

Trail 321

South Fork

Sawtooth Mountain 6,763 ft.

Middle Mountain

Billiard Table Mountain 6,622 ft.

(primitive Route)

56

Squaw Peak 6,167 ft.

Pillick Ridge Trail 1036

To Big Eddy Campground and 200

To Noxon and 200

Miles and Directions

- **0.0** Ross Creek Trailhead.
- **0.4** End of Ross Creek Cedars Interpretive Trail.
- **2.0** Ross Creek.
- **4.0** Ross Creek Trailhead.

Options: At the Ross Creek ford, it may look like a trail continues up the northwestern bank, but it crosses the creek. Watch for a blaze on the other side of the creek. This ford might be a serious task in spring. If you take this hike in May or June, you might not want to risk the ford.

Bill and three good friends. They aren't too talkative, but are always there for him. Marnie Schneider

After fording Ross Creek, you also cross the South Fork of Ross Creek. At 2.4 miles, there's an unmarked trail junction. A maintained trail goes left (south) past a large (12 feet in diameter) twin cedar tree, and the right (west) trail continues up the main fork of Ross Creek. Although I did not hike up the North Fork, the trail looks similarly maintained as the South Fork trail.

Once in the South Fork, the trail goes steeply uphill on a soft bedding of western hemlock cones. At 4.8 miles the good trail ends beside a beautiful cascade along the South Fork of Ross Creek.

If you want some real adventure, a partially flagged social trail continues to climb through dense forest until breaking out into what might best be described as overgrazed meadows. As the trail peters out, you can turn back, continue up to Sawtooth Mountain via a steep scramble, or bushwhack your way up to the ridge for a trip to Pillick Ridge.

To climb Sawtooth Mountain from Ross Creek Cascade (adding 8 difficult miles to your hike), continue up on a faint trail through devil's club, alder, and snowbrush. The faint trail crosses the creek, and if you find yourself looking up the right slope, you're off course. Cross the creek or follow the creek until you pick up the trail again. When we hiked this, someone had flagged the route.

This faint trail dead-ends in some large elk meadows. Here you should look around the valley and look at your watch to make sure you have enough time to climb Sawtooth Mountain, which requires another six hours to beat nightfall back to the trailhead.

You can climb Sawtooth Mountain via two routes. The best way is to hike up the creek about another quarter mile and find a dry creek bed to follow up the north slope, directly toward Sawtooth Mountain. If you choose carefully, this path should take you to the avalanche bowl below the summit and a small melt pond. From that point, take either ridge of talus slope and do some intermediate rock scrambling to the top. You'll gain almost 2,500 feet from the valley floor to the top in about 2 miles.

Once on top, angle down toward the talus slope on the opposite side of the South Fork of Ross Creek drainage. This bushwhack can be nasty, but the place is packed with elk, and we found many good elk trails to follow on the way back to the trail. Once back on the trail, it's another two hours to the trailhead and (if you planned well) the cold beer waiting in your vehicle, which you'll deserve after this mammoth hike.

Another route up Sawtooth Mountain is to continue all the way up the valley to the divide between the South Fork of Ross Creek and Blue Creek. There was a pond on top in late September 1998 (a dry year). From there you can walk the ridge up and over Middle Mountain to the summit.

Again, both routes involve serious bushwhacking and heart attack elevation gain, so use caution. These options are for well-conditioned and experienced hikers only.

Sawtooth Mountain offers a panorama of the glacially carved upper North Fork of Ross Creek drainage and excellent views of Billiard Table Mountain toward Pillick Ridge and Spar Peak in the opposite direction. I also thought this view of the Cabinets was the best I've ever seen. In addition, this peak is a crucial part of what will, we hope, be designated the proposed Scotchman Peak Wilderness Area.

The Pillick Ridge option requires a vehicle left at Pillick Ridge Trailhead. It has little water and a trail for only the last 11 miles of this hike.

To get to Pillick Ridge Trailhead, continue south on MT 56 for another 15 miles and watch for a possibly marked logging road to the right (west) 6.5 miles before the junction with MT 200. The trailhead may or may not be signed. (Unfortunately, trailhead signs are often stolen or vandalized.)

This option is strictly for woods-wise hikers with topographic maps and compass. I think this trip is best described as a true Montana wilderness experience, and brutal and dangerous for the unprepared or unconditioned. Hikers who don't mind rugged country with little water and who appreciate truly wild scenery and solitude should like this trip. Pillick Ridge is the pristine southeastern spur of the Scotchman Peaks and forms the scenic western backdrop to the Bull River Valley.

From the divide ridge between the Blue Creek and South Fork of Ross Creek drainages, follow the rugged, trailless ridge for 6 miles to the top of Squaw Peak. You stand a good chance of seeing deer and possibly a few mountain goats. In addition, the southern slopes of the ridge have an abundance of dry-site wildflowers. Take plenty of water, especially if camping. Subalpine basins below the northeast side of the ridge have water and possible campsites (there was water on the divide between Blue and South Fork of Ross Creeks in September of a dry year). Once off the ridge, however, the terrain becomes very steep and brushy, so don't expect easy going or an abundance of level camping spots.

From Squaw Peak, maintained Pillick Ridge Trail 1036 follows the crest for 11 miles to Pillick Ridge Trailhead. Although the going is very rugged, the view is excellent and solitude everywhere. Be on the alert for elk and mountain goats or possibly one of the few grizzlies still in this area. (Originally contributed by John Westenberg, re-hiked by the authors.)

4 Boulder Lakes

A day hike or overnighter into a lush lake basin

Start: 30 miles north of Libby or 7 miles west of Lake Koocanusa Bridge

Distance: 5.6 miles to Lower Boulder Lake; 10.6 miles to Purcell Marsh; out and back

Difficulty: Easy to Lower Boulder Lake; moderate to Purcell Marsh

Maps: USGS Boulder Lakes; Kootenai National Forest Map

Finding the trailhead: Drive southwest from Eureka for about 14 miles on MT 37, then turn west across the Lake Koocanusa Bridge. (Koocanusa is not an Indian name. It combines the first three letters of the words Kootenai, Canada, and USA, hence the name *Koo-can-usa*.) Once across the bridge, turn north onto FR 92 for 2.7 miles and then turn left, heading west on Boulder Creek Road. Follow Boulder Creek Road 337 for less than a mile, then follow the left fork on FR 7183. Go about 2 miles past this junction to the junction of FR 7183 and FR 7229, and park here. The road levels out after the trailhead, so if you find yourself driving on the level, you may have missed the trailhead. Limited parking at the trailhead, but be careful not to block the road; no toilet; only undeveloped camping. GPS: N48 49.717' / W115 24.533'

The Hike

You used to be able to drive 1.3 miles up FR 7229 to the trailhead, but in recent years this section of road has been closed to vehicles to protect grizzly bear habitat, so now it's become an excellent trail. In fact, if you want to see a subalpine lake without vehicle access in Kootenai Country, this may be the easiest hike you could take. It's only 2.6 miles to the Lower Boulder Lake along a slight incline—about 440 feet of elevation gain.

The trail is well maintained, and it stays in the woods most of the way. At 1.3 miles the old road, now being reclaimed rapidly by nature, ends. Turn left here and continue about a hundred yards up another old road to the junction with Trail 62, with a seemingly out-of-place steel gate. At 2.6 miles, just before the lake, the trail forks. Go left

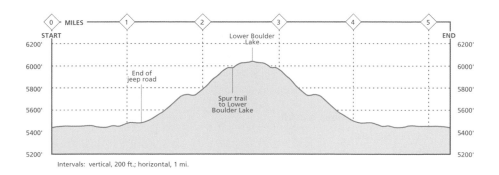

Lower Boulder Lake. BILL SCHNEIDER

(south) about a quarter mile more to the lower lake. The right-hand trail continues to Purcell Marsh. Bring drinking water; it can be dry until you reach the lower lake.

The first part of the trail on the abandoned road is as flat as a flapjack, but then you start a moderate 700-foot climb to the lower lake. The last part of the trail has been designated a National Recreation Trail, with motorized vehicles prohibited.

Lower Boulder Lake has fair fishing for pan-size cutthroats. Boulder Lakes country hosts the same diversity of wildlife found throughout northwestern Montana—deer, black bears (and a few grizzlies), moose, elk, and all the rest. Around the lakes you will find beargrass, glacier lilies, and a variety of other wildflowers.

Miles and Directions

0.0 Trailhead.

1.3 End of closed jeep road.

2.6 Spur trail to Boulder Lakes; turn left.

2.8 Lower Boulder Lake.

5.6 Trailhead.

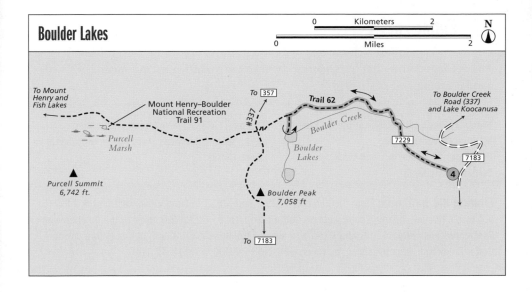

Boulder Lakes

Kilometers 0 2
Miles 0 2
N

To Mount Henry and Fish Lakes

Mount Henry–Boulder National Recreation Trail 91

Purcell Marsh

Purcell Summit 6,742 ft.

To 357

#337

Trail 62

Boulder Creek

Boulder Lakes

Boulder Peak 7,058 ft

To 7183

To Boulder Creek Road (337) and Lake Koocanusa

7229

7183

4

Side Trips: If you're an experienced hiker, you may want to add 5 miles to the trip and take an interesting side trip to Purcell Marsh. From Lower Boulder Lake, backtrack about a quarter mile and take Trail 62 west to Boulder Ridge at the head of Basin Creek, which is about a 500-foot climb. (From the top of the ridge, you can also make a side trip to the top of Boulder Peak by heading south along the ridge for less than a mile.) To continue on to Purcell Marsh (or Fish Lakes and beyond), from the junction with Trail 337 on top of Boulder Ridge, drop 900 feet to Purcell Marsh. Here you find few signs of human presence, and you have an excellent chance to see moose. It's an extra 5-mile round-trip to Purcell Marsh from Boulder Lakes. At Purcell Marsh you might find the uncommon alpine bog kalmia.

You can continue on the Mount Henry–Boulder National Recreation Trail past Purcell Marsh all the way to Fish Lakes Canyon, but the area around Mount Henry crosses several logging roads and harvest areas before dropping into the pristine canyon. It's another 10 miles to Fish Lakes from Boulder Lakes and another 6 miles to Vinal Lake Road. See Hike 2, Fish Lakes Canyon. (Originally contributed by Linda and Tom Hurlock, re-hiked by the authors.)

5 Cedar Lakes

An excellent overnighter or moderate day hike to two fish-filled mountain lakes with good camping

Start: 9 miles west of Libby in the Cabinet Mountains Wilderness
Distance: 11.0-mile out-and-back
Difficulty: Moderate

Maps: USGS Scenery Mountain; Cabinet Mountains Wilderness Map; Kootenai National Forest Map

Finding the trailhead: From the junction of US 2 and MT 37 in Libby, drive west on US 2 for 4.4 miles. Turn left, heading southwest on Cedar Creek Road 402 for 2.4 miles to the junction with Parmenter Creek Road 4727, where you turn left. The trailhead is on your right just before crossing Cedar Creek with limited parking, no toilet. GPS: N48 24.000' / W115 42.100'

The Hike

Cedar Creek Trail 141 climbs steadily on stream grade up Cedar Creek Valley. As you might guess, many young cedar trees surround the trail, creating a shady walk, perfect for a hot summer day. The trail was once lined with stately old cedars, but now you see only the stumps.

The trail is in excellent condition and sometimes used by stock parties. It stays on the north side of Cedar Creek all the way to the lakes. If you go in August, plan on taking an extra hour to gorge yourself in the abundant huckleberry patches.

Soon after leaving the trailhead (0.7 mile), turn left (west) at the junction with the Scenery Mountain Trail. At 4.4 miles, turn left (west) again at the new trail up Grambauer Ridge.

After 5 miles you'll see a spur trail going left to the lower lake. You can follow this trail down to Lower Cedar Lake and continue up a steep climb to Upper Cedar Lake, about a half mile up the trail. The trail climbs above the lower lake, and you get a great view from it.

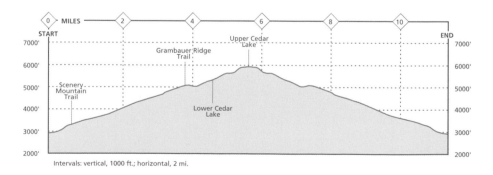

Intervals: vertical, 1000 ft.; horizontal, 2 mi.

You need to know the roll cast to catch fish on some mountain lakes. BILL SCHNEIDER

Both lakes have well-used campsites. To reduce resource damage, use existing campsites rather than create new ones. The Cabinets still supports a few grizzly bears, but this remnant population is severely endangered. Black bears are common, however, so be sure to keep a zero-impact camp.

Both lakes have a few small rainbow trout, but you might need some patience to catch them.

Miles and Directions

0.0   Trailhead.

0.7   Junction with Scenery Mountain Trail 649; turn left.

4.4   Grambauer Ridge Trail 383; turn left.

5.0   Spur trail to Lower Cedar Lake.

5.5   Upper Cedar Lake and Trail 140 to Parmenter Creek.

11.0 Trailhead.

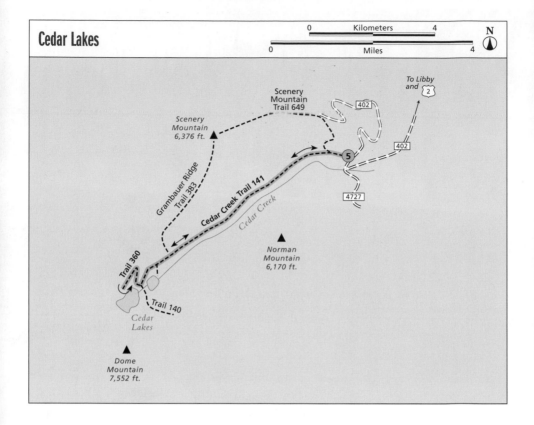

Cedar Lakes

Kilometers
0 ————————————— 4
Miles
0 ————————————— 4

N

To Libby
and 2

Scenery
Mountain
Trail 649

402

402

Scenery
Mountain
6,376 ft.

5

4727

Grambauer Ridge
Trail 383

Cedar Creek Trail 141

Cedar Creek

Trail 360

Norman
Mountain
6,170 ft.

Trail 140

Cedar
Lakes

Dome
Mountain
7,552 ft.

Options: You can make a loop of this hike by taking the new trail along Grambauer Ridge (not shown on the Cabinet Mountains Wilderness Map) to Scenery Mountain and back to the trailhead on Scenery Mountain Trail 649 instead of retracing your steps down Cedar Creek. Make sure you have enough time, though. This option makes your trek a long day hike of about 13 miles with more elevation gain.

The entire Kootenai National Forest is under a food storage order to reduce confrontations with wild animals, especially bears. You can find details at trailhead information boards or by contacting any district office on the Kootenai National Forest. Also, maximum party size is eight, including hikers and horses or mules. (Originally contributed by John Westenberg, re-hiked by the authors.)

6 Leigh Lake

A short but steep day hike to the largest lake in the Cabinet Wilderness (nearly a mile across) with stunning views of Snowshoe Peak, the highest peak in Montana west of Glacier National Park

Start: 12 miles south of Libby
Distance: 3.0-mile out-and-back
Difficulty: Moderate

Maps: USGS Snowshoe Peak; Kootenai National Forest Map

Finding the trailhead: Drive 8 miles south on US 2 from its junction with MT 37 in Libby and turn right (west) on the paved Bear Creek Road 278 (which is 80 miles from Kalispell). After 5.2 miles, turn right on Leigh Lake Trail 132 (FR 4786 on the map). From here it's 2.1 miles to the end of the road, where the trail starts. You can make it to the trailhead in any vehicle, but the last 2 miles are rough. Because of the heavy logging activity, the numerous roads in this area can change periodically, and sometimes (such as the day I hiked this route) signs can be MIA. Make sure you have a current Forest Service map or, better yet, check with the Forest Service before leaving for the trailhead. There is a trailhead information board at the west end of the small parking area, which has no room for horse trailers. GPS: N48 13.450' / W115 37.767'

The Hike

Leigh Lake is in the Cabinet Mountains Wilderness and receives heavy use. The Forest Service reports hiker visits as high as 2,400 people per year.

Leigh Lake Trail 132 climbs steeply uphill through thick forest with breaks providing views of Leigh Creek Valley. It's only 1.5 miles to the lake, but the steep grade and rocky trail make it an hour-long trip, and longer with an overnight pack. Along the trail you'll see some massive western hemlocks, a beautiful tree you don't see often in Montana. The vegetation is wonderfully lush all along the route.

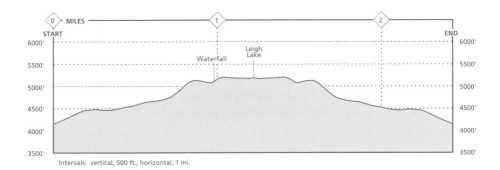

Intervals: vertical, 500 ft.; horizontal, 1 mi.

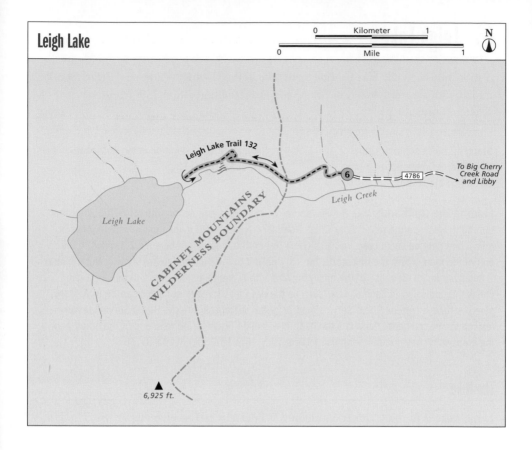

Less than a half mile before the lake, you get a great view of a gorgeous waterfall. Just before the falls, the trail turns right and goes straight up. This short section is extremely steep and requires handholds in a few places—not fun with a heavy pack.

After climbing about 1,000 feet in 1.5 miles (a tough Category 2 hill), the trail ends at Leigh Lake, a 5,144-foot-elevation lake with marginal fishing. If you're a hardy soul, you can pack in a small rubber raft to improve your chances.

This area gets phenomenal amounts of snow—as much as 20 to 30 feet. In July the lake still has ice floes, sometimes carved into strange shapes by wind and waves, and forming a striking contrast with the deep blue water.

This route is more suited for day hiking, but you can camp at the lake. Good campsites are hard to find, and local regulations prohibit camping and campfires within 300 feet of the lake, with a maximum party size of eight. The Forest Service prohibits horses on this trail because of unsafe conditions.

Miles and Directions

0.0 Trailhead.

1.1 Waterfall.

1.5 Leigh Lake.

3.0 Trailhead.

Side Trips: At the west end of the lake is a massive, 3,000-foot wall, the high point being 8,712-foot Snowshoe Peak, the highest peak in the Cabinet Range and the highest peak between Glacier National Park and the Cascades.

You can climb this peak from the lake, but it takes most of a day and would definitely be classified as strenuous. From the outlet of the lake, head northwest straight up the face of a large eastern ridge. Once on the ridge, follow it southwest to the main ridge, being careful to note Blackwell Glacier to the right and also being careful not to fall in that direction. After intersecting the main ridge, work your way up along the western side of this ridge until it levels out at the peak. Do not venture out onto the snowfields on the eastern side of the main ridge unless you are properly trained and equipped for ice climbing. (Originally contributed by Pat Caffrey, re-hiked by the authors.)

7 Baree and Bear Lakes

A day hike or overnighter (which could be stretched into a two-night backpack) to several mountain lakes with fish, alpine ridge walks, and a side trip up to Baree Peak

Start: Baree Lake Trailhead, 30 miles south of Libby
Distance: 10.0-mile loop
Difficulty: Moderate

Maps: USGS Goat Peak and Silver Butte Pass; Cabinet Mountains Wilderness Map; Kootenai National Forest Map

Finding the trailhead: Drive west of Kalispell on US 2 for 58 miles and turn left, heading southwest on Silver Butte Road (FR 148). After 3.4 miles, stay right past a private drive to the left and continue on FR 148. After 9.2 miles, pass the turnoff for Bear Lakes Trailhead and continue straight on FR 148 for another mile. At 10 miles, turn right and drive 0.2 mile to Baree Lake Trailhead. The turnoffs to both Bear Lakes and Baree Lake are mildly confusing. The signs say TRAIL when it's an obvious road. In both cases the roads go only a short distance (less than a quarter mile) and end at the trailheads under the power line that parallels the road. Ample parking; no toilet; only undeveloped camping. GPS: N47 57.067' / W115 29.550'

The Hike

If you don't like to retrace your steps and dislike the difficult two-car logistics that most point-to-point hikes involve, you should like this hike. The trailheads to the two lakes are only a mile apart, and the lakes are connected by a spectacular trail along the Cabinet Divide. Make sure you have your map and compass or GPS because most junctions are unsigned.

It's 3 miles and a 1,700-foot elevation gain on Baree Creek Trail 489 to Baree Lake. Watch for an unsigned spur trail heading left down to the lake, where you'll find a snow-gauging station. The lake is gorgeous and offers views up to the Cabinet Divide along slopes covered with beargrass and huckleberries. In fact, getting to the lake can be pitifully slow unless you have a strong will and can resist browsing

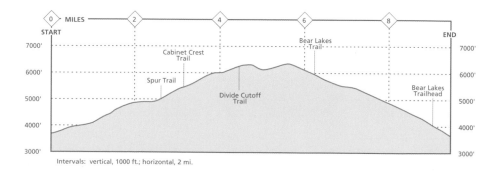

Intervals: vertical, 1000 ft.; horizontal, 2 mi.

Enjoying serene Baree Lake. BILL SCHNEIDER

on huckleberries. The lake also has a nice population of small cutthroats, so bring a fly rod.

After Baree Lake, the trail makes a steady climb to the Cabinet Divide. At 3.5 miles—about half a mile beyond the lake—turn right (north) onto Cabinet Crest Trail 360 (another unsigned junction) and follow it along the divide. The view from the ridge is terrific, particularly to the west and the northwest into Swamp Creek, Wanless and Buck Lakes, and the peaks surrounding them. A few grizzlies still survive along the Cabinet Divide, so be bear aware.

After about a mile of magnificent ridgeline hiking, turn right (east) at yet another unmarked junction on Divide Cutoff Trail 63 to Bear Lakes. The trail that continues left along the ridge appears to be more heavily used than this route down. This trail runs just below the top of a spur ridge off the Cabinet Divide.

Follow Divide Cutoff Trail 63 for another 1.5 miles on a gentle downward traverse to the junction (with the only sign I saw on this route) with Iron Meadows Trail 630 and Bear Lakes Trail 178 (labeled 531 on some signs). Turn left here toward Iron Meadows if you want to see Bear Lakes, but only go about a quarter mile before

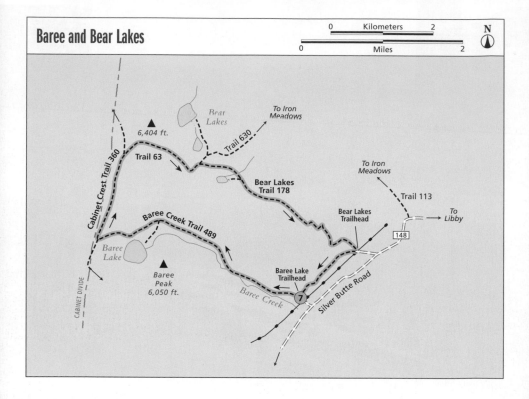

Baree and Bear Lakes

turning left again on an unsigned spur trail to the two uppermost lakes in Bear Lake Basin. (*Note:* Mileage to Bear Lakes is not included in total distance.)

After seeing or staying at one of the lakes (and catching a few small cutthroats), retrace your steps back to the junction and turn left onto Trail 178. From here it's 3 miles through mature unburned forest down to the Bear Lakes Trailhead. A mile or so after the junction, watch for a short spur trail to the right over to the lowermost Bear Lake.

After reaching the power line corridor that runs parallel to Silver Butte Road, follow it southwest for a mile to Baree Lake Trailhead and your vehicle.

Miles and Directions

0.0   Baree Lake Trailhead.

3.0   Spur trail to Baree Lake.

3.5   Cabinet Crest Trail 360; turn right.

4.5   Junction with Divide Cutoff Trail 63 to Bear Lakes; turn right.

6.0   Junction with the trail to Iron Meadows/Big Bear Lake and Bear Lakes Trail 178; turn right.

9.0   Bear Lakes Trailhead.

10.0 Baree Lake Trailhead.

Hiking along the spectacular Cabinet Divide. BILL SCHNEIDER

Options: The Trail Creek and Iron Meadows areas to the north and east of Bear Lakes offer interesting variations on the Baree and Bear Lakes hike. One variation requires leaving a car at Silver Dollar Trailhead, 9 miles up West Fisher River Road (4 miles north on US 2). Rather than returning to Silver Butte Road from Bear Lake, take Divide Cutoff Trail 63 east for 1.5 miles to Iron Meadows. You will walk through some of the best elk country in the Kootenai National Forest. From Iron Meadows, take Silver Dollar Trail 114 to your vehicle. (Originally contributed by John Westenberg, re-hiked by the authors.)

8 Ten Lakes

A long day hike or moderate overnighter (which could be stretched into a three-day backpacking trip) through lake-sprinkled alpine scenery in one of the last roadless areas in the Whitefish Range

Start: Bluebird Trailhead, 50 miles north of Whitefish
Distance: 10.5-mile loop

Difficulty: Moderate
Maps: USGS Ksanka Peak and Stahl Peak; Kootenai National Forest Map

Finding the trailhead: Drive north of Whitefish on US 93 for 41.5 miles (8 miles south of Eureka) and turn northeast onto paved Grave Creek Road (FR 114). After 10 miles the pavement ends; stay right past the Stahl Creek Road turnoff, continuing on FR 114. After 13.8 miles, continue straight on FR 319 after FR 114 takes a sharp right. After 24.7 miles from US 93, FR 319 reaches the junction with FR 7086. To reach the Bluebird Trailhead, take the left fork at the junction with FR 7086 (which goes to the Wolverine Lakes Trailhead and Rainbow Lake) and continue for about 2 more miles before turning right onto FR 7085, the road to Little Therriault Lake and Horse Camp. Drive by the campground for another half mile or so to the end of the road, where you'll find the Bluebird Trailhead. Ample parking; no toilet; two developed campgrounds nearby. GPS: N48 56.520' / W114 54.187'

The Hike

The Ten Lakes Scenic Area is a remote hiking area, but worth the drive. It gets buried with snow, however, so don't attempt this hike before July. Some of the lakes in this area receive heavy summer use, so if you're staying overnight, be sure to set up a zero-impact camp.

From the Bluebird Trailhead, be sure to get on Clarence Ness Trail 82, which comes in on the right side of the trailhead. Trail 82 climbs gradually through unburned forest and huckleberry patches until you reach Paradise Lake and the junction with Highline Trail 339. Turn left here, and either take a nice rest at Paradise Lake as you walk along the south shore or wait and go about a quarter mile up the trail to Bluebird Lake. You can't see Bluebird Lake from the Highline Trail, but watch for a good social trail to the left just past Paradise Lake, which leads to the lake. Bluebird Lake has several excellent campsites and a hungry population of small cutthroats.

From Bluebird Lake, Highline Trail 339 switchbacks over the ridge into the Wolverine Lakes Basin. The views are expansive in all directions, with glimpses of the ice-clad Bugaboos far into Canada.

At 4 miles, turn right (northeast) onto Wolverine Lakes Trail 84 and follow it down to the first Wolverine Lake and the ranger cabin. If you're camping, you can stay here or take the short spur trail to the left over to the other Wolverine Lake. Both lakes have good campsites and good fishing for cutthroats.

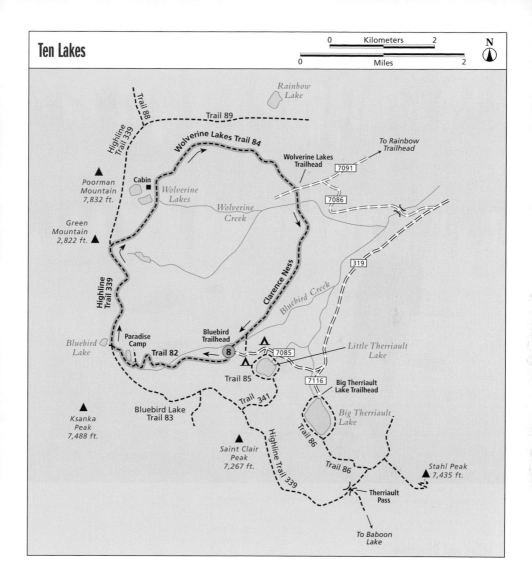

From Wolverine Lakes the trail drops steadily for 2.5 miles to the Wolverine Lakes Trailhead. This is a confusing point. Take the trail that starts directly across the road. There is no sign on the fairly distinct trail, but this is Clarence Ness Trail 82.

You cross Wolverine Creek (no bridge) about a half mile down the trail and continue through mature forest all the way to the Bluebird Trailhead. You'll see a junction 0.5 mile from the trailhead, with the left fork going to Horse Camp. Go right here. If you miss this fork and come out at Horse Camp, no big problem; just walk 0.4 mile up the road to the trailhead.

Enjoying the last light at Wolverine Lake. BILL SCHNEIDER

Miles and Directions

0.0   Bluebird Trailhead.

2.2   Paradise Lake and junction with Highline Trail 339, turn left.

2.5   Bluebird Lake.

4.0   Junction with Wolverine Lakes Trail 84; turn right.

5.0   Wolverine Lakes.

7.5   Wolverine Lakes Trailhead, start of Clarence Ness Trail 82.

10.0   Junction with trail to Horse Camp; turn right.

10.5   Bluebird Trailhead.

Options: If you have two vehicles or have stashed a bicycle, you can make a 7.5-mile shuttle out of this trip by skipping the last 3 miles from Wolverine to Bluebird Trailheads. (Originally contributed by Bill Cunningham, re-hiked by the authors.)

Lolo National Forest

9 Hub Lake

A fairly easy day hike or overnighter through beautiful subalpine country on a scale small enough to be easily enjoyed by families with small children

Start: 90 miles northwest of Missoula
Distance: 5.0-mile out-and-back
Difficulty: Moderate

Maps: USGS McGee Peak and Deborgia South; Lolo National Forest, Superior Ranger District Map

Finding the trailhead: From Missoula, take I-90 west for 80 miles to exit 25 (11 miles west of St. Regis). Immediately get back on the freeway going east, heading toward Missoula for 2 to 3 miles, and take exit 26 onto Ward Creek Road 889. (Sorry, no exit 26 going west.) Follow Ward Creek Road for about 6.5 miles to the trailhead on your right (west) just before crossing Ward Creek. Limited parking, so don't take two spots; no toilet. GPS: N47 17.633' / W115 20.017'

The Hike

The Ward–Eagle Peaks area offers small doses of the medicine that gives Montana's mountains their healing power—beautiful forests, waterfalls, wildlife, berries, interesting history, and fishing. Moreover, they're accessible to all hikers. You could call this a "pocket wilderness" that, in spite of its small size, holds many scenic and recreational attractions. Better yet, despite all of these attractions, this trail receives little use.

Most of western Montana's big-game species are found in this area, and if you're alert, you'll have a chance of seeing them. Although grizzlies are gone from the Bitterroots, a good population of black bears remains.

From the trailhead, follow Ward Creek Trail 262 along Ward Creek as it enters a beautiful, fern-bottomed cedar grove with some cedars over 6 feet across at the base—and a few monarchs close to 10 feet in diameter. That's something very rarely seen nowadays. This stretch of trail is like walking among the "old wise ones" and a glimpse of what much of western Montana used to look like before the logging age.

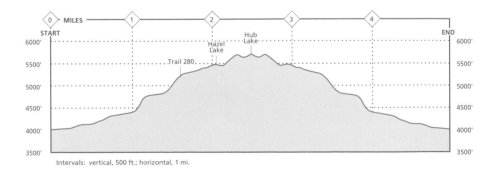

Intervals: vertical, 500 ft.; horizontal, 1 mi.

Hub Lake. Jacquelyn Corday

Soon after leaving the grove, the trail overlooks Dipper Falls, a pleasant spot for a break. The first part of the trail is mostly flat, but the grade kicks up slightly as you approach the lakes. Allow an extra half hour for grazing the abundant fields of huckleberries.

At 1.5 miles turn right (west) at the junction with Hub-Hazel Trail 280. The next mile of walking is steep, consuming most of the 1,500 feet of altitude gained on the way to Hub Lake, made even longer by the weakness of most hikers—not being able to go by a field of huckleberries without stopping. About 2 miles from the trailhead, the trail passes Hazel Lake, which has pan-size cutthroat trout, but its shores are too steep and brushy for camping.

Hub Lake is only about a half mile beyond Hazel Lake. Note the remains of an old prospector's cabin, now almost hidden in brush, between the trail and an abandoned mine that overlooks the upper end of the lake.

Hub Lake offers good fishing for easy-to-catch but small westslope cutthroat. The small lake sits in a picturesque subalpine setting.

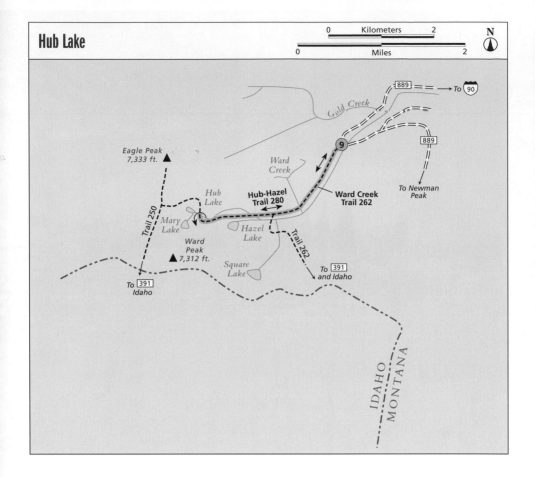

Miles and Directions

0.0 Trailhead.

1.5 Junction with Hub-Hazel Trail 280; turn right.

2.0 Hazel Lake.

2.5 Hub Lake.

5.0 Trailhead.

Side Trips: Hub Lake is also a good jumping-off point for day hikes to Ward or Eagle Peaks or fishing trips to Clear (small brook trout), Gold (rainbows), Square (brookies), and Hazel (cutts) Lakes. You won't catch anything large, but you can definitely have fish for dinner. You'll want a USGS quad for the cross-country hiking needed to reach some of these lakes. Mary Lake, in the cirque below Ward Peak, has no fish, but it's a pleasant stop en route to Ward Peak. (Originally contributed by John Westenberg, re-hiked by the authors.)

10 Bonanza Lakes

A day hike or overnighter into easily accessible subalpine country in the Bitter-root Range

Start: 50 miles west of Missoula
Distance: 5.6-mile out-and-back
Difficulty: Easy

Maps: USGS Illinois Peak; Lolo National Forest, Superior Ranger District Map

Finding the trailhead: From Missoula, take I-90 west to Superior. Take exit 47 and turn left (south) under the freeway. Take another left (east) just beyond the underpass onto a paved county road. After 1.2 miles, turn right (south) onto Cedar Creek Road (FR 320). Follow FR 320 for 24 miles of winding dirt road to the Bitterroot Divide (pavement ends after 2.4 miles) and the trailhead for Stateline National Recreation Trail, shortly after passing the Missoula Lake Campground turnoff. The Stateline Trail runs northwest and southeast from where Cedar Creek Road crosses the divide into Idaho. The parking area is on your left as you crest the divide, the same trailhead used for the Illinois Peak hike (Hike 11). The trail starts on your right. Ample parking; toilets, drinking water, and camping at nearby Missoula Lake Campground. GPS: N47 03.667' / W115 07.250'

The Hike

Most Montanans visualize the spectacular eastern front of the Selway–Bitterroot Wilderness when thinking of the Bitterroot Mountains. However, from Lolo Pass north to Lookout Pass lies a section of the Bitterroots with different but equally appealing character. The northern Bitterroots are less craggy than the southern peaks and heavily dotted with lakes. There are more than forty fishable lakes, most easy walks from a trailhead.

From the trailhead, take Stateline Trail 738 to the northwest, which takes off just to the Idaho side of the divide. Just after leaving the trailhead, Stateline Trail forks; stay right, continuing along the contour to the northwest (the Idaho side of the ridge). Stateline Trail forks again 1.5 miles beyond the trailhead. Take the right (northeast)

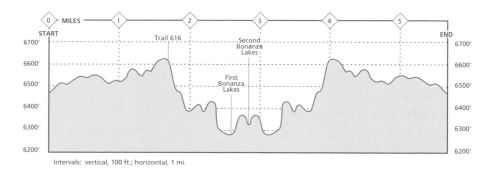

Intervals: vertical, 100 ft.; horizontal, 1 mi.

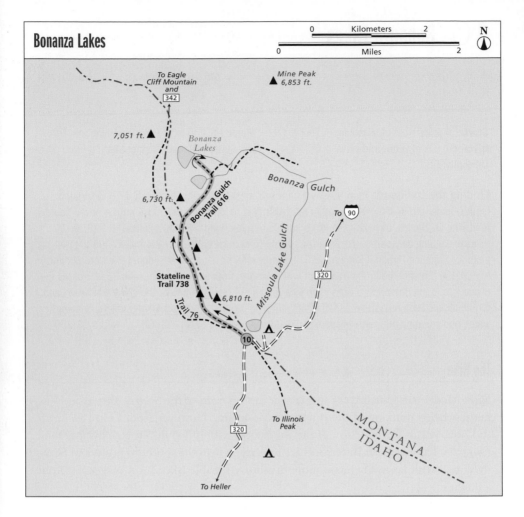

fork and follow Bonanza Gulch Trail 616 (no sign at this junction when I hiked this, but there was a large cairn) across the divide into Montana and through a grassy basin for about a mile to the first Bonanza Lake.

The big meadow before the lakes is awash with paintbrush and many other wildflowers. The second Bonanza Lake is about a quarter mile beyond the first. Both lakes have small brookies and several good campsites.

Miles and Directions

0.0 Trailhead.

1.5 Junction with Bonanza Gulch Trail 616; turn right.

2.5 First Bonanza Lake.

2.8 Second Bonanza Lake.

5.6 Trailhead.

Calypso orchid. Jacquelyn Corday

Options: Back on the divide, the Stateline Trail, which was designated a National Recreation Trail in 1981, continues northwest beyond Bonanza Lakes along the divide past Eagle Cliff. This makes an excellent shuttle hike if you leave another vehicle on Dry Creek Road 342 where it crosses the Bitterroot Divide. However, that involves a long dirt-road shuttle and you may want to do an out-and-back instead. (Originally contributed by John Westenberg, re-hiked by the authors.)

11 Illinois Peak

A day hike or overnighter through spectacular—and seldom seen—mountain scenery along the Bitterroot Divide

Start: 45 miles west of Missoula
Distance: 10.0-mile out-and-back
Difficulty: Moderate

Maps: USGS Illinois Peak and Hoodoo; Lolo National Forest, Superior Ranger District Map

Finding the trailhead: From Missoula, take I-90 west to Superior. Take exit 47 and turn left (south) under the freeway. Take another left (east) just beyond the underpass onto a paved county road. After 1.2 miles, turn right (south) onto Cedar Creek Road (FR 320). Follow FR 320 for 24 miles of winding dirt road to the Bitterroot Divide (pavement ends after 2.4 miles) and the trailhead for Stateline National Recreation Trail, shortly after passing the Missoula Lake Campground turnoff. The Stateline Trail runs northwest and southeast from where Cedar Creek Road crosses the divide into Idaho. The parking area is on your left as you crest the divide, the same trailhead used for Bonanza Lakes (Hike 10). The trail starts on south side of the road at the parking area. Ample parking; toilets, drinking water, and camping at nearby Missoula Lake Campground. GPS: N47 03.667' / W115 07.250'

The Hike

Perhaps because the higher portions of the Bitterroot Mountains north of Lolo Pass aren't visible from a major highway, they remain relatively overlooked and underrated. None of the peaks exceed 8,000 feet, but because they're among the westernmost of Montana's mountain ranges, the Bitterroots receive an abundance of rain and snow. The result is a lot more alpine scenery at lower elevations than in most mountain ranges. Many ridgeline trails are dry and parched, but this hike goes through a lush, green landscape.

At 7,690 feet, Illinois Peak is one of the highest peaks in the northern Bitterroots. The fairly easy walk to the top goes through subalpine country and offers many scenic views, as does the peak itself.

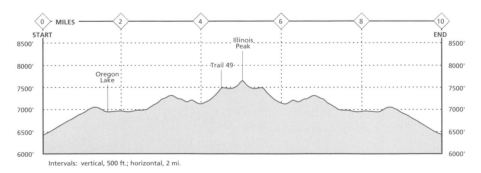

Intervals: vertical, 500 ft.; horizontal, 2 mi.

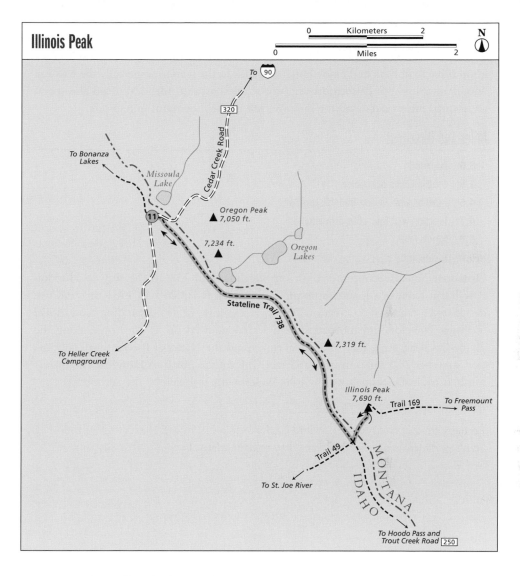

From the trailhead, take Stateline Trail 738 and head southeast from the parking area. The trail and the pass are dry, so bring water. The trail stays close to the divide all the way.

At 4.5 miles, watch carefully for the junction with St. Joe Trail 49. The sign is on your right and could be missed. Shortly after the junction with Trail 49, watch for Trail 169 going off to your left (east). There was no sign when we hiked this route. You don't want to miss it and end up on Hoodoo Pass.

Try to do this hike early in the morning. The first light of the day adds beauty to an already beautiful landscape. It'll be cooler too. Early departures also give you a better chance of avoiding afternoon thunderstorms, and you definitely don't want to be on this divide when the lightning starts flashing.

Illinois Peak, 1,200 feet higher than the trailhead, offers a sweeping view of much of the proposed Great Burn Wilderness to the southeast. Illinois Peak's grassy top is a good place to sit back and enjoy lunch and soak in the scenery, especially the Mission Mountains, southern Bitterroots, and vast roadless areas in Idaho. You can also spend an hour or more reading all the messages left in the mountaintop registers.

Miles and Directions

0.0 Trailhead.

1.5 Oregon Lakes overlook.

4.5 Junction with St. Joe Trail 49; turn left.

4.7 Junction with Trail 169; turn left.

5.0 Illinois Peak.

10.0 Trailhead.

Options: You can continue south on Stateline Trail 738 all the way to Hoodoo Pass, but it requires a long shuttle on Trout Creek Road 250. In 1981 this trail was designated a National Recreation Trail in recognition of its outstanding recreational qualities. Therefore, no motorized vehicles are allowed on it. The route along the divide has been used since aboriginal times, and the National Recreation Trail portion stretches 18.3 miles from near Eagle Cliff on the north to Hoodoo Pass on the south. (Originally contributed by John Westenberg, re-hiked by the authors.)

12 Heart Lake

An easy day hike or overnighter to a tranquil lake basin with lots of trout in the lakes and huckleberries along the trail

Start: 70 miles west of Missoula in the proposed Great Burn Wilderness
Distance: 4.0-mile out-and-back

Difficulty: Easy
Maps: USGS Straight Peak; Lolo National Forest, Superior Ranger District Map

Finding the trailhead: Drive west from Missoula on I-90 and turn south on Trout Creek Road 250 from Superior exit 47. The first 6 miles are a paved frontage road. After 20 miles the road makes a sharp switchback to the right. At this switchback, Heart Lake Trail 171 leads off to your left (south). Limited parking; no toilet; several undeveloped campsites along Trout Creek Road. GPS: N46 58.950' / W114 58.733'

The Hike

The proposed Great Burn Wilderness sprawls almost 40 miles along the Bitterroot Divide. This short hike is sure to tantalize you with the hiking possibilities in this 200,000-acre area, one of the wildest roadless areas in Montana.

From the trailhead, Heart Lake Trail 171 climbs some 1,200 feet in 2 miles to the shore of Heart Lake, crossing the South Fork of Trout Creek several times—all on bridges except the last crossing just before the lake. This is a beautiful trail that climbs gradually (except one little hill just before the lake) through a lush, green forest all the way to the lake.

When you get to the stream crossing just before the lake, be careful you don't miss the trail sign pointing to the lake. It's immediately after crossing the stream. If you miss it, you'll head up toward the Bitterroot Divide and have to backtrack to find the lake. A hundred yards after you turn left (south) at this junction, you're at the lake.

From mid-August through early September, ripe huckleberries line the trail and make this hike one of the most edible you've ever taken. Heart Lake has a good

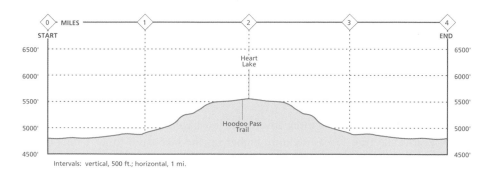

Intervals: vertical, 500 ft.; horizontal, 1 mi.

Heart Lake, a lonely gem deep in the northern Bitterroots. JACQUELYN CORDAY

population of cutthroat and brook trout, and it makes a good turnaround point for day hikers. Late summer is the best time for this hike—when the bugs are gone, the berries are ripe, and hunting season hasn't started.

Miles and Directions

0.0 Trailhead.
1.9 Junction with Hoodoo Pass Trail; turn left.
2.0 Heart Lake.
4.0 Trailhead.

Options: If you need a little more adventure, you have three options. Your first is to follow Pearl Lake Trail 175 as it climbs higher up the lake basin (only 1 mile to the lake but on a very brushy trail), past Pearl Lake, and over a low pass to Dalton Lake.

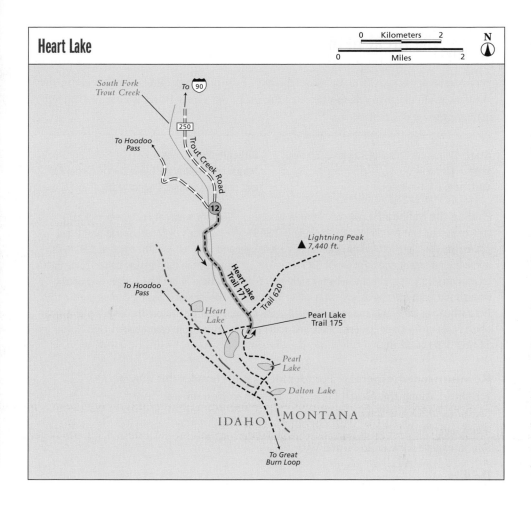

Pearl and Dalton Lakes support small cutthroat trout and have the advantage of being more remote (and less fished) than Heart Lake.

A second option is a steep trail that leads westward from Heart Lake to the Bitterroot Divide and the Idaho border, providing astounding views of vast roadless country in the forested mountains of Idaho. You can connect with either Illinois Peak (Hike 11) to the northwest or The Great Burn (Hike 13) to the southeast along the divide. You can also come down off the divide to Pearl Lake and then back to Heart Lake to make a small loop.

A third option is Trail 620, unmarked and primitive, which leads to the 7,440-foot summit of Lightning Peak, just east of Heart Lake, and eventually drops down into Cement Gulch and returns to Trout Creek Road. However, most hikers will want to return to their vehicles by way of Heart Lake and skip this 8-mile-long side trip. (Originally contributed by Bill Cunningham, re-hiked by the authors.)

13 The Great Burn

An extended backpacking vacation through beautiful subalpine country along the Bitterroot Divide through the heart of the proposed Great Burn Wilderness, including rare groves of giant cedars

Start: Clearwater Crossing Trailhead, 30 miles west of Missoula
Distance: 31.4-mile loop

Difficulty: Strenuous
Maps: USGS Straight Peak; Lolo National Forest, Superior Ranger District Map

Finding the trailhead: Drive west from Missoula on I-90, turn south at Fish Creek exit 66 (before Tarkio), and get on Fish Creek Road (FR 343), which passes by Montana's largest living ponderosa pine. Turn left (south) after about a half mile and then left (south) again at 1.9 miles, where the pavement ends. Follow FR 343 a total of 10.1 miles from the freeway before going right (south) on FR 7750 and continuing for another 5.6 miles to Hole in the Wall Lodge. Go straight through the lodge (driving slowly) for another 1.2 miles to Clearwater Crossing Campground and the trailhead at the end of the road. The trail starts on your right just before the large parking area, which is set up for horse trailers. Toilets and water are available in the campground. GPS: N46 54.467' / W114 48.500'

Recommended itinerary: For four nights out, consider this itinerary:
First night: Along the North Fork, 6 to 8 miles from trailhead
Second night: Goose Lake
Third night: Fish Lake
Fourth night: Halfway down the West Fork

The Hike

The Great Burn is a huge roadless area of almost 200,000 acres straddling the Idaho–Montana border. This superb loop hike takes you through long, timbered valleys and along open subalpine country on the Bitterroot Divide. However, even this 31-mile hike touches only a small portion of the backcountry hiking in the Great Burn. This description goes counterclockwise up the North Fork of Fish Creek (Trail 103) and along the Bitterroot Divide (Stateline Trail 738), then returns to the trailhead via the West Fork of Fish Creek (Trail 101).

With all the forest fires of recent years, especially in the Bitterroots, it's hard to find a trail that doesn't go through a burned forest. Ironically, the Great Burn loop, named for the famous 1910 fire, has mostly remained unburned since then.

From the trailhead, take Trail 103 along the North Fork of Fish Creek as it curves north and then west up to the Bitterroot Divide. Go right after 1 mile at the first junction with the trail up Straight Creek. Continue about 5 more miles and then turn left at the next two junctions up Greenwood (Trail 176) and French Creeks (Trail 143) at the 6- to 7-mile marks. Here, the trail passes through formerly private

Nothing like the first big backpacking trip. BILL SCHNEIDER

land next to the Greenwood Cabin. The area included patented mining claims dating back to early 1900s.

Prepare for wet crossings up Greenwood and French Creeks. Also prepare to see a few stands of mature western red cedars, always a rare treat, especially a big grove around French Creek. Seeing these great cedars exploding out of a lush carpet of ferns is worth the trip.

It's a steep and brushy 1,000-foot ascent out of the upper North Fork basin to a low pass on the state line. At 10.7 miles you reach Stateline Trail 738, where you turn left (south). Continuing south on Stateline Trail for about a half mile, you descend into Idaho and Goose Lake. Fill with water here, since the trail stays high and dry for the next 9 miles. Goose Lake is in a big meadow and has lots of campsites, but like the rest of this loop, it's heavily used by stock parties.

From the low point on the pass near Goose Lake (only 5,840 feet in elevation), the Stateline Trail rolls up and down over the minor summits of the northern Bitter-root Range, eventually reaching a high point of 7,334 feet. Some of the short pitches on the divide can really stretch out your calves and get your heart rate up. The trail crosses broad meadows and knife-edged ridges as it follows the crest of the divide south to Fish Lake. Above Straight Lake the trail goes through two small burns, both fairly old, that give the landscape an aura of mystery as you pass through groves of ghost trees.

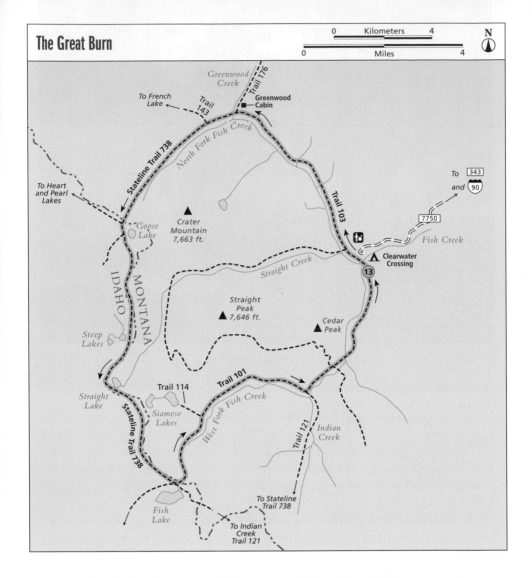

Kilometers

Miles

N

To French Lake

Trail 143

Greenwood Creek

Trail 176

Greenwood Cabin

Stateline Trail 738

North Fork Fish Creek

To Heart and Pearl Lakes

Trail 103

To 343 and 90

7750

Goose Lake

Crater Mountain 7,663 ft.

Fish Creek

IDAHO

MONTANA

Straight Creek

Clearwater Crossing

13

Straight Peak 7,646 ft.

Cedar Peak

Steep Lakes

Trail 114

Trail 101

Straight Lake

Stateline Trail 738

Siamese Lakes

West Fork Fish Creek

Trail 121

Indian Creek

To Stateline Trail 738

Fish Lake

To Indian Creek Trail 121

Here you're in the center of the proposed Great Burn Wilderness, with great views in every direction. On clear days the tops of the Mission Mountains appear far to the east; the crumpled ranges of the huge Bighorn-Weitas roadless country stretch off to the west in Idaho. Expect a spectacular wildflower display early in the summer, and ghostly snags remind the hiker of the Great Burn that sped through this country in August 1910.

At 17.5 miles you'll see a spur trail heading steeply down to Upper Siamese Lake. Continue on Stateline Trail unless you're camping here or have time for a side trip to catch a few cutthroats.

After about 20 miles of hiking, you reach the junction with Trail 101, which heads northward up the West Fork of Fish Creek. From this junction, it's about 11 miles down to Clearwater Crossing and your vehicle. The central portion of this stretch can be boggy and might slow your progress. Trail 101 also passes through groves of old western red cedar, western larch, and big lodgepole pine, which make this valley hiking more pleasant.

The Bitterroot Divide gets more precipitation than most of Montana, so don't attempt this loop before early July. Check with the Forest Service on snow conditions before trying an early-July hike in a heavy snow year. Being wet country, bugs can be way too numerous, so bring something to keep them at bay.

When we did this trip, several junctions were unsigned, so be alert not to miss any. And the signs that are there don't have mileages, which only adds to the special aura of wildness engulfing the Great Burn.

Miles and Directions

0.0 Clearwater Crossing Trailhead.

1.0 Junction with Straight Creek Trail; turn right.

5.0 Greenwood Cabin and junction with St. Pats Trail 176; turn left.

6.0 Junction with French Creek Trail 143; turn left.

10.7 Bitterroot Divide and junction with Stateline Trail 738; turn left.

11.2 Goose Lake and junction with Goose Creek Trail 414; turn left.

17.5 Spur trail to Siamese Lakes.

20.2 Junction with Trail 101; turn left.

21.7 Junction with Siamese Lakes Trail 114; turn right.

26.2 Junction with Indian Creek Trail 121; turn left.

26.3 Junction with Trail 104; turn left.

28.0 Bridge over West Fork and junction with Trail 110; turn left.

31.4 Clearwater Crossing Trailhead.

Options: You can do this loop in reverse with about the same level of difficulty. Also, you can skip Fish Lake and take the unmaintained social trail down and around Siamese Lakes and then take Trail 114 down to Trail 101. (Originally contributed by Ed Madej, re-hiked by the authors.)

14 Stuart Peak

A long, hard day hike with vistas of at least four mountain ranges from the summit of Stuart Peak

Start: Just north of Missoula in the Rattlesnake National Recreation Area and Wilderness
Distance: 18.0-mile out-and-back
Difficulty: Strenuous

Maps: USGS Northeast Missoula and Stuart Peak; Lolo National Forest, Missoula Ranger District Map; Rattlesnake National Recreation Area and Wilderness Map

Finding the trailhead: Drive north on Van Buren Street from the Van Buren exit off I-90 in Missoula, bearing to the right until you find yourself on Rattlesnake Drive. Turn left onto Sawmill Gulch Road (about a half mile beyond Wildcat Road and 4 miles total from I-90). The trailhead and entrance to the upper Rattlesnake area are located at the mouth of Sawmill Gulch, just a few yards beyond the bridge over Rattlesnake Creek. A large (but still full at times) parking lot with a toilet and information board with a map of the area; no drinking water; no camping near the trailhead. GPS: N46 58.800' / W113 50.150'

The Hike

Probably no other city has such a spectacular yet accessible wild area as Missoula with its backyard paradise, the 61,000-acre Rattlesnake National Recreation Area (NRA) and Wilderness. This hike takes you through a lot of that wild country and up to a vista above a scattering of alpine lakes in the most remote part of the wilderness.

The recreation area is open to mountain biking, so hikers can see how non-problematic it can be to share the trails with other human-powered recreationists. Multiuse trails work well as long as all recreation is nonmotorized, and here is a great example of it. Local mountain bikers in cooperation with the Forest Service have developed a code of riding ethics and posted it at the trailhead, and have put up several ride-friendly signs at key trail junctions.

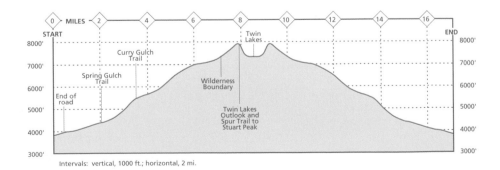

Intervals: vertical, 1000 ft.; horizontal, 2 mi.

The heavy use of this giant urban playground has made a few special regulations necessary. Depending on the time of year, dogs are either prohibited or must be on a leash for the first part of the trail, and shooting, camping, and campfires are prohibited in the south zone of the NRA, but allowed beyond the south zone as you get deeper into the NRA and the Rattlesnake Wilderness. And no motor vehicles allowed. At the end of the "three-mile zone," these restrictions no longer apply, except the ban on motorized recreation. Pick up a brochure at the information board at the trailhead, which has a map of part of the trail system and summarizes the regulations.

Beginning hikers like the Rattlesnake because they feel comfortingly close to civilization. Indeed, from time to time en route, one is within sight—and sometimes even the sound—of Missoula. This route is physically challenging for first-timers, however. It's a long, uphill grind (9 miles one way) to Stuart Peak.

Start the hike on the old road (FR 99) heading up Rattlesnake Creek at the far end of the parking area by the information board. Stay on the road for about a half mile before turning left (northwest) on Stuart Peak Trail 517. You can continue up the road for another half mile or so and take the Spring Gulch Trail, which stays on the east side of Spring Gulch, but it might be better to save this for the return trip.

The first 2 miles up the bottom of Spring Gulch are quite easy. The route goes past the sites of homesteads established a century or more ago, though all that remain are traces of foundations and hearths, a few persistent lilac bushes and apple trees, and two alien Lombardy poplars. Spring Gulch is a popular descent for mountain bikers, so keep your head up and yield for safety. At 2 miles the trail from the east side of the creek crosses a bridge and joins the Stuart Peak Trail. There's a toilet just across the bridge, but that's about the last sign that you're in a heavily used, semi-developed area. From this point on, the trail steadily climbs to the shoulder of Stuart Peak. At 3 miles you reach the top of Sawmill Gulch, where the "three-mile zone" restrictions end. At 3.5 miles turn right (north) where the Curry Gulch Trail rejoins.

After the gradual climb to the top of Spring Gulch, the Stuart Peak Trail winds relentlessly upward for another 5 miles to an overlook on the flanks of Stuart Peak. Take lots of water because you might not find any along the trail. At about 5.5 miles, the trail goes through a series of long, annoyingly flat switchbacks, which probably add a mile to the length of the trip. At 7 miles you leave the Rattlesnake National Recreation Area and enter the Rattlesnake Wilderness. All this means is no more mountain bikes; otherwise, you won't notice the difference. The trail is in as good a shape as a trail can be and is nicely suited for trail running.

When you get to the overlook into Twin Lakes at 8.5 miles, take a 0.5-mile spur trail to your right to the top of 7,960-foot Stuart Peak. The summit isn't actually that far from the sights and sounds of the city, but it seems like you're in the middle of a huge wilderness, which you are. Much of the Rattlesnake high country remains without trails or is served by only faint tracks. Despite the Rattlesnake's popularity, secluded, almost undiscovered basins and lakes dot its far reaches.

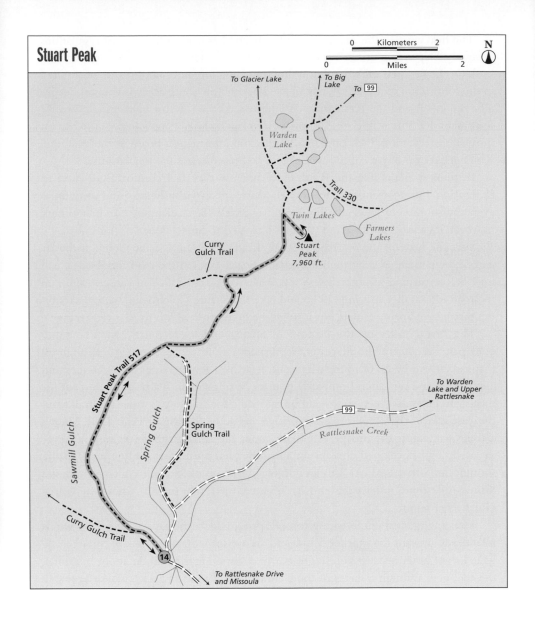

Stuart Peak

0   Kilometers   2

0   Miles   2

N

To Glacier Lake
To Big Lake
To 99

Warden Lake

Trail 330

Twin Lakes

Farmers Lakes

Curry Gulch Trail

Stuart Peak 7,960 ft.

Stuart Peak Trail 517

Sawmill Gulch

Spring Gulch

Spring Gulch Trail

99

Rattlesnake Creek

To Warden Lake and Upper Rattlesnake

Curry Gulch Trail

14

To Rattlesnake Drive and Missoula

Miles and Directions

0.0 Trailhead.

0.5 Junction with Stuart Peak Trail 517; turn left.

1.1 Junction with Curry Gulch Trail; turn right.

2.0 Junction with Spring Gulch Trail from east side of stream; turn left.

3.0 Top of Sawmill Gulch and end of special restrictions.

3.5 Junction with Curry Gulch Trail; turn right.

7.0 Wilderness boundary.

8.5 Overlook into Twin Lakes and spur trail to Stuart Peak; turn right.

9.0 Stuart Peak.

18.0 Trailhead.

Options: The remote Rattlesnake can also serve as a remote base camp. If you decided to lug an overnight pack all the way up to the overlook, drop down about another quarter mile to the junction with Trail 330, where you turn right (north) and descend for about a half mile to Twin Lakes. From here, or from one of the other lakes in the immediate area, you can spend days exploring the many lakes and peaks in the upper reaches of the Rattlesnake Wilderness.

No fish swim in Twin Lakes, but Farmers Lakes support cutthroat trout, as do most nearby lakes (McKinley, Warden, Carter, Big, and Sheridan). You might also pick up a few rainbows in some of them. The lake basin, beyond the junction with Trails 517 and 330, is closed to stock parties.

Proximity to Missoula results in high use of much of the area. This location—plus the fragile nature of the high country itself and the area's status as Missoula's municipal watershed—demands that you take every precaution to leave no trace of your visit. Evidence of high-country campsites is proliferating. Make every effort to pass lightly over this fragile terrain; don't add to the blight of fire rings; and take a few minutes to help repair the damage made by others.

On the way back, cross Spring Gulch and take the eastside trail back to the trailhead. It will probably be late afternoon, and you'll find a bit more shade here.

You also have the option of making a big loop out of this trip by taking either Trail 534 or 502 down to the trail down Rattlesnake Creek, which merges with FR 99 and goes back to the trailhead. Most of this route is still open to mountain bikers, and if you take it, expect to see more people, as this is the main thoroughfare of the Rattlesnake National Recreation Area.

Side Trips: The must-do side trip is the top of Stuart Peak, where you get a fantastic vista of the entire area. After that's done, take your choice from the many lakes and mountaintops to explore. (Originally contributed by Joseph A. Mussulman and Bill Brown, re-hiked by the authors.)

THE VIEW FROM HERE: SWITCHBACKING GONE AMOK

Who doesn't like switchbacks, those zigs and zags that make the hills easier? Nobody. Everybody likes them, including yours truly. But as often happens, we sometimes carry a good thing too far.

Lately, during trail reconstruction, land managers have started to put in what I call "mall walk" switchbacks, the nearly level and looonnnng variety. They can transform a 2-mile Category 1 hill into a gradual ascent, but in the process, they can also turn a 2-mile hike into a 4-mile hike. I much prefer switchbacks that turn a 2-mile hike into a 2.5- or 3-mile hike and allow me to get to camp sooner so I can spend more time fishing, day hiking, or napping.

People who go hiking expect to have hills, so it isn't necessary to make these switchbacks so easy and long. A few good examples of mall walk switchbacks in this book are Stuart Peak, Louise Lake, the Upsidedown Creek Trail coming out of the Lake Plateau, and the Hidden Lake Trail coming out of the Edith-Baldy Basin.

These mall walk switchbacks are not only unnecessary, but it also seems to me that they actually create environmental damage by first, disturbing a much larger slice of wild country during construction, and second, seducing some hikers into switchback cutting to save time, probably causing as many or more erosion problems than the original trail did.

Let's get back to more sensible zigs and zags with water bars that get us up a hill without a heart attack but don't deface the entire mountainside—and get us to our destination an hour sooner.

15 Boulder Lake

A day hike or overnighter into a high mountain lake in a lightly used section of the Rattlesnake Wilderness

Start: West Fork of Gold Creek Trailhead, 15 miles north of Missoula on the west edge of the Rattlesnake Wilderness
Distance: 10.0-mile out-and-back
Difficulty: Moderate

Maps: USGS Gold Creek Peak and Wapiti Lake; Lolo National Forest, Missoula Ranger District Map; Rattlesnake National Recreation Area and Wilderness Map

Finding the trailhead: Drive north of Bonner (east of Missoula) on MT 200 along the Blackfoot River. Turn left (northwest) and continue on Gold Creek Road (FR 126) for 6 miles. (This is private land, so be courteous of commercial logging operations.) Then turn left (west) onto FR 2103. Follow FR 2103 for 5 miles until it forks. Take the left (west) fork onto FR 4323 as it switchbacks up the left side of the valley before dropping to the valley floor and ascending the north side of the valley to the West Fork of Gold Creek Trailhead, 16 miles total from the MT 200. Limited parking along the road; be careful not to block it; no toilet or camping. GPS: N47 00.850' / W113 45.667'

The Hike

In 1980 Congress established the Rattlesnake National Recreation Area and Wilderness to provide a place where water, wilderness, wildlife, and recreational and educational values (four of the five "multiple uses" listed in the Wilderness Act of 1964) are preserved. Boulder Lake offers all. This hike presents a stark contrast between land preserved as wilderness and land open to timber cutting. All along the 16-mile unpaved road to the trailhead and along the first 1.5 miles of the hike, you go through an ocean of clear-cuts before escaping into the solitude of the Rattlesnake Wilderness.

From the trailhead, Trail 333 heads north for 2.5 miles on relatively flat terrain with two creek crossings. This area is partially private land, so be respectful. Watch for

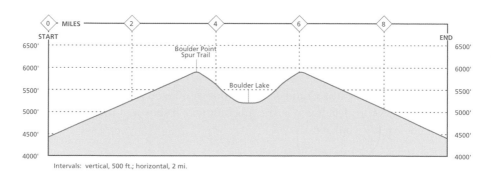

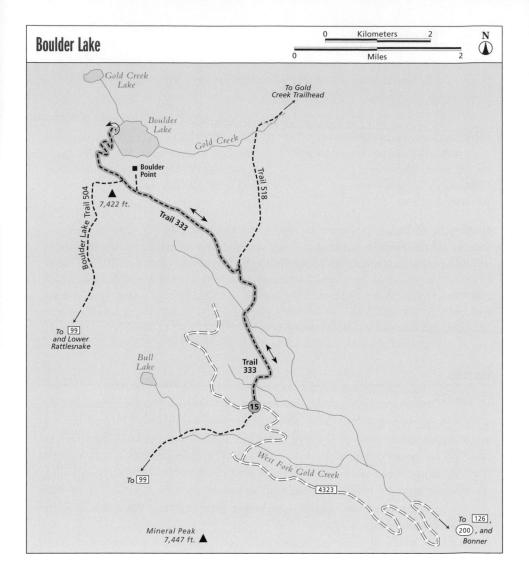

Gold Creek
Lake

To Gold
Creek Trailhead

Boulder
Lake

Gold Creek

■ Boulder
Point

Trail 518

Boulder Lake Trail 504

▲
7,422 ft.

Trail 333

To 99
and Lower
Rattlesnake

Bull
Lake

Trail
333

15

West Fork Gold Creek

To 99

4323

Mineral Peak
7,447 ft. ▲

To 126,
200, and
Bonner

trail markers and cairns while crossing a logged area. The trail follows a logging road for about 100 yards before turning right. A cairn marks the turnoff.

At 1.5 miles is the junction with Trail 518 from Gold Creek; take a sharp left, heading west. At the junction there is a small creek, and filtering water at this point would be a good idea. Past the junction the trail climbs gradually for 2.5 miles before the trail turns right (northwest) and descends another mile on steep trail into Boulder Lake. At 3.5 miles turn left (west) at the junction with a spur trail to Boulder Point. Save this side trip for your return.

Boulder Lake is the largest lake with fish in the Rattlesnake Wilderness. Some of the campsites are showing serious signs of overuse, so if staying overnight, leave zero impact of your visit.

Miles and Directions

- **0.0** West Fork of Gold Creek Trailhead.
- **1.5** Junction with Trail 518 from Gold Creek; turn left.
- **3.5** Junction with spur trail to Boulder Point; turn left.
- **5.0** Boulder Lake.
- **10.0** West Fork of Gold Creek Trailhead.

Side Trips: Before descending to the lake, a spur trail veers right to Boulder Point. An old fire lookout was standing at the top when we were there in 2002. Regrettably, a forest fire claimed the lookout in 2003, but the view is still there. The panoramic view of the lake and the view of the Mission Mountains to the north are well worth the short walk to the point. (Originally contributed and re-hiked by the authors.)

16 Welcome Creek

A day hike or overnighter into one of Montana's smallest wilderness areas, the Welcome Creek Wilderness

Start: Welcome Creek Trailhead, 25 miles southeast of Missoula in the Sapphire Mountains
Distance: Up to 14.0-mile out-and-back
Difficulty: Moderate

Maps: USGS Cleveland Mountain and Grizzly Point; Lolo National Forest, Missoula Ranger District Map

Finding the trailhead: Drive east from Missoula for 25 miles on I-90 and turn right (south) at Rock Creek exit 126. Go south on Rock Creek Road 102 for 14 miles (11.5 paved) and watch for a sign on your right (west) marking Welcome Creek Trail 225. Ample parking; toilet, camping, and drinking water at nearby Welcome Creek and Dalles Campgrounds. GPS: N46 33.603' / W113 42.243'

The Hike

Besides offering scenic, timbered hiking trails, the Welcome Creek Wilderness has a rich history. Mined extensively around the turn of the twentieth century, the area has many haunting reminders, now abandoned and decaying into the landscape, to greet you.

From the trailhead, Welcome Creek Trail 225 crosses Rock Creek on a suspension bridge. Veer right, following the creek downstream for about a quarter mile before turning, crossing Welcome Creek on a bridge and turning west. From here follow the stream until you feel like camping or turning around. Trail 225 continues 7 miles to the low summit of Cleveland Mountain. The trail is rocky (not for trail running), and the grade is so gradual that you don't realize you're climbing.

This valley is steep and narrow. It has a mystery and loneliness of its own as you walk by old mining sites and watch the forest gradually reclaiming them. This is a wet area with a beautiful old-growth forest and a lush understory (including, regrettably,

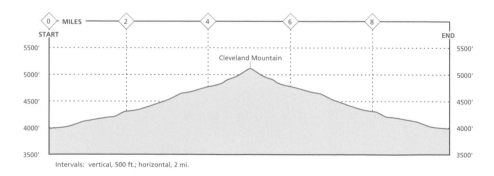

Start the Welcome Creek hike by crossing the cool suspension bridge over Rock Creek.
BILL SCHNEIDER

a good crop of nettles), so wait until July for hiking. If you go earlier, expect a boggy trail and mosquitoes out in force. Finding drinking water poses no problem, though. Although Welcome Creek has small brook trout, the fishing there takes a backseat to the famous Rock Creek running past the trailhead.

Although some people who opposed Wilderness designation for Welcome Creek claimed the area had too many signs of civilization to qualify for wilderness, the reverse is true. Man's hold on the area has long faded into history. Now, the ghosts of old-timers (such as outlaw Frank Brady, who was shot in 1904 in Welcome Creek) only enrich the wilderness experience. The area also provides an excellent example of how quickly nature heals the wounds of past carelessness. (Originally contributed by Don Berg, re-hiked by the authors.)

Welcome Creek

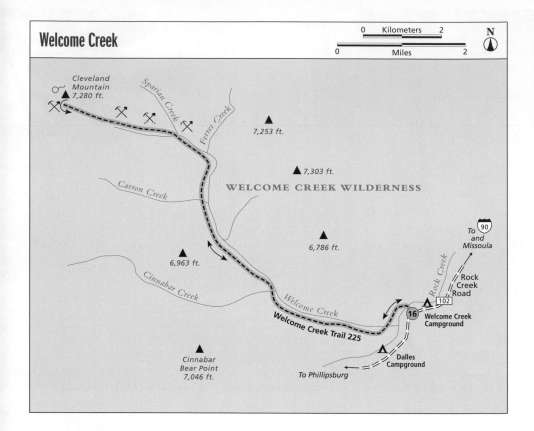

Miles and Directions

0.0   Welcome Creek Trailhead.

7.0   Cleveland Mountain.

14.0 Welcome Creek Trailhead.

17 Pyramid Lake

A day hike or overnighter into the Swan Range

Start: 10 miles northeast of Seeley Lake
Distance: 12.0-mile out-and-back
Difficulty: Moderate

Maps: USGS Morrell Lake and Crimson Peak; Lolo National Forest, Seeley Lake Ranger District Map

Finding the trailhead: From Seeley Lake, turn east on Cottonwood Creek Road 477 on the north edge of town. After 1.2 miles turn left (northeast) on Morrell Creek Road 4353. After driving 7.1 miles from Seeley Lake, turn right (east) on Pyramid Pass Road 4381 and follow it to the large trailhead where it ends. The sign in Seeley Lake says it's 9 miles to the trailhead, but it was 10.4 on our odometer. The large trailhead is set up for horse trailers and has ample parking and a toilet. GPS: N47 16.433' / W113 24.900'

The Hike

This trail, Trail 416, is one of the major entry points to the Bob Marshall Wilderness, so it gets heavy horse traffic. The trail is dry, though, so no horse bogs, and it's in great shape all the way. For the first mile or so, you're on an old logging road converted to a trail. After that it's mostly a gradual climb, broken up by a few switchbacks, that doesn't seem as steep as it actually is.

About a quarter mile below Pyramid Pass, at mile 4.7, you'll see an unnamed lake on your left. After you go over the low-profile pass, turn left (northeast) at the junction with Trail 278. Shortly thereafter, turn left on the spur trail to Pyramid Lake. If you aren't alert, you can miss this spur trail and keep heading into the depths of the Bob. This isn't an official Forest Service trail, and it wasn't marked when I hiked this route. Watch for it directly after crossing the first stream after coming over the pass. You can't see the lake from here, even though it's only about a quarter mile more.

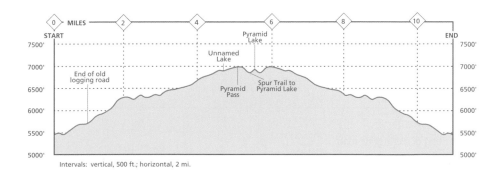

Pyramid Lake. JACQUELYN CORDAY

Pyramid Lake is big, round, and filled with cutthroats. Mighty Pyramid Peak looms over the lake to the west to provide a scenic backdrop.

Miles and Directions

0.0 Trailhead.

1.0 End of old logging road.

4.7 Unnamed lake.

5.0 Pyramid Pass and wilderness boundary.

5.5 Junction with Trail 278; turn left.

5.6 Junction with spur trail to Pyramid Lake; turn left.

6.0 Pyramid Lake.

12.0 Trailhead.

Side Trips: If you're energetic, try the scramble up to Pyramid Peak. It isn't dangerous and goes mostly through open country, but it's quite strenuous. (Originally contributed by the authors.)

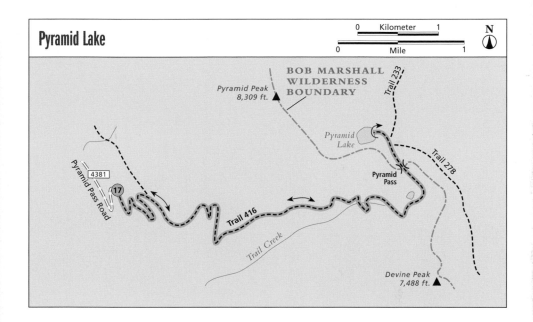

Bitterroot National Forest

18 Peterson Lake

A day hike or overnighter to several high mountain lakes with stunning views of Sweeney Canyon and the surrounding peaks

Start: 8 miles west of Florence
Distance: 10.0-mile out-and-back
Difficulty: Moderate

Maps: USGS Carlton Lakes, Dick Creek, and St. Mary's Peak; Selway-Bitterroot Wilderness Map

Finding the trailhead: Drive south of Missoula for 18 miles on US 93 to Florence and then another 1.5 miles south. Turn right, heading west on Sweeney Creek Road (FR 14), a paved road, which veers to the left 0.9 mile later. Stay right on unpaved FR 1315 at this junction and then right again 0.4 mile later, and drive another 6.4 miles to the trailhead (7.7 miles total from US 93). Sweeney Creek Road climbs steeply from the valley floor, and the last section of switchbacks on FR 1315 might stretch the limits of a low-clearance, two-wheel-drive vehicle. Limited parking (please avoid taking two spaces), with no room for horse trailers; no toilet. GPS: N46 37.333' / W114 08.933'

Peterson Lake from the trail above. JACQUELYN CORDAY

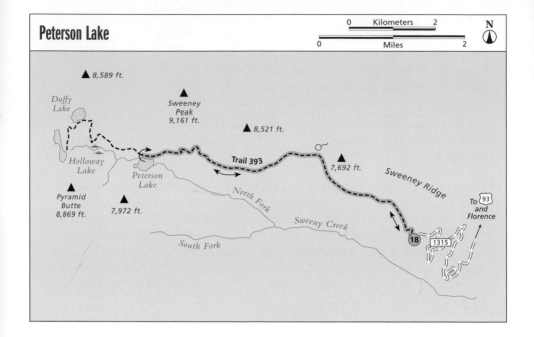

The Hike

This pleasant hike is close to Missoula, so you might see other hikers on busy summer weekends. It's also an excellent overnight trip to absorb the joys of ancient trees and mountain lakes. Duffy, Holloway, and Peterson Lakes all have fish. At Peterson Lake, however, there isn't much room for a backcast except at the inlet.

From the trailhead Trail 393 climbs steadily west along Sweeney Ridge for 2 miles before reaching a natural spring. Be sure to carry enough water for the climb. Along the way you may want to note the girth of some of the remaining Douglas fir and ponderosa pine trees; some are 4 feet in diameter. In addition, midway to the spring, there is a large rock overlook perfect for pictures. If you use the right camera angle, it'll look as if you were atop a mountain above the Bitterroots. From this overlook and a few more along the way, you get a great view of the upper Sweeney Creek Valley and Pyramid Butte.

From the spring the trail levels off, and then over the next 2 miles gradually descends before it drops steeply for the last mile or so to the lake. The trail is in great shape all the way, but rocky enough to make it marginal for trail running. A spur trail takes you to the inlet of the lake, where you'll find a few heavily used campsites. Avoid creating new impacts by using existing campsites. Bring the bug dope and head net; Peterson Lake has more than its share of mosquitoes.

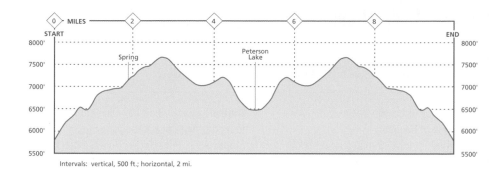

Intervals: vertical, 500 ft.; horizontal, 2 mi.

Miles and Directions

0.0 Trailhead.

2.0 Spring.

2.5 Wilderness boundary.

5.0 Peterson Lake.

10.0 Trailhead.

Side Trips: If you feel ambitious, continue on to Duffy and Holloway Lakes. Duffy is another 2 miles of climbing on a much rougher and less maintained trail. The farther from civilization you travel, the less wary fish get. (Originally contributed and re-hiked by the authors.)

19 Blodgett Canyon

A fairly easy trek through spectacular scenery with famed rock climbing; anything from a short day hike to a weeklong backpacking adventure

Start: Blodgett Canyon Trailhead, 5 miles northwest of Hamilton
Distance: Up to 25.0-mile out-and-back

Difficulty: Easy (short day hikes) to moderate (long day hikes or backpacking trips)
Maps: USGS Printz Ridge; Selway-Bitterroot Wilderness Map

Finding the trailhead: In Hamilton, turn west onto Main Street (also Highway 531) and continue through town for 1.1 miles; turn right on Ricketts Road. Drive another 0.5 mile and then turn left on Blodgett Camp Road when Ricketts Road turns right. Go another 2.4 miles to a junction with the road to the Overlook and Canyon Lake trailhead. Turn right here, following the sign to Blodgett Canyon Campground. Go another 1.5 miles until the road dead-ends at the trailhead, just before the entrance to the campground. (The road is paved all the way to the trailhead.) Ample parking and toilet; vehicle camping in the nearby Blodgett Canyon Campground. GPS: N46 16.133' / W114 14.617'

The Hike

There's a tendency to think that hiking is something you do to get somewhere. In Blodgett Canyon no destination is necessary beyond the hike itself. Just a hundred yards from the vehicle, you will be walking along a beautiful stream and looking up at spectacular canyon walls. These basic scenic ingredients continue throughout the hike. Because there is no need to get to any particular point, a hike up Blodgett Canyon is ideal for families and anyone who enjoys unhurried walking with lots of pleasant stops.

Blodgett Canyon is the most spectacular of the many canyons penetrating the eastern front of the Selway-Bitterroot Wilderness. The vertical relief from canyon bottom to ridgetop is nearly 4,000 feet. Blodgett Creek itself, like all the streams in the Bitterroots, is clear and cold. It also has good fishing for pan-size rainbow trout. Think catch-and-release on the lower, heavily fished sections.

The never-steep trail goes through a pleasant forest environment, sometimes crossing talus slopes, and always close to Blodgett Creek. Sheer granite faces of 500 to 600 feet are common on the north side of the canyon, and there are several waterfalls between 3 and 6 miles up the canyon.

Because the trail stays low by the creek, snow gives it up earlier than many routes. Although you can hike a full 12.5 miles up the canyon to Blodgett Lake, most hikers take shorter hikes. Go until you feel like stopping and either pick a campsite (use zero-impact methods if you have a fire) or turn back to the trailhead.

Although Blodgett Canyon is surrounded by the Selway-Bitterroot Wilderness, only the upper portion (7 miles from the trailhead) is part of it. When the

Blodgett Canyon

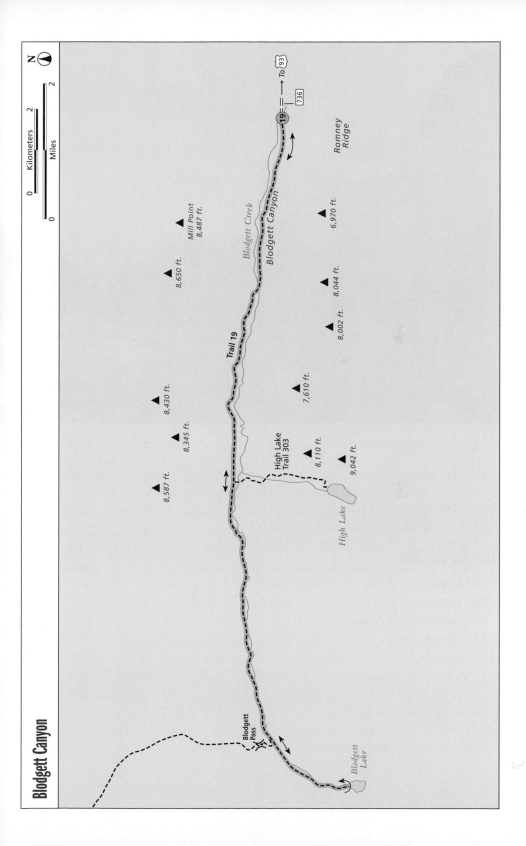

N

0   Kilometers   2

0   Miles   2

To 93

736

19

Romney Ridge

Blodgett Creek

Blodgett Canyon

Mill Point
8,487 ft.

6,970 ft.

8,650 ft.

8,044 ft.

8,002 ft.

Trail 19

8,430 ft.

8,345 ft.

7,610 ft.

High Lake
Trail 303

8,110 ft.

8,587 ft.

9,042 ft.

High Lake

Blodgett Pass

Blodgett Lake

Blodgett Canyon. JACQUELYN CORDAY

Selway-Bitterroot Wilderness was set aside in 1939, most of Blodgett Canyon was excluded because it was considered a possible site for a dam and reservoir for Bitterroot Valley water users. Lower Blodgett Canyon was included in the proposed 1988 wilderness bill vetoed by President Reagan.

Miles and Directions

0.0 Trailhead.

3.6 Waterfall.

6.0 High Lake Trail 303; turn right.

12.5 Blodgett Lake.

25.0 Trailhead.

Side Trips: If you're willing to tackle the steep 1,400-foot climb up to High Lake on the south rim of the canyon, you have a good chance of seeing mountain goats. If you're up for it, turn left (west) at 6 miles onto High Lake Trail 303 to make that trek, which is on a poorly maintained trail that can be hard to follow. (Originally contributed by John Westenberg, re-hiked by the authors.)

20 Blodgett Canyon Overlook

A great day hike on a newly rebuilt trail with an incredible view and interpretive displays

Start: Canyon Lake Trailhead, 5 miles west of Hamilton
Distance: 3.0-mile out-and-back

Difficulty: Easy
Maps: USGS Printz Ridge; Selway-Bitterroot Wilderness Map

Finding the trailhead: In Hamilton, turn west onto Main Street (also Highway 531) and continue through town for 1.1 miles; turn right on Ricketts Road. Drive another 0.5 mile and then turn left on Blodgett Camp Road when Ricketts Road turns right. Go another 2.4 miles to a junction with the road to the Overlook and Canyon Lake trailhead. Turn left here onto a good gravel road (passable with any vehicle) and follow it for 3 miles (steadily climbing all the way) until it deadends at the trailhead. Ample parking and a toilet; vehicle camping in the nearby Blodgett Canyon Campground. GPS: N46 15.167' / W114 14.817'

The Hike

The Forest Service rebuilt this trail after the dramatic Bitterroot fires of 2000. In addition to offering up the best possible view of fabulous Blodgett Canyon, it gives you a good education on the dynamics of forest fires. The Forest Service has put up six interpretive stations keyed to a free brochure you can pick up at the trailhead. The brochure tells about the different types of forest fires, impacts on plants and wildlife, and how we can reduce the impact of fires. Along the trail you can clearly see how nature is reclaiming the landscape after the fire.

The Blodgett Canyon Overlook trail gradually switchbacks up from the Canyon Lake Trailhead to the ridge overlooking Blodgett Canyon, the next valley to the north. On top be sure to watch children and pets carefully, because the overlook is on the edge of a steep cliff.

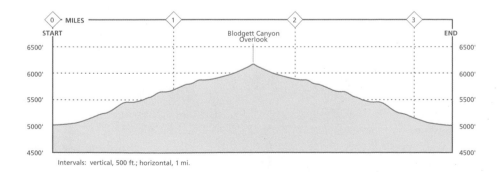

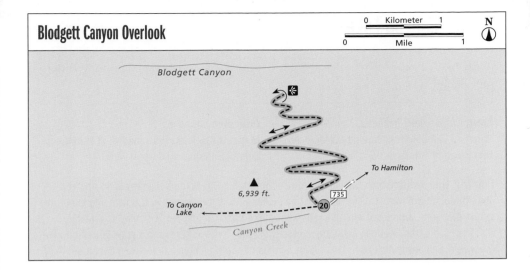

This could be a 0.5-mile steep climb, but the switchbacks make it an easy, 1.5-mile ascent suitable for any hiker. If you get tired along the way, rest on one of the benches installed by the Forest Service, enjoy the view, and think about the ecology of forest fires. (Originally contributed and re-hiked by the authors.)

Miles and Directions

0.0 Canyon Lake Trailhead.

1.5 Blodgett Canyon Overlook.

3.0 Canyon Lake Trailhead.

◀ *Stunning view from Blodgett Canyon Overlook.* SHUTTERSTOCK

21 Canyon Lake

A day hike or overnighter into one of the most scenic mountain lakes in the Bitterroot Range

Start: Canyon Lake Trailhead, 7 miles west of Hamilton in the Selway-Bitterroot Wilderness
Distance: 11.0-mile out-and-back

Difficulty: Strenuous
Maps: USGS Printz Ridge and Ward Mountain; Selway-Bitterroot Wilderness Map

Finding the trailhead: In Hamilton, turn west onto Main Street (also Highway 531) and continue through town for 1.1 miles; turn right on Ricketts Road. Drive another 0.5 mile and then turn left on Blodgett Camp Road when Ricketts Road turns right. Go another 2.4 miles to a junction with the road to the Overlook and Canyon Lake trailhead. Turn left here onto a good gravel road (passable with any vehicle) and follow it for 3 miles (steadily climbing all the way) until it dead-ends at the trailhead. Ample parking and a toilet; vehicle camping in the nearby Blodgett Canyon Campground. GPS: N46 15.167' / W114 14.817'

The Hike

Canyon Creek drains one of the smaller canyons penetrating the east side of the Bitterroots, but what it lacks in size, it makes up for in scenic beauty—definitely one of the gems in the vast Selway-Bitterroot Wilderness. The 2000 fires spared this valley, with the exception of a short stretch of burned forest about a mile from the trailhead.

From the trailhead, Trail 525 stays to the northern side of the creek, avoiding stream crossings and ascending gradually through a mature, unburned forest for about 4 miles. Along the trail on the first two-thirds of the hike, you might want to harvest some huckleberries, because you'll need the energy for the last third of the trip. At 4 miles the trail turns steeply uphill, climbing about 1,200 feet over the

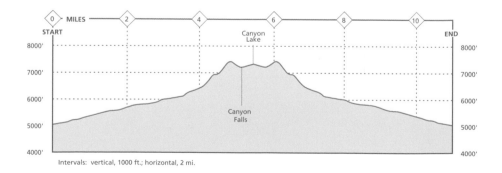

Canyon Lake. JACQUELYN CORDAY

next mile, a Category 1 hill—and on a very rough trail. About a half mile before the lake, you crest the ridge and go down into the lake. Just before the lake, you can see Canyon Falls, which is actually a series of cataracts with a total drop of 200 feet, off to your left.

If you're out for more than a tough day hike, you can camp at Canyon Lake, which has been made larger by an artificially created rock-and-wood dam. You'll find a few campsites at the lower end of the lake. The lake supports enough cut-throat trout to keep anglers happy.

Miles and Directions

0.0   Canyon Lake Trailhead.

5.0   Canyon Falls.

5.5   Canyon Lake.

11.0   Canyon Lake Trailhead.

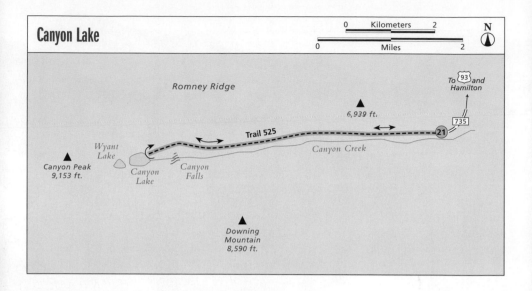

Side Trips: From Canyon Lake it's a short climb up the canyon to Wyant Lake. If you're interested in a little mountaineering, you can go beyond Wyant Lake and climb Canyon Peak (9,153 feet) via its rocky southern ridge. (Originally contributed by Don Reed, re-hiked by the authors.)

22 Trapper Peak

A climb to the summit of the highest peak (10,157 feet) in the Selway–Bitterroot Wilderness

Start: Trapper Peak Trailhead, 15 miles southwest of Darby
Distance: 12.0-mile out-and-back

Difficulty: Strenuous
Maps: USGS Trapper Peak and Boulder Peak; Selway-Bitterroot Wilderness Map

Finding the trailhead: Drive south of Darby on US 93 for 5 miles. Just before crossing the Bitterroot River, turn right onto West Fork Road (Highway 473). Head southwest on West Fork Road for 11 miles (just past mile marker 11) and turn west onto FR 5630. Follow FR 5630 for about a mile until it splits. Turn left onto FR 5630A and stay on it for another 5.5 miles until it ends at the trailhead, 6.4 miles total from West Fork Road. The road is steep and narrow. You could probably make it in any vehicle, but you'd be more comfortable with high clearance and low gears. Limited parking (be careful not to block the road); no toilet. GPS: N45 50.816' / W114 15.866'

The Hike

Until July, if not mid-July, snow covers much of the trail. The almost 4,000 feet of elevation gain in 6 miles makes this hike hard but exciting because of the destination. From the top of Trapper Peak, the world falls away into endless cascades of rocky ridges.

Trail 133 climbs abruptly from the parking lot, along the ridge above Boulder Creek to the south. The first part of the hike involves two steep climbs with a bit of flat relief in between, just enough to lower your heartbeat out of the danger zone. At early rest stops, take the extra time to walk the 20 feet to the edge of the ridge for a taste of the view from the top. The Boulder Creek Valley was formed by glaciation, creating a long, narrow, ice-gouged trough common to the eastern slope of the Bitterroots.

After the steep ascent in the first 2 miles, gaining most of the 1,300-foot elevation gain from the trailhead, the trail climbs gradually. A little less than halfway up is a small

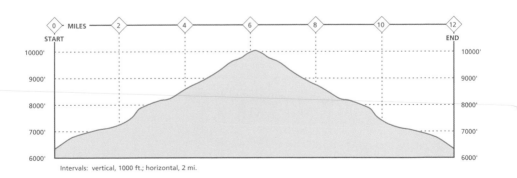

Intervals: vertical, 1000 ft.; horizontal, 2 mi.

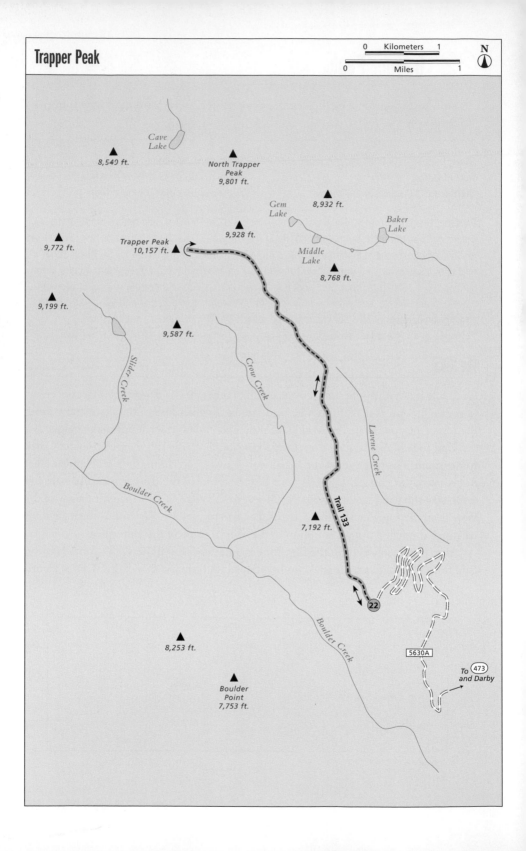

Trapper Peak

Cave
Lake

▲
8,549 ft.

▲
North Trapper
Peak
9,801 ft.

▲
8,932 ft.

Gem
Lake

Baker
Lake

▲
9,772 ft.

▲
9,928 ft.

Trapper Peak
10,157 ft. ▲

Middle
Lake

▲
8,768 ft.

▲
9,199 ft.

Slider Creek

▲
9,587 ft.

Crow Creek

Lavene Creek

Boulder Creek

▲
7,192 ft.

Trail 133

22

▲
8,253 ft.

Boulder Creek

5630A

To 473
and Darby

▲
Boulder
Point
7,753 ft.

0   Kilometers   1

0   Miles   1

N

The increasingly rare pika, a symbol of high and wild Montana. JACQUELYN CORDAY

spring to the right of the trail. The gurgling water is audible from the trail, and a small path veers off to the right. This is a good spot to replenish water bottles.

After the spring, the trail climbs steadily up and out of the trees. The view opens up to a world of ice-sculptured granite peaks and high-altitude weather patterns. Montana is known for unpredictable weather, and at the summit of Trapper Peak, 10,157 feet, it can snow any day of the year.

Once out in the open, follow cairns marking the trail, which often can be hard to follow as it passes over exposed rock. The route traverses the south face of Trapper Peak, angling toward the summit.

From the top, look for the sharp glaciated ridgelines and peaks of the Selway-Bitterroot Wilderness. More than 500,000 acres of this 1.3-million-acre wilderness are located in the Bitterroot National Forest (the rest are in Idaho). Unprotected areas such as parts of Trapper Creek to the north warrant future Wilderness designation. The hike down can be hard on the knees and toenails. (Originally contributed by the authors.)

Miles and Directions

- **0.0** Trailhead.
- **6.0** Trapper Peak.
- **12.0** Trailhead.

23 Tin Cup Lake

A long hike to a large, trout-filled subalpine lake deep in the Selway–Bitterroot Wilderness

Start: 5 miles southwest of Darby
Distance: 20.0-mile out-and-back
Difficulty: Strenuous

Maps: USGS Como Peaks, Trapper Peak, and Tin Cup Lake; Selway-Bitterroot Wilderness Map

Finding the trailhead: On the south edge of Darby, turn west onto Tin Cup Road (FR 639). After about 3.4 miles (pavement ends at 1.5 miles), turn left (south) on FR 639A as FR 639B continues straight. Watch for a hiker icon sign marking this turn. The trailhead is on the right (west) just after crossing Tin Cup Creek, 0.1 mile after turning on FR 639A. Park in the large parking area on your left across from the trailhead. Ample parking; no toilet. GPS: N46 0.800' / W114 13.466'

The Hike

The jagged peaks of this portion of the Bitterroots are the highest mountains in the entire range, which stretches more than 300 miles along Montana's western border. This hike will take you in to see many of them, such as El Capitan, the Lonesome Bachelor, and the Como Peaks.

From the trailhead, follow Tin Cup Trail 96 as it travels through dense timber in the lower reaches of the canyon, crossing Tin Cup Creek three times. Sorry, no bridges. These crossings can be tricky early in the summer and after heavy rains, so you might want to wait until mid-July.

The trail follows beautiful Tin Cup Creek, a large mountain stream, all the way to the lake. The grade kicks up a bit in the last 2 miles, but most of the route is a very gradual ascent. There are no steep sections, and you hardly notice the elevation gain. It's a long day with an overnight pack, though, so start early. The trail is in great shape and stays in the shady, unburned forest for the entire 10 miles.

You can choose from several campsites at the lower end of this large lake, which is filled with hungry cutthroat trout.

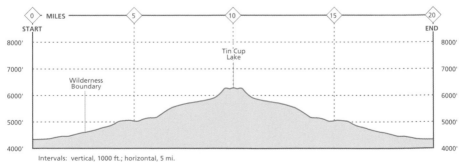

The high country of the Tin Cup Basin. JACQUELYN CORDAY

Miles and Directions

0.0 Trailhead.

2.5 Wilderness boundary.

3.0 First stream crossing.

5.5 Second stream crossing.

8.0 Third stream crossing.

10.0 Tin Cup Lake.

20.0 Trailhead.

Side Trips: About 6 miles from the trailhead and just before reaching the Kerlee drainage, you can leave the main trail and bushwhack up to Kerlee and Goat Lakes. You might be able to find a primitive social trail, but don't bank on it. For this side trip, you'll need a topo map, compass, and route-finding skills. Kerlee Lake has great scenery, with special views of the high, rocky peaks to the north of the lake.

If you're really ambitious, you can attempt to scramble to the summit of massive El Capitan, 2 miles to the northwest. Climb the hillsides to the northwest of Kerlee Lake, making sure to stay low enough to avoid the vertical rock walls on the southern slopes of the Lonesome Bachelor. After reaching a low pass between the Bachelor and

Tin Cup Lake

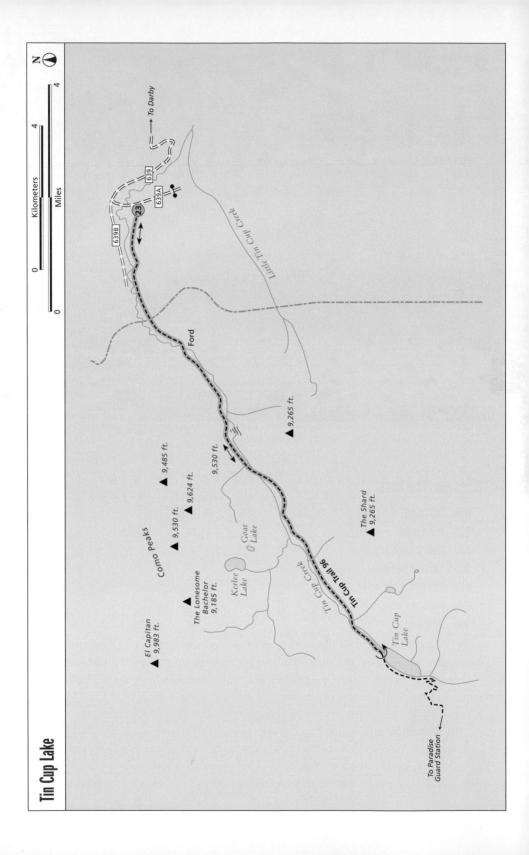

Hiking the Tin Cup Basin Trail. JACQUELYN CORDAY

El Capitan, cautiously follow the eastern ridge to the windswept summit, 9,983 feet high. Here are stupendous views of the Como Peaks, the Lonesome Bachelor, and the lakes in the Little Rock Creek drainage below. To the west lie the forested ridges of the mighty Selway-Bitterroot Wilderness thrown out in all its vastness and the canyons of the wild Selway River. To the south is a sawtooth ridge with granite towers separating the valley of Tin Cup Creek from the North Fork of Trapper Creek. Few views get better than the one from the summit of El Capitan.

Technical rock climbers will find challenging routes on the many faces of El Capitan, the Lonesome Bachelor, and Como Peaks. If you aren't trained in rock climbing, you should avoid the more difficult routes and limit yourself to the eastern slope of El Capitan. This trip makes a superb three-day or longer introduction to the high country of the Selway-Bitterroot. (Originally contributed by Don Reed, re-hiked by the authors.)

24 Overwhich Falls

A long day hike or overnighter to see 200-foot Overwhich Falls

Start: Porcupine Saddle Trailhead, 8 miles southwest of Sula

Distance: 17.0-mile shuttle

Difficulty: Moderate

Maps: USGS Medicine Hot Springs and Piquett Mountains; Bitterroot National Forest Map

Finding the trailheads: Drive south of Missoula on US 93 for about 80 miles to the Indian Trees Campground (5.4 miles south of Sula). After 0.6 mile, just as the roads turns to pavement and you're about to enter the campground, turn left on FR 8112 with the sign that says PORCUPINE TRAILHEAD 8. Turn right when the road splits after about a mile (junction with FR 729) and then right again at 6.5 miles, where the sign directs you to the Porcupine Saddle Trailhead where the road ends.

Be forewarned: A big part of the adventure of doing this hike is getting to the Porcupine Saddle Trailhead. The road is long, steep, rocky, narrow, and best suited for four-wheel-drive vehicles. You could probably make it in a small all-wheel-drive SUV, but you probably won't be too comfortable doing it. Ample parking; no toilet. GPS: N45 44.666' / W113 58.728'

Leave a vehicle or have somebody pick you up at the Crazy Creek Campground. To find this campground, drive 2.8 miles north of Sula on US 93 to Medicine Springs Road 5728, which turns directly across from Spring Gulch Campground. Turn left, heading southwest, and follow FR 370 past Warm Springs Campground for 4.1 miles to Crazy Creek Campground (the first mile or so is paved). The trail starts in the middle of the campground, where you see a sturdy stock bridge over Crazy Creek. Ample parking (park in the lot on your right as you enter the campground); nearby vehicle campgrounds with toilets and drinking water. GPS: N45 48.897' / W114 04.237'

The Hike

Since there isn't a steep climb—as is the case with most long hikes—the Overwhich Falls trip is suitable for all hikers. Most hikers are interested in a leisurely hike and take at least two days, but ambitious hikers could do this in one day and enjoy a scenic trek that's downhill most of the way.

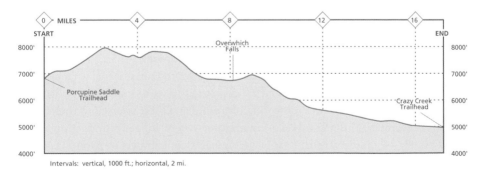

Intervals: vertical, 1000 ft.; horizontal, 2 mi.

On this hike, driving to the trailhead is a big part of the adventure. Yes, that's where the road goes. BILL SCHNEIDER

From the trailhead, take Porcupine Saddle Trail 196, which leads through lodge-pole pine forest for 0.8 mile, to the junction with Warm Springs Ridge Trail 177. Turn left, heading south on Warm Springs Ridge Trail, which merges with Shields Creek Trail 673 at mile 2.8. Then, after descending into the Shields Creek Valley, the trail joins Coulter Creek Trail 606 from the southeast. Stay right on Shields Creek Trail for another 2.5 miles downstream to Overwhich Falls. All of these trails are generally well maintained, and most junctions are well marked.

The highlight of the trip is, of course, 200-foot Overwhich Falls, which can be viewed from the trail. For a closer look, drop your pack and bushwhack a short way to the creek below the falls.

Shortly after passing the falls, reach the junction with Trails 103 and 248/400. You can take a short side trip up Trail 400 to Pass and Capri Lakes. Although both lakes have a few cutthroat trout, fishing is considered marginal, as it is in the streams along the way, with the possible exception of Warm Springs Creek, which can be good. The area is noted for its large, productive huckleberry patches, so consider substituting berry picking for fishing.

From the junction of Shields Creek Trail and Trails 103 and 248/400, turn north on Trail 103 and stay on it all the way to Crazy Creek Campground (about 9 miles).

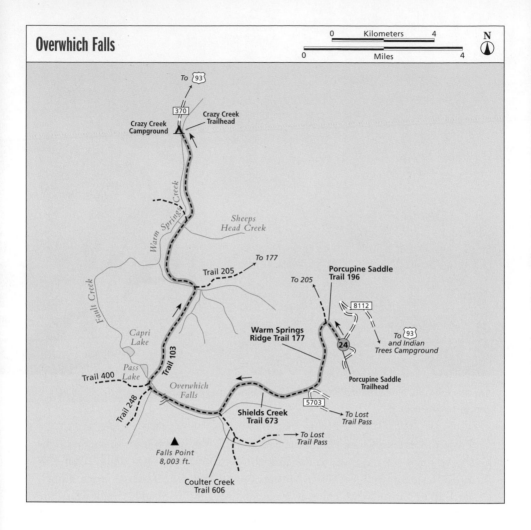

Trail 103 follows streams most of the way, but since the lower portions are grazed by domestic cattle, you should be sure to treat water before drinking. (Originally contributed by Wayne Avants, re-hiked by the authors)

Miles and Directions

0.0 Porcupine Saddle Trailhead.

0.8 Junction with Warm Springs Ridge Trail 177; turn left.

2.8 Junction with Shields Creek Trail 673; turn right.

5.25 Junction with Coulter Creek Trail 606; turn right.

8.0 Overwhich Falls, junction with Trail 103; turn right.

11.5 Three Forks Junction Trail 205; turn left.

17.0 Crazy Creek Campground trailhead.

25 Blue Joint

A long loop backpack through remote wilderness meadows, mountains, and wild country seldom seen

Start: Nez Perce Pass, 35 miles southwest of Hamilton on the Idaho-Montana border
Distance: 36.0-mile loop
Difficulty: Strenuous

Maps: USGS Blue Joint, Painted Rocks Lake NW, and Nez Perce Peak; Bitterroot National Forest Map. Also useful is the Forest Service's River of No Return Wilderness Map.

Finding the trailhead: Drive south from Darby on US 93 for 3 miles. Just before you cross the Bitterroot River, turn right onto West Fork of the Bitterroot Road (FR 473). Follow FR 473 southwest for 33 miles until you reach Nez Perce Pass on the Montana-Idaho border. At the pass, turn left (south) into the large parking lot (with toilet) where the trail starts. Check out the nifty interpretive displays before starting to hike. GPS: N45 43.016' / W114 30.166'

The Hike

You can take this 36-mile loop starting and ending at Nez Perce Pass Trailhead in either direction, but it seems easier to take Stateline Trail 16 first and then come back to the trailhead by hiking down Blue Joint Trail 614 and back up to the pass via Jack the Ripper Trail 137.

From the trailhead, start hiking on Stateline Trail 16 to the south. After 0.3 mile, stay right (south) at the junction with Castle Rock Trail 627, continuing south. Jack the Ripper Trail 137 down Jack the Ripper Creek takes off to the left about a mile from the trailhead. This trail will bring you back to your vehicle three days later.

Except for a small creek at about 5 miles and Two Buck Springs at about 11 miles from the trailhead, there is no water until you reach Reynolds Lake. So carry plenty of water and fill up again at Two Buck Springs (farther from the ridge than shown on the map), which is also a good place to spend the first night. The entire Stateline (or Divide) Trail is in great shape, either flat or with a few short hills. It goes through

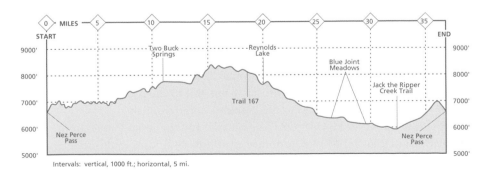

Columbia Clematis. JACQUELYN CORDAY

the mature forests of the Frank Church–River of No Return Wilderness but doesn't offer many vistas along the way. This is subalpine country, featuring whitebark pine and lots of standing snags.

Unless you stop at the stream at about 5 miles or can make it to Two Buck Springs, the first night out could be a dry camp, so be prepared for this possibility. It's about 9 miles from Two Buck Springs to Reynolds Lake, a good choice for the second night out. At 9 miles turn left (south) at the junction with Trail 8 to Hell's Half Acre. Don't miss the Trail 167 junction just before Reynolds Lake. It occurs in a small, grassy valley with water. Take the left-hand trail to the lake. Reynolds Lake has fishing for cutthroat trout to add to the evening's entertainment.

After leaving Reynolds Lake, continue on Trail 158 for about 2 miles to the junction with Blue Joint Trail 614. A primitive road (FR 044) leads to this trail junction, and it's possible to leave a vehicle here to make this a point-to-point hike. However,

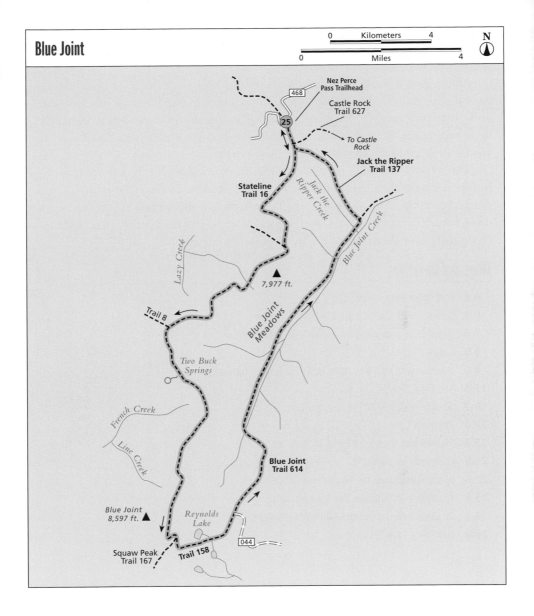

Blue Joint

0   Kilometers   4

0   Miles   4

N

Nez Perce
Pass Trailhead

468

Castle Rock
Trail 627

25

To Castle
Rock

Jack the Ripper
Trail 137

Stateline
Trail 16

Jack the
Ripper Creek

Lazy Creek

Blue Joint Creek

7,977 ft.

Trail 8

Blue Joint
Meadows

Two Buck
Springs

French Creek

Line Creek

Blue Joint
Trail 614

Blue Joint
8,597 ft.

Reynolds
Lake

044

Squaw Peak
Trail 167

Trail 158

it would be a loss to miss Blue Joint Trail, which winds through a wide valley with grassy meadows and along a meandering wilderness stream. The stream has good fishing for small cutthroat. Blue Joint Meadows, a good choice for the third night out, is about 7 miles past Reynolds Lake.

Jack the Ripper Trail 137 takes off about 5 miles from Blue Joint Meadows. Watch carefully for this junction. It juts off to the left just after a creek crossing, and it might not have a sign. Jack the Ripper Trail gradually climbs along troutless Jack the Ripper Creek for about 3 miles through small but gorgeous meadows. The last half mile gets steep as you approach the ridgeline. Then, retrace your footsteps from three days earlier back to Nez Perce Pass and your vehicle, leaving some of Montana's most spectacular, yet gentle, backcountry behind you.

Although you won't see grizzly bears on this hike, black bears are common. Be careful with your food and keep a clean camp. The area also has most other wildlife associated with western Montana, including mountain lions, mountain goats, elk, deer, and moose. Mosquitoes usually aren't a big problem after June. You'll want to wait until at least July anyway to let the snow melt.

The 61,400-acre Blue Joint Wilderness Study Area is actually a portion of the immense Frank Church–River of No Return Wilderness country that extends across the Idaho border into Montana. The 2.2-million-acre wilderness area is the largest designated wilderness in the Lower 48, and Blue Joint would make a fine addition. (Originally contributed by Bob Oset, re-hiked by the authors.)

Miles and Directions

0.0 Nez Perce Pass Trailhead.

0.3 Junction with Castle Rock Trail 627; stay right.

1.0 Junction with Jack the Ripper Trail 137; stay right.

5.0 Creek.

9.0 Junction with Trail 8 to Hell's Half Acre Spring; turn left.

11.0 Two Buck Springs.

18.0 Squaw Peak Trail 167; turn left.

20.0 Reynolds Lake.

22.0 FR 044 and Blue Joint Trail 614; turn left.

27.0 Blue Joint Meadows.

32.0 Junction with Jack the Ripper Trail 137; turn left.

35.0 Junction with Stateline Trail 16; turn right.

35.7 Junction with Castle Rock Trail 627; turn right.

36.0 Nez Perce Pass Trailhead.

Flathead National Forest

26 Thoma Lookout

A day hike in the North Fork of the Flathead River wildlands with panoramic views of the Kintla Massif in Glacier National Park

Start: 40 miles north of Columbia Falls
Distance: 6.0-mile out-and-back
Difficulty: Moderate

Maps: USGS Mount Hefty; Flathead National Forest Map (north half)

Finding the trailhead: Drive north of the Nucleus Avenue/US 2 junction in Columbia Falls on Outside North Fork Road for 49.5 miles (paved to the Glacier Rim access and partially paved before the Polebridge turnoff) past the Ford River access and turn left, heading west on Trail Creek Road 114. Follow this dirt road for 3.3 miles past the old Mount Hefty Trailhead (shuttle option). After another 1.5 miles, the road forks. Follow FR 114A to the right (may not be passable with a two-wheel-drive vehicle) for another 3 miles to where the road dead-ends past an unmaintained jeep trail and a sharp curve. Limited parking; no toilet or water. GPS: N48 57.433' / W114 34.583'

The Hike

The hardest part of this hike is the long, long dirt-road drive to the trailhead, which makes this a lesser-used trail, but it's a great short hike for those who brave the drive.

Thoma Lookout lies in an area between Trail Creek Road and the Canadian border, west of North Fork Flathead Road and east of the Whitefish Range. The previous winter's snowpack dictates when this trail is passable, but wait at least until July to avoid walking through snowbanks. The trail isn't heavily used at any time, although hunters use it in the fall.

Grizzly bears frequent the area. In fact, this part of the North Fork of the Flathead has one of the densest grizzly concentrations in the state, so stay alert.

Thoma–Colts Creek Trail 18 begins as an old logging road past the trailhead gate and winds gradually uphill past an old harvest area. The road may have some downfall on it and is slightly clogged with alder growth, but it's easy to follow. After about a half

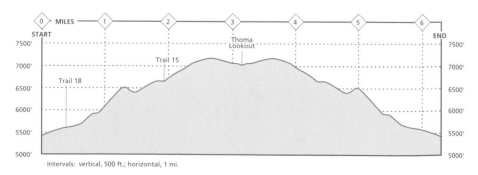

Intervals: vertical, 500 ft.; horizontal, 1 mi.

Thoma Lookout

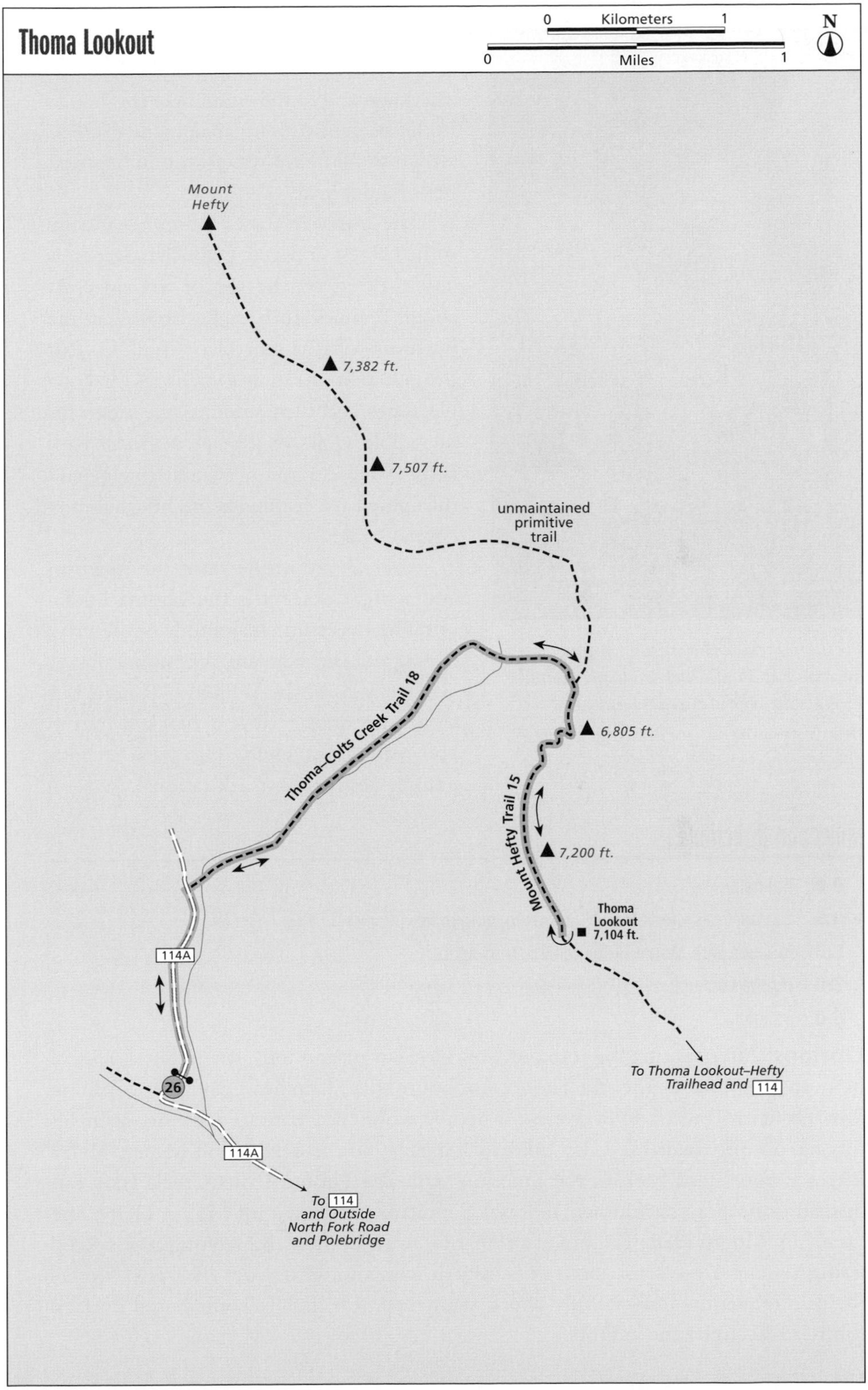

0 Kilometers 1
0 Miles 1
N
Mount Hefty
7,382 ft.
7,507 ft.
unmaintained primitive trail
Thoma–Colts Creek Trail 18
6,805 ft.
Mount Hefty Trail 15
7,200 ft.
Thoma Lookout 7,104 ft.
114A
26
114A
To Thoma Lookout–Hefty Trailhead and 114
To 114 and Outside North Fork Road and Polebridge

Western anemone, or western pasqueflower, not rare but an unusual wildflower found throughout northwestern Montana.
BILL SCHNEIDER

mile, a cairn indicates a trail junction, and a well-maintained trail is visible descending down and to the right. Take this trail as it climbs gently along an unnamed creek, which should have water even in September of a dry year.

The route up passes through a mature spruce forest and gets gradually steeper as you close in on the top of the ridge. At about 2 miles, turn right (south) at the junction with Mount Hefty Trail 15. Past the junction the trail switchbacks a couple times and then summits the ridge for incredible views of Glacier National Park and beyond. A forest of whitebark pine and subalpine larch highlights this huckleberry-covered ridge.

After about a mile from the junction and a slight descent is the Thoma Lookout. The sweep and magnitude of the view is magnificent. East are the mountains of Glacier; west is the Whitefish Range; but to the north, the view is blocked by the bulk of Mount Hefty. The view is both grandly aesthetic and educational.

Miles and Directions

0.0 Trailhead.

0.5 Thoma-Colts Creek Trail 18 leaves logging road.

2.0 Junction with Mount Hefty Trail 15; turn right.

3.0 Thoma Lookout.

6.0 Trailhead.

Options: After visiting the lookout, you have several options. If you left a vehicle or mountain bike at the old Thoma Lookout–Hefty Trailhead, you can continue down to it on Trail 15. However, most people would not want to drive two vehicles this far on dirt roads for a day hike, so I suggest you instead climb Mount Hefty. Retrace your steps back to the junction with the Thoma–Colts Creek Trail, but instead of heading back down, follow a primitive trail north up Mount Hefty. The "trail" up Mount Hefty is more of an off-trail route at times, but as long as you keep going up and are careful about your return, you should not get off track. Nonetheless, frequently and carefully check your map. (Originally contributed by Jack Johns, re-hiked by the authors.)

27 Great Northern

A mountain ascent on a well-established social trail with truly spectacular vistas— very likely the premier hike in all of northwestern Montana, if not the entire state

Start: 30 miles east of Kalispell in the Great Bear Wilderness
Distance: 8.0-mile out-and-back
Difficulty: Very strenuous; for experienced and well-conditioned hikers only

Maps: USGS Mount Grant; Flathead National Forest Map; Bob Marshall, Great Bear, and Scapegoat Wilderness Complex Map

Finding the trailhead: From Columbia Falls, drive east on US 2 through Hungry Horse. Turn right 0.9 mile past Hungry Horse, heading south on East Side Hungry Horse Road (paved for first 2 miles, then good gravel). Drive south through Martin City for 15.2 miles to a three-way junction. Here, take a sharp left onto FR 1048 (no sign when we were there in 2012) for about a half mile to a parking area before the bridge over Hungry Horse Creek. The main trail starts at the end of a pullout on the other side of the bridge. Ample parking and filterable water; no toilet. GPS: N48 20.025' / W113 49.860'

The Hike

Although named for a railroad, the name of the mountain suggests exactly what it is. Its graceful curves and broad faces are irresistible to anybody who has acquired a taste for high places. Even with the incomparable peaks of Glacier Park nearby, this great mountain attracts many hikers solely on the merits of its own beauty.

There are at least three routes to the summit of Great Northern, but no official trail. All three routes are rough and strenuous, either on social trails or rugged off-trail hiking with some difficult bushwhacking—and all only for the adventurous among us. The most popular route, described here, has a well-defined social trail (more defined than many official trails, in fact) all the way to the summit, but it's still extremely difficult and a bit nerve-wracking. It will be the steepest trail you've ever hiked.

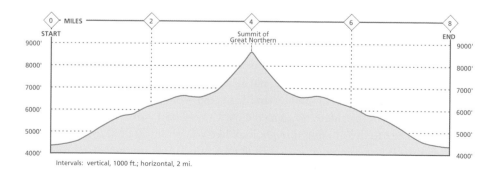

Intervals: vertical, 1000 ft.; horizontal, 2 mi.

The trail to Great Northern, not for the beginning hiker. BILL SCHNEIDER

Regardless of the route you chose, be absolutely sure to pack significantly more water than you'd normally bring on an 8-mile hike. You'll need it; absolutely no water is available on this route. Also, this hike is for bluebird days only. Don't even think about going up here on a stormy day. And try to start at first light. You'll probably need most of the day to make the climb, enjoy the incredible scenery, and get back before any afternoon thunderstorm rolls in.

It's only about 4 miles to the summit, but don't be fooled. That's an elevation gain of 4,400 feet, most of it in the first 1.5 miles, which is off my elevation chart and probably would be classified as something like a Category HHH climb.

From the trailhead on the north side of Hungry Horse Creek, an easy-to-follow social trail charges straight up the mountain, angling off to the north away from the creek. It may seem like you're on the wrong route, but don't fret. Stay on the social trail until it finally breaks out into the open about 1.5 miles later. You'll hope for a switchback or two, but no. It's nothing but straight up all the way to the ridge.

After about a half mile of scenic—and less steep—hiking, still on the social trail, you reach the top of the ridge and an incredible view of both Great Northern and the rest of your route to the summit. It might look like you're almost there, but you're not.

After a good rest, continue on the social trail, which follows the logical ridgeline route all the way to the summit. It's less difficult than it appears, but there is one short, three-point section and several stretches on a knife-edge ridge with steep cliffs on both sides.

Stanton Glacier clings to the east slope of mighty mountain, gradually melting away into beautiful Stanton Lake far below. Past Stanton Lake, to the east, the Middle Fork of the Flathead River flows north to its juncture with the North Fork to form the main Flathead River. On the horizon, across the river, is a seldom-seen array of peaks in southern Glacier Park, combining into a serrated skyline rivaled by none other.

One unusually monstrous mountain rises far above its competition. The southern portion of this peak is pyramid shaped, with a chopped-off ridge to the north. This is Mount Stimson, at 10,142 feet the second-highest peak and one of the most exhausting (but not technically challenging) climbs in the park. It's just north of Church Butte, a flat-topped rectangle. Saint Nicholas, a few miles south of Mount Stimson, is easy to spot because, quite literally, it sticks out like a sore thumb. Moreover, it appears impossible to climb.

Despite all these impressive peaks in the neighborhood, Great Northern maintains its own magical allure, and you're unlikely to feel deprived by not being on the summit of Mount Stimson or Saint Nicholas instead.

After enjoying a long stay on the summit, simply retrace your steps back to the trailhead. Be careful on the way down the forested section of the descent; the footing can be difficult on the extremely steep grade. If you haven't clipped your toenails, two or three will be black the following week.

Miles and Directions

0.0 Trailhead.

2.0 Top of ridge.

4.0 Great Northern summit.

8.0 Trailhead.

Options: We've also hiked up Great Northern on the off-trail route that starts by the parking area before you cross the bridge over Hungry Horse Creek on FR 1048. This is a shorter, but more difficult, route.

When you look south of the bridge over Hungry Horse Creek, you see impenetrable thickets of brush and small trees. After briefly considering the wisdom of trying this route, charge into these thickets. They don't last long and are the hardest part. Climb the ascending ridge on the southern side of Hungry Horse Creek. Pick your way straight up the hill, following game trails to help escape this jungle. Initially, work to the south, climbing and contouring to get out of the brush and windfalls on the northern side of the ridge. If you're hiking this route in early August, you'll need a lot of willpower to not delay too long in the massive huckleberry patches.

After the first very steep mile, you top out on the ridge, where a faint trail develops. Follow this ridge for another mile to where it tops out at timberline. From a knob, just before dropping into Dudley Bowl, you get a view of marshy meadows, a small timbered saddle, and, of course, a stunning view of Great Northern.

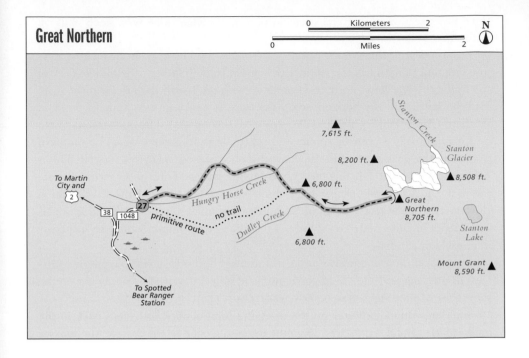

Kilometers 0 2

Miles 0 2

N

7,615 ft.

8,200 ft.

Stanton Creek

Stanton Glacier

8,508 ft.

To Martin City and

2

38 1048

27

6,800 ft.

Hungry Horse Creek

Primitive route

no trail

Dudley Creek

6,800 ft.

Great Northern 8,705 ft.

Stanton Lake

To Spotted Bear Ranger Station

Mount Grant 8,590 ft.

From here you have a choice of two routes. Note the rocky, open spur ascending to the right of the bowl along a ridgeline directly to the peak. Save this route for the descent. It's loose scree, and with great care and concentration, you can make a fast descent. Now note another ascending spur to the left (north) of the main peak, with clumps of gnarled trees reaching almost to the summit ridge.

After deciding to follow the left route up, you may want to consider a trip down into the bowl to filter water, if you didn't bring enough. When we did this hike in September of a dry year, there was still water in the creek. Then, head up and into the trees along the left (north) to the top of the ridge. The going is steep and involves some non-technical rock climbing. Once on top of the ridge, pick up the social trail to the summit.

After summiting and enjoying a long, scenic rest, head down the southern ridge toward Dudley Bowl. The scree is uneven, so rapid travel may be difficult, but it's surely faster than the way you came. Once back down in the bowl, climb the knob back on the ridge and follow the ridge down. One note on the return bushwhack: Err to the north (your right) as you head down, and remember your baselines, Hungry Horse Creek and FR 1048. If you find yourself on flat ground, even though you didn't cross flat ground on the way up, you have drifted too far south and should head north to the road and your vehicle.

There is also an off-trail route from the east to the top of Great Northern, but we have not hiked it. We're told, though, that you can hike an established trail to Stanton Lake (Hike 28) and then find an off-trail route to the summit of Great Northern. (Originally contributed by Pat Caffrey, re-hiked by the authors.)

28 Stanton Lake

A fairly easy day hike to a gorgeous lake in the Great Bear Wilderness with good fishing and incredible views of Great Northern and Stanton Glacier

Start: 13 miles southeast of West Glacier
Distance: 2.4-mile out-and-back
Difficulty: Easy

Maps: USGS Stanton Lake; Great Bear Wilderness Complex Map; Flathead National Forest Map

Finding the trailhead: From West Glacier, take US 2 east for 16 miles until just past Stanton Creek Lodge, where Stanton Lake Trail 146 begins on your right (west), next to the highway. Ample parking; no toilet or camping. GPS: N48 23.933' / W113 42.750'

The Hike

Even though it's a short hike, instead of hurrying up to the lake, take your time and enjoy the preserved forest of the Great Bear Wilderness—and dine on the abundance of thimbleberries along most of the route. This hike is ideal for beginners or families with young children. Be sure to have the kids bring their fishing poles so they can catch a few of the lake's cutthroats.

Stanton Lake Trail 146 is well maintained and gently climbs through larch-fir forest to the lake. At 0.9 mile is a junction with Grant Ridge Trail 339. The Grant Ridge Trail to the left climbs steeply up Grant Ridge for views of Great Northern and Mount Grant. Stay right (southwest) at this junction, and after a little hump, you reach the foot of Stanton Lake, which has a logjam at the outlet. If you need a little more exercise, the Stanton Lake Trail continues to the head of the lake around the west shore to your right.

There is no drinking water until you reach the lake, and the trail receives heavy use. Remember to bring your insect repellent in June and July. This is bear country, so be bear aware.

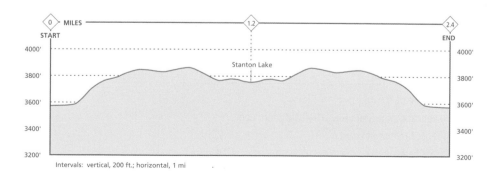

Primary hiking partner, Marnie, and grandchildren Josie and Casey, having lunch at Stanton Lake. BILL SCHNEIDER

From the foot of the lake, you have a postcard vista of mighty Great Northern and Stanton Glacier to its eastern slope. You might also get a glimpse of a moose at the head of the lake or a beaver in the beaver ponds where the stream leaves the lake. Wildflowers are common: beargrass, wild hollyhocks, cow parsnip, and many others. You might also be treated to a little serenade from the loons frequently found at Stanton Lake.

Some hikers carry in small rubber rafts or float tubes to fish, which is usually worth the effort, making it easier to hook larger rainbow and cutthroat trout. For mountain bikers, this might seem like a great trail, but it's closed to mountain biking.

Miles and Directions

0.0 Trailhead.

0.9 Junction with Grant Ridge Trail 339; turn right.

1.2 Foot of Stanton Lake.

2.4 Trailhead.

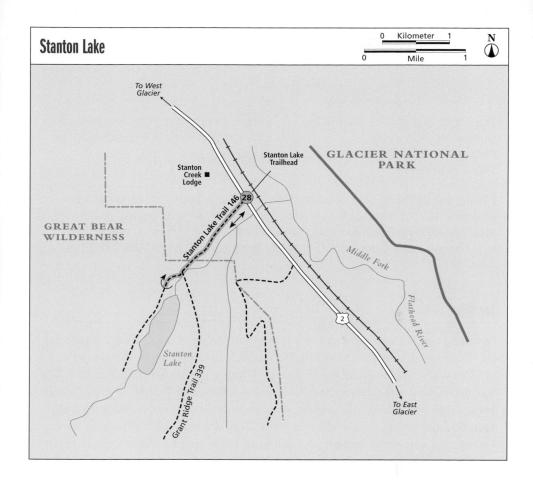

Stanton Lake

To West Glacier

GLACIER NATIONAL PARK

Stanton Lake Trailhead

Stanton Creek Lodge ■

Stanton Lake Trail 146   28

GREAT BEAR WILDERNESS

Middle Fork

Stanton Lake

Grant Ridge Trail 339

2

Flathead River

To East Glacier

Side Trips: If you have some extra time and energy, hike up along the north side of Stanton Lake to the head of the lake, which will only add about a mile to your hike. The trail continues up Stanton Creek for about another mile above the lake. (Originally contributed by Elaine and Art Sedlack, re-hiked by the authors.)

29 Marion Lake

A high-altitude lake deep in the Great Bear Wilderness

Start: South edge of Glacier National Park near the Izaak Walton Inn

Distance: 3.4-mile out-and-back

Difficulty: Moderate

Maps: USGS Pinnacle; Great Bear Wilderness Complex Map; Flathead National Forest Map (north half)

Finding the trailhead: Drive east of West Glacier on US 2 for about 28 miles to the turnoff for Essex Road 1640. Head south as the road crosses the railroad tracks and forks. Take the left (east) fork and follow Essex Creek Road 1640 for 1.5 miles to the trailhead on the right, just before crossing Marion Creek. Limited parking and filterable water; no toilet. GPS: N48 16.283' / W113 38.100'

The Hike

Marion Lake is easily accessible and has good fishing. Consequently, it probably receives more use than most other mountain lakes in designated Wilderness areas.

The way to Marion Lake is a steady, uphill pull along Marion Lake Trail 150. The trail gains about 1,800 feet in less than 2 miles, a Category 1 climb. The trail is well maintained, with plenty of drinking water and usually a tolerable number of mosquitoes. Since this lake lies within the Great Bear Wilderness, the hike has a remote feeling, and motorized vehicles and mountain bikes are prohibited. Like all of the Great Bear Wilderness and surrounding wildlands, be bear aware, as the area has a high population of both black bears and grizzlies. Wait until July unless you want to risk hiking through snowbanks.

At the head of the lake lies a gorgeous, grassy slope blanketed with wildflowers—beargrass, fireweed, wild hollyhocks, dogwood, bunchberry, and many others. The

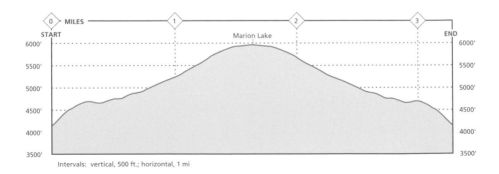

Intervals: vertical, 500 ft.; horizontal, 1 mi

Glacier lilies. JACQUELYN CORDAY

main trail comes to the foot of the lake, but a faint trail circles about a half mile around to the head of the lake.

Fishing at the lake is good, particularly in June when the ice breaks up. The lake has a healthy population of cutthroat and rainbow trout. Each winter, a few avid anglers ski or snowshoe to the lake to fish through the ice, and they usually have good success.

Miles and Directions

0.0 Trailhead.

1.7 Foot of Marion Lake.

3.4 Trailhead.

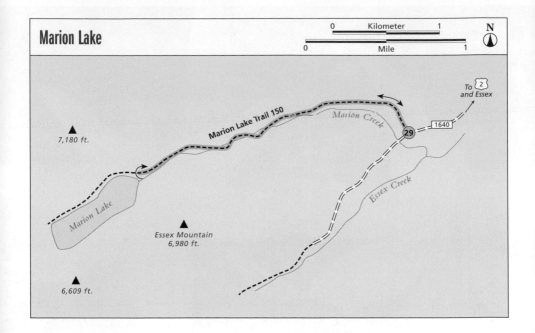

Marion Lake

0 — Kilometer — 1

0 — Mile — 1

N

Marion Lake Trail 150

7,180 ft.

Marion Creek

To ② and Essex

29 — 1640

Essex Creek

Marion Lake

Essex Mountain
6,980 ft.

6,609 ft.

Side Trips: You can extend your hike about a half mile by following the trail as it continues along the shoreline to the head of the lake. Also, for an excellent side trip, work your way through the meadowy slope to the pass on the horizon. It is only about a half mile from where the trail hits the lake. At the top you can look down over 1,000-foot cliffs into the headwaters of Essex Creek. (Originally contributed by Elaine and Art Sedlack, re-hiked by the authors.)

30 Jewel Basin

An easy trip into a popular hiking and fishing area in the Swan Range near the northwestern corner of the Bob Marshall Wilderness, suitable for both day hiking and backpacking, and ideal for an extended base camp trip

Start: Camp Misery Trailhead, 13 miles northeast of Bigfork

Distance: 8.6-mile out-and-back with loop options

Difficulty: Moderate

Maps: USGS Jewel Basin, Big Hawk Mountain, and Crater Lake; Forest Service's Jewel Basin Hiking Area map/brochure

Finding the trailhead: From Bigfork, drive north for 3 miles on MT 35 and turn right (east) onto MT 83 for 2.3 miles. Turn left (north) at the Echo Lake Cafe on Foothills Road, also called the Echo Lake Road. Follow this road past Echo Lake for 3 miles, turn right (east) onto Jewel Basin Road (FR 5392), and follow this dirt switchback road 7 miles to the Jewel Basin Hiking Area parking lot. The route is well marked, but the final stretch is bumpy, featuring whoop-dee-dos (abrupt mounds of dirt), and not recommended for RVs or trailers. The road extends beyond the Camp Misery Trailhead and parking lot, but it is closed to motorized use at the trailhead. The trailhead has a large parking lot, but it fills up on summer weekends. There is a toilet and a little cabin with a volunteer interpretive ranger often on duty, but no camping or drinking water. GPS: N48 9.316' / W113 56.750'

The Hike

Jewel Basin is ideal for a base camp hike, with many hiking options and fishing opportunities along the network of trails and lakes found throughout the area. Most years, snow does not give up the area until at least early July, and sometimes mid-July, so be sure to check on snow levels before heading for the trailhead.

Jewel Basin isn't a designated wilderness, but the Forest Service manages it like one—no logging, mountain bikes, motorized vehicles, or development. Because of the easy access from the Flathead Valley, this area can get crowded, but mainly

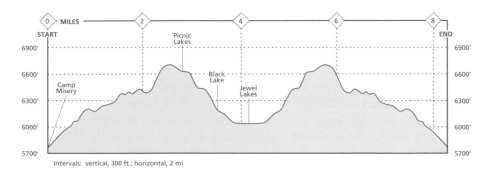

Intervals: vertical, 300 ft.; horizontal, 2 mi

Fishing and backpacking often go together, especially for grandkids. BILL SCHNEIDER

on weekends. The area has a maze of trails, so you definitely need a map, and the special hiking map/brochure published by Glacier National History Association is by far the best.

The first order of business on this hike is to pick your base camp. Two excellent options are Black Lake, 8 miles out and back, or any one of the four Jewel Lakes, a 9-mile out-and-back trip. An even easier choice would be Twin Lakes, a stunningly beautiful pair of "jewels" in a small basin only a 5-mile round-trip from the trailhead.

Two trails leave the trailhead. You can get to Black Lake and Jewel Lakes on either one with no extra distance. If you prefer to hike on a trail instead of a road, take Trail 8 by the ranger cabin. After 0.6 mile, turn right (south) onto Trail 68 unless you have decided to base camp at Twin Lakes, in which case go left. When Trail 68 junctures with Mount Aenes Trail 725, turn left (east) and climb up to the rim of Jewel Basin. Two trails depart at this point. You can get to Black Lake and Jewel Lakes on either one, but I prefer to go right (south), which seems to be a more scenic route through Picnic Lakes, where you turn left (north) onto Trail 392. Follow this trail to a junction with Trail 1 at Black Lake. Turn right (east) onto Trail 1 and drop down to Black Lake

But it can turn into extra work for Grandpa. BILL SCHNEIDER

(if you like this one for your base camp) or follow it just back from Black Lake to a junction with Trail 719, where you turn left (north). When you reach the Jewel Lakes, find a suitable base camp on one of the four lakes.

After you find your way through the labyrinth of trail junctions and get your base camp set up, start checking the map for suitable day trips. You could spend a week hiking in this area. When we hiked the loop around Clayton Lake, the trail was very brushy and hard to find, but in recent years the Forest Service has done some serious brush removal and other work on that trail, so it should be in good shape now—still a long, hard hike, though.

Jewel Basin is bear country, including the possibility of seeing a grizzly, so be bear aware—and be especially careful with food and garbage. Campsites are not officially designated, but they are well established. To leave less impact, use one of the established camps instead of camping in a virgin site—and practice zero-impact camping principles.

Most lakes in the basin are filled with cutthroat and a few rainbow trout, but they have seen lots of artificial flies and lures and might not be cooperative. To lower the impact, you might want to carefully release your fish so they can be caught again.

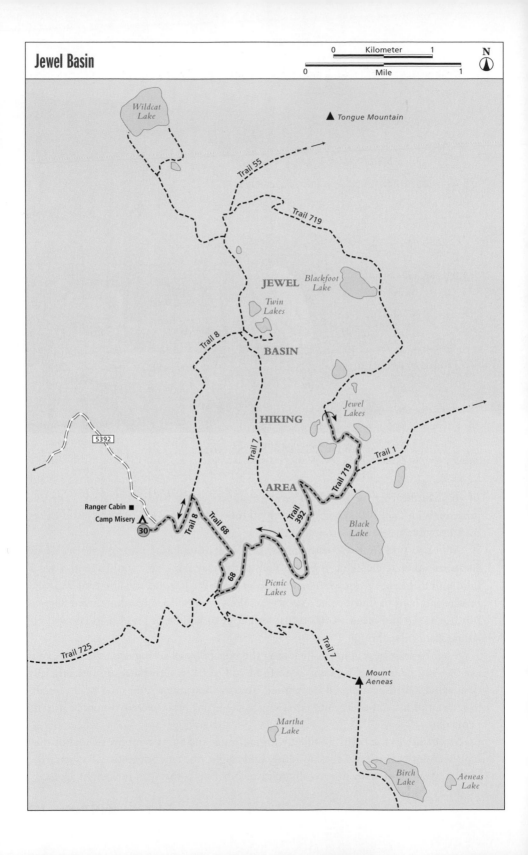

Jewel Basin

0 Kilometer 1
0 Mile 1

N

Wildcat Lake

▲ *Tongue Mountain*

Trail 55

Trail 719

JEWEL

Blackfoot Lake

Twin Lakes

Trail 8

BASIN

HIKING

5392

Trail 7

Jewel Lakes

Trail 1

Trail 719

AREA

Ranger Cabin ■
Camp Misery ⛺
30

Trail 8

Trail 68

Trail 392

Black Lake

68

Picnic Lakes

Trail 725

Trail 7

Mount Aeneas
▲

Martha Lake

Birch Lake

Aeneas Lake

Note the special regulations at the trailhead information board: Dogs must be on leashes; no campfires at Birch, Crater, Picnic, and Twin Lakes; and no more than twelve people in a party.

Miles and Directions

0.0 Trailhead.

0.6 Junction with Trail 68; turn right.

1.4 Junction with Mount Aenes Trail 725; turn left.

2.3 Junction with Alpine Trail 7; turn right.

2.7 Picnic Lakes and junction with Trail 392; turn left.

3.4 Junction with Trail 1; turn right.

3.7 Black Lake.

4.0 Junction with Trail 719; turn left.

4.3 Jewel Lakes.

8.6 Trailhead.

Options: This does not have to be a base camp trip. You could move your camp from lake to lake, but since the distances are so short, a base camp provides a less strenuous option. You can also make this a loop trip. Instead of retracing your steps to the trailhead, take the small loop through the basin via Black Lake, Jewel Lakes, Blackfoot Lake, and Twin Lakes, departing the basin on either Trail 7 or Trail 68.

Side Trips: Numerous side trips are possible throughout the basin. Check the map and find one that matches your interest and ability. If you need a long trip, you can head over to Crater Lake or Wildcat Lake, but there are also choice short trips to Blackfoot Lake, Twin Lakes, and Birch Lake. A 2003 forest fire burned a section of the trail around Blackfoot Lake. (Originally contributed and re-hiked by the authors.)

31 Crater Lake

A popular Jewel Basin hike through subalpine terrain to a good fishing lake; a long day hike or moderate overnighter

---

Start: Camp Misery Trailhead, 13 miles northeast of Bigfork
Distance: 12.0-mile out-and-back
Difficulty: Moderate

Maps: USGS Jewel Basin and Crater Lake; Jewel Basin Hiking Area Map; Flathead National Forest Map.

Finding the trailhead: From Bigfork drive north for 3 miles on MT 35 and turn right (east) onto MT 83 for 2.3 miles. Turn left (north) at the Echo Lake Cafe on Foothills Road, also called the Echo Lake Road. Follow this road past Echo Lake for 3 miles, turn right (east) onto Jewel Basin Road (FR 5392), and follow this dirt switchback road 7 miles to the Jewel Basin Hiking Area parking lot. The route is well marked, but the final stretch is bumpy, featuring whoop-dee-dos (abrupt mounds of dirt), and not recommended for RVs or trailers. The road extends beyond the Camp Misery Trailhead and parking lot, but it is closed to motorized use at the trailhead. The trailhead has a large parking lot, but it fills up on summer weekends. There is a toilet and a little cabin with a volunteer interpretive ranger often on duty, but no camping or drinking water. GPS: N48 9.316' / W113 56.750'

The Hike

To reach high-elevation lakes, you usually have to make a healthy climb. Crater Lake is an exception. The trail starts high, so it's 6 easy miles to this scenic fishing lake. The Forest Service adequately maintains this trail all summer. The trail is very popular, so expect to see other hikers.

Two trails leave the parking lot. Take the major trail (actually an old road) near the big information board on the east side of the lot (noting the special regulations there), not the singletrack trail leaving the north end near the ranger cabin. Follow the road

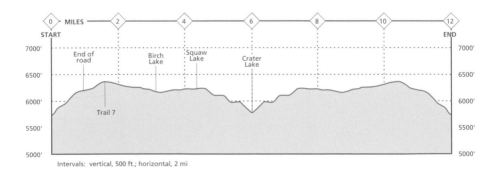

Intervals: vertical, 500 ft.; horizontal, 2 mi

Alpine Trail above Strawberry Lake. BILL SCHNEIDER

this high-altitude hike, allow three days. Although the trail is remote and primitive, it's well maintained and easy to follow. You have a good chance of spotting elk or deer, and a great variety of wildflowers greet you every summer, particularly in mid-July. Be careful not to miss them as you marvel at the incredible vistas in every direction.

Snow may block this trail until mid-July. You can find plenty of water along the trail with, depending on the year, some dry stretches on the northern half of the hike. Mosquitoes are there for you early in the season, but less bothersome than in many other areas. Find drinking water and shelter from the wind by dropping off the ridge to the east into the high meadows.

The first 2 miles on Trail 5 from the Strawberry Lake Trailhead are very steep (but not nearly as steep as starting at the other end of the hike at the Columbia Mountain Trailhead). Then, about a mile before Strawberry Lake, the grade levels out and stays fairly easy until you reach the lake. If you started late in the day, you can camp here, but there isn't a good choice of campsites, so you might want to continue on for the first night's camp.

Strawberry Lake probably should be called Huckleberry Lake. I found huge patches of huckleberries all around the lake, but not a single strawberry. Strawberry Lake is a very popular day hike for locals and tourists, so plan on seeing a few hikers,

Hiking the Columbia Mountain section of the Swan Crest Trail. MARNIE SCHNEIDER

mountain bikers, and horses along the trail, and regrettably, even a few motorcycles. As sad as it seems, the Swan Crest is open to motorcycles.

At the foot of the lake, you hit the junction with the famous Alpine Trail 7. Turn left here. From here to Columbia Mountain, the trail follows the Swan Crest, up and down, with probably a little more up than down, but no big climbs. You'll encounter several junctions, some official, some not; ignore all of them and stay on the ridge on Alpine Trail 7. The Swan Crest is actually quite lush, and you'll also encounter a wide variety and abundance of wildflowers, including a lot of one of my favorites, the western anemone (also called western pasqueflower).

Lamoose Lake, about 3 miles from Strawberry Lake, might also be a good first night's camp. It's only about a quarter mile from Alpine Trail 7 to the right at a signed junction.

Doris Lakes, about another 5 miles farther along the ridge, is a likely candidate for the second night's camp. That would make a long last day, but it's mostly downhill. Fawn Lake and Jenny Lake are also good camping choices.

When you reach the junction with Trail 51, turn left and drop steeply for 8 miles to the Columbia Mountain Trailhead. Before you do, though, take the short spur trail

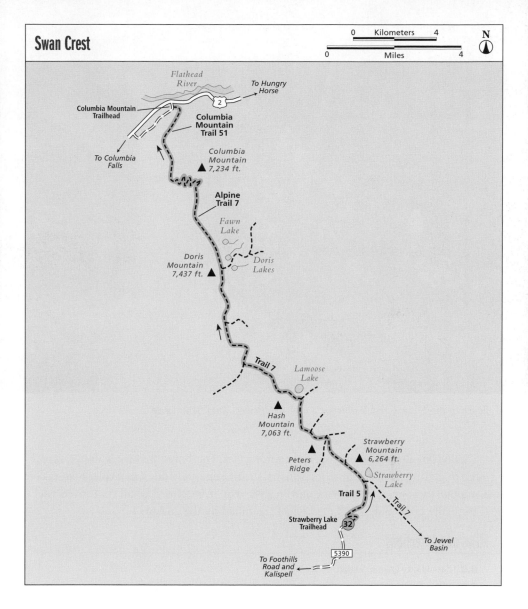

to the right to the top of Columbia Mountain for one last incredible vista (Hungry Horse Reservoir, the peaks of Glacier, and the vast expanse of the Flathead Valley) before plunging down to the trailhead.

Although you can catch a few small trout in Strawberry and Lamoose Lakes, this hike isn't well known for its fishing. It is, however, well known as prime bear country, and you'll probably see proof of it along the way, in the form of piles of recently recycled huckleberries. The likelihood of an encounter might be higher here than on most trails in Montana's national forests, so be bear aware.

Much of the Swan Crest Trail is lined with wildflowers. BILL SCHNEIDER

Sadly, this amazing trail is open to motorcycles. The Forest Service is always interested in getting feedback from forest users, so after enjoying this spectacular hike, take a minute to contact the agency and suggest that it be closed to all motorized use. (Originally contributed by Loren Kreck, re-hiked by the authors.)

Miles and Directions

0.0 Strawberry Lake Trailhead.

3.0 Strawberry Lake and junction with Alpine Trail 7; turn left.

7.0 Lamoose Lake.

10.5 Doris Lakes.

12.5 Junction with Trail 51; turn left.

20.5 Columbia Mountain Trailhead.

33 Palisade Lake

A backpacking trip through mixed old-growth forest with scenic views of the Swan and South Fork of the Flathead River Valleys

Start: 40 miles southeast of Kalispell, just northeast of Condon in the wild Swan Range
Distance: 22.0-mile out-and-back

Difficulty: Strenuous
Maps: USGS Swan Peak and Sunburst Lake; Flathead National Forest Map (south half)

Finding the trailhead: Drive south on MT 83 18 miles south of Swan Lake or 36 miles north of Seeley Lake to mile marker 52. Turn east onto Lion Creek Road 9769. Follow this road for 3 miles to the trailhead on the left, taking lefts at major forks at 0.5 and 1.8 miles. The road continues as an access to private land adjacent to the creek; there's no public access. Ample parking; no toilet. GPS: N47 40.197' / W113 44.582'

The Hike

In contrast to most hiking in the rugged Swan Range, the trail up Lion Creek climbs gradually from the Swan Valley to the large basin beneath the Swan Divide.

From the trailhead, Trail 25 descends and crosses the creek on a bridge and then ascends gently through an open forest of old ponderosa pine and larch trees. At 0.8 mile a trail enters from the left, an extension to Van Lake Road; stay right (east) on the main trail. The trail leaves the main Swan Valley, climbing rocky benches sprinkled with old ponderosa pines. After a short drop, an outfitter trail enters from the right; stay left, continuing east on Trail 25.

The trail is heavily used by horses and becomes wide and muddy, even during dry periods, as it enters the narrow canyon of Lion Creek. At about 5 miles is the first of several waterfalls on Lion Creek, which cascades down from the glaciers and snowfields of Swan and Union Peaks.

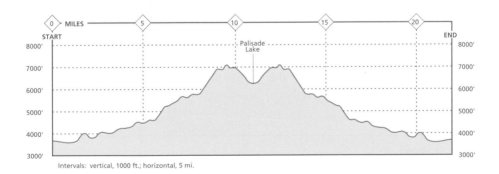

Intervals: vertical, 1000 ft.; horizontal, 5 mi.

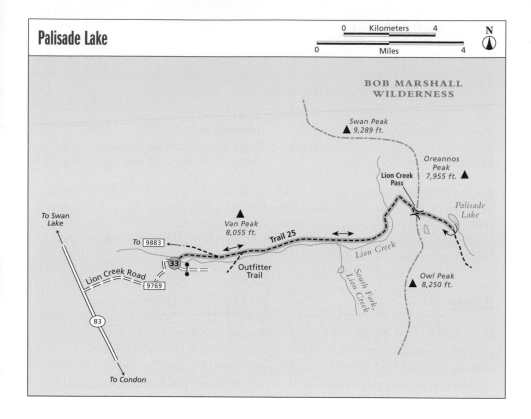

Continuing on, the trail passes through a majestic grove of old western red cedars. After the grove, another series of falls appears on the creek just after the South Fork of Lion Creek joins the main stream.

It's 9.5 miles from the trailhead to Lion Creek Pass and the Bob Marshall boundary. Palisade Lake, 1.5 miles farther on in the Bob Marshall Wilderness, is a popular destination, and when you reach it, you'll know why.

The trail is not maintained past Palisade Lake, making trip extensions difficult. Remember that when you enter Lion Creek Canyon, you enter the grizzly's domain: Be bear aware.

A small portion of the lower trail crosses private land, with access currently granted by an operating agreement between the landowner and the Forest Service. Please show your respect when on this private property. (Originally contributed by John Gatchall, re-hiked by the authors.)

Miles and Directions

0.0 Trailhead.

0.8 Trail enters from Van Lake Road; stay right on main trail.

1.5	Outfitter Trail joins main trail.
5.0	Waterfall.
9.5	Lion Creek Pass.
10.0	Small ponds.
11.0	Palisade Lake (end of maintained trail).
22.0	Trailhead.

THE VIEW FROM HERE: A HIKER'S BEST FRIEND?

When you hike Montana's trails nowadays, probably about half the people you meet on the trail have the family dog (or dogs) with them. I have no problem with dogs and have had one most of my life, but I do have a problem with people taking dogs into the backcountry and not keeping them under control.

Fortunately, most dogs are well behaved, and most dog owners are responsible and aware that not everybody loves their dogs as much as they do. Like so many things, however, the few can ruin it for the many. This is why we have restrictions on dogs in many hiking areas.

I'm sorry to say that in recent years I've experienced a growing number of problems. I have, in fact, twice been bitten by dogs while out on trails. I've had the stuffing scared out of me by a pack of four dogs charging out of nowhere and looking menacing. I've seen dogs scare little kids to tears. I've seen dogs chasing deer. I've lost my lunch to a dog that was quicker than I was (which is not difficult for a dog). I've seen dogs annoy people with incessant crotch sniffing. And I've spent a few sleep-deprived nights in the tent listening to dogs barking in a nearby campsite. All of this is irresponsible dog owner behavior.

Most dog owners who I discuss this subject with think their dog is "under control," but that's almost never the reality. So unless you're positive your dog responds quickly and firmly to voice commands, use a leash.

In any case, if you take your dog with you in the backcountry, please be a responsible dog owner and keep your dog closely under control or leashed—and quiet—while enjoying Montana's hiking trails, so others can enjoy their wilderness experience as much as you do.

34 Cold Lakes

An easy day hike to experience Mission Mountain beauty and fish in high mountain lakes

Start: South of Swan Lake, near Condon in the Mission Mountains Wilderness

Distance: 4.4 miles to lower lake, 5.0 miles to upper lake, out and back

Difficulty: Easy to lower lake; moderate to upper lake

Maps: USGS Piper Crow Pass and Peck Lake; Flathead National Forest Map

Finding the trailhead: Drive south of Swan Lake on MT 83 for 23 miles and turn right on Cold Creek Road (FR 903A), which is near mile marker 47. Drive southwest on FR 903A for 3 miles and turn right on FR 9568, then after 3 miles more, turn left on FR 9599. Go 1.5 miles more to the end of the road and the trailhead. It's 7.5 miles from MT 83 to the trailhead. Ample parking, filterable water, a pit toilet, and primitive camping. GPS: N47 35.597' / W113 46.725'

The Hike

This hike is an example of the positive changes taking place in the wilderness, even with increased use. Lower Cold Lake had been severely damaged by years of high-impact camping. With the Mission Mountains Wilderness designation, the Forest Service has made an effort to help areas like Cold Lakes recover from past abuses. This Wilderness Restoration Project has been a success so far. Native vegetation has regrown over old campsites. Camping is not allowed within 0.25 mile of either lake; however, it's a nightmare to find a suitable campsite that distance away. The brush is too thick, and there are few flat spots to put up a tent. Therefore, this makes this a great day hike but a marginal overnighter.

The Forest Service has rerouted the trail to Cold Lakes. When originally hiked, it followed the creek, but a major blowdown prompted the rerouting to the slopes above the creek. Now Trail 121 climbs through a mature spruce forest for about a mile before leveling off and then descending slightly into Lower Cold Lake.

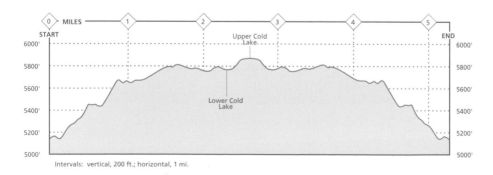

Intervals: vertical, 200 ft.; horizontal, 1 mi.

Checking out Cold Lake. MARNIE SCHNEIDER

At Lower Cold Lake, you'll find roped-off vegetation recovery areas and a great place to rest and enjoy the wilderness, but you might have company because it's a popular destination for day hikers. The fishing is good, but good fly-casting spots are scarce. Dense foliage grows tight against the lake on most of the shoreline.

If you're looking for an easy day hike, enjoy the lake for a while and then turn around and hike out. If you want a little more, follow the faint trail to Upper Cold Lake. It circles the north side of Lower Cold Lake and follows the stream up to the upper lake. The hard part is getting around the lake. Thick brush and deadfall cover the trail, including a few fallen 4-foot Engelmann spruce—always fun to crawl over. It's only 0.3 mile to the upper lake, but it can be exhausting to reach it.

Some have suggested that this trail should be maintained, but having a bush-whacking barrier minimizes the impact of hikers on the upper lake. Not as many people get there as would if the trail were maintained.

Once you make it around the lower lake to the inlet, it gets easier; the stretch between the lakes is gentle. The outlet of the upper lake is a logjam. If you choose to

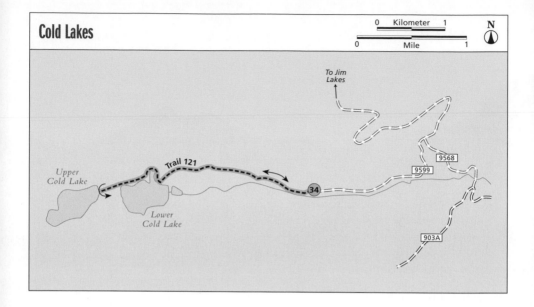

Cold Lakes

Upper
Cold Lake

Trail 121

Lower
Cold Lake

To Jim
Lakes

9568

9599

34

903A

cross it or fish from it, be careful of unstable logs. The fishing is better at the upper lake, with a good population of nice-size cutthroat and more casting spots.

The view from the upper lake is breathtaking. The glaciated peaks of the Missions rise sharp and rugged above the lake, carved from uplifted sedimentary rock. The surrounding cliffs offer a home to mountain goats. Bring your binoculars and see if you can spot one. This is also the home of the mighty grizzly, so be bear aware. (Originally contributed and re-hiked by the authors.)

Miles and Directions

0.0 Trailhead.

2.2 Lower Cold Lake.

2.5 Upper Cold Lake.

5.0 Trailhead.

35 Crescent Lake

A day hike or overnighter into a forested lake basin in the Mission Mountains Wilderness

Start: 25 miles northwest of Seeley Lake
Distance: 7.0-mile out-and-back
Difficulty: Moderate

Maps: USGS Gray Wolf Lake and Hemlock Lake; Forest Service's Mission Mountains Wilderness Map

Finding the trailhead: Drive 22 miles north of Seeley Lake or 32 miles south of Swan Lake on MT 83, between mile markers 37 and 38, then turn west onto FR 561 (also called Kraft Creek Road). From here it's 11.5 unpaved miles to the large trailhead. Several roads turn off, but stay on well-signed FR 561, the main road. Ample parking and a toilet. GPS: N47 22.775' / W113 47.970'

The Hike

This is a heavily used area, so be sure to check the information board at the trailhead to review current regulations. For example, the shoreline of Glacier Lake is open to day use only; no camping within 0.25 mile of the lake.

For the first mile you go gradually uphill on a stream grade through mature forest on Trail 690, crossing Glacier Creek twice, both on bridges. Go right (west) at the junction with the spur trail to Glacier Lake, unless you want to take a short side trip on the way in, which you should because you'll be rewarded with a spectacular view of a large and beautiful wilderness lake. After the junction, the trail climbs above Glacier Lake and gives you another great view of the lake.

At the junction with Turquoise Lake Trail 708 at mile 2.5, go right (west) again. From here Trail 690 goes up long, forested switchbacks, most lined with huckleberry bushes, so plan on extra time for grazing. The last mile of trail to Crescent Lake gets fairly brushy. The trail continues along the south side of Crescent Lake to Heart Lake.

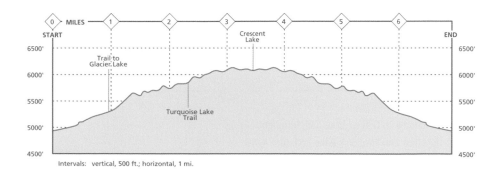

Intervals: vertical, 500 ft.; horizontal, 1 mi.

Glacier Lake, a nice rest stop on the way to Crescent Lake. MARNIE SCHNEIDER

Crescent Lake has a few heavily impacted campsites, but it's still better camping than Heart Lake. Both lakes have a few hungry cutthroats to keep you busy fishing after supper.

Miles and Directions

0.0 Trailhead.

1.0 Junction with Glacier Lake Trail; turn right.

2.5 Junction with Turquoise Lake Trail; turn right.

3.5 Crescent Lake.

7.0 Trailhead.

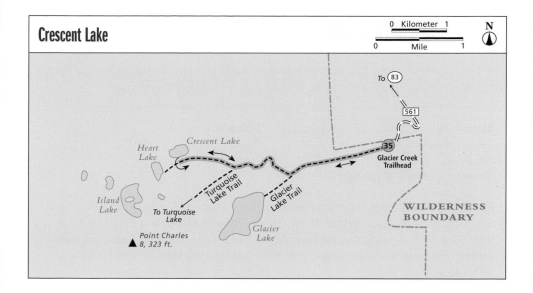

Side Trips: You'll be disappointed if you don't take the short (0.5 mile) side trip to Glacier Lake. Also, you can continue past Crescent Lake for 0.8 mile to Heart Lake. If you're experienced and ambitious, you can bushwhack up to Island Lake, the next lake up the drainage above Heart Lake. (Originally contributed and re-hiked by the authors.)

36 Sapphire Lakes

A long day hike or backpacking trip with several side-trip options to a high alpine lake with scenic views of the Swan Range and the Mission Mountains

Start: Holland Lake Lodge, 20 miles north of Seeley Lake on the edge of the Bob Marshall Wilderness

Distance: 14.8-mile lollipop loop

Difficulty: Strenuous

Maps: USGS Holland Lake; Flathead National Forest Map

Finding the trailhead: Drive north from Seeley Lake for about 20 miles on MT 83 and turn right (east) onto Holland Lake Road (FR 44), between mile markers 35 and 36. Follow this road for about 4 miles, staying left around the north shore of the lake, until it dead-ends just past Holland Lake Lodge at a large trailhead with ample parking and a toilet. GPS: N47 27.144' / W113 36.316'

The Hike

This hike describes the second-busiest access route into the Bob Marshall Wilderness (Benchmark in the Rocky Mountain Front is the busiest), so the main trail can get crowded at times. To avoid the hordes, take this loop hike as early in the season as snow conditions will allow. Once off the main drag and onto the Sapphire Trail, the crowds drop off dramatically.

The trail to Sapphire Lakes is a spectacular loop, but it's complicated, with numerous junctions and spur trails, so keep your map out to make sure you stay on the correct route. The hike can be a long day hike, or you can camp overnight at Sapphire Lakes for one or more nights. The mosquitoes in the Swan are well known for their voraciousness, so bring lots of bug dope to keep them under control.

Start up the main East Holland Connector Trail 415, which leads through dense forest for a mile and begins to climb into the Swan Range. Just after you start hiking, you reach the junction with Trail 416, which leads off to the right along Holland

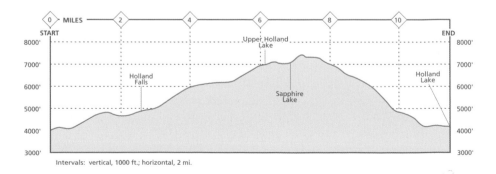

Holland Lake from the Sapphire Lakes Trail. MARNIE SCHNEIDER

Lake to Holland Falls; stay left (east), climbing on East Holland Connector Trail 415. (Turn right if you'd like to take the 1.5-mile spur trail along the Holland Lake shoreline to the base of Holland Falls before continuing your hike.)

At the 1.2-mile mark at the junction with Trail 192, stay right (east) on Trail 415, and then right again 0.1 mile later at the junction with your return route, Trail 42, staying on Trail 415. Along the main trail, the route cuts across steep sidehills, which offer beautiful views of lower Holland Lake, the Swan Valley, and the Mission Mountains.

The roar of water becomes overwhelming as the path passes above Holland Falls. After passing the falls, Trail 415 crosses Holland Creek and climbs to the junction with Holland Gordon Trail 35 on the south side of the canyon. Turn left (east) onto Trail 35 and start climbing parallel to Holland Creek. Several other waterfalls and cascades greet you as the stream rushes down the abrupt western slope of the Swan Range. In late June the thunder of the stream will be almost deafening and will almost drown out the buzzing of early-season mosquitoes.

At 5.4 miles you reach Upper Holland Lake, situated in a gorgeous subalpine basin beneath the crest of the Swan Range. Hike around the north shore to the junction with Trail 120 to Sapphire Lakes.

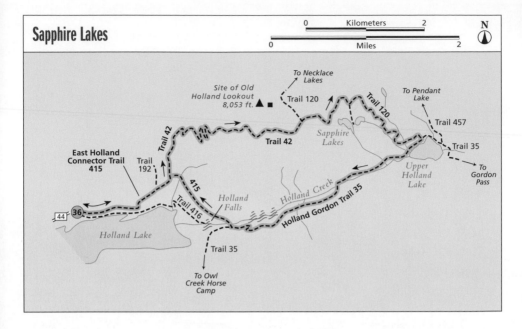

Sapphire Lakes

0   Kilometers   2

0   Miles   2

N

Site of Old
Holland Lookout
8,053 ft. ▲ ■

To Necklace
Lakes

Trail 120

To Pendant
Lake

Trail 120

Trail 457

Trail 42

Sapphire
Lakes

Trail 35

East Holland
Connector Trail
415

Trail
192

Trail 42

Upper
Holland
Lake

To
Gordon
Pass

415

Holland Creek

44   36

Trail 416

Holland
Falls

Holland Gordon Trail 35

Holland Lake

Trail 35

To Owl
Creek Horse
Camp

Turn left (north) on Trail 120, which leads upward from the north shore of the lake, passing through sparse stands of spruce and fir and meadows filled with glacier lilies. For the next 3 miles, the trail is a hiker's delight, with views opening up to the south along the Swan Range and distant vistas of huge mountains appearing to the east, deep within the Bob Marshall Wilderness. About a mile from Upper Holland Lake, the trail reaches the rumpled plateau on which several ponds and Sapphire Lakes are located.

Just before Sapphire Lakes, you'll see a spur trail veering off to your left to the lakes. This is an out-and-back spur trail. Trail 120 doesn't skirt the north shore of the lake, as shown on some maps. Instead, it stays north of the lakes.

After leaving the upper basin above Sapphire Lakes, the trail ascends a steep slope to a notch in a high ridge. Once through the notch, the trail continues along a south-facing slope, with the great pyramid of Carmine Peak rising over the deep canyon of Holland Creek below you. This spectacular skywalk through the alpine meadows on the western slope of the Swan Range brings you almost to eyeball level with the Mission Mountain peaks across the valley.

Stay left (west) at the junction where Trail 120 meets Trail 48 and left again 0.4 mile later at the junction with Trail 42, continuing down endless switchbacks on Trail 42. After 4.5 miles of downhill walking, some of it quite steep, you come to the junction with Trail 415 and the completion of the loop section of your hike. From here, retrace your steps back to the trailhead.

This entire hike is outside the western boundary of the Bob Marshall Wilderness, but it has been proposed as an addition to the wilderness.

Miles and Directions

0.0 Trailhead.

0.2 Junction with Trail 416 to Holland Falls; turn left.

0.8 Junction with East Foothill Trail 192; turn right

1.3 Junction with Holland Lookout Trail 42; turn right.

2.8 Junction with Holland Gordon Trail 35; turn left.

7.0 Upper Holland Lake and junction with Trail 120; turn left.

8.6 Sapphire Lakes.

8.7 Junction with Trail 48; turn left.

9.1 Junction with Trail 42; turn left.

13.5 Junction with Trail 415; turn right.

13.9 Junction with Trail 192; turn left.

14.8 Trailhead.

Options: If you want to avoid the traffic on the Holland Gordon Trail and you enjoy climbing steep switchbacks, the trip can be done as an out-and-back trip on Trail 42. You can also take this loop in reverse, but it might seem more difficult. This hike is also a good choice for an extended backpacking trip. Set up a base camp at Sapphire Lakes, Upper Holland Lake, or Necklace Lakes and spend a day or two exploring and fishing the lakes in the area.

Side Trips: At the junction with Trail 120, 0.9 mile past Sapphire Lakes, you can turn right and hike up to the ridge to see the old Holland lookout. A must-see side trip would be the 1.5-mile (one-way) trail over to Holland Falls. It follows the shoreline of Holland Lake most of the way and the falls are impressive, especially in early summer. (Originally contributed by Ed Madej and Rosemary Rowe, re-hiked by the authors.)

Glacier National Park

37 Boulder Pass

A long, scenic route starting in Canada and ending in the United States, with incredible alpine scenery and remoteness; a classic backpacking trip

Start: Goat Haunt in Glacier National Park
Distance: 30.6-mile shuttle
Difficulty: Strenuous

Maps: USGS Kintla Lake, Kintla Peak, Porcupine Ridge, and Mount Carter; either the USGS or Trails Illustrated map for the entire park

Finding the trailheads: To reach the Goat Haunt trailhead, cross through customs into Canada at the Chief Mountain border station, drive to the Waterton town site in Waterton Lakes National Park, and, for a modest fee, take the tour boat to Goat Haunt (6.7 miles one way), which also has a visitor center and restrooms. The boat leaves from the marina on Emerald Bay (also called Divers Bay). There is ample parking at the marina. The cruise runs two or three times daily and takes about two hours and fifteen minutes. Contact the Waterton Shoreline Cruise Company (403-859-2362; www.waterton cruise.com) for an updated schedule and fees. You can hike from the Waterton town site along the west shore of Waterton Lake, but the cruise is worth the money. GPS: N48 57.533' / W113 53.950'

Leave a vehicle or arrange for a pickup at Kintla Lake Campground at the foot of Kintla Lake. To reach this trailhead, drive north of Columbia Falls on CR 486 (known locally as Outside North Fork Road) for 30 miles until you see the sign for Polebridge. Turn right here and cross the North Fork of the Flathead River at the Polebridge Ranger Station. After you pass through the National Park Service (NPS) facilities, you intersect with the gravel road along the east side of the North Fork within the park. Turn left (north) here and drive 13 miles to the end of the road at the Kintla Lake Campground. Kintla Lake has a vehicle campground and toilets but limited parking, so be careful not to take more than one space. GPS: N48 56.133' / W114 20.767'

Recommended itinerary: Take the earliest boat you can (probably leaving about 10 a.m.) so you have time to reach Lake Francis, which has a nicer campsite than those at Waterton River, Lake Janet, or Hawksbill.
First night: Lake Francis
Second night: Boulder Pass or Hole-in-the-Wall
Third night: Upper Kintla Lake
Fourth night: Lower Kintla Lake

The spacing of the campsites on the west side of Boulder Pass makes deciding between a three- or four-night trip a difficult choice. You could cut back to a three-night trip by hiking from Boulder Pass Camp to Lower Kintla Lake, 11 miles, almost all downhill. If you can't reserve the Boulder Pass Campsite and stay at Hole-in-the-Wall, it's best to take four nights.

Getting a permit: To have the rare opportunity to experience Boulder Pass, you need a backcountry camping permit from the NPS. Since the demand is so great and since the NPS rightfully limits use for environmental reasons, getting a permit isn't easy. You must use designated campsites on this route. All have pit toilets and food/garbage storage devices.

One way to get a backcountry camping permit is to walk into one of the park's ranger stations or visitor centers, apply right there, and pay the backcountry camping fee. However, waiting until the last minute is risky because many popular campsites, such as those on Boulder Pass, are reserved long in advance.

The safest (but by no means the easiest) way to get your permit is by using the NPS's advance reservation system. Refer to Glacier's website (www.nps.gov/glac/activity.htm) for details on the reservation system. You can also download an application from the website. The NPS issues reservations on a first-come, first-served basis, so apply early. However, no applications are accepted if they are postmarked earlier than mid-April. Call the backcountry office (406-888-7857) or check the website for the specific date, which varies slightly from year to year. Plan on paying a modest fee for the permit.

If you get a permit for Boulder Pass and can't make it to Glacier for the trip, please call the backcountry office and cancel your reservation so others might enjoy these campsites.

The Hike

Boulder Pass is a truly classic backpacking trip and has achieved some widespread popularity because of it. The NPS limits use with the number of designated campsites and permits, so if you're lucky enough to get one, you won't feel crowded.

The hike itself is difficult to beat, but the preparation and shuttle can test your mettle. Use the park's backcountry permit reservation system to try for a permit in advance. Showing up at a ranger station looking for a permit to start the hike the next day means you'll probably be hiking somewhere else. Once you have your permit, you have to arrange a long, problematic shuttle. The best way to manage this logistical challenge is to take this trip with another party, so you can start at opposite ends of the route and meet at Boulder Pass or Hole-in-the-Wall camps to exchange car keys. Then, of course, you both have to get permits, thus requiring even more patience.

Be sure to watch the weather forecast. You really don't want to be up on Boulder Pass in a summer snowstorm. Because of the elevation, snow rules the area until at least late July, even early August in big snow years. And it can come back to claim the area any summer day. Even with a good forecast, be prepared for winter weather. Keep in mind that this is prime grizzly country, so study up on bear awareness before hitting the trail. But take some solace in the fact that this route is worth any amount of frustration in planning and preparation!

The first leg of the Boulder Pass Trail climbs gradually through the lush Olson Creek valley, thick with thimbleberry and false hellebore. If you leave early, before the sun gets a chance to dry the dew, plan on getting as wet as if it had rained. There are plenty of water sources here and throughout this hike.

Shortly after leaving the trailhead, turn right (west) at the junction with the spur trail to Rainbow Falls. At 3.1 miles at Lake Janet, you get a great view of the Sentinel over the lake, but at 5.6 miles you get a poor view of Lake Francis from the trail. Just

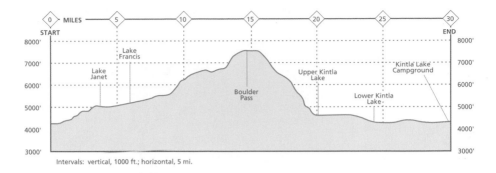

Intervals: vertical, 1000 ft.; horizontal, 5 mi.

past Lake Francis, at the foot of an unnamed lake, the trail starts switchbacking out of the forest into the alpine wonderland you'll enjoy until you plunge down to the Kintla Valley on the other side of Boulder Pass.

Here you break out of the thimbleberry jungle onto a wildflower carpet. Off to your left (south), Thunderbird Falls cascades down from the mountain and glacier of the same name (originating from several Indian legends about a great bird spirit with lightning flashing from its eyes that creates thunder by flapping its wings) into the unnamed lake. You might think this is scenery at its best, but it gets even better as you proceed uphill. It's a gentle, Category 4 climb to Brown Pass.

When you reach the junction with the Brown Pass Trail at 7.7 miles, which heads down to Bowman Lake, bear right. If you have a permit for the Brown Pass Campsite, you must have bug netting and repellent to survive the infamously vicious Brown Pass mosquitoes—little brown mutants that go right for your eyeballs.

After Brown Pass you gradually climb for about 5 miles to Boulder Pass, again only a Category 4 climb. About 2 miles from the pass, the wildflowers give way to sheer rock, with a few hardy phlox hanging on to the soilless landscape. Mighty Kintla Peak and its slightly shorter but more austere companion, Kinnerly Peak, dominate the southern horizon most of the way to the top. You can look back and see the park's highest peak, Cleveland, and nearby Stoney Indian Peaks with their thirteen distinct spires.

The trail is in great shape considering the rugged environment. You have to follow cairns in a few places, but the route is easy to find. Earlier in the season (mid to late July), you may encounter a few dangerous snowbanks.

After enjoying some special time on top of Boulder Pass, start down the giant decline of 5.8 miles to Upper Kintla Lake. This trail is rougher, rockier, and steeper than the east-side trail, but it isn't as brushy.

Along Upper Kintla Lake you get a constant postcard view of the Matterhorn-like Kinnerly Peak. With the exception of a small hill between the lakes and a few hills along Lower Kintla Lake, it's essentially a gradual downhill the rest of the trip. It's about 5.5 miles between the Upper and Lower Kintla Lake Campsites. Watch for bald eagles around the upper end of Lower Kintla Lake, but be careful not to disturb them.

At 27 miles you reach the junction with Kishenehn Creek Trail. Turn left (south) and enjoy the last 3.6 miles to the Kintla Lake Campground trailhead. Then,

Thunderbird Mountain dominates the southern horizon on much of the Boulder Pass adventure.
Courtesy of NPS

go somewhere and celebrate. You just finished one of America's best backpacking routes.

Normally this route doesn't attract anglers, but Lake Francis has some good fishing for rainbows. They can get large but are difficult to catch. You can also fish Lower Kintla Lake, where you stand a good chance of getting a nice cutthroat from the west shore. Upper Kintla Lake is closed to fishing.

Miles and Directions

- **0.0** Goat Haunt Trailhead.
- **0.4** Junction with Rainbow Falls Trail; turn right.
- **0.6** Waterton River Campsite.
- **0.9** Junction with Boulder Pass Trail; turn left.
- **3.1** Lake Janet and Campsite.
- **5.6** Lake Francis and Campsite.
- **6.2** Hawksbill Campsite.
- **7.7** Junction with Brown Pass Trail and Brown Pass Campsite; turn right.
- **10.5** Trail to Hole-in-the-Wall Campsite; turn right.
- **13.0** Boulder Pass.
- **13.6** Boulder Pass Campsite.

Boulder Pass

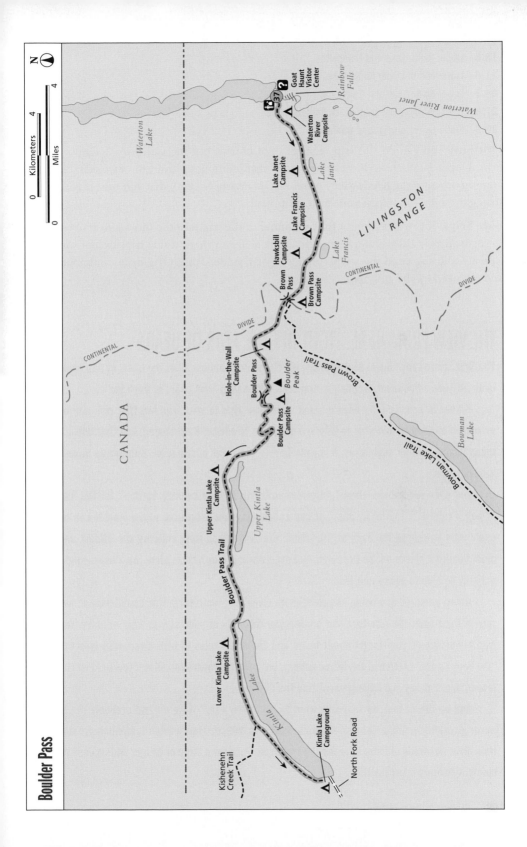

18.8	Upper Kintla Lake and Campsite.
21.6	Lower end of Upper Kintla Lake.
24.3	Lower Kintla Lake and Campsite.
27.0	Junction with Kishenehn Creek Trail; turn left.
30.6	Kintla Lake Campground trailhead.

Options: You can do this trip in reverse, of course, but the Category 1 climb up from Upper Kintla Lake is more strenuous than coming up from the east side. Plus, coming down to the Kintla Valley offers some fantastic scenery that you miss if you're struggling uphill staring at your next foot plant.

Side Trips: If you have time at the beginning of the trip, take the short spur trail over to see Rainbow Falls. Otherwise, there aren't really any logical side trips except some casual exploring amid the scenic grandeur of Boulder Pass. (Originally contributed and re-hiked by the authors.)

THE VIEW FROM HERE: FIGHT OFF THE FEAR OF BEARS

The first step of any hike in bear country, which includes almost all of the hikes in this book, is an attitude adjustment. Nothing guarantees total safety from bears or anything else.

Hiking in bear country adds a small additional risk to your trip, but that risk can be greatly minimized by adhering to this age-old piece of advice: Be prepared. And that doesn't mean having certain equipment; it means having the right information. Knowledge is your best defense.

You can—and should—thoroughly enjoy your trip to bear country, so don't let the fear of bears ruin it. If you let it, this fear can accompany you every step of the way. It can be constantly lurking in the back of your mind, preventing you from enjoying the wildest and most beautiful places left on the earth. And even worse, some bear experts think bears might actually be able to sense your fear.

Being prepared and being knowledgeable gives you confidence. This confidence allows you to fight back the fear that can burden you throughout your stay in bear country. You won't—nor should you—forget about bears and the basic rules of bear awareness (see the "Be Bear Aware" section in the introduction), but proper preparation allows you to keep the fear of bears at bay and let enjoyment rule the day.

And on top of that, do we really want to be totally safe? If we did, we probably would never go hiking in the wilderness—bears or no bears. We certainly wouldn't, at much greater risk, drive hundreds of miles to reach the trailhead. Perhaps a tinge of danger adds a desired element to our wilderness trip.

38 Akokala Lake

A remote lake filled with small, native cutthroat trout, secluded camping opportunities, and excellent views of Kintla-area peaks

Start: Bowman Lake Campground, 35 miles northwest of Columbia Falls in the North Fork region of Glacier National Park
Distance: 11.6-mile out-and-back

Difficulty: Moderate
Maps: USGS Quartz Ridge and Kintla Peak; either the USGS map or the Trails Illustrated map for the entire park

Finding the trailhead: From the junction of US 2 and Nucleus Avenue in Columbia Falls, drive north through town and turn right, heading northeast on Outside North Fork Road. After 35 miles of partially paved but mostly dirt-road driving, turn right, heading east for Polebridge. Drive through Polebridge and across the North Fork of the Flathead River for 2 miles to the junction with Inside North Fork Road (also called Glacier Route 7). Turn left, heading north on Inside North Fork Road for 0.1 mile, then turn right, heading east on Bowman Lake Road for 6 miles to Bowman Lake Campground. The last 6 miles are passable by a two-wheel-drive vehicle, but good tires and high clearance are recommended. (You could also take Inside North Fork Road from West Glacier, but it's bumpier, slower, and dustier, and you'd definitely want a high-clearance vehicle.) Bowman Lake Campground at the trailhead has toilets and drinking water. GPS: N48 49.883' / W114 12.116'

The Hike

The North Fork of the Flathead River forms the western boundary of Glacier National Park. Inside the park several lakes drain into the river, with Akokala being one of the smallest. This hike goes through typical North Fork country with lodgepole pine forests and rolling ridges, but without the snowcapped crags found elsewhere in the park.

The trail starts from the north edge of Bowman Lake Campground; it's about 5.8 miles to Akokala Lake on an easy-to-follow trail. You have one big hill near the beginning of the hike (easy grade, only gaining about 600 feet) and a few more small

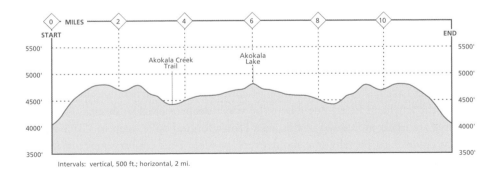

Intervals: vertical, 500 ft.; horizontal, 2 mi.

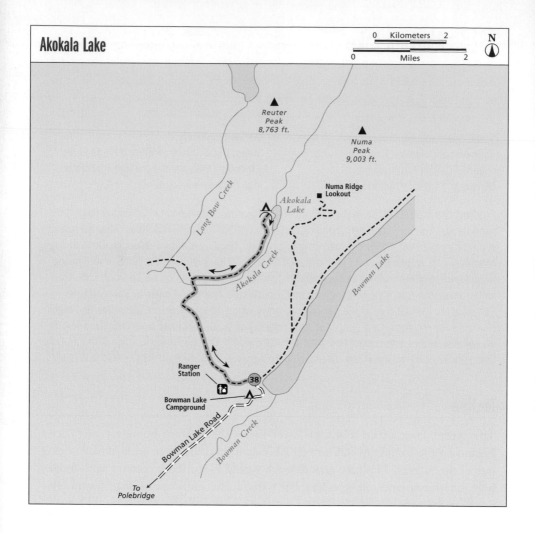

Reuter
Peak
8,763 ft.

Numa
Peak
9,003 ft.

Numa Ridge
Lookout

Long Bow Creek

Akokala Lake

Akokala Creek

Bowman Lake

Ranger
Station

38

Bowman Lake
Campground

Bowman Lake Road

Bowman Creek

To
Polebridge

climbs later. When you reach Akokala Creek, you'll see a junction with a trail follow-ing the creek. Turn right (northeast) and follow Akokala Creek upstream to the lake. The left-hand fork is maintained as a fire-access trail and was used on the Red Bench Fire in 1988. It leads through several burned areas.

The first half of this hike can be dry in late summer or early fall, but there's plenty of filterable water during the last half. Be sure to bring your insect repellent, especially in June, as the Bowman Lake area is infamous for its fierce mosquitoes.

Akokala Lake has a good population of cutthroat trout. The fishing is best halfway around the left-hand (west) side where the water deepens close to shore.

Fires are often prohibited in this area. Don't forget you're deep in Glacier Park grizzly country, so be religious about every possible bear country precaution and sanitary rule.

Granddaughter Josie and a native cutthroat she caught in Akakola Lake. Russ Schneider

You need a backcountry permit to stay overnight. (Originally contributed and re-hiked by the authors.)

Miles and Directions

0.0   Bowman Lake Campground.

3.6   Junction with old Akokala Creek Trail; turn right.

5.8   Akokala Lake.

11.6   Bowman Lake Campground.

39 Iceberg Lake

A beautiful lake in a spectacular setting with more than its share of mountain goats and grizzly bears, and lots of humans

Start: Many Glacier area of Glacier National Park
Distance: 10.0-mile out-and-back
Difficulty: Moderate

Maps: USGS Many Glacier; either the USGS map or the Trails Illustrated map for the entire park

Finding the trailhead: Drive 8 miles north from St. Mary to Babb on US 89 along the eastern boundary of Glacier National Park, then 12 miles west on Glacier Road 3 into the park to Many Glacier. The trail starts from a parking lot behind Swiftcurrent Motel. Full visitor services are available nearby. GPS: N48 47.883' / W113 40.683'

The Hike

More people see grizzly bears along the Iceberg Lake Trail than any other hiking route in this book, partially due to the high concentration of relatively unafraid grizzlies in the Many Glacier Valley. Be extra careful to make noise and stay on the trail. Because of the high bear population, no overnight camping is allowed at Iceberg Lake.

Technically, Iceberg Lake does not have icebergs, but it comes as close as any place in Montana. Chunks of ice float around in the lake, usually until September, but the "icebergs" are larger and more scenic in July and August.

This trail climbs only 200 feet per mile, a rate most people find comfortable. Wide and relatively smooth, the trail leads through fields of wildflowers. Large flickers with pronounced reddish coloring and swooping flight patterns nest in the ghost trees along the trail. On the last segment of this hike, mountain goats and bighorn sheep are commonly seen on the grassy slopes above the trail.

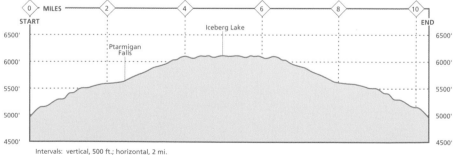

Intervals: vertical, 500 ft.; horizontal, 2 mi.

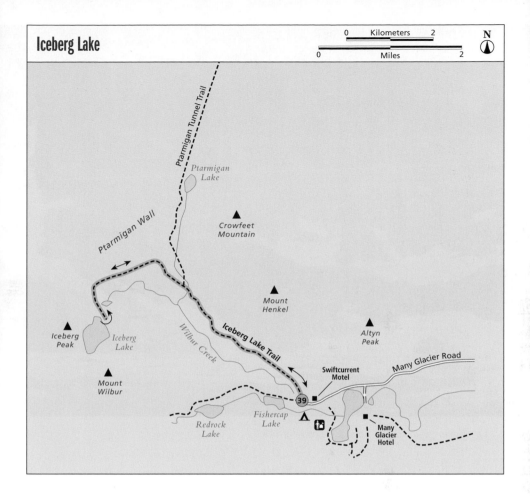

0 Kilometers 2

0 Miles 2

N

Ptarmigan Tunnel Trail

Ptarmigan Lake

Ptarmigan Wall

▲ *Crowfeet Mountain*

▲ *Mount Henkel*

▲ *Iceberg Peak*

Iceberg Lake

Wilbur Creek

Iceberg Lake Trail

▲ *Altyn Peak*

Many Glacier Road

Swiftcurrent Motel

▲ *Mount Wilbur*

39

Redrock Lake

Fishercap Lake

Many Glacier Hotel

At the 2.5-mile mark, you pass lovely Ptarmigan Falls as it plunges over rocky layers to a deep emerald pool. Shortly thereafter, a clearly marked trail junction indicates a right turn for those wishing to see Ptarmigan Lake and Tunnel and willing to make the steep, 2.5-mile climb to get there. Iceberg Lake Trail goes straight (west) for another 2.5 miles to the lake.

During the summer the National Park Service (NPS) installs a bridge over Iceberg Creek just before the lake. This bridge is removed each fall to prevent it from washing out in the spring.

Miles and Directions

0.0   Trailhead.

2.5   Ptarmigan Falls and junction with Ptarmigan Tunnel Trail; turn left.

5.0   Iceberg Lake.

10.0   Trailhead.

The "icebergs" in Iceberg Lake. Courtesy of NPS

Options: You may sacrifice solitude, but you can take this trip with a group. An NPS ranger conducts walks almost every morning in July and August, a good option for people who can't overcome their fear of bears.

Side Trips: If you have the time and energy, treat yourself by making the steep climb up to Ptarmigan Tunnel and the incredible views you'll find there, including a sweeping vista of the Upper Belly River Valley. (Originally contributed by Mike Sample, re-hiked by the authors.)

40 Granite Park

A very popular and super-scenic route (often called the Highline Trail) along the Continental Divide in the alpine heart of Glacier National Park; a long day hike or overnighter at a chalet

Start: Visitor center on Logan Pass on Going-to-the-Sun Road in Glacier National Park
Distance: 15.2-mile out-and-back with shuttle option

Difficulty: Moderate
Maps: USGS Ahern Pass, Logan Pass, and Many Glacier; either the USGS or Trails Illustrated map for the entire park

Finding the trailhead: The trailhead is across the highway from the Logan Pass Visitor Center. The visitor center has drinking water, toilets, and a large parking lot, which can be full on any summer day. GPS: N48 41.767' / W113 43.033'

The Hike

The first 3 miles of the trail go along the Garden Wall directly above Going-to-the-Sun Road. Some of it is on a ledge, which can be a little nerve-racking but beautifully unique. Then the trail gradually climbs up to Granite Park Chalet across the flanks of Haystack Butte and in the shadow of mighty Mount Gould to the north. (There has never been a haystack on Haystack Butte, but it looks like one.)

To the south, Heavens Peak, Longfellow Peak, and others dominate a fantastic horizon. You can also see McDonald Creek tumbling down to the huge lake with the same name. The entire route is on or near the Continental Divide. Don't forget to look behind you on this section for some stunning views.

The hike is mostly flat with a few small upgrades, but nothing serious. It's also extremely popular, so plan on seeing lots of people—and maybe a few mountain goats and bighorn sheep, too, that have become accustomed enough to hikers to freely show themselves. The trail is always in great shape. It opens in early July, and if

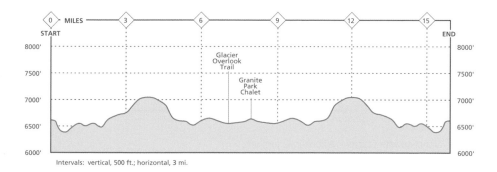

Granite Park Chalet and Heaven's Peak. Courtesy of NPS

you go soon after the opening, you may have to traverse a few lingering snowbanks that can be dangerous, so be careful.

You can see the wonderfully positioned Granite Park Chalet about 1.5 miles before you get there. Locals appropriately call this stretch of trail Bear Valley because you can often see grizzly bears here from the trail and the chalet. Alpine wildflower enthusiasts will think they're in heaven.

Turn left (west) at the junction with the Glacier Overlook Trail, 0.8 mile before the chalet.

If you're out for a long day hike, have lunch at the chalet and then return to Logan Pass. If you plan to stay overnight, make sure to make reservations at the chalet in advance. Rooms are wonderfully rustic and reasonably priced. Get more information at graniteparkchalet.com and make reservations by calling (800) 521-7238. You can also carry your backpack, of course, and stay at the campsite near the chalet, but you'll need a backcountry camping permit to do so.

Miles and Directions

0.0   Trailhead.
6.8   Junction with Glacier Overlook Trail; turn left.
7.6   Granite Park Chalet.
15.2 Trailhead.

The Nyack Loop

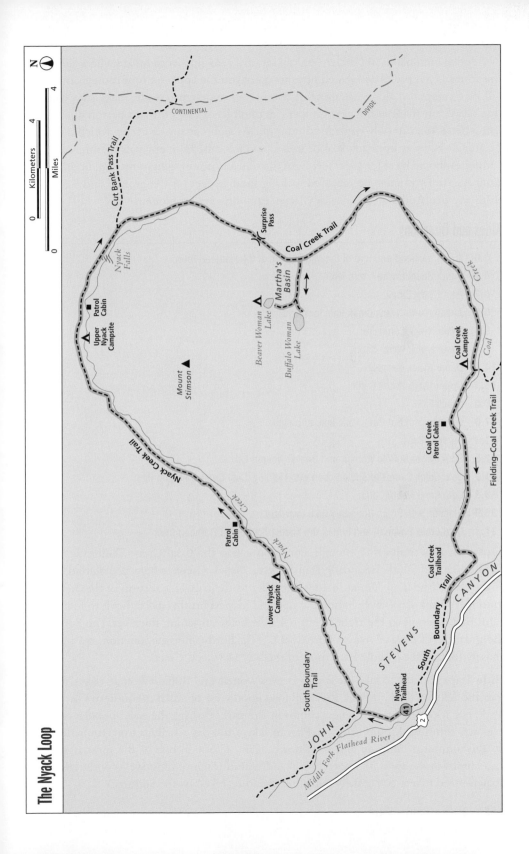

N

Kilometers 0 4

Miles 0 4

CONTINENTAL DIVIDE

Cut Bank Pass Trail

Nyack Falls

Surprise Pass

Coal Creek Trail

Upper Nyack Campsite

Patrol Cabin

Beaver Woman Lake

Martha's Basin

Buffalo Woman Lake

Mount Stimson

Coal Creek Campsite

Coal Creek

Nyack Creek Trail

Coal Creek Patrol Cabin

Fielding–Coal Creek Trail

Nyack Creek

Patrol Cabin

Lower Nyack Campsite

Coal Creek Trailhead

South Boundary Trail

STEVENS CANYON

JOHN

Nyack Trailhead
41

South Boundary Trail

Middle Fork Flathead River

2

Unlike most places in Glacier, you can set up a zero-impact camp anywhere along this route. If you prefer designated sites, however, you can apply for four campgrounds (all nice campsites) along the route. If you use an undesignated site, make sure you don't leave any mark so the next camper can think he or she is the first person to ever camp there. You can only stay a maximum of two nights at any campsite, which must be at least 100 feet from any lake or stream and 0.5 mile from any patrol cabin. Also, campsites should be at least 150 feet from the trail and out of sight of the trail or other campers. And you must be prepared to hang food 12 feet off the ground and 6 feet from any tree. And as in the rest of Glacier, campfires are prohibited.

Miles and Directions

0.0 Nyack Trailhead and ford of the Middle Fork of the Flathead River.

0.1 South Boundary Trail; turn left.

0.7 Ford Nyack Creek.

0.8 Junction with Nyack Creek Trail; turn right.

5.4 Lower Nyack Campsite.

7.4 Lower Nyack Patrol Cabin.

14.4 Upper Nyack Campsite.

15.4 Upper Nyack Patrol Cabin.

16.0 Nyack Falls.

17.0 Junction with Cut Bank Pass Trail; turn right.

21.7 Surprise Pass.

22.5 Spur trail to Buffalo Woman and Beaver Woman Lakes.

31.2 Coal Creek Campsite and junction with Fielding-Coal Creek Trail; turn right.

33.3 Coal Creek Patrol Cabin.

36.9 Junction with South Boundary Trail; turn right.

37.3 Coal Creek Trailhead and ford of the Middle Fork of the Flathead River.

Options: If 37 miles isn't enough, once you get to the Coal Creek Trailhead, you could take the South Boundary Trail back to Nyack Creek where you started, to make this a true loop. Doing so adds 4.5 miles to the trip. This section of the South Boundary Trail is, however, lightly traveled and may be brushy and difficult to follow. This trail takes off to the right (west) 0.4 mile before reaching the river. The South Boundary Trail heads down to ford Coal Creek shortly after the junction and then closely follows the Middle Fork most of the way to Nyack Creek.

Side Trips: Be sure to take the trip to Beaver Woman and Buffalo Woman Lakes. You can also hike up the Cut Bank Pass Trail for a good view of much of southern Glacier Park, but it's one of the toughest climbs in the park. Perhaps the most popular side trip is a climb up Mount Stimson. Plan to take a full day to climb from timberline to the summit of Stimson and back down again. Although one of the most rigorous climbs in the park, it's nontechnical and within reach of most well-conditioned, experienced hikers. (Originally contributed and re-hiked by the authors.)

42 Triple Divide Pass

A difficult day hike to a unique mountain pass

Start: Cut Bank Trailhead in the Two Medicine area of Glacier National Park near East Glacier
Distance: 14.4-mile out-and-back
Difficulty: Strenuous

Maps: USGS Cut Bank Pass and Mt. Stimson; either the USGS map or the Trails Illustrated map for the entire park

Finding the trailhead: Drive south of St. Mary on US 89 for 15 miles and turn right (west) onto the unpaved Cut Bank Road. Follow the unpaved road for 5 miles until it ends at the campground and trailhead. You'll find a toilet, drinking water, campground, and ranger station at the trailhead. GPS: N48 36.085' / W113°23.088'

The Hike

Triple Divide Peak, which hovers above Triple Divide Pass, is the only place in Montana where water flows into three oceans—Atlantic, Pacific, and Hudson Bay (Arctic Ocean), which are, appropriately, the names of the three streams flowing off the mountain.

From the trailhead, the Cut Bank Creek Trail gradually climbs all the way to the Pitamakan Pass Junction at 3.9 miles. The southern horizon is dominated by Bad Marriage Mountain, named for a Blackfeet chief, not an old ranger's marital problems. You follow sparkling and slow-moving Cut Bank Creek all the way.

At the junction, turn right (west) toward Medicine Grizzly Lake. About a half mile later, you pass through Atlantic Creek Campground. Shortly after the campground, at 4.6 miles, turn right (north) again onto the Triple Divide Pass Trail. At this point you leave the thick, lush, unburned forest of the Medicine Grizzly Valley and start the long (2.6-mile) Category 2 grind up to the pass, remarkably without switchbacks.

The trail climbs above Medicine Grizzly Lake, which is a blue jewel in a green ocean in the shadow of the mountain by the same name and Razoredge Mountain hosting the Continental Divide west of the lake. This valley is streaked with avalanche

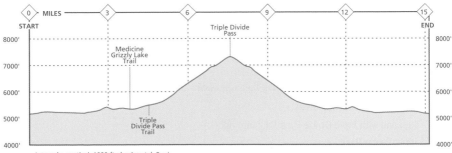

Intervals: vertical, 1000 ft.; horizontal, 3 mi.

Triple Divide Peak. SHUTTERSTOCK

chutes and flush with succulent vegetation, all such great grizzly habitat that the National Park Service had to close the campsite at the lake and consolidate camping at Atlantic Creek. You can also see a small, unnamed lake in a huge gouge out of the side of Medicine Grizzly Lake, a place lots of people probably think about visiting, but I doubt anybody ever does.

At Triple Divide Pass, you'll probably see some bighorn sheep grazing in the flats on the south side of the pass, and you'll definitely get some great views into the Red Eagle Valley to the north dominated by Split Mountain, on the flanks of which you can see tarns with little icebergs in them. In summary, you're walking through a moving postcard.

This trail is popular, so don't expect to have it to yourself. On the pass, watch your pack because the ground squirrels and marmots have, regrettably, been fed by hikers and now realize they can always find treats like gorp and granola bars in packs. Don't make the situation worse by letting them have any crumbs.

Miles and Directions

0.0 Trailhead.
3.9 Junction with Medicine Grizzly Lake Trail; turn right.
4.3 Atlantic Creek Campground.
4.6 Junction with Triple Divide Pass Trail; turn right.
7.2 Triple Divide Pass.
14.4 Trailhead.

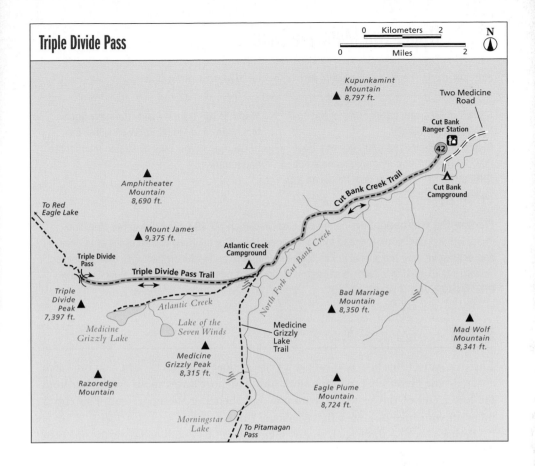

Triple Divide Pass

0 — Kilometers — 2
0 — Miles — 2

N

Kupunkamint Mountain
▲ 8,797 ft.

Two Medicine Road

Cut Bank Ranger Station

42

Cut Bank Campground

Amphitheater Mountain
8,690 ft.

To Red Eagle Lake

Cut Bank Creek Trail

Mount James
▲ 9,375 ft.

Triple Divide Pass

Atlantic Creek Campground

Triple Divide Pass Trail

North Fork Cut Bank Creek

Triple Divide Peak ▲
7,397 ft.

Atlantic Creek

Medicine Grizzly Lake

Lake of the Seven Winds

Bad Marriage Mountain
▲ 8,350 ft.

Medicine Grizzly Lake Trail

Mad Wolf Mountain
8,341 ft.

Medicine Grizzly Peak
8,315 ft.

Razoredge Mountain

Eagle Plume Mountain
8,724 ft.

Morningstar Lake

To Pitamagan Pass

Side Trips: The logical side trip is Triple Divide Peak, but don't try it unless you've left at first light and hurried up to the pass. If you didn't, you probably won't have enough time to make the ascent and get back to the trailhead before darkness. The Cut Bank/Medicine Grizzly area has such a high grizzly population that you definitely don't want to be hiking out at night. You can stay overnight at Atlantic Creek to make it easier, but you should still leave as early as possible in the morning; you should be fit and experienced at off-trail hiking. And, of course, make sure you have good weather.

Another good side trip is Medicine Grizzly Lake, which adds only about 3 miles to the total distance. This trail is, however, frequently closed because of bear problems. (Originally contributed and re-hiked by the authors.)

43 Upper Two Medicine Lake

An easy day hike or overnighter into a spectacular mountain lake

Start: Two Medicine Lake in Glacier National Park near East Glacier
Distance: 3.8-mile out-and-back with boat ride; 10-mile lollipop loop with no boat ride
Difficulty: Easy with boat ride; moderate with no boat ride

Maps: USGS Dancing Lady (formerly Squaw Mountain) and Mount Rockwell; either the USGS map or the Trails Illustrated map for the entire park

Finding the trailhead: Drive north from East Glacier on MT 49 for 4 miles to Two Medicine Road. Turn left and follow the road to Two Medicine Lake. The trailhead is west of the boat dock and parking lot near the shoreline. The trailhead features the Two Medicine Camp Store, a ranger station, lots of parking, a toilet, a campground, and boat rides with Glacier Park Boat Company. GPS: N48 29.250' / W113 22.133'

The Hike

The first part of this hike is as easy as it gets—a boat ride. After 9 a.m. you can catch a ride on the Hiker's Express for a small sum. The boat leaves about every hour from the lower end of the lake to a boat ramp and shelter at the upper end. This cuts 3 miles off your hike to Upper Two Medicine Lake.

Perhaps because this is such an easy hike that can be combined with a scenic boat ride, it's extremely popular. On a warm summer day, hundreds of people will take the boat ride and walk as far as Twin Falls, and many of them will extend their day hike to Upper Two Medicine Lake.

From the boat ramp at the west end of the lake, hike west on the well-marked trail. You'll find a pit toilet about a quarter mile later, just past the first junction with the South Shore Trail. A little more than a half mile farther, you'll see a major spur trail veering off to the right to Twin Falls, a magnificent waterfall you won't want to miss.

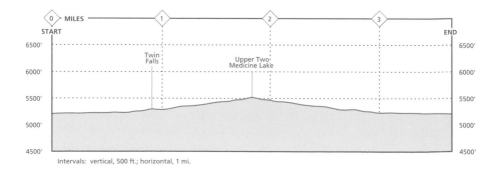

Intervals: vertical, 500 ft.; horizontal, 1 mi.

Upper Two Medicine Lake

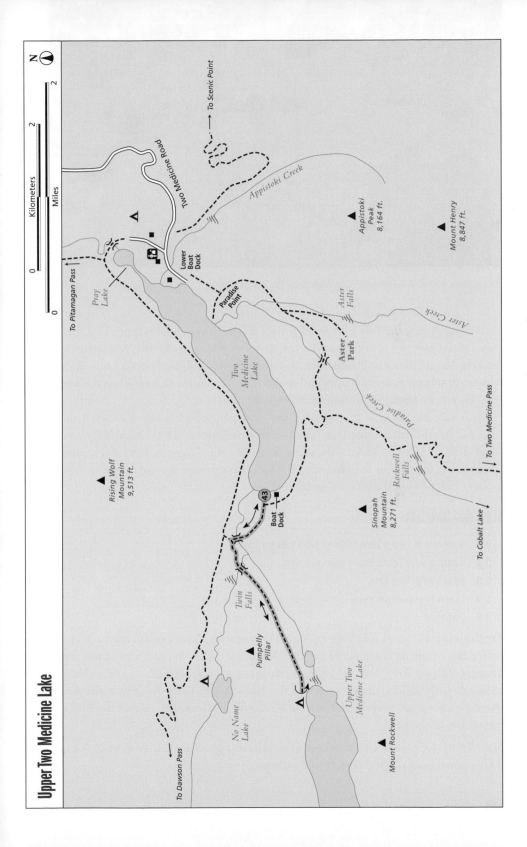

The reason people hike so slowly in Montana. BILL SCHNEIDER

After enjoying the falls, hike another mile to the lower end of Upper Two Medicine Lake, a blue jewel in the heavily forested mountains of the Two Medicine area. Massive Mount Rockwell rises from the south shore, and precipitous Lone Walker Mountain juts up from the upper end of the lake. Late in the season when the water recedes, you can walk all or most of the shoreline.

You can also camp at the lake, but most people don't because it's such a short hike and heavily visited lake. It is, however, an excellent choice for backpackers with small children or those making their first overnight trip. There are three backcountry campsites at the foot of the lake, with the food area strangely close to the trail, preventing much privacy while eating dinner.

Miles and Directions

0.0   Trailhead at Upper Boat Dock of Two Medicine Lake.

0.3   Junction with South Shore Trail; turn right.

0.9   Spur trail to Twin Falls.

1.9   Upper Two Medicine Lake.

3.8   Trailhead.

Options: If this short hike isn't enough exercise, add 3 miles by hiking back along either the north or south shore of Two Medicine Lake. You can also make this a 10-mile lollipop loop hike by hiking both shores. Since both the north and south trails generally follow the shoreline of the lake, they're fairly flat. From the south shore you get a great view of awesome Rising Wolf Mountain, one of the bulkiest mountains in the park.

Side Trips: Definitely take the short spur trail for a good look at Twin Falls. (Originally contributed and re-hiked by the authors.)

44 Lake Isabel

An extended backpacking trip over magnificent Two Medicine Pass to one of the most remote lakes in Glacier National Park

Start: Two Medicine Lake in Glacier National Park near East Glacier
Distance: 30.0-mile out-and-back
Difficulty: Strenuous

Maps: USGS Dancing Lady Mountain (formerly Squaw Mountain) and Mount Rockwell; either the USGS map or the Trails Illustrated map for the entire park

Finding the trailhead: Drive north from East Glacier on MT 49 for 4 miles to Two Medicine Road. Turn left and follow the road to Two Medicine Lake. The trailhead is west of the boat dock and parking lot near the shoreline. The trailhead features the Two Medicine Camp Store, a ranger station, ample parking, restrooms, a campground, and boat rides on Two Medicine Lake with Glacier Park Boat Company. GPS: N48 29.250' / W113 22.133'

The Hike

The thought of Glacier National Park often conjures up images of bumper-to-bumper traffic on the Going-to-the-Sun Road or people on every trail; Hidden Lake (on Logan Pass) doesn't seem so hidden and wildlife not so wild. Much of the park is truly wild, however, and you only have to get off the beaten path to experience it.

There are three ways to get away from the crowds. First, go somewhere no one wants to go. Second, go somewhere few people know about. Third, go somewhere that is too hard for most people to go. The third way works for this hike. There are two routes to Lake Isabel. One is a 16.9-mile flat and in-the-trees hike up Park Creek from the west side of Glacier; the other is the scenic but more difficult 15-mile grunt over Two Medicine Pass from Two Medicine Lake. The latter is described here.

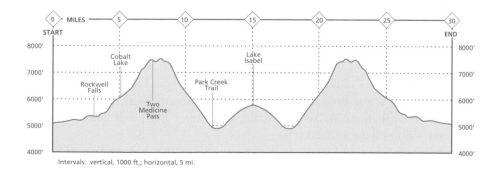

Intervals: vertical, 1000 ft.; horizontal, 5 mi.

The difficulty of this route reduces use, of course, but in addition, the National Park Service (NPS) has only one campsite at the lake, and it's usually reserved. That, too, helps make this trip a true wilderness adventure where you'll have all the solitude you could ever want.

In fact, there's nothing easy about getting to Lake Isabel, including getting the permit. The route is really too much for one day with a full pack. The only alternative, however, is staying at Cobalt Lake, but getting a reservation for this campsite is extremely difficult because this destination is so popular. You can also stay the first night at the Upper Park Creek Campsite, which is not particularly scenic, but people who make it this far tend to prefer toughing it out another 2.3 miles to Lake Isabel.

Having said all that, let's be clear on one point: Lake Isabel is worth the effort to get there.

From the Two Medicine Camp Store parking lot, head west along the southern shore of Two Medicine Lake. The South Shore Trail stays in the trees, climbing slightly. Several trails intersect the main trail. Stay left (southwest) at the junction with Paradise Point. Stay right (southwest) at the junction with Aster Falls Trail. After crossing a suspension bridge over Paradise Creek, turn left (southwest) at the junction with the Two Medicine Pass Trail and head for Cobalt Lake.

After 3.4 miles, Rockwell Falls offers a good rest stop. Rockwell Falls is a series of cascades in the shadow of Sinopah Mountain. Be sure to drink lots of water here; you'll need to be fully hydrated for the Category 1 climb up to Two Medicine Pass.

The climb beside Rockwell Falls is fairly steep but short. Then the hike steadily ascends to Cobalt Lake with many huckleberry patches along the way to keep your mind off the climb. Follow the creek through the fir-clad slopes until you're within sight of Cobalt Lake. At the trail junction at the lake, at 5.7 miles, turn right for Two Medicine Pass. The left trail goes to the campsite at Cobalt Lake. In July and August Cobalt Lake has a one-night stay limit.

Again, be sure you have enough water for the climb, although snowmelt might provide some relief. The trail gains serious altitude for the next mile. After the climb to the saddle next to Mount Rockwell, the trail remains relatively flat over Chief Lodgepole Peak. From almost anyplace here, notice the view of Paradise Park down and to the left. To the right, Park Creek Valley extends for as far as the eye can see. This evidence of glaciation, along with the cirque containing Lake Isabel across the valley, alludes to a much more harsh and powerful time.

Check your map to name and count the surrounding peaks. Start with Grizzly Mountain above Paradise Park and work to your right: Eagle Ribs Mountain, Mount Despair, across Park Creek to Statuary Mountain, Vigil Peak above Lake Isabel, Caper Peak, Lone Walker Mountain, and Mount Rockwell. The mountains surround you in divine council.

From above Chief Lodgepole Peak, continue along the ridge to Two Medicine Pass at 7.9 miles. Be careful to follow the cairns; they mark the trail that drops down

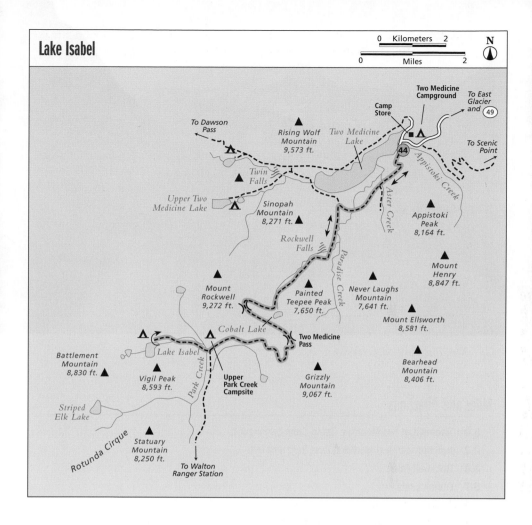

Lake Isabel

and to the right into Park Creek Valley. Also watch for mountain goats, numerous in the area.

The trail descends for almost 4 miles of easy switchbacks to the Upper Park Creek Campsite. On the return trip this climb is the hardest part of the hike. The switchbacks last for about a mile, then the trail drops through a thick undergrowth of ferns, bushes, and devil's club. When you reach the Park Creek Trail, turn right (west) and hike the last hill up to Lake Isabel.

Unfortunately, the NPS prohibits fishing in Park Creek, but you should still bring your fly rod because it's only another 2.3 miles to Lake Isabel, where the oversize cutthroats rise to anything you cast out there. The water in this lake is remarkably clear, and Vigil Peak provides a scenic backdrop.

The return hike is tough. Carry and drink plenty of water. (Originally contributed and re-hiked by the authors.)

Two Medicine Lake. SHUTTERSTOCK

Miles and Directions

0.0 Trailhead at Two Medicine Camp Store parking lot.

2.3 Junction with Two Medicine Pass Trail; turn left.

3.4 Rockwell Falls.

5.7 Cobalt Lake.

7.9 Two Medicine Pass.

12.7 Junction with Park Creek Trail; turn right.

15.0 Lake Isabel.

30.0 Trailhead.

45 Three Passes

A long day hike or moderate backpacking trip through outstanding mountain scenery, mostly above timberline. With three mountain passes, it's definitely one of the most scenic and popular hikes in Glacier National Park.

Start: Two Medicine Lake in Glacier National Park near East Glacier
Distance: 18.8-mile loop
Difficulty: Strenuous

Maps: USGS Cut Bank Pass, Mount Rockwell, and Dancing Lady Mountain (formerly Squaw Mountain); either the USGS map or Trails Illustrated map for the entire park

Finding the trailhead: From East Glacier, drive north on MT 49 about 4 miles to a well-marked turnoff for Two Medicine Road. Turn right for Two Medicine Campground. Drive through the campground to the bridge over Two Medicine River at the outlet of Pray Lake, a small lake below the outlet of Two Medicine Lake. (Pray Lake is named after Charles N. Pray, one of the congressmen who pushed hard for the establishment of Glacier National Park.) The Pray Lake Trailhead is at the outlet of the two lakes. The trailhead features the Two Medicine Camp Store, a ranger station, ample parking, toilets, a campground, and boat rides on Two Medicine Lake with Glacier Park Boat Company. GPS: N48 29.250' / W113 22.133'

The Hike

Where else can you hike over three spectacular passes in 4 miles of scenic hiking? I'm not sure if there is any other opportunity, so be sure to take this one.

From the trailhead parking lot, cross the bridge below Pray Lake and turn right toward Oldman Lake, 6.4 miles down the trail. In the first 2.4 miles, you hike around the base of a towering mastiff called Rising Wolf Mountain (shortened version of a Blackfeet term for "the way the wolf rises") and across the bridge over Dry Fork Creek to a marked trail junction, where you turn left (west). From here, you face a steady climb up an open valley. The very wet Dry Fork Creek cascades the length of the valley, and several smaller streams drop out of hidden cirques to add to the volume. Paintbrush and lupine add splashes of color to the scene.

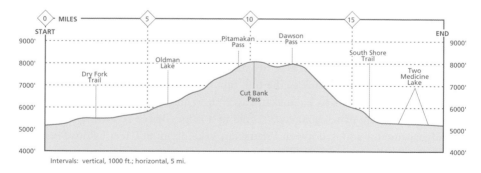

Intervals: vertical, 1000 ft.; horizontal, 5 mi.

Distinctive Sinopah and Painted Teepee Peaks loom above Two Medicine Lake. Courtesy of NPS

At the head of the valley, you enter a blister rust–plagued whitebark pine forest. The trail splits shortly before Oldman Lake. The right fork heads directly for Pitamakan Pass, while the left fork leads to the campsites on the lake. Flinsch Peak dominates the western skyline. At Oldman Lake you might see a family of beavers at the far end of the lake in the twilight hours, and 20-inch Yellowstone cutthroats cruise the shoreline. On the northern slopes above the lake, a white cloud of beargrass stands as thick as anywhere in the park in late July. The area around Oldman Lake is prime habitat for grizzlies. Play it safe.

From Oldman Lake to No Name Lake, the trail is nearly devoid of water by early August; make sure you have full bottles before starting this segment. To reach Pitamakan Pass from Oldman Lake, take the short cutoff trail almost straight north from the toilet instead of going back to the trail junction.

The Category 2 climb to Pitamakan Pass is short and steep—more than 1,000 feet up in 1.8 miles. The pass is actually a saddle in a ridge. Before following the trail up the ridge, pause for a look down at Pitamakan Lake, about 800 feet below. *Pitamakan* is, incidentally, Blackfeet for "running eagle."

Very soon after leaving the saddle, you encounter two well-marked junctions. In each case, turn left (west). Just after the second junction, you reach Cut Bank Pass and cross the Continental Divide. Due west stands mighty Mount Stimson, rising 6,000 feet above the Nyack Creek Valley.

From here the trail goes in a southerly direction, paralleling the Continental Divide along the shoulders of Mount Morgan and Flinsch Peak to Dawson Pass (named for an early surveyor of the park), where you cross the divide again. While nearly level through this section, the trail traverses steep slopes of roller-bearing scree, which is dangerous when wet. Some sections of the trail follow ledges with steep drops, so watch your step. Because dangerous snow bands lie across these slopes until late June or early July, the National Park Service opens this trail later than most. Check with the Two Medicine Ranger Station before planning an early trip.

Grandkids perched above Oldman Lake on the way to Pitamakan Pass. KIMBERLY SCHNEIDER

Dawson Pass is a favorite hangout for mountain goats, which are quite tame. Don't feed them and make the situation worse. You might also see bighorn sheep.

Dawson Pass is also a popular cutoff spot for people who wish to make the steep walk up the south face of Flinsch Peak. While you're up high on these passes, watch the weather. You don't want to get caught in a thunderstorm (like we did).

From Dawson Pass the trail drops rapidly through Bighorn Basin to No Name Lake. The lake deserves a more descriptive name, such as Gorgeous Lake or Mountain Jewel Lake. It lies at the base of sheer Pumpelly Pillar, named after an early geologist in the park. It is an evocative pool, especially in the first moments of sunlight on a quiet morning.

Leaving No Name Lake, you move down the valley about 1.5 miles to a trail heading up to Upper Two Medicine Lake, Twin Falls, and South Shore Trails. Turn left (east) and follow the trail along the north side of Two Medicine Lake back to the Pray Lake Trailhead.

If you decide to backpack, make this a two-night trip, staying at Oldman and No Name Lakes, but apply for your permits as early as possible. They're a hot ticket.

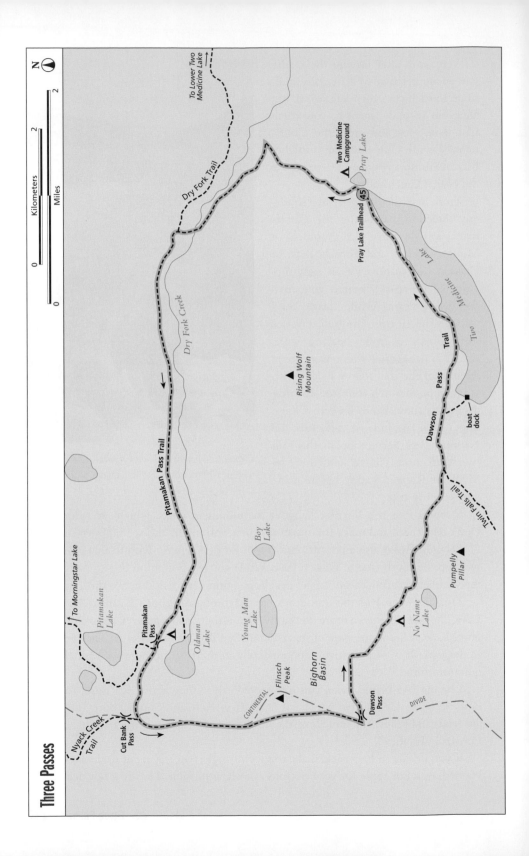

Three Passes

To Lower Two Medicine Lake

Dry Fork Trail

Dry Fork Creek

Pitamakan Pass Trail

To Morningstar Lake

Pitamakan Lake

Pitamakan Pass

Oldman Lake

Nyack Creek Trail

Cut Bank Pass

CONTINENTAL

Flinsch Peak

Young Man Lake

Boy Lake

Bighorn Basin

Dawson Pass

DIVIDE

No Name Lake

Pumpelly Pillar

Rising Wolf Mountain

Dawson Pass Trail

Twin Falls Trail

boat dock

Two Medicine Lake

Pray Lake

Pray Lake Trailhead 45

Two Medicine Campground

N

0   2
Kilometers
0   2
Miles

As far as fishing goes, Oldman Lake has some nice-size Yellowstone cutthroats, and you might also attract a few fish to your fly in the stream below the lake. No Name Lake has small brookies and rainbows and can be fair fishing when conditions are right. You can also stop to fish Two Medicine Lake on the way back—you might catch a few rainbows or brookies. The brook trout can grow big in Two Medicine Lake, but you need a float tube or canoe to increase your chances of catching a big one.

The name Two Medicine, incidentally, comes from the Blackfeet history that refers to two medicine lodges built in the area for performing the Sun Dance. The exact site of the lodges has not been discovered.

Miles and Directions

0.0 Pray Lake Trailhead/Two Medicine Campground.

2.4 Junction with Dry Fork Trail; turn left.

6.4 Oldman Lake.

8.2 Pitamakan Pass and junction with Cut Bank Creek Trail; turn left.

8.5 Junction with Nyack Creek Trail; turn left.

8.8 Cut Bank Pass.

12.4 Dawson Pass.

14.0 Junction with No Name Lake Trail; turn left.

15.5 Junction with Twin Falls/Upper Two Medicine Lake/South Shore Trails; turn left.

18.8 Pray Lake Trailhead/Two Medicine Campground.

Options: You can just as easily hike this loop in reverse, and the availability of campsites might make this option necessary.

From the lower end of Two Medicine Lake, you can take a commercial tour boat to the trailhead—or back to the trailhead at the end of your hike. This cuts about 3 miles off your trip. Check on the arrangements at the boat dock near the trailhead before you leave on the hike or contact Glacier Park Boat Company at (406) 257-2426; glacierparkboats.com.

Side Trips: On the way back you can take the trail up to Upper Two Medicine Lake as a side trip. From the Dawson Pass Trail, it's about 1.3 miles to Upper Two Medicine Lake. Double this for the trip back, and you add 2.6 miles to your hike. You might want to at least take a break and take the short hike (about a mile round-trip) to see Twin Falls. You probably do not want to take side trips down the Cut Bank Creek or Nyack Creek Trails unless you like climbing huge hills to get back to this trail. (Originally contributed by Mike Sample, re-hiked by the authors.)

Beaverhead-Deerlodge National Forest

46 Stony Lake

A day hike or easy overnighter to a remote mountain lake in the shadow of Dome Shaped Mountain

Start: Crystal Creek Campground, 27 miles northeast of Hamilton near Skalkaho Pass in the Sapphire Mountains
Distance: 8.0-mile out-and-back

Difficulty: Moderate
Maps: USGS Mount Emerine, Burnt Fork Lakes, Skalkaho Pass, and Stony Creek; Beaverhead-Deerlodge National Forest Map (North)

Finding the trailhead: Take US 93 south from Missoula to its junction with Skalkaho Road (MT 38), 2 miles south of Hamilton. Turn left (east) onto this winding mountain road (first 17.5 miles paved), driving past Skalkaho Falls and over Skalkaho Pass for 27 miles. About 2 miles over the pass is Crystal Creek Campground. The trailhead, marked by a hiking icon sign, is across the road and slightly northwest of the campground, where two old logging roads start. Take the one on your left, which is FR 78578. Park in the overflow area in the campground and walk up the road to the trailhead; toilet and vehicle camping in the campground. GPS: N46 13.983' / W113 44.767'

The Hike

Part of the enjoyment of hiking in the Sapphires is the feeling that you have discovered an area most hikers would ordinarily drive past without a second glance. The Sapphires (once they have your attention) prove there's more to the "wilderness" than craggy peaks and snowfields. Stony Lake makes this point. It's one of the sapphires of the Sapphire Range.

At the trailhead, which is marked by a hiking icon sign, you'll see Crystal Creek on the right and a logged area on the left. The first 0.5 mile of the trail is on a primitive road (FR 78578), which is being converted to a trail and closed to motorized use. Then, the road ends and the singletrack starts. Turn right onto Trail 8010, which continues to follow Crystal Creek for about 1.5 miles to its beginning at the Sapphire Divide. The trail goes steadily but gradually uphill, much of the time through meadows.

Upon reaching the divide, Trail 8010 heads north for another mile before you reach the junction with Trail 8002 down to Stony Lake, where you turn right (east) and drop down to the lake.

Stony Lake offers average fishing for cutthroats and has a few nice but heavily used campsites.

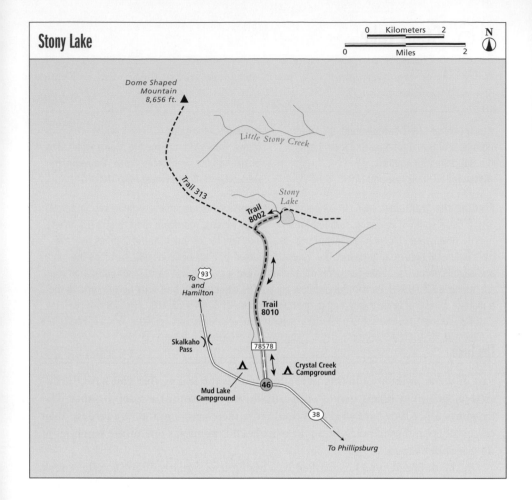

0   Kilometers   2

0   Miles   2

N

Dome Shaped
Mountain
8,656 ft.

Little Stony Creek

Trail 313

Stony
Lake

Trail
8002

To 93
and
Hamilton

Trail
8010

Skalkaho
Pass

78578

Crystal Creek
Campground

Mud Lake
Campground

46

38

To Phillipsburg

Miles and Directions

0.0 Trailhead.

0.5 FR 78578 changes to Trail 8010.

3.0 Junction with Trail 8002 to Stony Lake; turn right.

4.0 Stony Lake.

8.0 Trailhead.

Options: If you have an extra day or are a strong hiker, it's possible to return to Trail 8010 on the Sapphire Divide (where it becomes Trail 313 if you go north) and follow it north for approximately 4 miles to Dome Shaped Mountain, which has a broad, grassy summit crisscrossed with snowdrifts that may linger well into July. Also of interest are the thickets of whitebark pine on the summit ridge. The trail to Dome Shaped Mountain is lightly used and may be difficult to follow.

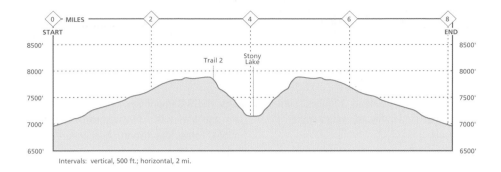

Intervals: vertical, 500 ft.; horizontal, 2 mi.

With the Skalkaho Fork Game Preserve on your left (west), you stand a good chance of seeing deer and elk. Although the Sapphires don't appear to be typical mountain goat country, a few hang out around Dome Shaped Mountain. The occasional open spots along the divide provide views of the Pintlers to the southeast, the Flint Creek Range to the northeast, the Bitterroots to the west, and to the south across Skalkaho Pass, the higher peaks of the Sapphire Mountains.

You can also get to Stony Lake by coming up Stony Creek on Trail 8002. The distance is about the same, but it's a gradual uphill all the way. (Originally contributed by John Westenberg, re-hiked by the authors.)

THE B-D NUMBERS GAME

Important Note: A few years ago, the Beaverhead-Deerlodge National Forest decided to change its trail numbers, making all of them four digits by adding the number of the ranger district (e.g., 8 for the Pintler Ranger District) to the beginning of the existing trail number, filling in zeros if necessary so all numbers are four-digit numbers. For example, Trail 29 becomes Trail 8029.

The problem is that some maps and signs still have the old numbers, and it will take a long time to make this conversion. On the other hand, you don't have to worry. It's the same trail. In this book all trail numbers have been converted to the new four-digit system.

You can go to this website and view the most updated forest maps where all numbers have been converted to the new system: www.fs.usda.gov/main/bdnf/maps-pubs.

So far, the Beaverhead-Deerlodge National Forest is the only national forest in Montana to adopt the new numbering system—except for the Continental Divide Trail, where the original one-, two-, or three-digit numbers have been retained. Yes, I know it's confusing, but in a few years, all signs and maps will be converted, and we'll all be using the same numbers.

47 Tamarack Lake

A moderate backpacking trek into the Anaconda–Pintler Wilderness

Start: Middle Fork Trailhead, 30 miles south-west of Anaconda in the Anaconda-Pintler Mountains
Distance: 22.5-mile loop (almost)
Difficulty: Strenuous

Maps: USGS Carpp Ridge, Moose Lake, Kelly Lake, and Warren Peak; Beaverhead-Deerlodge National Forest Map (North); Anaconda-Pintler Wilderness Map

Finding the trailhead: Take MT 1 south from Philipsburg for 6 miles (or 23 miles north of Anaconda) and turn west onto MT 38. After 9.2 miles, turn left (south) onto Middle Fork Road 5106 (also called Moose Lake Road) and follow the unpaved road until it ends 15.3 miles later at Middle Fork Trailhead, 4 miles past Moose Lake. Large parking area; toilet. GPS: N45 59.483' / W113 31.867'

This hike is almost a loop. Either leave a vehicle or bicycle at the Moose Lake Trailhead (GPS: N45 59.498' / W113 31.875'), which is on your left about 2 miles before the Middle Fork Trailhead, or plan on designating somebody to hike or jog back to the Middle Fork Trailhead at the end of the hike to retrieve your vehicle.

Recommended itinerary: For a two–night trip, spend the first night at Edith Lake and the second night at Tamarack Lake; you'll have a long hike on the third day. For a three–night trip, spend the third night at Carpp Lakes.

The Hike

This trip is nicely suited to families and other groups who want to take the next step from overnighters to a fairly easy three-night backpacking trip. It can be done in two nights, but the last day is a long, though mostly downhill, grind. The Anaconda–Pintler Wilderness is conveniently located and accessible to most western Montana urban areas.

At the trailhead, be sure to register—it's required. Also note the regulation limiting group size to twelve or less.

The first 3 miles on Falls Fork Trail 8029 gradually ascends through a mature forest on an excellent, heavily used trail. At 3 miles, turn left (east) at the junction with Hiline Trail 8111 going to Edith Lake. About a half mile up the trail, turn right onto Trail 8097, where you face a fairly serious, but short (about a mile), climb up to Edith Lake and your first night's camp.

The next morning, drop back down to Trail 8111 and turn right. After 3 miles, turn right onto Trail 8004 for a mostly uphill mile to Tamarack Lake, nestled in a beautiful cirque in the shadow of mighty 10,463-foot Warren Peak. Camp here your second night out.

The next morning, drop down again to Trail 8111, turn right again, and hike another 2.5 miles to Carpp Lakes, your third campsite and the junction with Trail

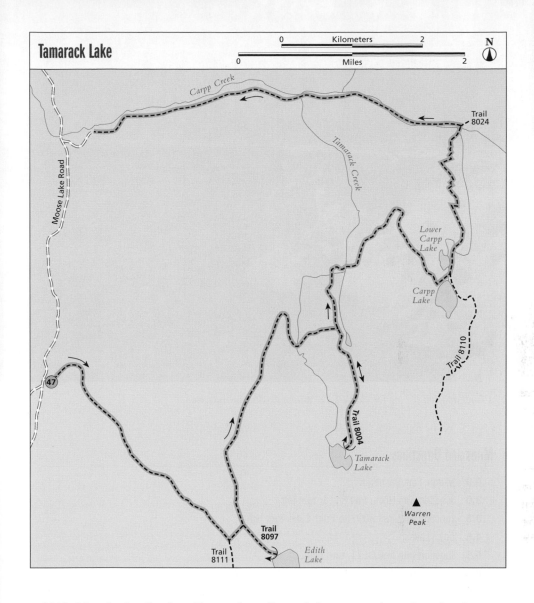

0   Kilometers   2

0   Miles   2

N

Carpp Creek

Trail 8024

Moose Lake Road

Tamarack Creek

Lower Carpp Lake

Carpp Lake

Trail 8110

47

Trail 8004

Tamarack Lake

Warren Peak

Trail 8097

Trail 8111

Edith Lake

8110. It's only 4 miles from Tamarack to Carpp Lakes, so you have time that day to explore the remote lake basin or, for the especially ambitious, climb Warren Peak (either from Tamarack Lake before you leave that morning or from Carpp Lakes in the afternoon).

At the junction between Lower Carpp Lake and Carpp Lake, take Trail 8110 for 2.5 miles to the junction with Trail 8024, where you turn left and follow Carpp Creek for 6 gradually downhill miles to the Moose Lake Trailhead.

Both Edith and Tamarack have decent populations of scrappy rainbows, but the Carpp Lakes do not appear to have a fishery.

Father and son fishing for Edith Lake rainbows. BILL SCHNEIDER

Miles and Directions

0.0 Middle Fork Trailhead.

3.0 Junction with Hiline Trail 8111; turn left.

3.5 Junction with Trail 8097 to Edith Lake, turn right.

4.5 Edith Lake.

5.5 Junction with Trail 8111; turn right.

8.5 Junction with Trail 8004 to Tamarack Lake; turn right.

10.0 Tamarack Lake.

11.5 Junction with Trail 8111; turn right.

14.0 Carpp Lakes and junction with Trail 8110; turn left.

16.5 Junction with Trail 8024; turn left.

22.5 Moose Lake Trailhead.

Side Trips: You should have time to at least see Upper Carpp Lake (continuing on Trail 8111), but the ultimate side trip would be the summit of Warren Peak. (Originally contributed by the authors.)

48 Heart of the Pintlers

A strenuous but ultra-scenic backpacking trek through the heart of the Anaconda-Pintler Wilderness

---

Start: Middle Fork Trailhead, 30 miles south-west of Anaconda in the Anaconda-Pintler Mountains
Distance: 23.5-mile loop
Difficulty: Strenuous

Maps: USGS Carpp Ridge, Moose Lake, Kelly Lake, and Warren Peak; Beaverhead-Deerlodge National Forest Map (North); Anaconda-Pintler Wilderness Map

---

Finding the trailhead: Take MT 1 south from Philipsburg for 6 miles (or 23 miles north of Anaconda) and turn west onto MT 38. After 9.2 miles, turn left (south) onto Middle Fork Road 5106 (also called Moose Lake Road) and follow the unpaved road until it ends 15.3 miles later at Middle Fork Trailhead, 4 miles past Moose Lake. Large parking area; toilet. GPS: N45 59.483' / W113 31.867'

Recommended itinerary: For a three-night trip, spend the first night at Johnson Lake; the second night at Hidden, Kelly, or Ripple Lakes; and the third night at Phyllis Lakes or Little Johnson Lake. For a four-night trip, spend the first night at Edith Lake; the second night at Oreamnos Lake or along Pintler Creek; the third night at Hidden, Kelly, or Ripple Lakes; and the fourth night at Phyllis Lakes or Little Johnson Lake.

The Hike

The Anaconda-Pintler is one of Montana's smaller wilderness areas—but one of the most spectacular. This route makes a convenient circuit around the scenic heart of this fairly accessible wild area. It's a great place for hikers from Butte, Missoula, or Helena to spend a three-day weekend. A myriad of possible side trips could turn it into a weeklong backpacking vacation.

At the trailhead, be sure to register. It's required. Also, note the regulation limiting group size to twelve or less.

The first 5 miles on Falls Fork Trail 8029 to Johnson Lake gradually ascends through a mature forest with some burned sections between the Edith Lake Trail and Johnson Lake. At 3 miles you'll reach the junction with Hiline Trail 8111 going to Edith Lake to your left; stay right on Trail 8029.

Johnson Lake is, perhaps unfortunately, in a logical place to camp for most routes using this trailhead. Consequently, the campsites show signs of heavy use, so please be extra careful to leave zero impact of your visit. The numerous campsites are marked on Forest Service locator maps posted in two places at the lake. Don't camp between the trail and the lake. The lake gets so much use that a few campground deer have become food-conditioned and hang around all day looking for food scraps and licking up urine.

Author's grandson Ryan enjoying a hiking in the Pintlers. BILL SCHNEIDER

Although a fire burned sections along the trail before the lake and the trail to Rainbow Pass, the lake itself escaped the fire. Johnson Lake has a few cutthroats in it, but they've gotten smart after seeing so many artificial flies and lures.

As you hike along the western shore of Johnson Lake, you'll reach the Johnson Inlet Trail 8096 junction at 5.2 miles. Turn left here. Then turn right at 5.4 miles onto Continental Divide Trail 9. The 2-mile, Category 2, 1,000-foot climb up to the Continental Divide and Pintler Pass isn't too difficult. As you drop down the other side of the pass, you'll note that the climb would be more difficult from the south.

At 7.5 miles you can turn right onto a spur trail for a quick visit to Oreamnos

Lake. Return to Trail 9 where, after 1.5 miles, you turn right (west) at the junction with Pintler Creek Trail 2037. Then, at 10.5 miles, turn right (west) again at the junction with Trail 3368, staying on the Continental Divide Trail.

Now you face a more difficult 1,300-foot climb over the Continental Divide again and down into the upper reaches of the East Fork of the Bitterroot drainage. A fairly long stretch of the trail on the Bitterroot side has been burned, including part of Trail 401 up to Hidden Lake, as well as part of the lakeshore. If you decide to camp there, it's a 0.5-mile, 500-foot climb, but you should be able to have fish for dinner.

At 13 miles turn right (west) onto Trail 313 and continue another 2.5 miles to the junction with Hidden Lake Trail 401. Turn right if you're going to the lake. Otherwise keep going on Trail 313. At 15.7 miles you come to the junction with Trail 433, which veers off to your left. Stay right on Trail 313.

When we hiked this, several signs were missing at the junctions through this section of the hike, so be alert. It's always safe to assume there won't be signs, lest you become dependent on them to find your way.

After turning right (north) at 16.2 miles at the junction with Trail 402 going to Kelly and Ripple Lakes (worth the side trip), hike 0.5 mile to the junction with Trail 8028. Turn right and onto Trail 8028 and you have an easy 0.5-mile climb up to Bitterroot Pass, where you'll find some stately whitebark pines and, when we were there, a beautiful weathered sign that a bear chewed up.

The section of Trail 8028 down to Little Johnson Lake is in great shape, as is the 1.2-mile stretch along Trail 8111 up to Phyllis Lakes, if you've decided to camp there. Trail 8111 goes to Upper Phyllis Lake, which has limited campsites. It's a precipitous, dangerous bushwhack down to the lower lake, but both lakes have good cutthroat populations.

The 5.7 miles down from Little Johnson Lake to the trailhead along Trail 8028 is a little boring and also muddy in spots because of the heavy horse traffic on this section of trail. You could lengthen the trip by going from Phyllis Lakes back to Johnson Lake and make a lollipop loop out of the hike, but you'll probably prefer seeing new territory by hiking down to the trailhead from Little Johnson Lake.

Miles and Directions

0.0   Middle Fork Trailhead.

3.0   Junction with Hiline Trail 8111; turn right.

5.0   Johnson Lake.

5.2   Junction with Trail 8111; turn left.

5.4   Junction with Continental Divide Trail 9; turn right.

7.0   Pintler Pass.

7.5   Spur trail to Oreamnos Lake; turn left.

9.0   Junction with Pintler Creek Trail 2037; turn right.

10.5 Junction with Trail 3368; turn right.

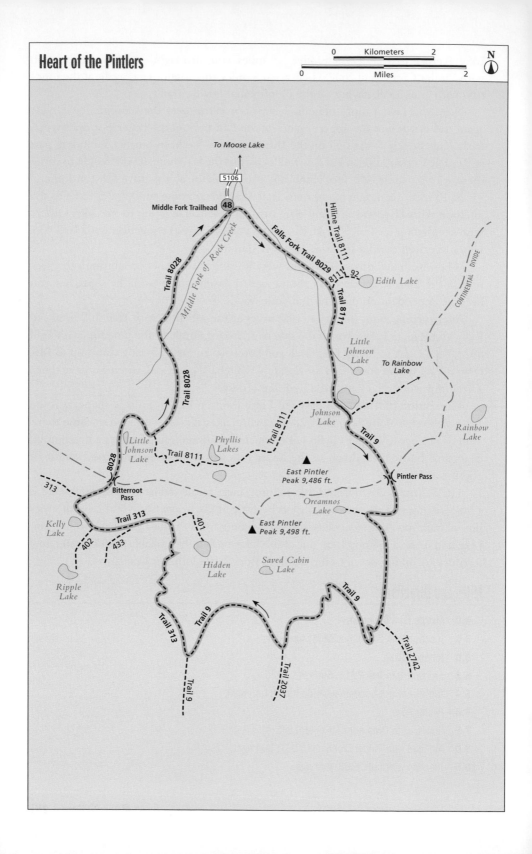

Heart of the Pintlers

Kilometers

Miles

N

To Moose Lake

5106

Middle Fork Trailhead 48

Hiline Trail 8111

Falls Fork Trail 8029

8111 92

Edith Lake

CONTINENTAL DIVIDE

Trail 8028

Middle Fork of Rock Creek

Trail 8111

Little Johnson Lake

Trail 8028

To Rainbow Lake

Trail 8111

Little Johnson Lake

Phyllis Lakes

Johnson Lake

Trail 9

Rainbow Lake

8028

Trail 8111

East Pintler Peak 9,486 ft.

Pintler Pass

313

Bitterroot Pass

Kelly Lake

402

Trail 313

433

401

East Pintler Peak 9,498 ft.

Oreamnos Lake

Ripple Lake

Hidden Lake

Saved Cabin Lake

Trail 9

Trail 313

Trail 9

Trail 9

Trail 2142

Trail 2037

13.0 Junction with Trail 313; turn right.

15.5 Junction with Hidden Lake Trail 401; turn left.

15.7 Junction with Trail 433; turn right.

16.2 Junction with Trail 402 to Ripple and Kelly Lakes; turn right.

16.7 Junction with Trail 8028.

17.2 Bitterroot Pass.

17.8 Little Johnson Lake.

19.0 Junction with Hiline Trail 8111; turn left.

23.5 Middle Fork Trailhead.

Side Trips: If you aren't camping at Oreamnos, Hidden, Ripple, Kelly, or Phyllis Lakes, they all make great side trips. Also, if you're staying at Johnson Lake, take on the switchbacks up to 9,040-foot Rainbow Pass after supper or hike to Edith Lake on the way in.

If you want to stay an extra night at Johnson Lake, you can make the long side trip over Rainbow Pass to Rainbow Lake, a popular destination for hikers and anglers. Snow usually clings to Rainbow Pass until at least late June, so mid-July or later is best for this hike. From the pass you're treated to a nice view of the ominous, broad pyramid of 10,793-foot West Goat Peak, highest point in the Pintler Range. You can also see the trail twisting down to the 8,215-foot-long Rainbow Lake, about a mile below. And yes, it has rainbow trout. (Originally contributed by the authors.)

49 Trask Lakes

A day hike or short backpacking trip to a lake-filled basin, and a good choice for a family outing

Start: Rock Creek Lake, 15 miles west of Deer Lodge in the Flint Creek Range
Distance: 12.6-mile out-and-back
Difficulty: Moderate

Maps: USGS Rock Creek Lake, Pike's Peak, and Pozega Lakes; Beaverhead-Deerlodge National Forest Map (North)

Finding the trailhead: Since none of the junctions are signed, watch your odometer. Drive down the main street of Deer Lodge and turn west onto Milwaukee Avenue. Follow this road for 1.7 miles until it splits. Stay right, continuing straight on the Old Stage Road (unsigned). After 7.2 miles from the bank in Deer Lodge, turn left when the road forks and continue on FR 006 (also unsigned). After 9.5 miles, what is now FR 168 splits; stay right for Rock Creek Lake. After 2.5 miles, you reach the dam that makes Rock Creek Lake and drive around the north shore for another mile to the trailhead. (You may need a four-wheel-drive or high-clearance vehicle to make the last mile and to get to the established campsites.) The 2.5 miles down to the dam is very steep and narrow, so try not to meet a horse trailer. After 13 miles total from Deer Lodge, park your vehicle where the road is closed just before a cluster of cabins. It might look like you can drive farther, but don't try it. Limited parking; no toilet; several excellent campsites on the north side of the reservoir. GPS: N46 24.883' / W112 57.650'

The Hike

From the trailhead, follow an old jeep road through the Daphne Lode patented mining claims past several cabins. About a half mile up this road at Rock Creek Falls is the closure-area boundary—no motorized vehicles beyond this point except for snowmobiles. From this point, the jeep road becomes the maintained Rock Creek Trail 8053.

At 2.3 miles Trail 8053 continues straight, but you must turn left, crossing Rock Creek on a sturdy bridge, and follow the South Fork of Rock Creek on Trask Lakes Trail 8063.

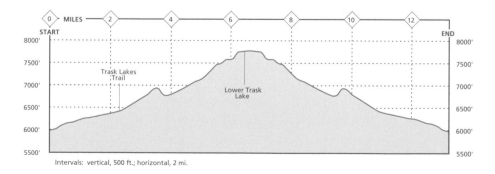

Intervals: vertical, 500 ft.; horizontal, 2 mi.

Trask Lakes

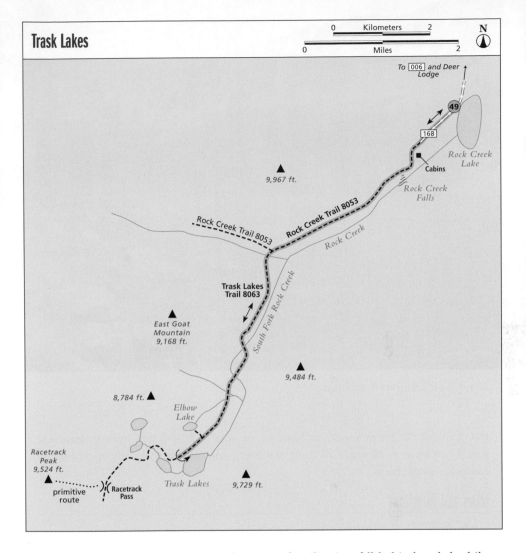

Once you're off the jeep road, the signs of civilization fall behind, and the hike becomes more of a higher-quality backcountry experience, a nice walk-in-the-woods through mature, unburned forest with an understory of huckleberries and fairly lush most of the way. The trail has a few rocky sections but is well defined and climbs gradually for 4 miles to Lower Trask Lake, one of four lakes (plus several ponds) in this small, gorgeous cirque. The Forest Service did a great job on the trail to Trask Lakes, including bridges over all major stream crossings and puncheon walkways.

Trask Lakes, at 7,700 feet, offer excellent fishing for small brook trout. Fish are abundant, and even the youngest angler can expect a good catch. (The fishing is also good in the main Rock Creek along the jeep road in the first 3 miles of the hike.) The good fishing and moderate, nearly 13-mile round-trip (1,800-foot elevation gain, only a Category 1 grade) make Trask Lakes ideal for family backpacking.

Lower Trask Lake. Bill Schneider

Don't forget the insect repellent, however, or your kids will not want to leave the tent. There's plenty of water all along this route, and numerous excellent established campsites in the basin.

Miles and Directions

0.0 Trailhead.

0.5 Rock Creek Falls; Rock Creek Trail 8053 begins.

2.3 Junction with Trask Lakes Trail 8063; turn left.

6.3 Lower Trask Lake.

12.6 Trailhead.

Side Trips: After you get bored with hauling in fish, you might try an interesting side trip to Racetrack Peak. Stay on Trask Lakes Trail for 3 miles past the lakes until it climbs to the top of 8,507-foot Racetrack Pass. Then turn right (west) and make a 1-mile scramble to the summit of 9,524-foot Racetrack Peak for an outstanding view of the entire area. Also, on the way out, take the short side trip over to see Elbow Lake. (Originally contributed by Frank Culver, re-hiked by the authors.)

50 Dolus Lakes

A fairly easy day hike or overnighter to two forested lakes

Start: Rock Creek Lake, 15 miles west of Deer Lodge in the Flint Creek Range
Distance: 4.6-mile out-and-back

Difficulty: Moderate
Maps: USGS Rock Creek Lake; Beaverhead-Deerlodge National Forest Map (North)

Finding the trailhead: Since none of the junctions are signed, watch your odometer. Drive down the main street of Deer Lodge and turn west onto Milwaukee Avenue. Follow this road for 1.7 miles until it splits. Stay right, continuing straight on the Old Stage Road (unsigned). After 7.2 miles from the bank in Deer Lodge, turn left when the road forks and continue on FR 006 (also unsigned). After 9.5 miles, what is now FR 168 splits; stay right for Rock Creek Lake. After 2.5 miles, you reach the dam that makes Rock Creek Lake and drive around the north shore for another 0.3 mile to the trailhead. (You may need a four-wheel-drive or high-clearance vehicle to make the last 0.5 mile and to get to the established campsites.) The 2.5 miles down to the dam is very steep and narrow, so try not to meet a horse trailer. After 12.5 miles total, park near the trailhead. Very limited parking; no toilet; several excellent campsites on the north side of the reservoir. GPS: N46 24.883' / W112 57.650'

The Hike

From Rock Creek Lake, Trail 8115 climbs steeply with a few switchbacks to the junction with Doney Lake Trail 8138 about a half mile later. This is the toughest part of the hike.

After your turn left (west) at this junction, Trail 8138 flattens out and follows an old mining ditch in places as it gradually ascends to the lower lake. The trail is well defined all the way but gets rocky in places. The trail between the first two lakes is less defined and brushy but still fairly easy to follow.

You can catch pan-size cutthroats in both lakes, but the shoreline is brushy, so watch your backcast. You can find a few campsites at both lakes that aren't heavily

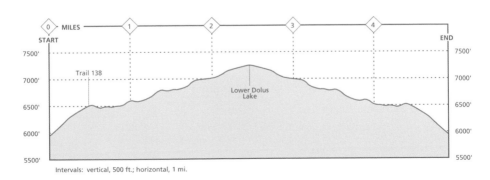

Intervals: vertical, 500 ft.; horizontal, 1 mi.

Dolus Lakes

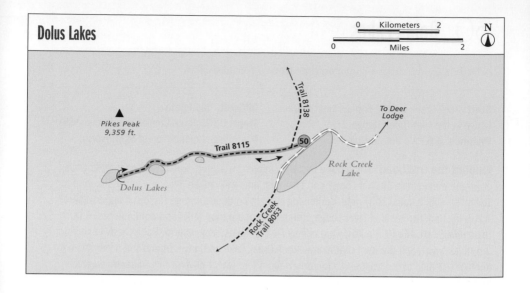

used, because most people day hike into Dolus Lakes instead of staying overnight. If you camp, you'll probably have the place to yourself that night.

Miles and Directions

0.0 Trailhead.

0.5 Junction with Doney Lake Trail 8138; turn left.

2.0 Lower Dolus Lake.

2.3 Upper Dolus Lake.

4.6 Trailhead.

Options: From Upper Dolus Lake an adventuresome hiker can bushwhack another mile up to the third and highest Dolus Lake. (Originally contributed by the authors.)

51 Bobcat Lakes

A day hike or overnighter into the West Pioneers and one of the few lakes still supporting the rare southern grayling

Start: Lacy Creek Trailhead, 20 miles south of Wise River and 60 miles southwest of Butte in the West Pioneer Mountains
Distance: 9.0-mile out-and-back with loop options

Difficulty: Moderate
Maps: USGS Odell Lake and Shaw Mountain; Beaverhead-Deerlodge National Forest Map (Central)

Finding the trailhead: Drive south of Wise River on the Pioneer Mountains National Scenic Byway for 17 miles (all paved) or 28 miles from the south end (also all paved) and turn west on Lacy Creek Road 1299. Drive 4 miles to Lacy Creek Trailhead, where the road ends. Ample parking; toilet; developed camping nearby. GPS: N45 36.266' / W113 10.283'

The Hike

From Lacy Creek Trailhead, the main trail into Bobcat Lakes starts up Pioneer Loop Trail 2750. Follow this trail for 0.1 mile and turn right (north) onto Bobcat Lakes Trail 2050 just after crossing Bobcat Creek. Trail 2050 up Bobcat Creek Canyon passes through stands of lodgepole pine and Douglas fir most of the way, with occasional vistas across the broad slopes of the West Pioneers. It climbs steadily, and is steep and quite rocky in places, so progress can be slow. The trail is open to motorcycles but not ATVs.

About 4 miles from Lacy Creek Trailhead, you reach Lower Bobcat Lake. About a half mile up the trail, you'll find smaller Upper Bobcat Lake. If you're staying overnight, you'll probably want to camp at the lower lake, which has better (but heavily impacted) campsites and more fish.

The lakes lie in small glacial cirques in the middle of the gentle West Pioneer Mountains below Bobcat Mountain. At 9,165 feet, this peak is one of the higher points in the range. From the upper lake, a steep trail leads west to the ridge separating the Bobcat Creek and Pattengail Creek drainages, the latter dissecting the heart of the West Pioneers. Elk often frequent the small meadows that dot this high area. Farther west is a long ridge topped by Odell Peak. Several cirque lakes lie at the base of this ridge.

An interesting feature of Lower Bobcat Lake is its arctic grayling population. These rare native fish survive in limited numbers in the Big Hole River drainage. The grayling have specialized habitat requirements that make it hard for them to compete with other sport fish in lower-elevation waters. The remoteness of the Bobcat Lakes helps them survive. Please take care not to disturb the small stream that drains Lower Bobcat Lake—the grayling depend on the fine gravels in the streambed for spawning.

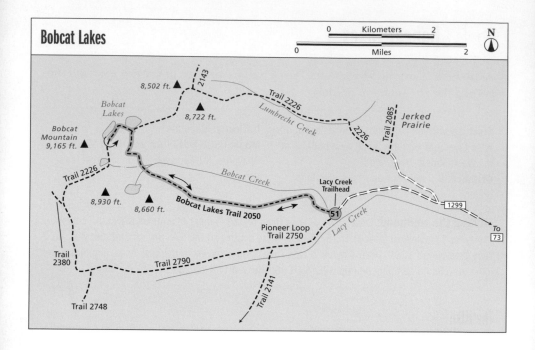

Bobcat Lakes

If you decide to catch a few of them (and they are fairly easy to catch), please carefully release them.

There's not much water along this trail, so start with enough to make it to the lake.

Miles and Directions

0.0 Lacy Creek Trailhead.

0.1 Junction with Bobcat Lakes Trail 2050; turn right.

4.0 Lower Bobcat Lake and junction with Trail 2226; stay on Trail 2050.

4.5 Upper Bobcat Lake.

9.0 Lacy Creek Trailhead.

Options: From Bobcat Lakes you have two options to avoid retracing your footsteps back to the Lacy Creek Trailhead. First, you can make an almost-a-loop trip by taking Trail 2226 from the lower lake toward Jerked Prairie. Trail 2226 heads east for less than 2 miles to a lovely meadow. Then, at the junction with Trail 2143 (to Kelley Cabin), turn right (southeast) and continue on Trail 2226 through thick stands of lodgepole pine, spruce, and Douglas fir. After following a small stream, Trail 2226 becomes a jeep road for the last mile to Lacy Creek Road. Where you rejoin Lacy Creek Road, stow your pack and walk a mile or so up the road to your vehicle.

Second, you can make a real loop out of the trip by taking the Pattengail Trail past the upper lake and over some dry switchbacks over the divide and down into Pattengail Creek. Turn left at both the Baldy and Odell Lake junctions. You pass by

Montana's state flower, the bitterroot. BILL SCHNEIDER

Grassy Lake (no problem knowing how it got its name) and later, between the two junctions, Schwingar Lake. This makes a nice 13-mile loop, with one exception. After the Odell Lake junction, the trail turns into a heavily used ATV road that, like most "troads," has been ground up, widened, and covered with loose rocks thrown up by ATVs, making walking difficult.

Some of these trails aren't on the topo map, so be sure to take the Forest Service map. (Originally contributed by Fred Swanson, re-hiked by the authors.)

52 Sawtooth Lake

A day hike or overnighter to a gorgeous lake graced with golden trout

Start: Near Elkhorn Hot Springs northwest of Dillon

Distance: 8.0-mile out-and-back

Difficulty: Moderate

Maps: USGS Elkhorn Hot Springs; Beaverhead-Deerlodge National Forest Map (Central)

Finding the trailhead: From Wise River, drive south on the Pioneer Mountains National Scenic Byway for 34 miles or 11 miles from the south (all paved). At Grasshopper Inn junction, turn east onto Wellman Creek Road (FR 7441), passing through the Taylor subdivision. Follow FR 7441 for 1.8 miles until it forks; stay right for 0.3 mile to the trailhead. Ample parking; toilet; developed camping nearby. GPS: N45 25.479' / W113 05.084'

The Hike

From the trailhead, Trail 1195 follows Clark Creek, crossing the creek twice, climbing gently and passing through mature lodgepole pine and Engelmann spruce. The Forest Service reconstructed this section of trail in 2009 and added hiking bridges to the stream crossings. After about 3 miles, Trail 1195 turns southeast toward Goat Mountain and climbs switchbacks to the lake.

Sawtooth Lake rests in a cirque surrounded by Goat, Highboy, and Sawtooth Mountains. Even in summer, light snows often accent the crags and their slopes above the cold lake. The lake has a few campsites, but they're heavily impacted, so please don't make it any worse than it is—and, in fact, try to remove a fire ring or two to make it better.

This hike is popular because of the unique species of fish that inhabit Sawtooth Lake. Golden trout are rare and colorful, and here they grow large. The south shore of the lake is a talus slope that offers an ideal place to fish. The 23-inch or larger goldens are temperamental but catchable.

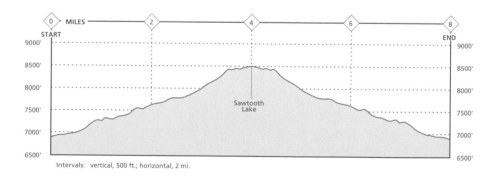

Intervals: vertical, 500 ft.; horizontal, 2 mi.

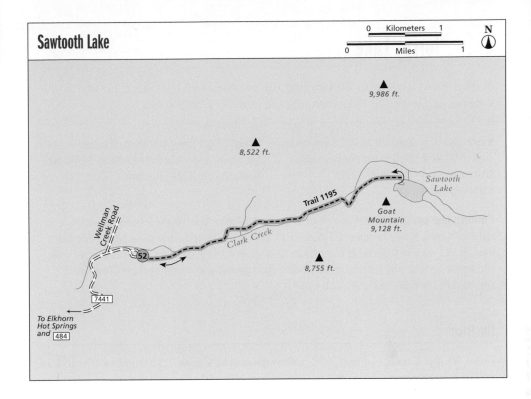

Sawtooth Lake

In 2003 a forest fire burned portions of this trail, so be prepared for a few dead trees across the trail. (Originally contributed by the authors.)

Miles and Directions

0.0 Trailhead.
4.0 Sawtooth Lake.
8.0 Trailhead.

53 Torrey Lake

A long, hard day hike or backpacking trip to a nearly 9,000-foot-high lake in the shadows of Torrey and Tweedy Mountains, both over 11,000 feet

Start: Jacobson Creek Trailhead, 25 miles north-west of Dillon in the East Pioneer Mountains
Distance: 17.0-mile out-and-back
Difficulty: Strenuous

Maps: USGS Torrey Mountain, Maurice Mountain, and Vipond; Beaverhead-Deerlodge National Forest Map (Central)

Finding the trailhead: From the north, drive south of Wise River on the Pioneer Mountains National Scenic Byway for about 22 miles or 23 miles north from the south (all paved) and turn east on FR 2465 for 0.3 mile to Mono Creek Campground and Jacobson Creek Trailhead on your left. Ample parking; toilet; filterable water; developed camping at nearby at Mono Creek Campground. GPS: N45 32.083' / W113 04.733'

The Hike

From Mono Creek Campground, follow Jacobson Creek Trail 1002 as it wanders through some open timber and then skirts Jacobson Meadows. After the meadows, it ducks back into the timber and, just before Jacobson Creek, turns right (southeast) at 2.5 miles at the junction with Torrey Lake Trail 2086.

The Torrey Lake Trail immediately drops down to cross Jacobson Creek and then heads up David Creek. You now have 4 miles of gentle climbing through lodgepole stands, intermittent meadows, and spruce bottoms. The last 2 miles ascend 1,000 feet (only a Category 2 climb) as the trail winds its way up through granite boulders to the lake.

The eastern portion of the Pioneer Range is a confusing jumble of formations, and geologists have yet to come up with a complete explanation for what happened here. Torrey Lake, at 8.5 miles, is in the middle of an area where molten rock intruded

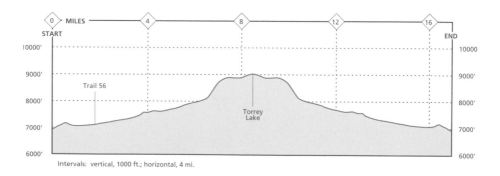

Intervals: vertical, 1000 ft.; horizontal, 4 mi.

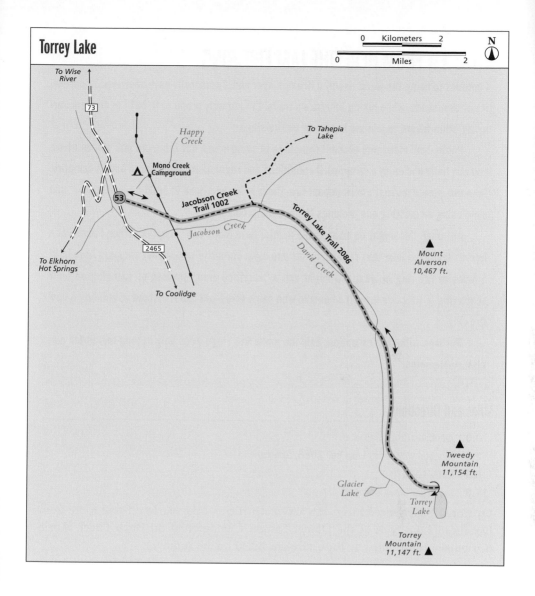

0   Kilometers   2

0   Miles   2

N

To Wise
River

73

Happy
Creek

To Tahepia
Lake

Mono Creek
Campground

53

Jacobson Creek
Trail 1002

Torrey Lake Trail 2086

Jacobson Creek

2465

David Creek

Mount
Alverson
10,467 ft.

To Elkhorn
Hot Springs

To Coolidge

Tweedy
Mountain
11,154 ft.

Glacier
Lake

Torrey
Lake

Torrey
Mountain
11,147 ft.

into the older formations from below and cooled there. Time and erosion removed the overburden of older rock and exposed the granite backbone of this range.

Looking south across the lake, you can see the ragged igneous hump of Torrey Mountain, 11,147 feet high. Behind to the northeast are the shredded granite cliffs and buttresses of Tweedy Mountain, 11,154 feet high. Granite towers stand on the divide between Tweedy and Torrey, west of Torrey. If you decide to climb around on the large rockslide between Torrey Mountain and the lake, note that this slide shifted dramatically in 1981 and may still be unstable. Avoid the steep pitches of rubble, which will start to slide under your weight.

THE VIEW FROM HERE: THE LAST FIRE RING

I confess to being the worst enemy a fire ring ever had. I personally have destroyed hundreds, if not thousands, while hiking Montana's trails. I'm not only proud of it, but I'm also encouraging other hikers to join me in my war on fire rings.

Public-land managers prohibit campfires in some areas, but there are still places where you can build and enjoy a campfire. If conditions and regulations allow you to have a campfire, however, please make it a zero-impact fire. There is never a need to build a new fire ring, and even using an existing one prolongs the age-old problem.

Although this might be an arguable point, I have made one exception. When I arrive at a heavily impacted lake that commonly has one main campsite where past campers have built a massive fire ring in what you might call a "sacrifice area." Instead of spending an hour scattering it, I usually leave it so people who camp there will use it instead of building a new fire ring.

Perhaps with that exception, help me make fire rings exist only in long memories and historical photos.

Miles and Directions

- **0.0** Jacobson Creek Trailhead.
- **2.5** Junction with Torrey Lake Trail 2086; turn right.
- **8.5** Torrey Lake.
- **17.0** Jacobson Creek Trailhead.

Options: Experienced hikers can also reach Torrey Lake via an off-trail route from Deadhead Lake. Start at the Dinner Station Campground on Birch Creek Road. (Originally contributed by Pat Caffrey, re-hiked by the authors.)

54 Grayling Lake

A day hike or overnighter to three peaceful lakes in the shadow of 10,144-foot-high Sharp Mountain

Start: Canyon Creek Campground at the end of Canyon Creek Road, 16 miles west of Melrose
Distance: 10.0-mile out-and-back

Difficulty: Moderate
Maps: USGS Vipond Park and Mount Tahepia; Beaverhead-Deerlodge Map (Central)

Finding the trailhead: Drive south of Butte on I-15 and take exit 93 for Melrose. From Melrose, follow the fishing access signs west across the Big Hole River, passing by a campground on the left, where the road turns to gravel. Continue across a second bridge and straight through a four-way intersection. After 1.5 miles from Melrose, the road forks. The left road goes to Cherry Creek, and the right road continues toward Canyon Creek. Go right. Follow the road straight up Trapper Creek for 5 miles to the old smelter town of Glendale. At the intersection in Glendale, turn right (uphill) on FR 187 (Canyon Creek Road) for Canyon Creek. After 8.5 miles from Melrose, cross Canyon Creek and then in 2.8 more miles, pass by the old Canyon Creek charcoal kilns, which were used to fire the Glendale Smelter around the end of the nineteenth century. Then, after 13 miles, turn left on FR 7401 for the last 4 miles to the trailhead. It's 16.5 miles of dirt roads from Melrose to Canyon Creek Campground and Trailhead. The road is rocky and narrow. You could probably make it in any vehicle, but you'd be better off and more comfortable with high clearance and low gears. Ample parking; toilet; vehicle camping. GPS: N45 37.500' / W112 56.667'

The Hike

You can start this hike right at the campground by parking near the entrance of the campground and just before the gate to the Canyon Creek Guest Ranch. Follow the trail along the fence, through some heavy brush, until you see a footbridge over Canyon Creek. Right after the bridge, the trail goes through a gate; be sure to close it behind you.

You can also start at a marked trailhead about a half mile before you reach the campground where you cross the creek on a sturdy stock bridge and walk along the south side of the creek on a good trail that joins the main trail just past the gate.

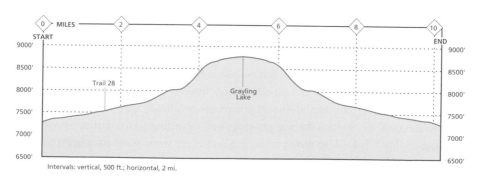

Grayling Lake. BILL SCHNEIDER

The first 1.5 miles gradually climb through unburned forest along Canyon Creek to a junction where Trail 2088 veers off to the right towards Canyon Lake. At this junction, stay left (south) on Trail 2028. From here, it's 3.5 miles to Grayling Lake. The first 2 miles continue along Canyon Creek at stream grade, then the trail turns west for the first stream crossing over Lion Creek. In the next 2 miles, the trail crosses Lion Creek four times; only the third one has a bridge. Unless you hike this early in the season when the streams are still high, you can rock hop across the other three crossings without getting wet feet. The next mile is a climb, the only real climb of the hike, mostly on switchbacks that are a bit too flat.

After the ascent, the trail crosses the flatlands below Vera Lake. You can easily reach the lake by navigating off-trail south and a little east after the fourth crossing of Lion Creek. Vera Lake used to have fish, but one visit will explain their absence: The lake isn't deep enough for fish to survive the winter freeze.

Grayling Lake (1,600 feet elevation above the trailhead) is about a half mile farther up the trail. It's listed as having grayling, but according to the Forest Service, the grayling couldn't make it, so now you have to settle for some good fishing for scrappy

Grayling Lake

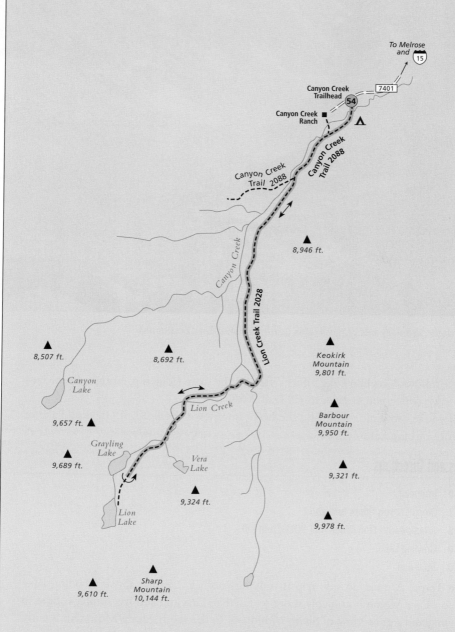

0 Kilometer 1

0 Mile 1

N

To Melrose and **15**

Canyon Creek Trailhead
54
7401

Canyon Creek Ranch

Canyon Creek Trail 2088

Canyon Creek Trail 2088

Canyon Creek

▲ 8,946 ft.

Lion Creek Trail 2028

▲ 8,507 ft.

▲ 8,692 ft.

▲ Keokirk Mountain 9,801 ft.

Canyon Lake

Lion Creek

9,657 ft. ▲

▲ Barbour Mountain 9,950 ft.

Grayling Lake

▲ 9,689 ft.

Vera Lake

▲ 9,321 ft.

▲ 9,324 ft.

Lion Lake

▲ 9,978 ft.

▲ 9,610 ft.

▲ Sharp Mountain 10,144 ft.

Lion Lake, definitely one of those lakes worth hiking to. BILL SCHNEIDER

little rainbows. Grayling Lake offers a view of the steep ridge separating it from Canyon Lake, which you can get to via Trail 2088.

If you're camping, you'll find the best campsites at the head of Grayling Lake or the foot of Lion Lake.

Miles and Directions

- **0.0** Trailhead.
- **0.1** Cross Canyon Creek and gate.
- **1.5** Junction with Lion Creek Trail 2028; turn left.
- **5.0** Grayling Lake.
- **10.0** Trailhead.

Side Trips: A must-do side trip is walking another 0.5 mile above Grayling Lake to Lion Lake, which is arguably more scenic than Grayling and has similar fishing to Grayling and a great view of Sharp Mountain. To the south, Sharp Mountain is fairly obvious and definitely sharp. Not too many people hike here, so be sure to do your part to keep the area pristine. (Originally contributed and re-hiked by the authors.)

55 Selway Mountain

Impressive views of southwest Montana and the site of an old fire lookout

Start: 40 miles west of Clark Canyon Reservoir, south of Dillon
Distance: 5.4-mile out-and-back
Difficulty: Moderate

Maps: USGS Selway Mountain and Kitty Creek; Beaverhead-Deerlodge National Forest Map (South)

Finding the trailhead: From Dillon, drive 19 miles south on I-15 to Clark Canyon Reservoir exit 44. Turn right onto Highway 324, heading west. After about 20 miles, watch for a national forest access sign and then another sign for Reservoir Lake Campground. Turn right onto FR 181 and follow the dirt road and signs 18 miles northwest to Reservoir Lake Campground. Trail 1034 starts in the boat trailer parking lot. Ample parking; toilet; vehicle camping at the trailhead. GPS: N45 7.333' / W113 27.216'

The Hike

Ascending this nearly 9,000-foot-high peak requires moderate effort in exchange for an outstanding view of far southwestern Montana. The trail is easy enough for inexperienced hikers but scenic enough for veterans. The mountain's proximity to Reservoir Lake Campground makes it an appealing day hike while camping on Reservoir Lake. In addition, moose often wander through the marshy Bloody Dick Creek, which runs along the road, and the surrounding Continental Divide area is prime elk habitat.

Trail 1034 begins at a gate and runs for about 200 feet along the lake before it forks. Take the right fork to Selway Mountain. (The other fork circles Reservoir Lake.)

The trail rises quickly on switchbacks up a hillside meadow for the next half mile or so. Stop here and there to soak in the view of Bloody Dick Creek and the lake

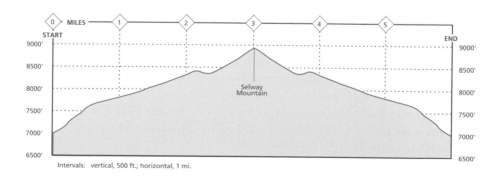

Intervals: vertical, 500 ft.; horizontal, 1 mi.

Hoary marmot, ready for a nap. SHUTTERSTOCK

below. Soon the trail flattens out and begins a long, steady climb for the next mile. The 1,900-foot gain over 2 miles makes this a Category 1 climb, so let's call it short but steep.

The woods are almost exclusively lodgepole pine, dotted with patches of blue mountain lupine. As the trail begins to turn sharply eastward, whitebark pines start taking over from the lodgepole. The trail then circles Selway Mountain on the northern side and follows the contour along the slope.

Through the trees you can see Bloody Dick Peak to the east. After about another quarter mile, the trail turns north to the summit. Some Douglas fir and spruce grow here, but slowly the trees thin out as you reach the top.

In 1942 the Forest Service built a 30-foot-high lookout tower on top of Selway Mountain. It was staffed for twenty-nine years and supported a heliport, but the FS demolished and burned it in 1976. The FS has since abandoned most of its lookouts and now relies on aircraft for spotting fires. You can see some remains of the tower at the summit, and the heliport itself remains intact. The site of the heliport is easy to find and makes a good spot for lunch, with a view to the south out across the Continental Divide. The bald south slope of the mountain is talus and extremely steep, dropping quickly into the woods and ridge below.

Once on top of Selway Mountain, it's easy to see why this shaved top made an ideal spot for a lookout tower. Off to the north, you can see past Black Mountain, the timber-covered peak just behind Selway, and across the Big Hole Valley all the way to the snowcapped Anaconda-Pintlers. To the west the view stretches past the Bitterroots and the Continental Divide to the jagged Lemhi Range in Idaho. Far past Bloody Dick Peak, to the northeast, are the high summits of the Pioneer Range: Torrey, Tweedy, and Baldy Mountains. And to the south, Bloody Dick Creek runs past Reservoir Lake toward Lemhi Pass and south to the Montana-Idaho border. (Originally contributed by Douglas Schnitzspahn.)

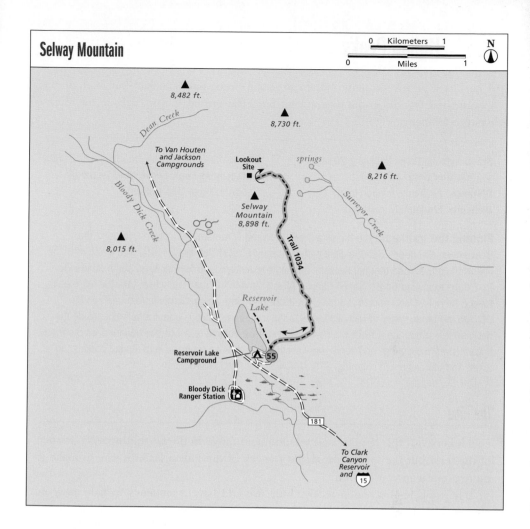

Selway Mountain

0   Kilometers   1

0   Miles   1

N

8,482 ft.

Dean Creek

8,730 ft.

To Van Houten
and Jackson
Campgrounds

Lookout
Site

springs

8,216 ft.

Bloody Dick Creek

Selway
Mountain
8,898 ft.

Surveyor Creek

Trail 1034

8,015 ft.

Reservoir
Lake

Reservoir Lake
Campground

55

Bloody Dick
Ranger Station

181

To Clark
Canyon
Reservoir
and

15

Miles and Directions

0.0 Trailhead.

2.7 Top of Selway Mountain.

5.4 Trailhead.

56 Italian Peaks

A backpacking adventure into the huge glacial cirque below Italian Peak, high on the Continental Divide, in the magnificent but little-visited Italian Peaks in far southwestern Montana

Start: Nicholia Creek Trailhead, 20 miles southwest of Lima
Distance: 23.0-mile lollipop loop
Difficulty: Moderately strenuous

Maps: USGS Scott Peak, Deadman Lake, and Eighteenmile Peak; Beaverhead-Deerlodge National Forest Map (South)

Finding the trailhead: The Nicholia Creek Trailhead is remote but easy to find using the Beaverhead-Deerlodge National Forest Map. Turn off I-15 at Dell exit 23, 45 miles south of Dillon. Follow the gravel road that parallels the interstate's western side for 1.5 miles south, where FR 257 turns westward up Big Sheep Canyon. After 18 miles the road branches; take the left branch toward Nicholia-Deadman. In 2.3 miles FR 3922 branches again. Continue to the left on FR 657 up the broad valley of Nicholia Creek to the trailhead, which is about a half mile inside the national forest boundary. You'll want a four-wheel-drive vehicle to get to this trailhead, as there are several stream crossings and some rocky sections. A primitive trailhead with limited parking, no toilet, and undesignated camping. GPS: N44 43.405' / W112 46.275'

The Hike

Few hikers visit this remote, isolated mountain range in the far southwestern corner of the state, but the spectacular alpine scenery of the Italian Peaks is sure to make it more popular in years to come.

The trails in this region receive little use and have a tendency to fade away in grassy meadows, making a few tips in order. Don't trust the trail as shown on the Scott Peak USGS quad, which is old and inaccurate. Do trust the official blazes on the trees, which look like upside-down exclamation points. The trail stays close to the stream, except in places where the trail is built above it to avoid avalanche debris.

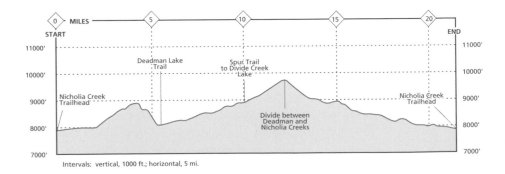

A green gentian and Eighteenmile Peak from Lower Nicholia Creek. Jacquelyn Corday

For the first 3 miles, the trail follows Nicholia Creek until you reach the junction with the Continental Divide Trail. Turn left (north) here and climb over a beautiful sagebrush plateau down into Deadman Creek. The Continental Divide Trail joins Trail 1091 about a half mile up the trail from Deadman Lake. The lake can also be accessed by a very rough jeep road, so you might see people car camping here.

From here, Trail 1091 follows Deadman Creek, which frequently goes dry or underground, so make sure you have enough water. The USGS quad shows two unnamed small lakes between Deadman Lake and the pass, but they dried up years ago and are now meadows.

The valley at this point begins to take on a more alpine character, showing signs of the glaciers that once carved the U-shaped upper canyon. If you have the energy, you can hike up to Divide Creek Lake, which lies in a rocky depression a few yards on the Idaho side of the Continental Divide but is invisible from the Deadman Creek side. The old trail used to climb the grassy slope up to a broad saddle on the divide to the lake, but it's now grown over. There is now a trail southeast of the grassy saddle as you head toward the pass on your left. It's only about a half mile to the lake, which, after mid-July, may be your only source of water in this area. Use your topo map, and you shouldn't have any problem. The lake is small but scenic and has some nice campsites.

For the amateur geologists among us, a breach anticline, deep in the Italian Peaks.
JACQUELYN CORDAY

From here Trail 1091 continues to climb gradually through the alpine meadows of the upper Deadman Creek drainage, with the steep rocky ridge of the Continental Divide looming overhead to the left. At one point a huge geological formation, called a breach anticline, forms a cliff along the divide, resembling a meteor-impact crater.

About 4 miles from the Divide Creek Lake turnoff, the trail reaches the pass between the Deadman and Nicholia Creek drainages. Here, at 9,400 feet, the alpine scenery is spectacular, with the knife-edged ridge of the divide rising up to the 10,996-foot summit of Italian Peak. Keep your eyes peeled for bighorn sheep and goats up on the high slopes.

The trail switchbacks down a steep talus slope into the alpine meadows at the base of the north wall of Italian Peak. A snowfield lingers year-round on Italian Peak's north wall, perhaps aspiring to become a glacier. This alpine basin makes a perfect second night's campsite and may convince you to spend an extra day exploring the meadows

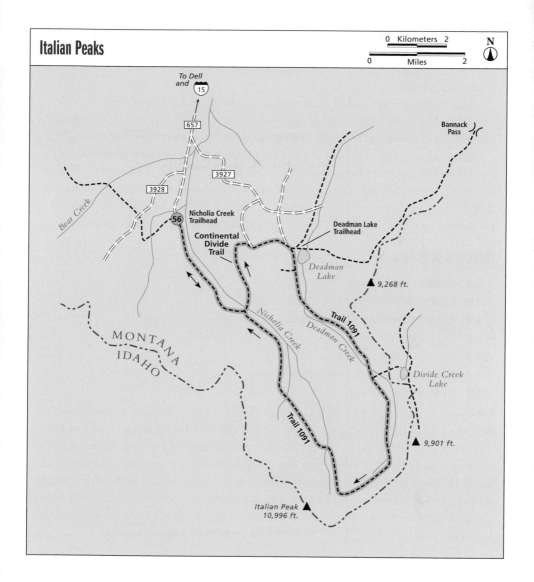

To Dell and **15**

657

3927

3928

Bear Creek

56

Nicholia Creek
Trailhead

**Continental
Divide
Trail**

Deadman Lake
Trailhead

*Deadman
Lake*

▲ 9,268 ft.

Nicholia Creek

Trail 1091

Deadman Creek

MONTANA
IDAHO

*Divide Creek
Lake*

▲ 9,901 ft.

Trail 1091

Italian Peak ▲
10,996 ft.

Bannack
Pass

and talus slopes of this huge cirque. This is the southernmost point in Montana—and surely one of the most stunning. If you brought your dog, please keep it on a leash or close by, as this meadow-filled valley is an elk calving area.

Going northward, the trail descends the broad, green valley of Nicholia Creek, staying on the western side of the stream just above the bogs in the creek bottom. Again, the trail often disappears in the meadows, but it's blazed through the forested parts. At one large meadow, about 3 miles from the cirque basin, the route is marked by a series of 5-foot-high posts.

Past this meadow, Trail 1091 enters the lower reaches of Nicholia Creek and becomes well defined, especially after it crosses to the eastern bank of the stream. For

6 miles the route follows an old, grass-grown jeep track through the sagebrush flats. Be sure to turn around frequently to see the changing views of Italian Peak and Scott Peak over in Idaho. After 9.5 miles from the cirque at the base of Italian Peak, you reach your vehicle.

Although there are several fresh springs in both Deadman and Nicholia Valleys, you should be prepared to treat or filter your water, since cattle graze the meadows along most of the route. The bugs can be bad as well, so bring insect repellent.

The high pass between Nicholia and Deadman Creeks is usually clear of snow by the Fourth of July, but check local conditions with the Forest Service office before heading for the trailhead. The Forest Service has proposed wilderness status for the Italian Peaks area. Parts of the trail in lower Nicholia Creek and the section between Nicholia Creek and Deadman Creek are open to motorcycle use but closed to ATVs.

Miles and Directions

0.0 Nicholia Creek Trailhead.

3.0 Continental Divide Trail; turn left.

4.5 Deadman Creek Trail 1091; turn right.

7.0 Deadman Lake.

10.5 Spur trail to Divide Creek Lake.

14.0 Pass between Deadman and Nicholia Creeks.

23.0 Nicholia Creek Trailhead.

Options: If you have two high-clearance vehicles, you can make a shuttle out of this trip. Check the Forest Service map for a primitive road going to Deadman Lake and leave one vehicle there, but be forewarned that this four-wheel-drive road can get rough and very slick when wet. You can start the shuttle at either trailhead with about the same level of difficulty. If you arrive at the trailhead late in the day, you can do the loop clockwise and find a nice campsite about 3.8 miles up the trail; just keep going straight at the junction of the Deadman Lake Trail. (Originally contributed by Ed Madej and Rosemary Rowe, re-hiked for authors by Jackie Corday.)

57 Hollow Top Lake

A day hike or overnighter to a mountain lake bordered on three sides by the high peaks of the Tobacco Root Mountains

Start: 55 miles west of Bozeman
Distance: 12.5-mile loop
Difficulty: Moderate

Maps: USGS Pony and Potosie Peak; Beaverhead-Deerlodge National Forest Map (Central)

Finding the trailhead: From the small rural community of Harrison on US 287, drive west 6 miles to Pony, an even smaller rural community. Drive through Pony (where the main street turns into FR 191) for 1 mile until the road forks; stay left until the road dead-ends at a trailhead loop about 2 miles from Pony. North Willow Creek Trail 6301 starts to the northwest, and Loop Park Trail 6302 returns from the southwest. Ample parking; no toilet or camping. GPS: N45 39.016' / W111 54.600'

The Hike

At the trailhead, you get a sense of the local interests. A large Forest Service sign welcomes ATVs and motorcycles, an ominous proclamation for hikers and backcountry horsemen, but it isn't quite as bad as it sounds. After 1.5 miles, most ATVs turn off and head up to Albro Lake. A few motorcycles go to Hollow Top Lake, but not many, and if you hike this during the week, you probably won't see any—and you'll have a nice hike to a beautiful lake basin.

From the trailhead, North Willow Creek Trail 6301 crosses a bridge and then gradually climbs along the north side of the creek. In the spring watch for fuzzy blue pasqueflowers in the grassy meadows.

For the first 1.5 miles, you must walk on an ATV road, but then the "troad" turns off to the left as Albro Lake Trail 6333 and heads up to Albro Lake. You stay right (west) at this junction and continue to follow Trail 6301, which turns into a single-track and continues along the north side of the creek through groves of spruce and

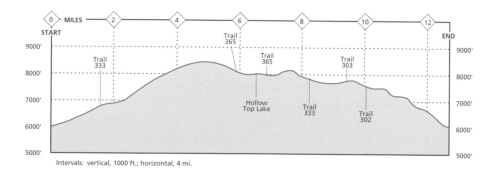

Intervals: vertical, 1000 ft.; horizontal, 4 mi.

fir and back into open meadows. You might see a few cows grazing in these meadows, and you go through a gate. Be sure to securely close it behind you.

About 3.5 miles from the trailhead, the trail again crosses the creek. Pause here to filter water. At this point the trail heads away from the main creek. This stream crossing can be tricky during early summer runoff. Later in the summer you can cross the stream on jammed logs. Above the crossing the trail climbs more steeply to Hollow Top Lake, passing through some beautiful, sloping meadows with great views east into the Gallatin Valley and the Spanish Peaks.

At about 4 miles, turn right (west) at the junction with Trail 6365. The last mile to the lake gets quite rocky and steep, which makes for rough walking but also makes it difficult for motorcycles to get to the lake.

Hollow Top Lake (which has pan-size rainbow trout) is the source of the stream you've been following. Northwest of the lake is Hollowtop Mountain, at 10,604 feet the highest point in the Tobacco Roots. Mount Jefferson (10,513 feet) lies west of the lake, and to the south is Potosi Peak (10,125 feet), named by miners after a fabulous mine in the Andes. All three mountains are technically easy scrambles, but prepare for rough weather on the windswept alpine slopes.

After Hollow Top Lake, you may wish to explore Deep Lake, the next lake up the drainage. Simply skirt Hollow Top Lake to the inlet on the northwest end and follow the trail found here about a quarter mile to Deep Lake.

Hollow Top Lake has lots of good campsites all around it. The flow from the outlet has been regulated with a small floodgate, which, regrettably, takes a nick out of the natural beauty of this mountain lake.

Instead of retracing your steps, you can make a loop out of this trip by dropping a mile down from the lake to the junction with Potosi Peak Trail 6365 and turning right (south). This trail goes through a lodgepole forest for 1.5 miles until it joins Albro Lake Trail 6333. Turn left (east) here, and follow the ATV road for 1.5 miles to the junction with Loop Park Trail 6302. (Take a left at North Willow Creek Trail 6303 about a half mile before Loop Park Trail 6302 junction.)

This 1.5-mile section is not much to write home about, but once you take a right (northeast) onto Park Trail 6302 and climb up to the top of a ridge into a huge meadow, you do have something to write about. This section of trail is closed to all motorized vehicles and is a real beauty. It goes along the open ridgeline for about 2 miles, and the scenery is outstanding. The mountains at the spine of the Tobacco Roots dominate the western horizon, and some fantastic old whitebark pines talk to you up close and personal as you hike by. Even during midday you can usually see elk and deer on this stretch. It's well worth enduring a short walk on the ATV road. It's long and dry, though, so make sure you still have enough water in your bottles.

Trail 6302 fades away in several places, but watch for well-placed cairns and fence posts to show the way. After a delightful trip along the ridge, the trail switchbacks another 1.5 miles down to the trailhead. (Originally contributed by Fred Swanson, re-hiked by the authors.)

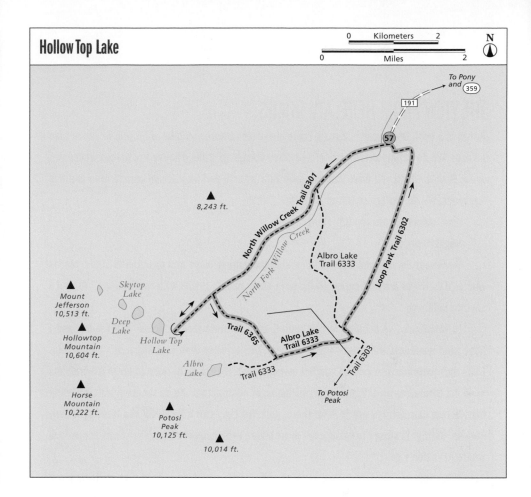

Hollow Top Lake

0   Kilometers   2
0   Miles   2

N

To Pony and (359)

191

57

North Willow Creek Trail 6301

8,243 ft.

Loop Park Trail 6302

North Fork Willow Creek

Albro Lake Trail 6333

Skytop Lake

Mount Jefferson 10,513 ft.

Deep Lake

Hollow Top Lake

Trail 6365

Albro Lake Trail 6333

Trail 6303

Hollowtop Mountain 10,604 ft.

Albro Lake

Trail 6333

To Potosi Peak

Horse Mountain 10,222 ft.

Potosi Peak 10,125 ft.

10,014 ft.

Miles and Directions

0.0   Trailhead.

1.5   Junction with Albro Lake Trail 6333; turn right.

4.0   Junction with Potosi Peak Trail 6365; turn right.

5.0   Hollow Top Lake.

6.0   Junction with Potosi Peak Trail 6365; turn right.

7.5   Junction with Trail 6333; turn left.

8.5   Junction with Trail 6303; turn left.

9.0   Junction with Trail 6302; turn right.

12.5   Trailhead.

THE VIEW FROM HERE: ATV ROADS

A trail is a trail. And a road is a road. Trails are places where you hike or bicycle or run or ride a horse. We do nonmotorized, muscle-powered things on trails. They're not places where you drive. Places where you drive vehicles with four wheels and an internal combustion engines are roads. We do motorized things on roads.

That seems simple enough, right?

Regrettably, no.

On Forest Service and Bureau of Land Management maps and directional signs, places where ATVs travel are still called trails, or in some cases, "trails with restrictions." To that I say: No kidding!

In this book I've decided to call routes open to motorized vehicles "ATV roads," and I hope land managers will start doing the same. This is more than semantics. It's public relations and customer service and conflict management. Hikers really need to know if a trail has been designated as an ATV route, which means, of course, that it's no longer a trail. Knowing this, hikers can still choose to hike there, just like they can hike along the freeway if they choose. Neither is closed to hiking, but most hikers will choose to hike elsewhere, someplace where ATVs don't go.

ATV roads are open to hiking—and in some cases might even be a nice walk—but you have an increased chance of social conflict that most hikers probably want to avoid. Anybody can spend time researching forest travel plans and maps to determine what routes are "trails with restrictions," but calling them roads would make it easier for everyone to know what to expect when we leave for the trailhead—where, incidentally, the directional signs (at the trailhead and along the road to the trailhead) still call these ATV roads "trails." In addition, the numbers used to identify trails and ATV roads are the same, which is also confusing.

I'm not saying we shouldn't have routes for ATVs. These recreationists have a right to travel on public land. I am saying this simple switch in our vernacular would help to greatly reduce conflict by making it clear to hikers that they're entering an ATV zone instead of letting them be surprised later, perhaps having a conflict, and then making that phone call the district ranger doesn't like to get.

58 Curly Lake

A day hike or overnighter to a popular subalpine lake in the Tobacco Root Mountains

Start: 40 miles southeast of Butte
Distance: 6.0-mile out-and-back
Difficulty: Moderate

Maps: USGS Manhead Mountain; Beaverhead-Deerlodge National Forest (Central)

Finding the trailhead: From exit 256 in Cardwell (east of Butte on I-90), drive south on Highway 359 for 5 miles. Then turn right, heading south on South Boulder Road (FR 107). The pavement ends after 2.7 miles. Stay on the main road (FR 107), through Mammoth, for 13.6 miles. Curly Creek Trail 7151 starts on your right just before crossing Curly Creek, 2.1 miles past the little gathering of cabins called Mammoth. South Boulder Road 107 is rough and rocky in places but passable, barely, by a two-wheel-drive vehicle. The first half mile or so of the trail is on a private inholding, so be respectful. Limited parking; no toilet; no camping at trailhead but vehicle camping nearby. GPS: N45 38.266' / W112 1.949'

The Hike

Curly Creek Trail 7151 begins by switchbacking up a steep sidehill, quickly gaining elevation with views of the South Boulder Valley to the east. After about a mile, the trail flattens out and crosses a series of meadows along Curly Creek. These meadows have a wealth of wildflowers.

After 2 miles, Curly Creek Trail climbs again through lodgepole pine forest. Many springs and seeps are found along this stretch. Next, the trail again levels out, crossing another hanging valley before a final climb to the Curly Lake basin.

After 2.5 miles, stay right on Curly Lake Trail 7159 to the lake. There is really only one good water source along the way, a small stream at about 2 miles. The trail is in great shape and would be a good choice for trail runners. It's a long 3 miles to the lake, which is on your right after the junction and past two smaller ponds.

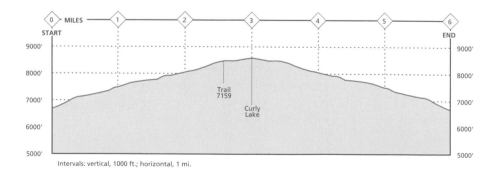

Intervals: vertical, 1000 ft.; horizontal, 1 mi.

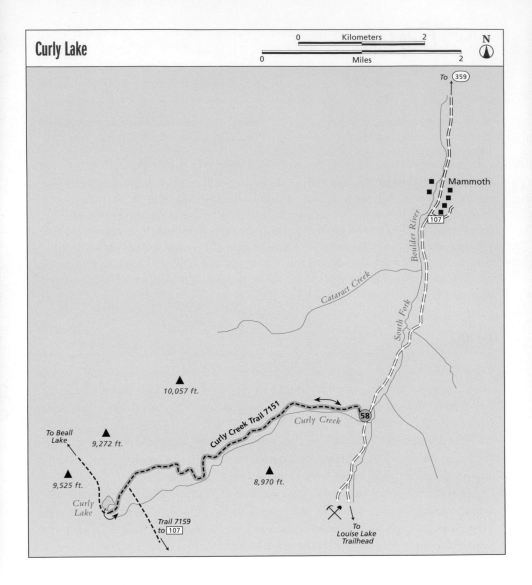

Curly Lake sits in a subalpine basin at 8,800 feet below several unnamed 10,000-foot peaks. The lake is tucked in the timber north of the trail. While the fishless lake is not unduly spectacular, the alpine meadows and meandering creek south of the lake are beautiful, offering views of alpine peaks to the south end of the cirque. Mountain bikers like the Curly Lake area, so expect to see a few on your hike. The Curly Lake Trail is also open to motorcycles except from May 1 to July 15.

Bighorn Sheep. COURTESY OF NPS

Miles and Directions

0.0 Trailhead.

2.5 Junction with Curly Lake Trail 7159; turn right.

3.0 Curly Lake.

6.0 Trailhead.

Options: You could take Trail 7159 down to the road and then jog about 2 miles on the road back to your vehicle, a good option for trail runners. (Originally contributed by Kim Wilson, re-hiked by the authors.)

59 Louise Lake

A nice family hike to a high lake deep in the Tobacco Root Mountains

Start: Lost Cabin/Louise Lake Trailhead, 40 miles southeast of Butte
Distance: 7.0-mile out-and-back

Difficulty: Moderate
Maps: USGS Waterloo; Beaverhead-Deerlodge National Forest (Central)

Finding the trailhead: From exit 256 in Cardwell (east of Butte on I-90), drive south on Highway 359 for 5 miles. Then turn right, heading south on South Boulder Road (FR 107). The pavement ends after 2.7 miles. Stay on the main road (FR 107) through the small community of Mammoth for 14.7 miles. Stay right when the road forks, continuing on FR 107. After 15.7 miles, you reach Bismark Reservoir and the trailhead for both Louise Lake and Lost Cabin Lake. As you approach the trailhead, the road has some rough sections where you might want a high-clearance, four-wheel-drive vehicle. This trail starts on a private inholding, so be respectful. Ample parking and vehicle camping at the trailhead; undeveloped camping and toilet nearby at the junction of FR 107 and Trail 7154. GPS: N45 36.428' / W112 03.190'

The Hike

The Tobacco Roots offer many short hikes, such as the one to Louise Lake, suitable for families, but wait until at least mid-July for the snow to melt. We went in early July, and the lake was still partially frozen.

From the Lost Cabin/Louise Lake Trailhead, Trail 7168 gradually climbs for 3.5 long miles, mostly on "mall walk" switchbacks, to the lake. You hardly notice the ascent on these nearly level switchbacks. Carry your drinking water, as there are only a few water sources along the way.

Louise Lake sits in a cirque with massive, 10,353-foot Middle Mountain to the south. The lake has a small population of large cutthroat trout that can be very fussy about which fly they might take. If you find the fly that works, catch only enough for supper, leaving the rest for the next angler.

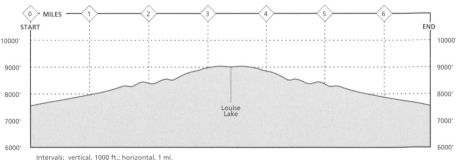

Intervals: vertical, 1000 ft.; horizontal, 1 mi.

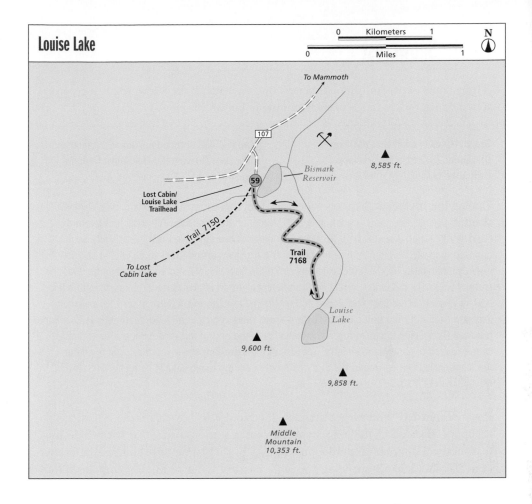

Louise Lake

0 Kilometers 1

0 Miles 1

N

To Mammoth

107

Bismark
Reservoir

8,585 ft.

59

Lost Cabin/
Louise Lake
Trailhead

Trail 7150

Trail
7168

To Lost
Cabin Lake

Louise
Lake

9,600 ft.

9,858 ft.

Middle
Mountain
10,353 ft.

The Forest Service has recognized this route as a National Recreation Trail for its outstanding scenery and exceptional recreational opportunities. It is closed year-round to all motorized vehicles. It is, however, open to mountain bikes and horses, so be sure to courteously share the trail if you meet any.

Miles and Directions

0.0 Lost Cabin/Louise Lake Trailhead.

3.5 Louise Lake.

7.0 Lost Cabin/Louise Lake Trailhead.

Side Trips: Peak baggers might be tempted to scramble up Middle Mountain, a nontechnical climb. (Originally contributed and re-hiked by the authors.)

60 Snowcrest

A long, super–scenic subalpine traverse along the apex of the Snowcrest Range, probably the nicest place in Montana that nobody knows about

Start: 40 miles southeast of Dillon
Distance: 23.0-mile lollipop loop
Difficulty: Moderately strenuous

Maps: USGS Antone Peak and Stonehouse
Mountain; Beaverhead-Deerlodge National
Forest (South)

Finding the trailhead: Follow the business route of I-15 south through Dillon, past Western
Montana College, and then turn left at Barrett Memorial Hospital. After 0.2 mile, turn left and
head southeast on Blacktail Deer Road for 6.6 miles, where the paved road turns into a wide
unpaved roadway. It's easy to drive too fast on this excellent gravel road, so be careful and stay
within your abilities. Washboarded sections can throw your vehicle into a spin, as can the loose
gravel if you make a sudden correction. Continue straight on FR 1808 for 27 miles, then turn left
and head east toward East Fork Blacktail Deer Creek Campground. After another 11.5 miles on a
less-improved dirt road (but passable by two-wheel-drive vehicle), the road dead-ends in East Fork
Blacktail Deer Creek Campground. The trailhead is at the end of this nice campground (managed
by the Bureau of Land Management). Because of the extra-long drive, you may want to spend
the night and get an early start the next day. Ample parking; toilet; vehicle camping. GPS: N44
50.183' / W112 11.567'

Recommended itinerary: Although spectacular to see, this route is difficult to
backpack. Because of the long, waterless center section, you're left with three less-
than-optimal options: (1) putting in a long (13- to 14-mile) day and two short days
(4 to 5 miles each), (2) spending one night in a dry camp, or (3) dropping down into
one of the side drainages off the crest to find water and then carrying your pack up
to the divide again the next morning—and in the process tacking 3 to 4 miles onto
the total distance. Of these three, I prefer the first option, keeping my pack as light
as possible, getting up early on my second day, and enjoying a long day on the gorgeous Snowcrest Divide, stopping on the high points to sit and soak in the essence

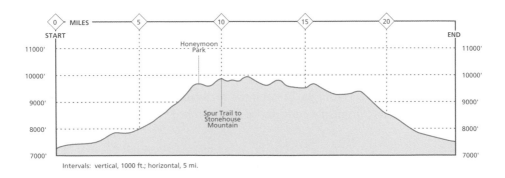

Taking a break along the seldom-visited Snowcrest Divide. JACQUELYN CORDAY

of this special place. Specifically, that means spending the first night along the East Fork below Honeymoon Park and the second night along Lawrence Creek about 5 miles from the trailhead. Or better yet, start at dawn and do it all in a very long, very rewarding day hike, which is what we did.

The Hike

When you hike hundreds of miles each summer, you sometimes go places that make you say, "I've already been here." While it's certainly true that every piece of wild nature is unique, that doesn't keep some mountains and lakes and streams from looking similar. Then, once in a great while, surprise, the stars are all aligned, and you end up in a place that blows you away like a 100 mph gust of wind and you say, "This is a truly special place." Such is the Snowcrest Range.

The Snowcrest is probably the nicest hike in Montana that nobody goes on. In fact, when we hiked it in late August 2003, we ran into a trail crew who told us we were the first hikers they'd seen all summer, even though this route had been in this book for twenty-five years. That's incredible, because we were standing on a 9,500-foot ridge amid scenery as amazing as Glacier or Grand Teton National Park or the Absaroka–Beartooth Wilderness, although different in nature—more gentle and peaceful and lonely.

The Snowcrest Range stretches for 20 miles north to southwest of the Gravelleys in the far southwestern corner of Montana. Because of the high wildlife populations, Snowcrest is the domain of big-game hunters and outfitters, but after experiencing the area, I wonder why it isn't more popular with hikers. The scenery is clearly world-class, and the heavy horse traffic during the hunting season keeps most trails nicely distinct all year.

This route takes you on a delightful circuit that covers most of the southern portion of the range, including 11 miles of the spectacular ridgeline, the area's namesake, mostly at elevations higher than 9,500 feet. Check in with the Forest Service about snow conditions if you're attempting the hike before mid-July.

The only problem with this hike is the confusing maze of trails and junctions (many without signs when we hiked it), and some trails visible only on the map. However, since we hiked it, the Forest Service has reconstructed some sections of the trail around Lewis Creek and Leadford Pass and from the BLM campground to Honeymoon Park. The Forest Service also improved signage, so it should not be as confusing now.

From the trailhead at the BLM campground, it's less than a mile along East Fork Blacktail Deer Creek Trail 6069 to a wet crossing of the East Fork. This section of trail that follows the stream is surprisingly lush. After a 40-mile drive through dry, sagebrush country, you might expect more dryness, but you get the opposite. The slow-moving, spring-fed stream winds through a green, lush valley full of moose and other wildlife. A few busy beavers have slowed the flow even more.

After 2 miles on Trail 6669 (incorrectly numbered 699 on some signs when I hiked this route), you reach the junction with trail 6069. Go left (north) here on trail 6069 and continue up the East Fork Blacktail Deer Creek Trail all the way to Honeymoon Park on the Snowcrest Divide. About halfway up, turn left (north) at the Two Meadows Trail 6074 junction to remain on Trail 6069.

In massive Honeymoon Park, turn right (east) onto Snowcrest Trail 6004 (left fork goes to the Notch Trailhead). Follow Snowcrest Trail 6004 for the next 11 miles, all on the Snowcrest Divide and through some of the most spectacular scenery in Montana. Whitebark pines surround Honeymoon Park and climb up small drainages to the ridgeline. Some of them even make it to the windswept divide, but they suffer the consequences come winter, as witnessed by the absence of west-side branches.

Like most ridgeline trails, you go up and down, up and down, but nothing too long or steep. At 9 miles Stonehouse Mountain is the highest point near the trail at 10,075 feet, and there is actually a "stone house," built long ago by shepherds. The trail goes right by it. Olson and Sunset Peaks, both higher than Stonehouse, dominate the western horizon, with Hogback Mountain a little farther off joining the celebration.

Before getting too wrapped up in the vistas, make sure you have plenty of water. There isn't any for the next 11 miles unless you drop down for a mile or two into

A Snowcrest Divide vista. JACQUELYN CORDAY

one of the creeks flowing from the ridge. This situation is especially problematic later in the season. If you go early in July, lingering snowbanks might provide a little water. Large cirque basins hug the eastern side of the crest as Trail 6004 skirts several minor summits along the divide, always remaining above 9,500 feet. And unlike any other trail I've ever hiked, there are several points along the ridge where you can see the entire 23-mile route covered by the trail description.

As you pass by a series of trail junctions (Mount Carey Trail 612, Two Meadows Trail 6074, Corral Creek Trail 6417, Divide Trail 6061), you need to do only two things: stay on the top of the ridge and keep your eyes peeled for the magnum cairns marking the way, each its own work of artful resourcefulness. In many places the trail fades away, but no matter. The magnificent cairns, all strategically located, can be seen a mile ahead. Watch for moose, elk, deer, golden eagles, and other wildlife along the way.

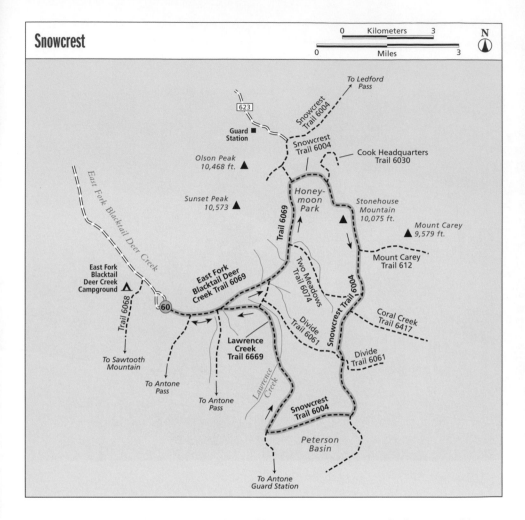

Near the end of this 11-mile slice of hiker's heaven, you might have a problem. When we hiked this route, the stretch from the junction where you turn right onto Lawrence Creek Trail 6669 (unsigned, basically invisible, and incorrectly marked 699 on the map when we were there) at 16.5 miles down to the junction with the East Fork Blacktail Deer Creek Trail 6069 at 21 miles, where you turn left, was very confusing. Between those two points are two left turns: at the junction with Lodgepole Trail 6073 at 19 miles and at the junction with Divide Trail 6061 at 19.5 miles. Keep the map out and be alert. Some trail sections, such as part of the Two Meadows Trail, have been rerouted, making the topo map inaccurate.

Fortunately, you're up high and can see where you're heading, so if you temporarily lose the trail, it should only be a minor problem. The terrain is open and easy bushwhacking, and the Forest Service has been working in the area to better mark the trails.

Miles and Directions

0.0 Trailhead at East Fork Blacktail Deer Campground.

0.7 Wet crossing of Blacktail Creek.

2.0 Junction with Lawrence Creek Trail 6669 (incorrectly marked 699); turn left.

5.5 Junction with Two Meadows Trail 6074; turn left.

7.5 Honeymoon Park and junction with Snowcrest Trail 6004; turn right.

8.0 Junction with Cook Headquarters Trail 6030; turn right.

9.0 Spur trail to the summit of Stonehouse Mountain; turn left.

10.5 Junction with Mount Carey Trail 612; turn right and stay on ridgetop.

11.5 Junction with Two Meadows Trail 6074; turn left and stay on ridgetop.

12.0 Junction with Corral Creek Trail 6417; turn right and stay on ridgetop.

13.5 Junction with Divide Trail 6061; go straight and stay on ridgetop.

16.5 Junction with Lawrence Creek Trail 6669 (incorrectly marked 699); turn right.

19.0 Junction with Lodgepole Trail 6073; turn left.

19.5 Junction with Divide Trail 6061; turn left.

21.0 Junction with East Fork Blacktail Deer Creek Trail 6069; turn left.

22.5 Cross Blacktail Deer Creek.

23.0 East Fork Blacktail Deer Creek Trailhead and Campground.

Options: Although it would be a nightmarish shuttle, you could drive to the Notch Trailhead just north of Honeymoon Park and day hike only the Snowcrest Divide Trail down to the East Fork Blacktail Deer Creek Trailhead, about 16 miles total distance. This would be an amazing day hike but a difficult and time-consuming shuttle. Perhaps the best way to do it would be to have somebody drop you off at the Notch Trailhead and then drive around to pick you up as you hike through the southern section of a hidden treasure called the Snowcrest Range.

You could also do a shorter loop hike from the Notch Trailhead by dropping off the ridge on the Two Meadows or Divide Trail and then climbing back up the East Fork to Honeymoon Park and back down to the Notch Trailhead.

Side Trips: One must-do side trip is a short scramble up to the top of Stonehouse Mountain on a well-marked spur trail. (Originally contributed by Bob Wagenknecht and Ed Madej, re-hiked by the authors.)

61 Antone Peak

A short but steep climb to 10,247-foot Antone Peak

Start: Antone Guard Station, 40 miles south-east of Dillon in the remote Snowcrest Range
Distance: 5.0-mile out-and-back

Difficulty: Easy to Antone Pass; strenuous to Antone Peak
Maps: USGS Antone Peak; Beaverhead-Deerlodge National Forest Map (South)

Finding the trailhead: Drive south from Dillon on I-15 for 47 miles to Lima exit 15. Head north through town and turn right, heading east on FR 205 toward Lima Reservoir. Follow FR 205 for 23.2 miles past Lima Reservoir to the junction with FR 202. Turn left (northwest) for Antone Guard Station. Drive northwest for 5.2 miles and turn right onto FR 325 (0.3 mile past Clover Divide). Drive 5.3 miles on FR 325 to Antone Guard Station. The Forest Service rents this cabin for a reasonable fee. Contact the Madison Ranger District in Ennis at (406) 682-4253 for information on this and other rental cabins. Ample parking; toilet; no camping or water. GPS: N44 46.85' / W112 12.683'

The Hike

Rough Creek Trail 6670 starts across the field from the Antone Guard Station parking lot. After leaving the guard station, the trail traverses the right side of the ridge, passing through open sagebrush meadows and limber pine, aspen, and fir forest. The trail is well maintained and popular with horse packers and hunters.

After what feels like a long mile, you reach 8,600-foot Antone Pass. Antone Pass is a grassy open saddle with excellent views north of the Snowcrest Range. Rough Creek Trail 6670 continues down the other side toward the East Fork of Blacktail Deer Creek.

At Antone Pass turn right, heading through the grass on the faint Meadow Creek Trail 6042. The trail is hard to follow, but look for trail markers and blazes along the left side of the meadows. When the blazes peter out, look uphill and to the left, up the

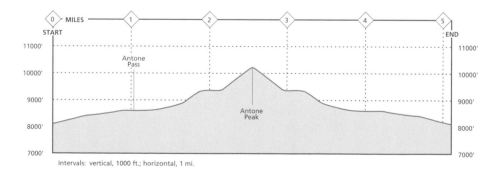

Intervals: vertical, 1000 ft.; horizontal, 1 mi.

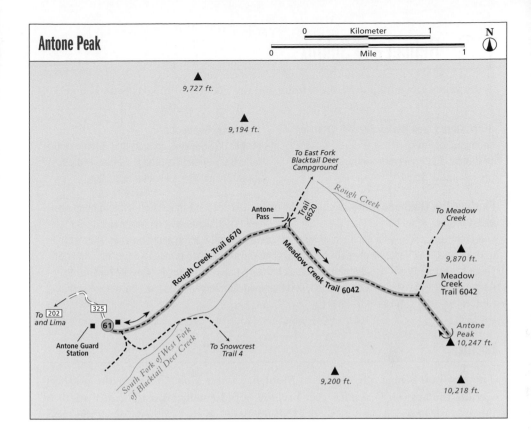

ridge. The trail drops into the bowl below Antone Peak. It's a short but very steep and strenuous climb up this bowl to the 10,247-foot summit of Antone Peak, a Category H ascent. The view here includes the rest of the Snowcrest Range stretching off to the north, the expanse of the Red Rock Valley, and the Centennial Mountains on the southern horizon. You also get a good look at Sawtooth Peak to the west, which looks like the teeth of a circular saw blade and could be termed "Sawteeth Peak." (Originally contributed by Herb B. Gloege, re-hiked by the authors.)

Miles and Directions

0.0 Antone Guard Station.

1.0 Antone Pass.

2.5 Antone Peak.

5.0 Antone Guard Station.

62 Helmet and Sphinx

A day hike or overnighter to the Sphinx and the Helmet in the Madison Range

Start: Bear Creek Ranger Station, 18 miles southeast of Ennis
Distance: 11.5-mile loop (without climbing the Helmet or Sphinx)

Difficulty: Strenuous
Maps: USGS Lake Cameron and Sphinx Mountain; Beaverhead-Deerlodge National Forest (South); Lee Metcalf Wilderness Map

Finding the trailhead: Drive south of Ennis on US 287 for 11.1 miles. Turn left and head east on Bear Creek Road (FR 327) at Cameron. Bear Creek Road heads east on pavement for 3 miles and then turns south on a good gravel road for 1.5 miles until it turns east and goes another mile to the Bear Creek Ranch. Turn south here again and travel less than a mile to a junction; turn left, heading east up Bear Creek to the Bear Creek Ranger Station. It's 8 miles from the highway to Bear Creek Ranger Station, Campground, and Trailhead. Ample parking; toilet; developed camping. GPS: N45 9.399' / W111 33.249'

The Hike

The Madison Range offers some of Montana's finest hiking. Yet only the northern section, the Spanish Peaks, has ever become popular with hikers. The area south of the Spanish Peaks all the way to the Hilgard Basin on the southern tip of the range has just as much if not more to offer hikers. The loop trail between the Sphinx and the Helmet nicely illustrates this fact.

Trail 6326 enters the Lee Metcalf Wilderness just beyond the Bear Creek Ranger Station and immediately crosses the Trail Fork of Bear Creek on a bridge. It then follows the stream for about 2 miles before it joins Trail 6327. It crosses the stream three more times—once on a bridge, twice without bridges—but the stream is usually small enough to let you keep your feet dry.

At the junction, turn left (northeast) on Trail 6327, which heads uphill toward the saddle between the Helmet and the Sphinx, which is another 3 miles. During

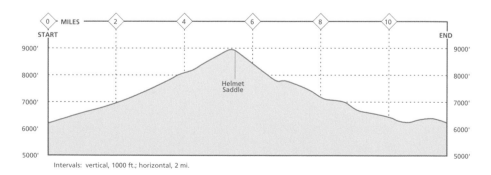

Intervals: vertical, 1000 ft.; horizontal, 2 mi.

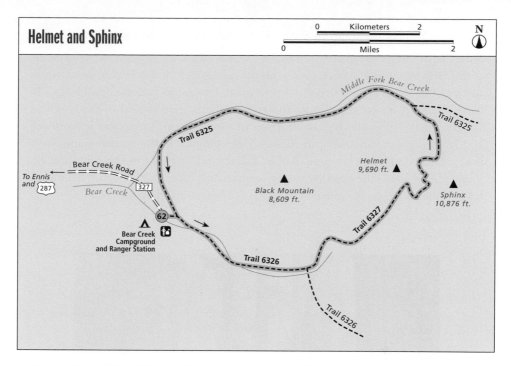

this portion of the hike, you'll experience most of the 2,300-foot elevation gain, a Category 1 climb.

From the saddle, continue down the north side on Trail 6327 into the Middle Fork of Bear Creek. From the saddle down to this junction, the trail drops sharply. From the T junction with Trail 6325 at 6.5 miles, where you turn left (west), Trail 6325 continues down the drainage 3.5 miles to a bridge across the creek (after five wet crossings!). From the bridge, Trail 6325 takes you south through mostly open country and directly back to the Bear Creek Ranger Station.

Once you pick up Trail 6325, it's about 5 miles out to the road, making this a tough, 11.5-mile hike, not including the mountain climbs. The Middle Fork and a smaller stream on the climb are the only reliable water sources, so plan on carrying water with you.

If you're camping, pick one of several good sites along the Middle Fork.

Miles and Directions

0.0 Bear Creek Ranger Station trailhead.

2.0 Junction with Trail 6327; turn left.

5.0 Helmet saddle.

6.5 Junction with Trail 6325; turn left.

10.0 Bridge across Middle Fork of Bear Creek.

10.5 Junction with North Bear Trail; turn left.

11.5 Bear Creek Ranger Station trailhead.

Options: You can make this an out-and-back hike by retracing your steps.

Side Trips: From the saddle you have two logical side trips—climbs to the summits of the Helmet and the Sphinx, which, untderstandably, do indeed resemble a helmet and a sphinx. Scaling the Helmet takes less than two hours and the Sphinx slightly more. They're both scrambles, with the Helmet the more technical of the two. The Sphinx has the edge on vistas, with much of the Madison Range visible from the 10,876-foot summit, including the Yellow Mules country to the northeast and Koch Peak, Shedhorn Ridge, No Man Ridge, and the Taylor Peaks to the south. At the summit, stay clear of the edge lest you fall over an incredibly steep cliff into the Indian Creek Valley. (Originally contributed by Pat Caffrey, re-hiked by the authors.)

Don't try this at home unless you're thirteen. BILL SCHNEIDER

Lewis and Clark National Forest

63 Gateway Gorge

A long backpacking loop in the Rocky Mountain Front and in the northeast corner of the Bob Marshall Wilderness with two fairly easy trips over the Continental Divide

Start: Swift Dam Trailhead, 35 miles northwest of Choteau
Distance: 39.5-mile lollipop loop
Difficulty: Moderate but long

Maps: USGS Morningstar Mountain, Swift Reservoir, Fish Lake, Gateway Pass, and Gooseberry Park; Bob Marshall Wilderness Complex Map

Finding the trailhead: Take US 89 to a rest area on the north edge of Dupuyer (36 miles south of US 2 and 32 miles north of Choteau) and turn left (west) onto FR 146 to Swift Dam. This road runs west for 18 miles to Swift Dam Trailhead—the main trailhead—on your left (south) at the foot of the dam. You can start the hike here or travel 2 miles farther around the north side of the reservoir on a rough road to a secondary trailhead. This road crosses the Blackfeet Reservation and may be closed or restricted, so check for signs near the dam. Also, a permit from the Blackfeet Tribe is required to park on the north side of the trailhead. You can buy one at the general store in Dupuyer. You can make it to the main trailhead in any vehicle, but you need high clearance to access the secondary trailhead on the north side of the reservoir.

The following description follows the route from the main trailhead at the foot of the dam. At the main trailhead, plenty of parking; toilet; developed camping. At the secondary trailhead, limited parking; no toilet; only undeveloped camping. GPS: N48 9.899' / W112 51.999'

Recommended itinerary: You can hike longer days on this trip because of the gentle terrain; a well-conditioned hiker could easily do this trek with three nights out. A four-night trip, however, would be less strenuous.

First night: Halfway up the South Fork of Birch Creek
Second night: Big River Meadows
Third night: Meadows just west of Badger Pass or Beaver Lake
Fourth night: Halfway down the North Fork of Birch Creek

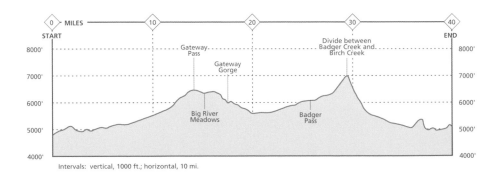

Intervals: vertical, 1000 ft.; horizontal, 10 mi.

The Hike

This trip typifies backpacking in the Bob. It goes through long, gentle, and mostly forested valleys and gradually climbs to low-elevation passes. If you develop a stronger interest in the Bob, you can expect more of the same on many other routes. On this route you pass over the Continental Divide twice, but both are so gradual, you hardly break into a sweat.

The Bob is horse country, so expect to meet stock parties. And expect very distinct trails because of the high horse traffic—too distinct in many places, where the trail becomes deeply rutted.

The route has adequate water sources, but some can dry up in August. Plan on carrying a full water bottle at all times. You can camp anywhere, but be sure to set up a zero-impact camp. This is grizzly country, so be bear aware and handle food and garbage properly. Anglers can find a few cutthroats in both the South Fork and the North Fork of Birch Creek, but this trip is not known for its fishing.

From the main trailhead you face a short, 200-foot hill to get your heart pumping before dropping down into the South Fork of Birch Creek for the long haul to Gateway Pass. Once you ford the stream (sorry, no bridges on this route), you follow a gradual upgrade all the way to the pass. You'll find six trail junctions and frequent social trails established by outfitters, but stay on the main trail, South Fork of Birch Creek Trail 105, for 14.5 miles to Gateway Pass, the most distinct choice in all cases. At the pass, Trail 105 becomes Trail 322.

The trail meanders through sparse forest of lodgepole and Douglas fir with frequent meadows, opening up more and more as you approach the pass. Be alert for campsites. You'll need to find one somewhere along the way, and there isn't an abundance of good choices.

Typically hikers expect a short, steep pull to get over a pass, but not so with Gateway. As you approach the pass, you'll be looking ahead trying to guess where the trail goes. And then, much to your surprise, you'll see a sign on a tree indicating you're standing on the low-elevation (6,478 feet) pass hidden in a small grove of mixed conifers.

Immediately after the pass, you start out on Trail 322 through Big River Meadows, a logical choice for your second night out. The meadow is gorgeous and so typically Bob, but it should be named Little Brook Meadows because there's no river.

After a pleasant night in Big River Meadows, you drop gradually toward the Gateway Gorge, taking a left (southeast) turn at 16.6 miles when Trail 371 up the East Fork of Strawberry Creek veers off to the right. As you approach the gorge, the trail climbs up onto the talus slope above the stream for a better view. The gorge is impressive but possibly overrated for its scenic beauty.

After the gorge the trail heads into a mature forest and stops there after you turn right (north) onto Trail 161 and begin the gradual upgrade along Strawberry Creek toward Badger Pass. The Fool Creek Fire of 2007 burned some parts of this section. As you approach the pass, the forest opens up into a series of meadows. You can pick one of these meadows for your next campsite or, if you're ambitious, go all the way to the pass at 24.5 miles and take a 1.5-mile spur trail (Beaver Lake Trail 147) over to Beaver Lake for your third night out. This side trip to Beaver Lake adds 3 miles to the total distance of this route.

Badger Pass resembles Gateway Pass, a gentle, forested, no-sweat pass that you hardly notice climbing—and close to the same elevation too. At the pass and shortly thereafter, stay alert to make sure you get on North Fork of Birch Creek Trail by going right (south or east) at both junctions—with Beaver Lake Trail 147 at 24.7 miles and with Badger Creek Trail 104 at 24.9 miles. You'll know you're on the right trail when you start the only serious climb of this trip out of Badger Creek over a mildly serious, Category 3 hill (about 600 feet in 1.5 miles), into the North Fork of Birch Creek.

When you reach the top, take a break and look around. To the north you get a panoramic view into the expansive Badger–Two Medicine area, currently proposed for wilderness status but also proposed for extensive oil and gas development. To the south you get a sweeping view of the North Fork of Birch Creek, the boundary line of the Bob Marshall Wilderness. This means all the wild country on the north side of the stream is part of a large undesignated wildland called the Rocky Mountain Front—expansive and stunning, proposed for Wilderness designation, but threatened by energy development.

On the way down the North Fork Trail, stay on campsite alert. Unless you have decided to hike out that day, you'll need to find one about halfway down for your fourth night out. As you watch the stream bottom for a campsite, you'll see the dramatic signs of a major flood that flushed out this area in 1964.

After you drop steeply for about 2 miles from the North Fork/Badger divide (making you happy you didn't do the trip in reverse), the trail settles into a stream-grade easy walk until you reach the road leading to the secondary trailhead on the north side of the reservoir. You probably won't see vehicles on this road as you walk along it for a quarter mile, because most users park in an open area above tiny Haywood Creek and don't drive on this last half mile or so of road before it turns into a singletrack. This section can be confusing, so be alert. You follow the road to the top of a ridge. When you see the road veering off to the left and heading down to Haywood Creek, you go straight on a distinct trail.

Shortly after you leave the jeep road, you drop down and get your feet wet fording the North Fork. Then you climb a short hill over the divide between the North Fork and South Fork, drop down again, and hook up with the trail back to the main trailhead and your vehicle.

Miles and Directions

0.0 Swift Dam Trailhead.

1.0 Junction with Trail 150; turn right.

2.1 Junction with Trail 150; turn right.

3.5 Junction with South Fork Birch Creek Trail 105; turn left.

5.0 Junction with Middle Fork Birch Creek Trail 123; turn left.

7.5 Junction with North Fork Teton Trail 107; turn right.

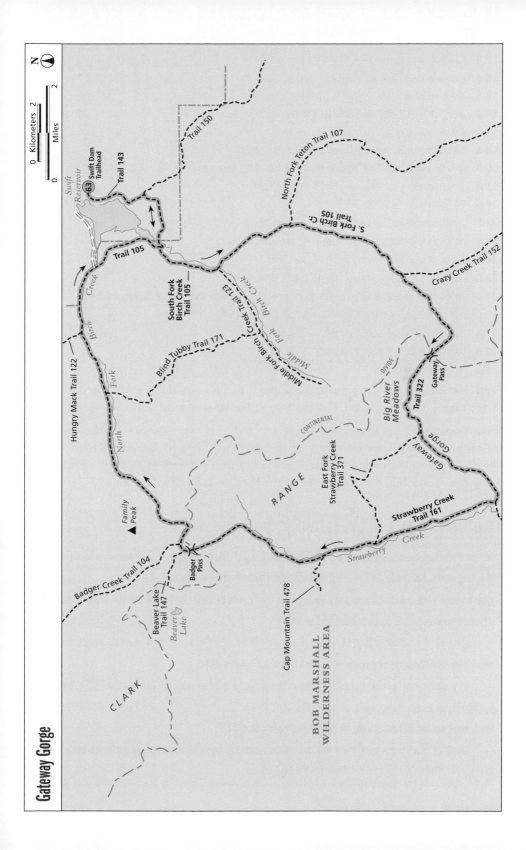

Gateway Gorge

N

0 Kilometers 2

0 Miles 2

Swift Reservoir

(63) Swift Dam Trailhead

Trail 143

Trail 150

Trail 105

Birch Creek

Hungry Mack Trail 122

North Fork

Birch Fork

South Fork Birch Creek Trail 105

Blind Tubby Trail 171

Middle Fork Birch Creek

Middle Fork Birch Creek Trail 122

S. Fork Birch Cr. Trail 105

North Fork Teton Trail 107

Crazy Creek Trail 152

Badger Creek Trail 104

Family Peak

CLARK

Beaver Lake Trail 147

Beaver Lake

Badger Pass

CONTINENTAL

RANGE

East Fork Strawberry Creek Trail 371

DIVIDE

Big River Meadows

Gateway Pass

Trail 322

Gateway Gorge

Cap Mountain Trail 478

Strawberry Creek Trail 161

Strawberry Creek

BOB MARSHALL WILDERNESS AREA

12.9	Junction with Crazy Creek Trail 152; turn right.
14.5	Gateway Pass; Trail 105 becomes Trail 322.
15.5	Big River Meadows.
16.6	Junction with East Fork Strawberry Creek Trail 371; turn left.
17.5	Gateway Gorge.
19.5	Junction with Strawberry Creek Trail 161; turn right.
20.0	Junction with East Fork Strawberry Creek Trail 371; turn left.
21.5	Junction with Cap Mountain Trail 478; turn right.
24.5	Badger Pass.
24.7	Junction with Beaver Lake Trail 147; turn right.
24.9	Junction with Badger Creek Trail 104; turn right.
30.5	Junction with Blind Tubby Trail 171; turn left.
32.0	Junction with Hungry Mack Trail 122; turn right.
34.0	Jeep road (Trail 121 on map) on north side of Swift Reservoir and secondary trailhead.
36.0	Junction with South Fork Birch Creek Trail 143; turn left.
37.4	Junction with Trail 150; turn left.
38.5	Junction with Trail 150; turn left.
39.5	Swift Dam Trailhead.

Options: You can do this route in reverse, but the climb over the North Fork/Badger divide makes it more difficult. The climbs over the passes would still be no sweat.

Side Trips: You can always find a side trip, but this route doesn't include many logical choices, with the exception of the short trip over to Beaver Lake. If you like mountaintops, try Family Peak from the top of the North Fork/Badger divide. (Originally contributed by Elaine and Art Sedlack, re-hiked by the authors.)

THE VIEW FROM HERE: FLIPPING ROCKS

When I worked on the trail crew in Glacier National Park long ago, I developed a habit of flipping rocks off trails as I walked down them. I didn't stop or change stride, but would just give a loose rock a little flip as I walked by. The trail crew did that to help keep the trails clear without wasting time by breaking stride.

Long after I left that job, I kept on flipping rocks every time I hiked. I started wondering what some of these rocky trails would be like if all hikers did it.

As a conservative estimate, I flip about three rocks off the trail for every mile I hike, and I probably average about 200 miles of hiking every summer and have since I started in 1965. Well, that's a lot of rocks—about 20,000 of them, in fact!

Think of what we'd have if we multiplied my numbers by millions of people who go hiking every year. Those rocky trails? Well, they'd be history.

64 Our Lake

A day hike or overnighter to a pristine mountain lake with good fishing and mountain goats inhabiting the slopes above the lake

Start: Headquarters Pass Trailhead, 30 miles west of Choteau
Distance: 5.0-mile out-and-back

Difficulty: Moderate
Maps: USGS Our Lake; Bob Marshall Wilderness Complex Map

Finding the trailhead: Drive 4.4 miles north of Choteau on US 89 and turn west on Teton River Road 144. Follow this paved road for about 16.5 miles until you see the sign for Ear Mountain Ranger Station or South Fork of the Teton River. Here turn left (south) on FR 109. After less than a half mile, you cross the Teton River and turn right (west) at a junction just after the one-lane bridge. Follow this road for 4 miles, turn right at another junction, and follow that road for 6 miles until it ends. You're on FR 109 all the way. Trails 184 to Our Lake and 165 to Headquarters Pass begin where the road ends. The large trailhead is set up for horse trailers and has lots of parking and a toilet. GPS: N47 50.800' / W112 46.933'

The Hike

This is a popular hike on a well-maintained trail with outstanding scenery, good fishing, and excellent opportunities to view wildlife.

When I last hiked this route, Our Lake wasn't on the trailhead signs, but that might have been fixed. In any case, take Trail 165 toward Headquarters Pass. About a half mile up the trail, take the right (north) fork onto Trail 184 to Our Lake, even though it might not be indicated on the sign. There's a big interpretive display about a quarter mile up the trail that tells the story of Our Lake, one of the few alpine lakes on the Rocky Mountain Front. Just below the lake, you pass by a fantastic waterfall.

It's only 2.5 miles to Our Lake. The trail climbs 1,500 feet to the lake (Category 2 hill), and the last half mile or so switchbacks up a steep slope that can be hazardous if tried before the snowbanks give it up, so wait until July or August for this hike.

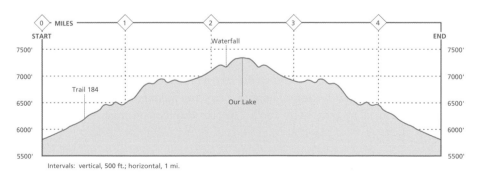

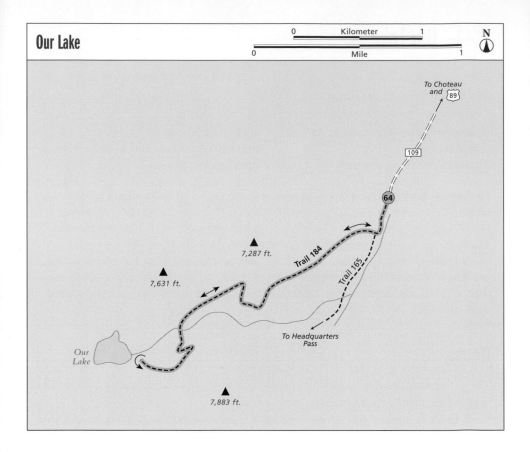

There is a good source of water at about the 2-mile mark, but the rest of the trail is dry, especially in late August and September.

Bears are common in the area, and you can usually spot mountain goats on the alpine slopes behind Our Lake. If you're lucky, you may also see bighorn sheep near Rocky Mountain, the highest peak in the Bob Marshall Wilderness (9,392 feet). In addition, expect to see marmots and pikas. Asters, daisies, and lupine seem to prevail among the abundant supply of wildflowers along this trail. Skunkflower is common on the alpine slopes above the lake.

In 1988 the Gates Creek Fire partially burned the basin, but spared the area around the lake. Since access is easy, the lake is heavily used, so the Forest Service prohibits camping within 1,000 feet of the lake to reduce impact.

Even though the fish see lots of lures and flies, the fishing remains good. Ten-inch rainbow trout make up most of the catch. The lake also has cutthroat trout, but they're harder to catch.

Miles and Directions

0.0 Headquarters Pass Trailhead.

0.2 Interpretive display.

0.5 Junction with Trail 184; turn right.

2.2 Waterfall.

2.5 Our Lake.

5.0 Headquarters Pass Trailhead.

Side Trips: For moderately experienced hikers, there's a good side trip to the saddle west of the lake above the basin. From this saddle, you can see the Chinese Wall, the backbone of the Bob Marshall Wilderness. The distance to the saddle is about a mile. This spectacular mountain country is part of the Teton Geographic Unit and is designated as roadless. (Originally contributed by Dave Orndoff, re-hiked by the authors.)

65 Mount Wright

A strenuous climb to one of the best mountaintop views of the northern Bob Marshall Wilderness Complex

Start: Mount Wright Trailhead, 30 miles west of Choteau

Distance: 6.0-mile out-and-back

Difficulty: Strenuous

Maps: USGS Wright; Bob Marshall Wilderness Complex Map

Finding the trailhead: Drive 4.4 miles north of Choteau on US 89 and take paved Teton River Road 144 west into the Rocky Mountain Front for 16.7 miles to the junction with South Fork of Teton River Road. Go straight on North Fork of Teton River Road (FR 144) and drive 18 more miles, past the Cave Mountain Campground and turnoff to the Teton Pass Ski Area, to the West Fork Ranger Station. Just before the bridge crossing the North Fork of the Teton River and after the bridge crossing the West Fork of the Teton River going toward the campground and ranger station, a small sign on your left points to Mount Wright Trailhead. Limited parking at the trailhead, but extra parking, vehicle camping, and toilet at nearby West Fork Teton Campground. GPS: N47 57.750' / W112 48.466'

The Hike

For those in good physical shape, the trail to the 8,855-foot summit of Mount Wright is the perfect hike to catch the views that stretch across the famous Rocky Mountain Front stretching from Glacier National Park to the Scapegoat Wilderness. For many years, there was a lookout on Mount Wright, but it's gone now. Instead, you'll find a small building housing radio repeater equipment.

At the trailhead the sign says West Fork Teton Trail 114, not Mount Wright, but this is the right trail. It starts out on a jeep road, but after only about a quarter mile, you reach a trail junction. Turn right (northwest) here onto Mount Wright Trail 160.

After the junction, you go through an old clear-cut on an old logging road. In 2007 the Fool Creek Fire burned much of this area, including the first part of the

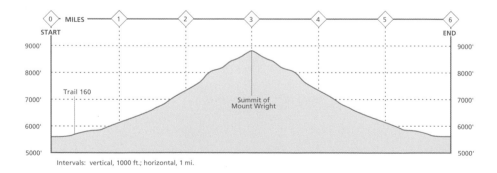

Intervals: vertical, 1000 ft.; horizontal, 1 mi.

From the summit of Mount Wright, the grandeur of the mighty Bob Marshall Wilderness unfolds before you. JACQUELYN CORDAY

Mount Wright Trail, but it's still a beautiful trip, with the forest reclaiming nicely and the carpet of fireweed adding color to the landscape.

The route through the clear-cut is well marked with cairns and directional signs. After about a half mile, the trail leaves the clear-cut and enters an uncut forest and starts switchbacking up the mountain, with the last half of the trip above timberline. The trail goes to a singletrack and is easy to follow, except in a few meadows where it fades away and is marked by cairns. Two miles from the trailhead, you reach a small pass to the east of the main summit. The trail continues over the pass to a low saddle on the north-south ridge ahead. Once on the ridge, it's a short climb to the summit.

The view from the summit rivals any in the Northern Rockies. Directly north is the knife-edged top of Mount Patrick Gass, named after a lieutenant in the Lewis and Clark Expedition. To the east is the thin, steep ridge of Choteau Mountain and the endless expanse of the northern Great Plains. You can pick out Mount Saint Nicholas

A wildflower landscape on the way to the summit of Mount Wright. JACQUELYN CORDAY

in Glacier Park, the long limestone cliffs of the northern Chinese Wall, and the large hulks of Old Baldy and Rocky Mountain Peak to the south. Literally hundreds of other peaks stretch across the horizon on a clear day, which is what you need to take this hike.

While ascending the southeastern slope, watch for mountain goats as the trail breaks out of the sparse tree cover. Also watch the weather closely. You don't want to be up on these windswept slopes in a thunderstorm, a good reason to start early in the morning.

The descent from the summit should take you less than two hours, while the ascent can stretch as long as four or five hours. The 3,500-foot elevation gain (a Category H climb) may deter families with young children, but the trail doesn't require any mountain climbing experience, just strong lungs and legs.

The route is totally waterless, so take an extra bottle. You can try this hike early in the season (late June or early July) and usually find a few tired snowfields still around

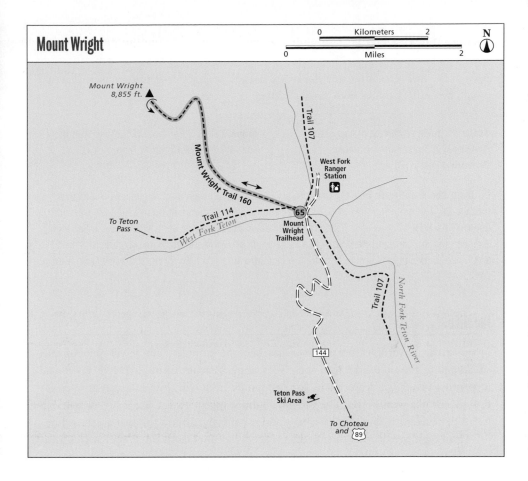

Mount Wright

0 — Kilometers — 2

0 — Miles — 2

N

Mount Wright
8,855 ft.

Trail 107

West Fork
Ranger
Station

Mount Wright Trail 160

To Teton
Pass

Trail 114

65

Mount
Wright
Trailhead

West Fork Teton

Trail 107

North Fork Teton River

144

Teton Pass
Ski Area

To Choteau
and 89

to slake your thirst near the summit. The exposed, south-facing slopes can make for a real scorcher in in August. (Originally contributed by Ed Madej and Rosemary Rowe, re-hiked by the authors.)

Miles and Directions

0.0   Mount Wright Trailhead.

0.3   Junction with Trail 160; turn right.

3.0   Summit of Mount Wright.

6.0   Mount Wright Trailhead.

66 Devils Glen

A day hike or overnighter to a gorgeous cascade on a super-scenic untamed river, a good choice for families with small children

Start: 15 miles southwest of Augusta
Distance: 7.0-mile out-and-back
Difficulty: Easy

Maps: USGS Steamboat Mountain; Bob Marshall Wilderness Complex Map

Finding the trailhead: Take Elk Creek Road 12 miles southwest from Augusta to Bean Lake (or take CR 434 north from MT 200, 27 miles southwest of Simms). At Bean Lake take Dearborn Canyon Road (FR 577) westward into the mountains until it ends at the trailhead 5.7 miles later, 2 miles past the Diamond Bar X Ranch. A large trailhead with separate parking areas for hikers and horse parties (hikers on the left; don't park in the area reserved for horse trailers) and a toilet. GPS: N47 15.866' / W112 31.9'

The Hike

Floating the lower Dearborn River has become popular, but fewer people take advantage of the nice hike into the river's upper reaches through Devils Glen—an interesting geological feature and an ideal family hike with low mileage, little elevation gain, and a scenic river. The canyon all the way to Devils Glen is spectacular, but it can be dangerous until high water subsides typically around the first week of June.

The Forest Service has obtained legal access to the Devils Glen Trail at this location. At the request of the private landowners, the Forest Service is advising hikers to stay on the trail until they reach the national forest boundary, which is well marked at 1.8 miles. The trail is closed to motor vehicles.

About a mile from the trailhead, Trail 206 crosses the Dearborn River on a sturdy bridge. A few years back, the Forest Service rerouted and reconstructed much of the

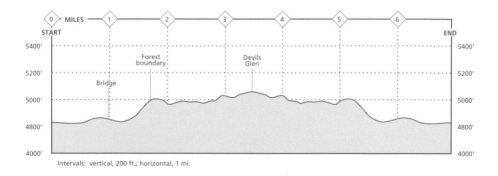

Viewing Devil's Glen from the trail. LAURA SCHNEIDER

trail from the bridge through Devils Glen. Beyond the bridge the trail stays on the north side of the river.

After about 3 miles, the trail begins to climb onto a rock pile coming off the southern slopes of Steamboat Mountain where the river has gouged out a stunning canyon called Devils Glen. In addition to frothing, cascading water, Devils Glen features a stunning display of wildflowers and a beautiful, moss-covered creek bottom, a carpet of green with crystal-clear water slicing through the center.

You'll see a trail veering off to the left, heading down to the canyon. Take it and enjoy a pleasant break at Devils Glen (or stay overnight) before heading back to the trailhead.

You can continue up the river for miles into the Scapegoat Wilderness, all scenic and worth the effort, and you can camp anywhere along the river at or beyond Devils Glen. On busy weekends, you might want to ford the stream and camp on the southern side in the trees or continue past Devils Glen for a mile or two more.

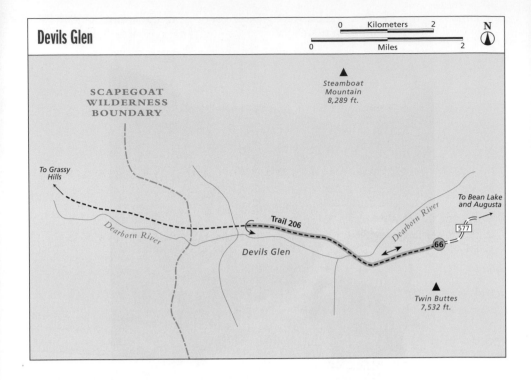

Devils Glen

Kilometers 0 — 2
Miles 0 — 2

N

SCAPEGOAT
WILDERNESS
BOUNDARY

Steamboat
Mountain
8,289 ft.

To Grassy
Hills

Dearborn River

Trail 206

Devils Glen

Dearborn River

To Bean Lake
and Augusta

577

66

Twin Buttes
7,532 ft.

This entire area is a recommended addition to the Scapegoat Wilderness, which starts about a half mile up the trail from Devils Glen. If enough people visiting the area talk to a member of Congress about it, perhaps it might be protected as it should be.

Miles and Directions

0.0 Trailhead.

1.0 Bridge over Dearborn River.

1.8 National forest boundary.

3.5 Devils Glen.

7.0 Trailhead.

Side Trips: If you're bored with fishing and river music, you can bushwhack north up the rocky slopes to the summit of Steamboat Mountain, which offers stunning views of the Rocky Mountain Front and the Great Plains. (Originally contributed by Ed Madej and Rosemary Rowe, re-hiked by the authors.)

67 Castle Mountains

A day hike through the heart of the little-visited Castle Mountains

Start: Grasshopper Campground Trailhead, 10 miles east of White Sulphur Springs
Distance: 10.0-mile out-and-back

Difficulty: Moderate
Maps: USGS Fourmile Springs and Manager Park; Lewis and Clark National Forest Map

Finding the trailhead: Drive northeast of White Sulphur Springs on US 89 for 3 miles, then turn right (east) onto US 12, go 4 more miles, and turn right (south) onto Fourmile Creek Road (FR 211) to Grasshopper Campground. Richardson Campground is about a mile farther down the road. Grasshopper and Richardson Campgrounds are great places to vehicle camp. Both offer quiet settings next to clear mountain streams, lush meadows, and dense forests—plus toilets, ample parking, and water at Grasshopper Campground. GPS: N46 32.666' / W110 44.866'

The Hike

Just east of White Sulphur Springs, there is a place where coyotes hunt and elk roam as they have for ages, but not many hikers venture. Here lie the Castle Mountains, a gentle, lodgepole-covered, island mountain range.

The trail leaves from the south end of Grasshopper Campground through a gate, which prevents the cattle intermingling with campers. The trail follows the East Fork of Grasshopper Creek for less than a mile before turning east and up the slope, passing through groves of trees and silent meadows. This hike is best early in the morning, when the sun has a chance to shine through beads of dew. At 1 mile the trail opens into Richardson Park, which is a meadow skirted with aspen. At 1.2 miles the trail intersects Elk Peak Trail 717 from Richardson Campground, where you turn right (south).

After walking through the trees for a short distance, the trail forks at 1.7 miles. Take the left fork (south), which is still Elk Peak Trail 717. (Trail 723 goes to the right.) Elk

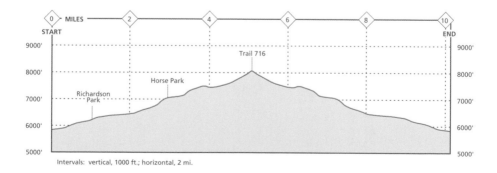

Intervals: vertical, 1000 ft.; horizontal, 2 mi.

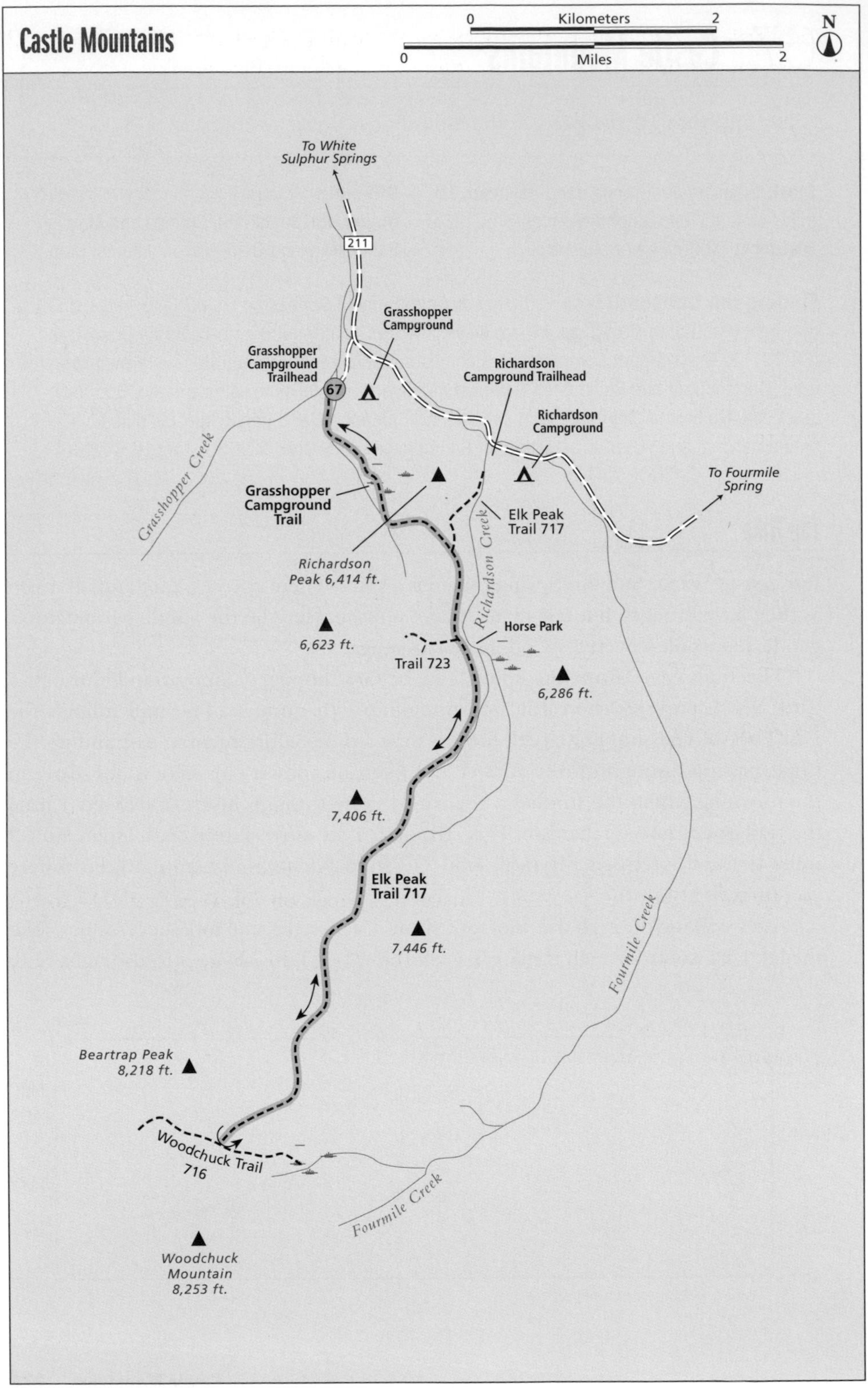

Castle Mountains

0   Kilometers   2

0   Miles   2

N

To White Sulphur Springs

211

Grasshopper Campground

Grasshopper Campground Trailhead

Richardson Campground Trailhead

Richardson Campground

67

Grasshopper Creek

Grasshopper Campground Trail

To Fourmile Spring

Richardson Creek

Elk Peak Trail 717

Richardson Peak 6,414 ft.

▲ 6,623 ft.

Horse Park

Trail 723

▲ 6,286 ft.

▲ 7,406 ft.

Elk Peak Trail 717

▲ 7,446 ft.

Fourmile Creek

Beartrap Peak 8,218 ft. ▲

Woodchuck Trail 716

Fourmile Creek

▲ *Woodchuck Mountain 8,253 ft.*

Peak Trail 717 descends quickly, following Richardson Creek into Horse Park miles. Horse Park is a series of beautiful mountain meadows studded with wil along the creek. The trail stays on the western side of Richardson Creek across Ho Park and fades away in places. Watch for blazes south across the meadows.

After Horse Park the signs of grazing disappear. Walk softly through the quiet forest and look for wildlife. This isn't bear country, so silence is acceptable. The trail climbs steadily, crossing several streams and meadows. The climb lasts between 2 and 3 miles. Bring water. This area dries out fast in late summer.

Once the trail flattens out, you're just east of Beartrap Peak. You might not even know it, because the mountain is just a continuation of the slopes above the trail. Curving around the mountain, the trail intersects Woodchuck Trail 716. From here retrace your steps to the trailhead.

This hike is dry in May. It's good physical conditioning and a great route for trail runners.

Miles and Directions

- **0.0** Grasshopper Campground Trailhead.
- **1.0** Richardson Park.
- **1.2** Junction with Elk Peak Trail 717; turn right.
- **1.7** Junction with Trail 723; turn left.
- **2.2** Horse Park.
- **5.0** Junction with Woodchuck Trail 716.
- **10.0** Grasshopper Campground Trailhead.

Options: On the way back, you can drop down to Richardson Campground and then walk a mile on the road back to your vehicle, which is about the same total distance, but you can see some new country.

You can also start from Richardson Campground, which makes the route a mile shorter but slightly steeper. Cross Richardson Creek on Elk Peak Trail 717 to the west shore, walk through a meadow turning south, and begin ascending the ridge. This 0.5-mile ascent is steep. At the top of the hill, the trail intersects the Grasshopper Campground Trail.

It's also possible to make a loop using Woodchuck Trail 716. Check your map. (Originally contributed and re-hiked by the authors.)

8 Sand Point

A backpacking loop through a large and little-used roadless area with major streams and 1,000-foot limestone cliffs

Start: 100 miles southeast of Great Falls in the Little Belt Mountains

Distance: 27.0-mile lollipop loop

Difficulty: Strenuous

Maps: USGS Sand Point and Ettien Springs; Lewis and Clark National Forest Map

Finding the trailhead: Take US 12 east from White Sulphur Springs for 20 miles until you reach the small town of Checkerboard. Go 6 miles east of Checkerboard and turn left (north) onto FR 274 to the Whitetail Guard Station—paved for the first 2 miles and then turning into an excellent gravel road. Go past the guard station and stay on FR 274 for 18.4 miles until you intersect FR 487. Turn left (north) here and follow FR 487 for 2.3 miles and then turn left again onto FR 821. Stay on FR 821 for about a half mile until you reach Holiday Camp Trailhead.

The actual trailhead is slightly difficult to find. You can start hiking right from Holiday Camp on a jeep road. When we were there, a sign indicated that a road leaving the north end of Holiday Camp was Trail 433, but in a few feet, the road forked with no sign. Start walking on the left-hand fork of the road, or you can also drive this road (if you have a high-clearance vehicle) for 1 mile to the actual trailhead, where there is very limited parking and no facilities, but there is a sign for Trail 433 to Burris Cabin.

The Holiday Camp Trailhead can also be reached via FR 487 from Utica on the north side of the Little Belt Mountains. The trailhead features a large parking area with toilet. GPS: N46 45.133' / W110 35.249'

The Hike

Of all the large roadless areas in Montana, the Middle Fork of the Judith River may be the least known to hikers, not because it doesn't offer good hiking, because it does. The 81,000-acre de facto wilderness has great stream fishing, a large wildlife population, and vistas to rival any wild area.

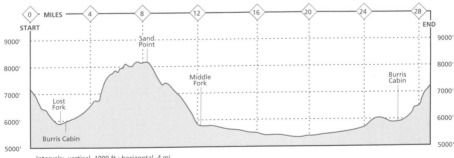

Intervals: vertical, 1000 ft.; horizontal, 4 mi.

Elk can be seen on many Montana hikes. SHUTTERSTOCK

It's uphill from Holiday Camp to the actual trailhead, but from here you lose elevation rapidly for 2 miles from the top of the ridge to the Lost Fork of the Judith River and to Burris Cabin, an abandoned homestead. Hikers, horses, and motorcycles heavily use this section of trail, which has been reconstructed with the addition of several new switchbacks (and probably about a half mile to the total distance).

If you started late in the day, you might want to camp along the Lost Fork above Burris Cabin. There are plenty of good sites, complete with firewood and a beautiful stream with native cutthroat plus a few rainbows and brookies. You can see the aftermath of the Sand Point Fire, which burned more than 11,300 acres in July 1985. You can also see that the beavers have been busy in this area, damming up the still-small river in several places.

At Burris Cabin the trail intersects with Lost Fork Trail 409, which follows the length of the Lost Fork. Turn left (west) and follow Trail 409 up the Lost Fork for about 2.5 miles until you reach Trail 422. Turn right (north) here and start a 4-mile uphill stretch to Sand Point, an 8,211-foot knob on the divide separating the Lost Fork and Middle Fork drainages.

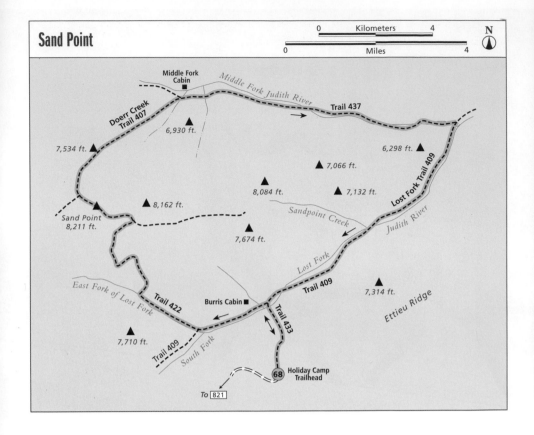

Middle Fork
Cabin

Middle Fork Judith River

Trail 437

Doerr Creek
Trail 407

6,930 ft.

7,534 ft.

6,298 ft.

Lost Fork Trail 409

7,066 ft.

8,084 ft.

7,132 ft.

8,162 ft.

Sandpoint Creek

Sand Point
8,211 ft.

Judith River

7,674 ft.

Lost Fork

East Fork of Lost Fork

Trail 422

Trail 409

7,314 ft.

Burris Cabin

Trail 433

Ettieu Ridge

7,710 ft.

Trail 409

South Fork

68 Holiday Camp
Trailhead

To 821

This part of the trip offers an opportunity to study the natural effects of fire on forested plant communities. Close examination reveals newly established lodgepole pine seedlings that launched from seeds released from storage in thousands of serotinous cones. Abundant forage stimulated by fire feeds wildlife, and beaver dams add stability to the riparian system by storing sediment.

After relishing the view from the top of Sand Point for a few minutes, go northwest for about a half mile to a trail junction. Take a right (northeast) here and head downhill on Doerr Creek Trail 407 about 3 miles to the Middle Fork of the Judith River.

You come out onto the bottomland at the Middle Fork Cabin. Don't camp on this private land. Take a right on Trail 437 and head downstream, selecting one of many good campsites along the Middle Fork.

Like the Lost Fork, the Middle Fork offers excellent small stream fishing and scenery, especially towering limestone cliffs. From the Middle Fork Cabin, you actually walk on a lightly traveled jeep road for about 6 miles downstream until you reach the point where the Lost Fork joins the Middle Fork. At the trail junction, take a right (southwest) back onto Lost Fork Trail 409 and follow the Lost Fork about 7 miles upstream to the Burris Cabin, where you must retrace your steps 2 miles uphill to your vehicle at the Holiday Camp Trailhead.

All told, this is a 28-mile loop that introduces you to the drainage of the Middle Fork of the Judith River. The Forest Service, in the Lewis and Clark National Forest Plan, has allocated most of the area for "semi-primitive recreation," which is a start, but Wilderness designation would be much better to truly protect this special place. (Originally contributed by Bill Cunningham, re-hiked by the authors.)

Miles and Directions

0.0 Holiday Camp Trailhead.

2.0 Burris Cabin and junction with Lost Fork Trail 409; turn left.

4.5 Junction with Trail 422; turn right.

8.5 Sand Point.

9.0 Junction with Doerr Creek Trail 407; turn right.

12.0 Middle Fork Cabin and junction with Trail 437; turn right.

18.0 Junction with Lost Fork Trail 409; turn right.

25.0 Burris Cabin and junction with Trail 433; turn left.

27.0 Holiday Camp Trailhead.

69 Big Snowies Crest

A nice, but difficult, loop through an eastern Montana island range with an ice cave and unrestricted views as far as you can see, all the way from the Missouri River Breaks to the Beartooth Plateau

Start: 20 miles south of Lewistown
Distance: 12.3-mile loop (including side trip to ice cave)
Difficulty: Strenuous

Maps: USGS Crystal Lake, Jump Off Peak, and Half Moon Canyon; Lewis and Clark National Forest Map

Finding the trailhead: Turn south from US 87/MT 200 onto Crystal Lake Road 275 about 8 miles west of Lewistown (or 5 miles east of Moore). Drive about 22 miles on Crystal Lake Road to Crystal Lake, the first 5.5 miles paved and the rest excellent gravel. There are several junctions, all well signed. The trailhead for Uhlhorn Trail 493 is at the south end of the lake just past the entrance to the campground. A large trailhead with plenty of parking, vehicle camping, toilet, and drinking water at Crystal Lake Campground. GPS: N46 47.733' / W109 30.750'

The Hike

Anybody who thinks there aren't any great hikes in eastern Montana hasn't hiked this route, now designated as the Crystal Lake Loop National Recreation Trail. The entire trailhead and campground are as clean, well developed, and well signed as any area in this book. It really couldn't be any better than this.

The Big Snowies consist of one massive, broad-based ridge flanked by cirques and streams. Up on the crest, the main ridge runs for 12 miles from east to west and ranges from 8,500 to 8,700 feet in elevation.

From the trailhead, go south on Uhlhorn Trail 493. This trail, named after long-time district ranger and Lewistown community leader Carl Uhlhorn, climbs more than 2,000 feet in 3 miles to the crest of the Big Snowies. At this point, the hiking

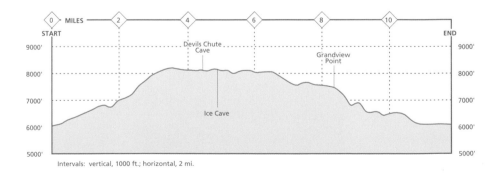

Intervals: vertical, 1000 ft.; horizontal, 2 mi.

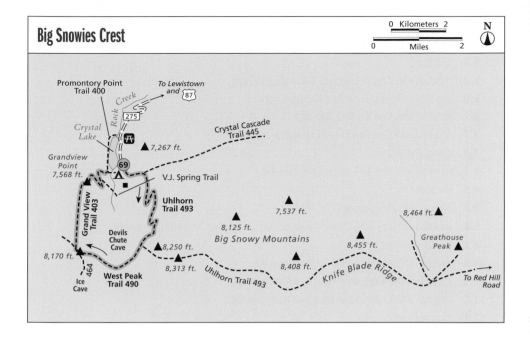

Big Snowies Crest

0 Kilometers 2

0 Miles 2

N

Promontory Point
Trail 400

To Lewistown
and 87

Crystal
Lake

Rock Creek

275

Crystal Cascade
Trail 445

▲ 7,267 ft.

Grandview
Point
7,568 ft.

69

V.J. Spring Trail

Uhlhorn
Trail 493

▲
7,537 ft.

▲ 8,464 ft.

Grand View Trail 403

Devils
Chute
Cave

▲
8,125 ft.

Big Snowy Mountains

▲
8,455 ft.

Greathouse
Peak ▲

8,170 ft. ▲

464

Ice
Cave

West Peak
Trail 490

▲ 8,250 ft.

▲ 8,313 ft.

Uhlhorn Trail 493

▲ 8,408 ft.

Knife Blade Ridge

To Red Hill
Road

becomes a stroll across level prairie-style tundra interspersed with mangled thickets of trees.

At the top, the Uhlhorn Trail becomes West Peak Trail 490 and Trail 493 goes off to the left on the ridge toward Greathouse Peak. Turn right (east) onto Trail 490, which goes toward the ice cave. You come to two more junctions along the way, but both are less distinct than the main trail, so stay to the right on the main route, which is marked by cairns in some cases.

At 4 miles you'll see Devils Chute Cave along the trail on your right. Then about a quarter mile later, take the short round-trip (about a half-mile) down and back on Trail 464 to see the ice cave, an incredible sight you'd never expect to see in this environment. Trust me—you'll be surprised. Please be very careful not to despoil it for others who'll follow you. A flashlight is useful but not necessary.

Once back on the crest trail, turn left (east) and head for Grandview Point. At 5.8 miles, at the junction with Dry Pole Creek Trail, West Peak Trail 490 becomes Grand View Trail 403 and goes down a super-scenic ridgeline marked by cairns and lined with whitebark pines. You can see forever out into the prairie in all directions.

At Grandview Point you get a stunning view of Crystal Lake below. From here the trail (called the Jack Milburn Trail) drops sharply down to the campground, going by several junctions. Follow the map and the turns indicated in the Miles and Directions to stay on the main route.

There's essentially no water on this route, so carry plenty.

Miles and Directions

0.0 Trailhead.

1.3 Junction with Crystal Cascade Trail 445; turn right.

3.0 Junction with West Peak Trail 490; turn right.

3.2 Junction with Red Hill Trail; turn right.

3.7 Junction with East Fork Blake Creek Trail; turn right.

4.0 Devils Chute Cave.

4.2 Junction with Trail 464 to ice cave; turn left.

4.5 Ice cave.

4.8 Back to Trail 490; turn left.

5.8 Junction with Dry Pole Creek Trail (becomes Grand View Trail 403); turn right.

8.1 Grandview Point.

10.4 Junction with spur trail to V.J. Spring; turn left.

11.1 Junction with Promontory Point Trail 400; turn right.

11.6 Junction with Crystal Lake Loop Trail 404; turn right.

12.1 Campground.

12.3 Trailhead.

Options: For the extra ambitious who want a very long day (or for trail runners), try to make it to Greathouse Peak on Trail 493. Greathouse Peak is the highest point of the Big Snowies at 8,681 feet. The route to Greathouse Peak holds one surprise after another. The trail crosses large expanses of alpine grasses that give incredible visual harmony to the endless prairies off to either side, 4,000 feet below. Then there is a stretch called Knife Blade Ridge, where the mile-wide crest narrows to a few feet and drops off abruptly on either side. In the center of Knife Blade Ridge, the trail dips into a primitive little pass where you'll find a four-way trail junction. Stay on the obvious ridge trail to reach the top of Greathouse Peak. From here, retrace your route back to Crystal Lake. (Originally contributed by Pat Caffrey, re-hiked by the authors.)

Helena National Forest

70 Heart Lake

An easily accessible lake for family fun in the southern tip of the Bob Marshall Wilderness

Start: Indian Meadows Trailhead, 62 miles northwest of Helena, near Lincoln
Distance: 8.2-mile out-and-back

Difficulty: Moderate
Maps: USGS Heart Lake, Stonewall, and Silver King; Helena National Forest Map

Finding the trailhead: Turn onto Copper Creek Road 330, 5.3 miles east of Lincoln or 4.7 miles west of the junction of MT 200 and Highway 279. Drive north on Copper Creek Road for 7.8 miles, taking a left when it splits with Landers Fork Road, and turn right onto FR 1882 at a well-signed turn for Indian Meadows Trailhead. After a total of 9.3 miles, you reach Indian Meadows Trailhead. Only the first 3.6 miles are paved, and if you see Snowbank Lake, you missed the turn to the trailhead. The trailhead has a pit toilet and a large parking area with separate facilities for hikers and recreational horse packers and outfitters. The signage at the trailhead could be better; Trail 481 starts just before you reach the hikers parking area. GPS: N47 05.369' / W112 38.546'

The Hike

It's 4.1 miles to Heart Lake, 6.7 miles to Webb Lake, and about 9 miles to Parker Lake. And you can take a trail to the right just before Parker Lake to Two Point Lake. But Heart Lake is the nicest of the bunch. Webb Lake is small and shallow. Parker Lake is very scenic, but also shallow compared to Heart Lake. Two Point is away from the trail and surrounded by forest, more so than the rest of the lakes. It's hard to fly fish at all of these lakes—no place for the backcast.

Trail 481 gets a lot of horse traffic. The trail is wide and easy to walk in most places, as long as you don't try it in the spring before it dries up or time your trip right after a few days of rain. Fortunately, this well-maintained trail features many bridges over marshy areas.

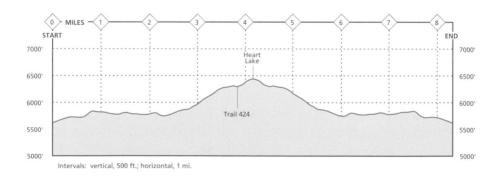

Intervals: vertical, 500 ft.; horizontal, 1 mi.

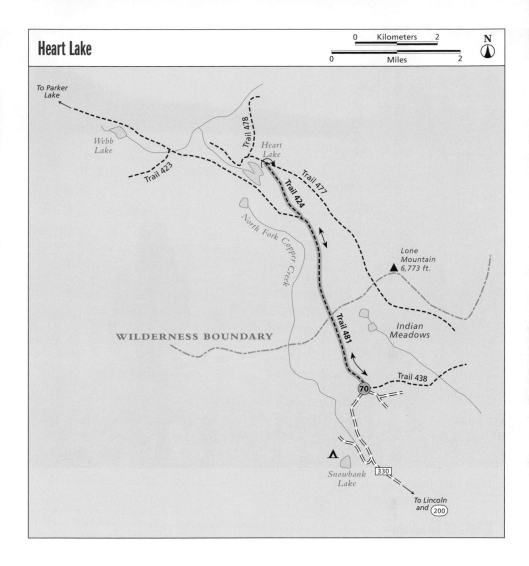

Actually, Trail 481 doesn't go directly to Heart Lake. At about the 3.1-mile mark, Trail 424 veers off to the right to the lake.

Heart Lake and Parker Lake are heavily used, so special regulations are in effect for horse use and camping at both lakes: no horses near the shoreline, and no camping on peninsulas in the lakes. Camping restrictions on the peninsulas not only reduce damage from camping, but also leave these beautiful areas open to everybody. If somebody camped there, which would be common, they would essentially be keeping everybody else out.

In 2002 a forest fire burned large sections of Trail 481 between the trailhead and the junction with Trail 424, but not around the lake. (Originally contributed and re-hiked by the authors.)

Heart Lake. Bill Schneider

Miles and Directions

0.0 Trailhead.

3.1 Junction with Trail 424 to Heart Lake; turn right.

4.1 Heart Lake.

8.2 Trailhead.

71 Bear Prairie

A long day hike or overnighter into the heart of the Gates of the Mountains Wilderness

Location: Refrigerator Canyon Trailhead, 20 miles northeast of Helena
Distance: 16.6-mile out-and-back
Difficulty: Strenuous

Maps: USGS Upper Holter Lake, Candle Mountain, and Hogback; Helena National Forest Map

Finding the trailhead: Drive northeast from Helena on Highway 280 for about 15 miles until you cross the Missouri River via the York Bridge. Then drive for about 4 miles to the tiny community of York. Turn left (north) at the York Bar and follow the well-maintained gravel road until it intersects with another gravel road at the small town of Nelson. Turn right (east) onto Beaver Creek Road and drive for about 5 miles until you see the well-marked trailhead for Refrigerator Canyon. The last 5 miles on Beaver Creek Road can be dangerous because of sharp, blind corners and large trucks. So if you are driving, do not be caught gawking at the scenery. Let the passengers take in the steep-walled Beaver Creek Canyon with its whitish limestone cliffs and beautiful stream. Limited parking; no toilet; no camping. GPS: N46 50.929' / W111 44.248'

The Hike

The 28,560-acre Gates of the Mountains Wilderness has open parks, deep canyons, and craggy peaks, but no lakes. More than compensating for this void, however, is the area's rich history.

From the Refrigerator Canyon Trailhead, Trail 259 gradually climbs about a quarter mile to Refrigerator Canyon. Even on the hottest summer day, it's cool in this extremely steep, narrow canyon, which is, of course, why the Lewis and Clark Expedition used it to store meat to delay spoiling.

After Refrigerator Canyon the trail gradually switchbacks for about 3 miles up to the junction with Trail 260. Trail 260 continues on to the right toward Willow Creek. Stay left (west) on Trail 259, which leads to Bear Prairie.

About 5 miles later, you reach the wildflower-carpeted Bear Prairie, one of the largest and most gorgeous mountain meadows in the Helena area. Through Bear Prairie the trail is level and well maintained.

After June the entire route is devoid of water with the exception of Refrigerator Canyon and a short section of Meriwether Creek at the head of the canyon. If you're staying overnight at Bear Prairie, carry enough water for a dry camp. On the plus side, the dry climate holds down the mosquitoes. The snow usually melts early in the year, even as early as late April in dry years. This is one of the few Montana hikes you can safely do in May and early June.

Hiking through Refrigerator Canyon on the way to Bear Prairie. BILL SCHNEIDER

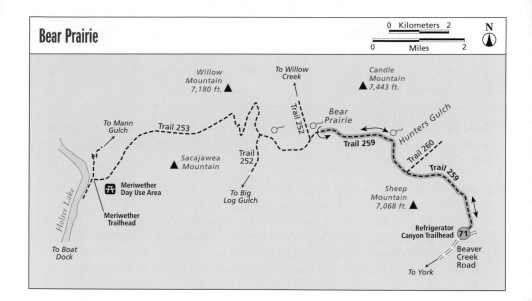

Bear Prairie

Miles and Directions

0.0 Refrigerator Canyon Trailhead.

0.3 Refrigerator Canyon.

3.5 Junction with Willow Creek Trail 260; turn left.

8.3 Bear Prairie.

16.6 Refrigerator Canyon Trailhead.

Options: Before 2007, you could continue through Bear Prairie and hike down 5 miles to the Meriwether Day Use Area on Holter Reservoir near the famous Gates of the Mountains formation. However, a major forest fire that year destroyed that section of trail. The Forest Service plans to rebuild it, so you might want to check to see if that has been done yet before taking this hike. If it has been reconstructed, you can make a nice, but logistically difficult, shuttle hike out of this route. (Originally contributed and re-hiked by the authors.)

72 Mann Gulch

A scenic and historical hike near the Gates of the Mountains Wilderness to the site of a tragic forest fire accident

Start: 20 miles north of Helenar
Distance: 6.0-mile out-and-back
Difficulty: Moderate

Maps: USGS Upper Holter Lake and Beartooth Mountain; Helena National Forest Map

Finding the trailhead: To get to the new trail to Mann Gulch, go to the famed Silver Bridge, 4 miles north of Wolf Creek, where Craig Frontage Road (also called Recreation Road) crosses the Missouri River. Turn southeast onto Beartooth Road, past Holter Lake Recreation Area, for 8.6 miles to the gate of the Beartooth Wildlife Management Area, the last 3.2 miles of this section on a good gravel road. From here, you'll need a high-clearance, four-wheel-drive vehicle, as the road worsens and gets rutted with a few steep pitches and a drive through Cottonwood Creek. In another 3.1 miles, turn left onto Willow Creek Road and follow it for 2.7 miles to the trailhead.

When I did this hike in 2013, there was only a fence post marking the trailhead—no sign, facilities, or even a parking area—but the Forest Service may sign this trailhead and carve out a small parking area before this edition is published. GPS: N46 59.116' / W111 48.068'

To get to the alternate Mann Gulch trailhead, drive 16 miles north of Helena on I-15 and take the Gates of the Mountains exit. Turn right (east) and drive for 2 miles to the Gates of the Mountains boat dock. Take your personal boat down the Missouri River to Meriwether Day Use Area.

You may also be able to take the tour boat to Meriwether Day Use Area, but in 2013, when this book was revised, the boat did not stop here. The Forest Service is currently trying to secure funding to build a dock capable of handling a commercial vessel the size of the tour boat, so the boat might again stop at Meriwether in the future. Be sure to check before planning on taking the tour boat, which usually leaves in two-hour intervals. If the tour boat is stopping at Meriwether, you can take an early boat and then, after your hike, catch a later one back to the boat dock. Call for current schedules and prices (Gates of the Mountains Boat Tours, 406-458-5241, www.gatesofthemountains.com). A cafe, toilet, and visitor services are available at the boat dock. GPS: N46 52.666' / W111 54.833'

The Hike

This is a brand-new trail, constructed by the Forest Service in 2012 to provide access to the Mann Gulch area that doesn't require a boat and doesn't go through an area heavily impacted by fire. It also gives you a great trip through the seldom-visited but amazing Beartooth Wildlife Management Area, a wildlife- and bird-watching paradise, probably worth the trip even if you didn't do the hike.

From the trailhead, you immediately cross Willow Creek, which in late summer can be done with one big step. For the first quarter mile or so, the trail is invisible as you hike across a big meadow with grass up to your waist. You can, however, easily

Roy Parkley, Helena National Forest recreation manager, at head of Mann Gulch.
BILL SCHNEIDER

follow the designated route by going from post to post until you start climbing up the ridge and the trail becomes easier to follow.

From here the trail gradually climbs (about 600 feet elevation gain) to the head of Mann Gulch, where thirteen men died trying to save it from a forest fire in 1949. You can hike off-trail here along the ridge to the thirteen crosses the FS erected to mark the exact places the firefighters died. Check the map for the location of the crosses; the tall grass hides them until you're close.

From the head of Mann Gulch, you can also continue up the trail for about another mile to a great viewpoint and a spiffy interpretive display explaining the Mann Gulch tragedy. This route doesn't go into the Gates of the Mountains Wilderness unless you continue up the trail to the interpretive display, but it skirts the north edge of the wilderness and gives you a great view of it. You'll probably see deer and elk along the trail, and early in the season, you'll also have an incredible wildflower show.

Take the hike as early as possible to take advantage of cooler temperatures (it can get hot), and be sure to bring water; you won't find any on this route. July and August aren't the best time for this hike because it gets so hot, but the route is a terrific choice for spring or fall.

Hiking up to Mann Gulch from Meriwether Day Use Area. BILL SCHNEIDER

Miles and Directions

0.0   Trailhead.

2.0   Head of Mann Gulch.

3.0   The crosses.

6.0   Trailhead.

Options: To take the water-based trailhead, take your boat or the tour boat to the Meriwether Day Use Area. From the day-use area, you can hike 4 miles to see the crosses marking the spots where thirteen firefighters died in the 1949 Mann Gulch Fire.

From the boat dock, walk up the gulch for several hundred yards to the Vista Point turnoff. Turn left (north) for Vista Point. When you reach the junction with the short spur trail to Vista Point, keep going uphill on the Mann Gulch Trail after taking a short 100-foot trip over to see the scenic vista, which is nice, but not as nice as several views you get as you climb out of Meriwether Canyon. From the junction, you climb a long 2 miles on well-designed switchbacks to the viewpoint and interpretive display explaining the Mann Gulch tragedy. The trail is in excellent shape and gives you increasingly better views as you climb, passing a deep undercut in a cliff called Devil's Kitchen at about the 1.5-mile mark. Unlike the rest of Meriwether Canyon,

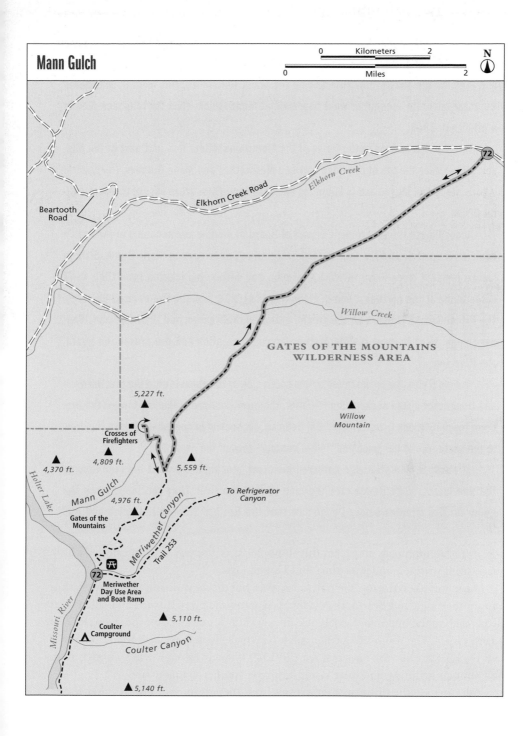

Mann Gulch

0   Kilometers   2

0   Miles   2

N

72

Beartooth
Road

Elkhorn Creek Road   Elkhorn Creek

GATES OF THE MOUNTAINS
WILDERNESS AREA

Willow Creek

5,227 ft.

Willow
Mountain

Crosses of
Firefighters

4,370 ft.   4,809 ft.   5,559 ft.

Holter Lake

Mann Gulch   4,976 ft.

Gates of the
Mountains

To Refrigerator
Canyon

Meriwether Canyon

Trail 253

72

Meriwether
Day Use Area
and Boat Ramp

Missouri River

Coulter
Campground

5,110 ft.

Coulter Canyon

5,140 ft.

THE MANN GULCH TRAGEDY

Interest in the Mann Gulch area has grown since the release of Norman Maclean's *Young Men and Fire* in 1992. In his book Maclean pieces together a picture of actual events and explains the controversy surrounding the Mann Gulch Fire. This book is considered the most accurate account of what happened at Mann Gulch when thirteen men died in a wildfire in 1949.

The fire was located in the Gates of the Mountains Wilderness just east of the Missouri River near the top of the ridge between Meriwether and Mann Gulches. The general area is steep and jagged and is known as one of the roughest areas east of the Continental Divide.

According to the government Report of Board of Review and accounts in Maclean's book, on August 5, 1949, a fire, started by lightning, developed in Mann Gulch. Sixteen smoke jumpers were flown in from Missoula, and fifteen parachuted from their C-47 cargo plane at the northeast end of Mann Gulch. At 3:10 p.m. the fire covered 60 acres. The fifteen smoke jumpers on the ground gathered their cargo, and their foreman, Wagner Dodge, went to meet the Meriwether Canyon recreation and fire prevention guard, Jim Harrison.

Around 5 p.m. the crew started up the south side of the gulch toward the fire. Harrison and Dodge met ahead of them. Shortly after, the crew continued climbing toward the fire. Upon reaching them, Dodge ordered Bill Hellman, his second-in-command, to take the crew to the north side of the gulch and "follow contour" toward the river.

At about 5:40 p.m. Dodge gathered his crew, placing Hellman at the rear to keep the line intact, while Dodge took the lead toward the river. They continued down the gulch for five minutes before Dodge saw that the fire had crossed the gulch and was

the 2007 fire minimally impacted this slope. Most of the way up you can get a little shade from mature ponderosa pines and Douglas firs.

Once you reach the top, the trail fades away, but the view does not. Willow Peak is east up the ridge, and Beartooth Mountain is across the river. Burned and fallen trees lie parallel on the opposite slope. Rockslides and thick grasses cover the steep slope of Mann Gulch. The south side of the gulch has small, densely packed ponderosa pines and Douglas firs like the ones that fed the 1949 blowup. Enough wind, enough heat, and enough lightning, and there could easily be another dramatic fire.

You can't see the thirteen stone crosses from the interpretive display; refer to the map for their location. A small talus slope marks the vicinity, but tall grass conceals

coming up the ridge toward them. They were less than 200 yards from the fire at 5:45 p.m. They then turned back up the gulch, and the race for the ridge began.

At 5:53 p.m. Dodge ordered the men to drop their heavy equipment. The fire roared closer. Dodge then stopped and did something that was critical to his survival. He lit the dry grass beneath him on fire and yelled desperately for the rest of his crew to enter the burned area with him. None listened. Sallee and Rumsey, the lone survivors from the crew, recalled that somebody said, "To hell with that, I'm getting out of here." If the crew had listened to Dodge, more might have survived. This was the first case in Forest Service history that a man had set his own escape fire. Dodge lay down in the burned area with a wet cloth over his mouth while the fire burned around him.

Sallee and Rumsey made it through an opening in the rimrock at the top of the ridge. That opening saved their lives. They stumbled over the other side of the ridge into the safety of a rockslide.

At approximately 5:56 p.m. eleven men died. It was at that exact time that the hands on Jim Harrison's watch stopped. Most of the victims suffocated before the fire charred their bodies. Although Hellman and Joseph Sylvia survived the fire and were carried out through Rescue Gulch on the opposite side of the ridge, they died later in Helena, burned beyond recovery.

Granite monuments and crosses mark where the men fell to remind hikers of nature's power. These men died because of a blowup: The fire exploded in size from 30 acres to 2,000 acres in just ten minutes. Just before the fire broke out, the air temperature in Mann Gulch was near 100 degrees Fahrenheit, the grass had dried to the consistency of hay, and the young ponderosa pine and Douglas fir were like kindling. Lightning struck, and the whirling winds did the rest.

the crosses. To reach them, hike off-trail up the ridge for 0.3 mile. Descend from the ridge, traversing northeast up the gulch, and angle over to the crosses. The opposite ridge is steep, and the crosses are near the top of the ridge.

The minimum reasonable amount of time you should allot for seeing the crosses from Meriwether Day Use Area is four hours. If you brought a picnic lunch, enjoy it at the day-use area before heading back to the Gates of the Mountains boat dock. (Originally contributed and re-hiked by the authors.)

73 Hanging Valley

A day hike to a deep, narrow canyon with impressive limestone towers

Start: Vigilante Campground, 20 miles northeast of Helena
Distance: 12.0-mile out-and-back

Difficulty: Moderate
Maps: USGS Hogback Mountain and Snedaker
Basin; Helena National Forest Map

Finding the trailhead: To get to York, take Highway 280 northeast of Helena for 15 miles,
crossing the Missouri River via the York Bridge. The trailhead starts at Vigilante Campground in
the Helena National Forest, 5 miles northeast of York on the old Figure Eight Route (FR 4137).
The Figure Eight Route used to go beyond Vigilante Campground until massive floods in May
1981 buried the road under tons of gravel in Trout Creek Canyon. The trailhead is at the far end of
the campground loop. Limited parking for hikers; vehicle camping, water, and toilets at Vigilante
Campground. GPS: N46 45.956' / W111 38.936'

The Hike

Hanging Valley is actually a dry tributary of Trout Creek. It enters the canyon from a
point high on the southern wall. You'll be able to pick out where you have been from
the bottom of Trout Creek Canyon after you've taken the hike. After exploring this
section of the Big Belt Mountains, you'll wonder how part of Utah, complete with
narrow canyons and unusual rock formations, ended up in Montana.

Trail 247 starts at the back of the campground and is marked with a National
Recreation Trail sign. The path slowly climbs a dry hillside for 3 miles to a low pass
between Trout Creek and Magpie Creek. During late May the trail is lined with hundreds of pink fairy slippers and blue clematis just below the pass.

At the pass you reach a junction with Trail 248, which veers off to the right. Turn
left to stay on Trail 247 and proceed to the top of the mountain that forms the southern rim of Trout Creek Canyon. The views here are tremendous on a clear day, with

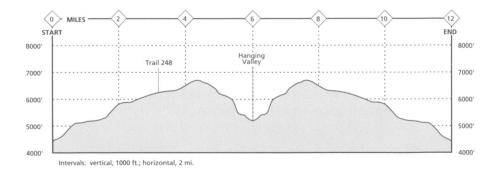

Intervals: vertical, 1000 ft.; horizontal, 2 mi.

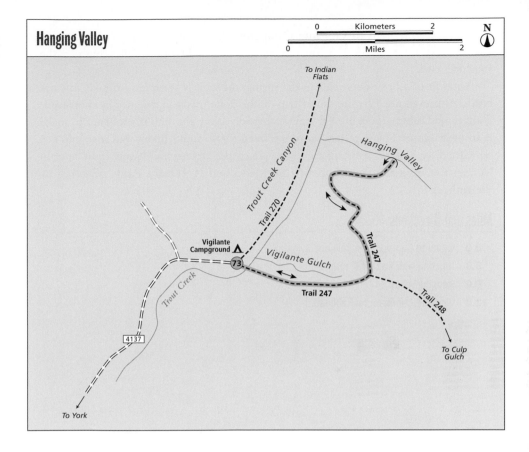

the Flint Creek Range appearing from over the Continental Divide to the west and the Spanish Peaks near Bozeman visible some 100 air miles to the south.

The trail is well constructed and practically impossible to lose. Past the summit the trail switchbacks down a heavily wooded slope for about a half mile into Hanging Valley and passes huge Douglas firs that have escaped wildfires. The trail follows the dry watercourse into the canyon.

Limestone pinnacles 50 feet tall tower over the trail, which soon becomes a route just a few feet wide at the bottom of a narrow canyon. After the trail passes under a small natural bridge, you must descend a 5-foot-high rock step in the trail, adding excitement to the trip. During heavy snow years, the trail at this point may be impassable until mid-June.

The trail dead-ends on the lip of a dry waterfall several hundred feet up a sheer rock face on the southern wall of Trout Creek Canyon, hence the name Hanging Valley. The canyon walls bear a close resemblance to those of Bryce Canyon in Utah. There's a small, fenced platform on the lip of the sheer cliff, which definitely makes this one hike where you know for sure you've reached the end of the trail.

Retrace your steps to Vigilante Campground, where you can briefly hike on Trail 270 up Trout Creek Canyon and try to pick out Hanging Valley, high on the southern rim.

Aside from a few snowfields in the spring, the trail is waterless, so take an extra bottle. Although the 12-mile round-trip can be done easily in one day by most well-conditioned hikers, there are a few dry campsites along the trail if you want to make it an overnighter. The trip may prove too steep for younger hikers, but it should not be missed by anyone wanting to see a part of the desert Southwest right here in Montana. (Originally contributed by Ed Madej and Rosemary Rowe, re-hiked by the authors.)

Miles and Directions

- **0.0** Vigilante Campground Trailhead.
- **3.0** Junction with Trail 248; turn left.
- **6.0** Hanging Valley.
- **12.0** Vigilante Campground Trailhead.

74 Trout Creek Canyon

An easy day hike up a very accessible canyon with a beautiful stream

Start: Vigilante Campground, 20 miles north-east of Helena
Distance: 6.0-mile out-and-back

Difficulty: Easy
Maps: USGS Hogback Mountain and Snedaker Basin; Helena National Forest Map

Finding the trailhead: To get to York, take Highway 280 northeast of Helena for 15 miles, crossing the Missouri River via the York Bridge. The trailhead starts at Vigilante Campground in the Helena National Forest, 5 miles northeast of York on the old Figure Eight Route (FR 4137). The Figure Eight Route used to go beyond Vigilante Campground until massive floods in May 1981 buried the road under tons of gravel in Trout Creek Canyon. The trailhead is at the far end of the campground loop. Limited parking for hikers; vehicle camping, water, and toilets at Vigilante Campground. GPS: N46 45.956' / W111 38.936'

The Hike

This might be the best easy day hike in the Helena area. It's also living proof that we can correct our mistakes, that development can be reversed. This trail used to be a road, and a well-traveled one at that, called the Figure Eight Route, a significant tourist attraction in the Helena area and promoted as such by the Helena National Forest and local chamber of commerce. Then in 1981 a flood washed away the road for the second time, and the Forest Service decided to make it a trail. After you hike through this picturesque canyon, send the agency a thank-you letter.

The first mile of the trail has been made passable for wheelchairs and is very pleasant. Beautiful Trout Creek flows through this limestone-walled canyon even in August of a dry year. After the first mile (at a picnic table), the trail narrows (no longer wheelchair accessible), and the stream may stop flowing.

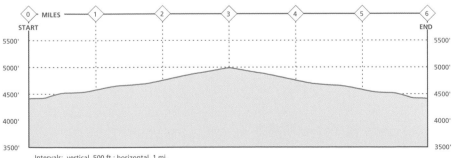

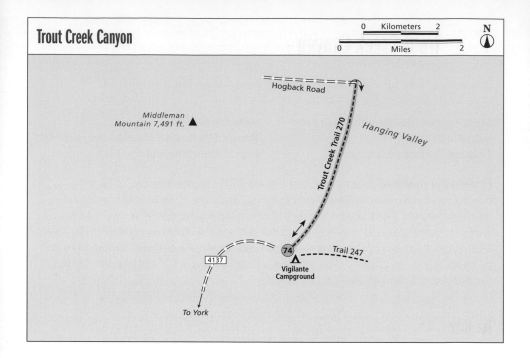

This is a great early-season hike, flush with fall colors in September and October, and always ideal for small children and senior hikers. The gradual uphill grade is so gentle, it seems flat. You can hike the entire 3 miles until you see Hogback Road heading off to the left, or you can turn around whenever you feel like it. (Originally contributed and re-hiked by the authors.)

Miles and Directions

0.0 Trailhead.

3.0 Tour around.

6.0 Trailhead.

75 Mount Helena Ridge

A scenic walk along a dry, forested ridge, perhaps the best urban trail in Montana

Start: Park City Trailhead, 5 miles south of Helena
Distance: 7.4-mile shuttle

Difficulty: Moderate
Maps: USGS Helena; Helena National Forest Map

Finding the trailheads: Drive south on Park Avenue, past the entrance to Reeders Village, until the road forks on the edge of town. Take the right fork (Grizzly Gulch) and drive 4.1 miles up the well-maintained dirt road to where another dirt road veers off to the right on an open area on top of a large hill. The upper trailhead (locally called Park City Trailhead after a long-gone ghost town) is about a half mile up this road. Look for a small sign marking the direction to the trail and the right turn. After turning right, drive a short distance uphill to a parking area. Start here and hike toward Helena. Limited parking; no toilet; no camping. GPS: N46 32.566' / W112 7.049'

To set up the shuttle, turn right (west) into Reeders Village, through the fairly new residential subdivision and up to the Mount Helena City Park parking lot. A large parking area (often full on weekend afternoons) and portable toilet; no camping. GPS: N46 35.233' / W112 2.983'

The Hike

When I wrote the first edition of this book, back in 1979, the Forest Service encouraged me to leave this trail out. A few years later, the agency designated this scenic, point-to-point trail as a National Recreation Trail. Go figure, eh?

From Park City Trailhead, follow Trail 373 as it climbs gently up a few long switchbacks along a grassy slope to the northeast. Small clusters of rural ranchettes dot the valley below. From here to Mount Helena, the trail is well marked and very well used. This is probably the most scenic part of the hike, with views of the Mount Helena ridge, Mount Helena, and the Helena Valley. The city of Helena also appears frequently in the distance. You'll see a few retired jeep roads heading off the ride, but you stay right on the ridge.

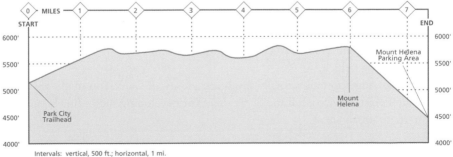

Intervals: vertical, 500 ft.; horizontal, 1 mi.

Taking in the view of the Helena Valley from the top of Mount Helena. BILL SCHNEIDER

At 5.4 miles you reach Mount Helena City Park, at 620 acres one of the largest city parks in the country, and its 20 miles of hiking trails. The first junction in the Mount Helena trail system is the Prairie Trail (stay right) and shortly after, the Prospect Shafts Trail (stay left), and then the 1906 Trail (stay right). All three junctions are within a 200-yard stretch of trail. Follow the 1906 Trail about a half mile farther to the top of Mount Helena.

From the summit, there are at least three ways to get down, but the most pleasant is to descend to the south on the Hogback Trail and turn left onto the Prospect Shafts Trail, descending gently down to the trail above the new Reeders Village subdivision and your waiting vehicle.

Since this ridgetop trail is totally dry, bring plenty of water. You might also want to give the Forest Service a call and thank them for developing such a fine hiking trail so close to an urban area.

Mount Helena Ridge

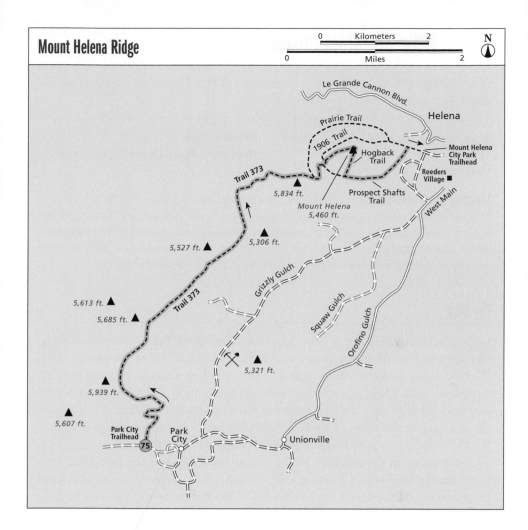

Miles and Directions

0.0 Park City Trailhead.

5.0 City park boundary.

5.4 Junction with Prairie, Backside, and 1906 Trails.

5.9 Summit of Mount Helena.

7.4 Mount Helena City Park Trailhead.

Options: During the summer months, the downtown business community runs a shuttle bus up to the Park City Trailhead, so take advantage of this and you won't need two vehicles for the shuttle. You can also do the hike in reverse, of course, but it has more climbing. (Originally contributed and re-hiked by the authors.)

76 Little Blackfoot Meadows

A day hike or overnighter to a large, marshy meadow in a subalpine basin along the upper reaches of the Little Blackfoot River

Start: Kading Campground, 20 miles south-west of Helena
Distance: 11.0-mile out-and-back

Difficulty: Easy
Maps: USGS Basin; Helena National Forest Map

Finding the trailhead: Turn south off US 12 about 1 mile east of Elliston onto FR 227. After 15 miles of gravel road, you pass Kading Campground on your left. Park just past the campground where the road turns into a jeep track. Park along the road just before the turnaround so that your vehicle does not interfere with horse trailers turning around. Very limited parking at trailhead; toilet and vehicle camping at Kading Campground. GPS: N46 25.533' / W112 29.166'

The Hike

Little Blackfoot Meadows, a large subalpine basin along the Continental Divide, receives heavy use during hunting season but not much the rest of the year.

Park on the road and continue on foot along the jeep track. At 1.3 miles the jeep track forks, with Kading Grade Trail going off to the right. Go left and stay on the jeep track. Shortly after, the road ends and turns into Trail 329, which heads gradually downhill to the banks of the Little Blackfoot, crossing a footbridge at 2.5 miles. Rainbow and brook trout frequent the pools along this stretch of stream.

Continuing up the east bank of the stream, the trail passes through some low-lying, marshy areas before climbing a dry sidehill. Good views of the meadows and the mountain-rimmed basin can be obtained by briefly leaving the trail and climbing uphill into an obvious open area just before the second crossing of the Little Blackfoot at 4 miles. Sorry, no footbridge.

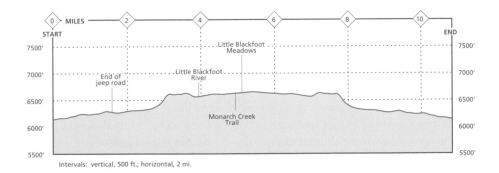

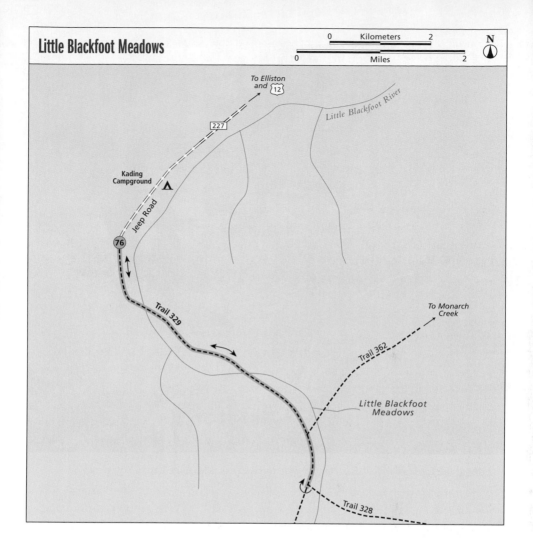

From this crossing it's an easy mile or so to the Little Blackfoot Meadows. On the way, at 5.3 miles, you'll come to a junction with Monarch Creek Trail 362. Turn right and continue about a quarter mile to the meadows.

The meadows have several nice campsites and make a good base camp for exploring the surrounding roadless country. Trails lead up to the rounded, rocky summits of Cliff Mountain, Electric Peak, Thunderbolt Mountain, and Bison Mountain on the Continental Divide. For those wanting a gentle introduction to hiking or overnight camping, this hike is a great choice. The Forest Service has a proposal to move the trailhead to Kading Campground—take a moment to support the agency's plan. (Originally contributed by Rosemary Rowe, re-hiked by the authors.)

Fishing the Little Blackfoot River on the way to Blackfoot Meadows. LAURA SCHNEIDER

Miles and Directions

0.0   Trailhead.

1.3   Junction with Kading Grade Trail; turn left.

1.5   End of jeep road.

2.5   Cross Little Blackfoot River on footbridge.

4.0   Ford Little Blackfoot River.

5.3   Junction with Monarch Creek Trail 362; turn right.

5.5   Little Blackfoot Meadows.

11.0   Trailhead.

77 Elkhorn and Crow Peaks

A mostly off-trail trek to two of the highest peaks in the Helena area

Start: The historic ghost town of Elkhorn, 35 miles southeast of Helena

Distance: 11.0-mile out-and-back

Difficulty: Strenuous

Maps: USGS Elkhorn; Helena National Forest Map

Finding the trailhead: The trail begins at Elkhorn, a historic mining camp and ghost town on the southern end of the Elkhorn Mountains. From Helena, drive 27 miles south on I-15 to Boulder. Take the Boulder exit off the interstate and go 6.5 miles south of town on MT 69, then turn left (east) onto a paved road marked by a large sign for Elkhorn. The road immediately crosses the Boulder River and turns right, at which point it turns into a good gravel road. Follow this road for about 13 miles to Elkhorn, bearing left at two junctions along the way. If you have a two-wheel-drive vehicle, park at the Forest Service picnic area on the state park site in town.

The trail, actually a jeep road, heads north out of town. If you have a four-wheel-drive vehicle, you can make it another 0.7 mile to a signed junction where you can park and take the right fork in the road. Start your hike here, even though you might see a Designated Route sign and the road looks decent, but don't be fooled. In reality the road to the Iron Mine, an abandoned mining camp, is way too rough for most vehicles—and most drivers. It gets rocky and rutted, so don't try it unless you have low range and high clearance—and don't mind driving at a 45-degree angle on a steep mountainside.

On the Forest Service map, the trail is marked as FR 258, but on some old maps and at the trailhead sign, it's Muskrat Creek Trail 72. Unfortunately, this old road is open to ATVs. GPS: N46 16.550' / W111 56.495'

The Hike

If you're an experienced hiker who likes off-trail hiking spiced with a little peak bagging, you'll enjoy this hike. About half of the hike is a cross-country route to the summits of the two highest peaks in the Helena area.

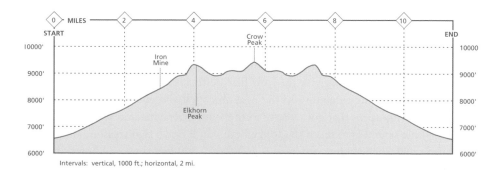

The "road" up to the Iron Mine, much better for hiking than driving. BILL SCHNEIDER

From the ghost town of Elkhorn, or the Muskrat Creek Trailhead, hike up the steep ATV road, which you could call the "Switchbacks-Are-for-Wussies" trail. It goes up and up and up with little relief until you get close to the Iron Mine. As you approach the Iron Mine, you pass through a whitebark pine forest that has been decimated by pine beetles.

At about the 2-mile mark, watch for an ATV road turning sharply right (no sign). Take this road and stay on it as it passes through a gate and some private property, which is signed NONMOTORIZED USE ONLY. After the gate, you pass by a secluded cabin with a sign that says HIPPIES USE THE BACK DOOR. Please respect this private property and stay on the trail. After the cabin, the ATV road turns into a singletrack and stays so until it emerges from the forest onto the ridge about a half mile later and rewards you with a sweeping view of your first destination, Elkhorn Peak.

As you head up the ridge toward the peak, bear left and you'll find a good social trail marked with cairns that goes nearly to the summit, leaving you with only about a quarter-mile scramble to reach the top, where you'll find a trail register and a small man-made rock shelter. Here, you're at 9,443 feet, 2,800 feet above Elkhorn, and the view is something to behold, especially to the north where you can see the entire

The last scramble to the summit of Elkhorn Peak. BILL SCHNEIDER

Tizer Basin, the glacier-carved heart of the Elkhorn Mountains. To the southeast lies 9,414-foot Crow Peak.

Pick your way to Crow Peak about a mile beyond Elkhorn Peak, along the saddle between the two mountains. Be sure to bear slightly to the north so that you can look down steep cliffs into Hidden Lake and, a little farther on, Glenwood Lake. Both lakes are nestled in steep, glacier-scoured cirques with sheer cliffs on three sides and openings only on the north.

You used to be able to regularly see mountain goats on Elkhorn and Crow Peaks, but in recent years that population has crashed. But you can still get a mild heart attack as a blue grouse flushes from the weather-beaten whitebark pines between the two peaks.

Unless you spend too much time taking in the vistas, you can easily make it to Crow Peak and back in a full day. However, this rugged cross-country hike may be too tough for small children or poorly conditioned hikers.

Bring drinking water, as there is only one small stream (about halfway to the Iron Mine), and even that one may dry up by late summer. Snow clings to the area into late June and even July in heavy snow years, so plan a late summer or early fall conquest.

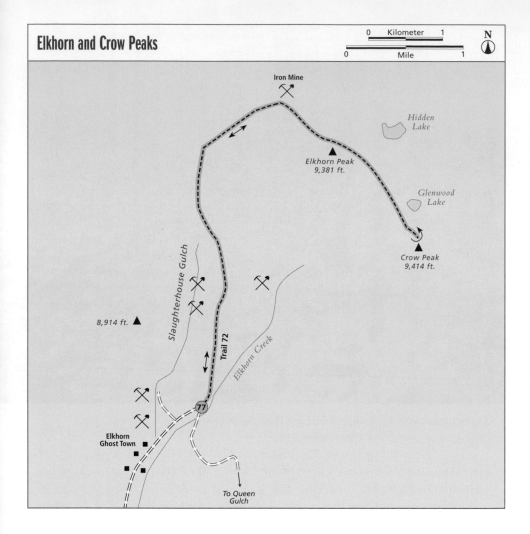

If you miss the ATV road up to the ridgeline or if the landowner decides not to allow access through this private property, don't fret. Just before you reach the Iron Mine, bushwhack up to the ridge, which is a fairly easy climb (less than a half mile) and then continue on up to Elkhorn Peak. (Originally contributed and re-hiked by the authors.)

Miles and Directions

0.0 Trailhead.

2.0 ATV road; turn right.

4.5 Elkhorn Peak.

5.5 Crow Peak.

11.0 Trailhead.

78 Crow Creek Falls

A day hike to a stunning waterfall in a place you don't expect it

Start: 35 miles southeast of Helena in the Elkhorn Mountains
Distance: 6.0-mile out-and-back

Difficulty: Easy
Maps: USGS Crow Creek Falls; Helena National Forest Map

Finding the trailhead: Drive 11 miles south of Townsend on US 287 and turn right (west) on the paved CR 285 for 9 miles to Radersburg. Go through Radersburg and onto a good gravel road (Crow Creek Road 424) and drive for 17 miles until you see the sign for Crow Creek Trail 109 on your right. Plenty of parking; no toilet; undeveloped camping at and near the trailhead. GPS: N46 19.285' / W111 45.861'

The Hike

This hike was in the first edition of this book, but it was removed after a maverick miner moved into this inholding in the Helena National Forest in 1981, dredged below the falls, and denied access to the public. In 2003 the area was acquired by a nonprofit organization, the American Land Conservancy, and reopened to the public. So, it seems, since this is such a wonderful hike, it was also time to put it back in *Hiking Montana*.

This is a terrific early-season hike that you can safely take in mid–May. The trail is in excellent shape all the way, and it's obvious the Forest Service is taking great care to make this route a nice hike.

The waterfall is truly remarkable. The force of the water casts up a fine mist that makes the entire area around the falls much more lush than the fairly dry environs all around it.

The hike starts out on Crow Creek Trail 109 with a sharp drop on two or three switchbacks down to Crow Creek. Just before the bridge over the creek, you'll see the junction with Hall Creek Trail 128. Turn right (east) here to stay on Crow Creek

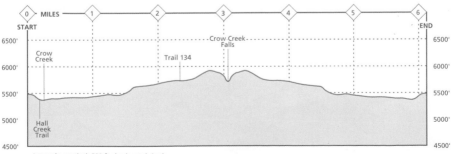

Intervals: vertical, 500 ft.; horizontal, 1 mi.

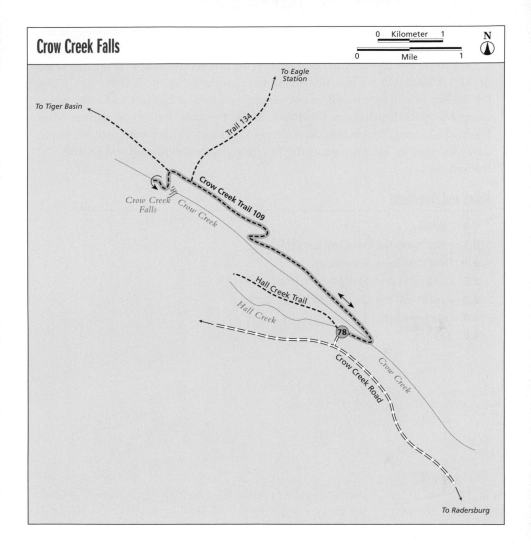

0   Kilometer   1

0   Mile   1

N

To Eagle
Station

To Tiger Basin

Trail 134

Crow Creek Trail 109

Crow Creek
Falls

Crow Creek

Hall Creek Trail

Hall Creek

78

Crow Creek

Crow Creek Road

To Radersburg

Trail 109 and cross Hall Creek and then Crow Creek. The trail then turns back west and closely follows the stream for about 1.5 miles. Two or three sections are mildly hazardous as the trail cuts through steep banks above the stream, enough for the Forest Service to discourage the use of horses on this section of trail, but it isn't too dangerous for hikers. If you have small children, though, watch them closely.

At about 1.5 miles, the trail climbs up to the bench above the stream onto an old jeep road that the FS is converting to a trail, part of it gone to singletrack already. You

◀   *Two of the author's grandchildren, Alex and Lucy, enjoying Crow Creek Falls, just like thousands of kids who have gone before them have done.* LAURA SCHNEIDER

stay on the bench until you drop sharply down to the falls, going left (west) at the junction with Trail 134 about a half mile before you get there.

Try to do this trip early in the morning, because it can get hot on the east slope of the Elkhorns. On the plus side, mosquitoes usually aren't too bad, but watch out for the horseflies. There is one sort of marginal campsite at the falls, and a few better campsites on the bench above the stream, so you can make this an overnighter. Most hikers don't camp, though, because it's hard to get much privacy with people coming down to enjoy an hour or two at the falls. (Originally contributed and re-hiked by the authors.)

Miles and Directions

0.0 Trailhead.

0.5 Junction with Hall Creek Trail; turn right.

0.7 Cross Crow Creek on log bridge.

1.5 Climb out of stream bottom to old jeep road; turn left.

2.2 Junction with Trail 134 to Eagle Station; turn left.

3.0 Crow Creek Falls.

6.0 Trailhead.

THE VIEW FROM HERE: THE LEGACY OF CROW CREEK FALLS

When I was young, I hiked to Crow Creek Falls many times. I went there with my wife before we started a family. Later I walked into the falls with my babies on my shoulders, and a few years later I walked with them, ever so slowly. This was a special place for me, my little piece of paradise, a family retreat, a mirage we always reached. It was probably the nicest, most popular short hike in the Helena area.

Then in 1981, one careless man destroyed Crow Creek Falls. He built an illegal road over public land. He drove in earth-moving equipment on that illegal road. He dredged the sparkling pool below Crow Creek Falls. He didn't find gold, so he abandoned the site, leaving behind the most sickening mess you could imagine.

The Forest Service let it happen. The Montana Mining Association let it happen. The politicians let it happen. They all let it happen because they felt they had to, because Crow Creek Falls was private land. It originally was public land, but the ancient, archaic Mining Law of 1872 still allows anybody who fancies himself or herself a miner to claim public land—even an extremely rare, irreplaceable public treasure like Crow Creek Falls. At best this law is an absolute embarrassment to a civilized society, and there is no better testimony to this description than the desecration of Crow Creek Falls.

So, for a long, long time, I didn't go to Crow Creek Falls. It hurt to go there. I even took the hike to Crow Creek Falls out of this book. Then the worm turned, perhaps because we really don't realize how valuable something is until it's gone.

Obviously I wasn't the only person who missed Crow Creek Falls, who had taken his or her children there so an appreciation of wild nature could take root in their souls. Lots of people did, and they all missed Crow Creek Falls. It was like a piece of us had been taken away, and we found it hard to fill in the void.

Well, it took a long, long time, but sometimes we are strong enough and smart enough to do the right thing, to do what sometimes seems impossible: to go back and correct our mistakes. We finally put the jewel of the Elkhorn Mountains, Crow Creek Falls, back in the public trust. We reclaimed the road. We cleaned up the disgusting mess left behind by one uncaring miner.

The resurrection was carried out by the same players as the destruction—the Forest Service, the mining association, the politicians. Decades ago they had made a tragic mistake by standing idly by and allowing the devastation of this natural wonder, but then they all realized the blunder and stepped forward to rectify it.

Now I go back to Crow Creek Falls. I take my grandchildren there. I put it back into this guidebook. And when I'm there I think about the legacy of Crow Creek Falls, which is: Nothing is a lost cause. We can admit our mistakes and correct them. We've made a lot of environmental mistakes through the years. This little story should give us incentive to correct more of them.

79 Boulder Basin

A day hike or overnighter to a basin with three lakes and views of the Missouri River Valley

---

Start: 10 miles north of Townsend in the Big Belt Mountains
Distance: 12.0-mile out-and-back

Difficulty: Moderate
Maps: USGS Boulder-Baldy; Helena National Forest Map

Finding the trailhead: Drive 2 miles east of Townsend on US 12 to Highway 284 and turn left, heading north for 11.5 miles to the Duck Creek Road turnoff. Turn right onto Duck Creek Road for 11 miles to FR 139-F1 and turn left. Drive 2 miles on FR 139-F1 until you reach the parking lot next to a spring. Plenty of parking; no toilet; only undeveloped camping. GPS: N46 30.549' / W111 17.416'

The Hike

These high mountain lakes offer scenery, solitude, and the simple joy of a good hike. As a bonus, you might be the only hikers on this trail.

As you climb up to the ridge, you enter a large forest of weathered whitebark pines, one of the largest groves I've ever seen. Regrettably, the pine beetle has killed most of the high-altitude icons, turning them into silvery ghost trees.

For wildflower lovers, the entire route puts on a good show—lots of lupine, arnica, paintbrush, and larkspur, but also lots of more rare flowers like mountain health, princess pine, mountain bluebells, and trapper's tea.

Trail 118 switchbacks up a steep slope for the first mile or so, traversing fields of sagebrush, a remarkable plant that flourishes at 8,000 feet without much water. Be careful to get on the official trail right at the trailhead. The first two switchbacks have become indistinct because of lack of use. After that, though, the trail is easy to follow the rest of the way.

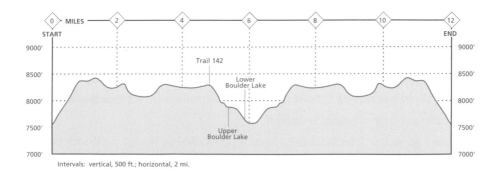

Lower Boulder Lake. BILL SCHNEIDER

There's no water along the ridgetop for the first 4.5 miles, so carry plenty. At about 4.5 miles you go over several small streams, which might be intermittent and dry in August. At 5 miles you hike along a delightful mountain stream, which provides the only reliable water source until you reach the lakes.

After the first mile of climbing, the trail goes up and down, up and down, through unburned forest, as you follow the ridgeline for about 4 miles, but with no major climbs. To the east you can see the Camas Creek Valley, which has been proposed for Wilderness designation. It has not been logged like the slopes along the drive up to the trailhead.

At about 3.5 miles, Trail 147 joins from the left (no sign when we hiked it). Keep following Trail 118 along the ridge.

To get to the lakes, turn left at the 5-mile point at the intersection with Boulder Lakes Trail 142. The main trail to the right continues up Boulder-Baldy Mountain and Camas Lake. After turning left, the trail descends almost 1,000 feet into the Boulder Basin. The upper lake is below Boulder Mountain to the south at 5.5 miles (watch carefully; it's easy to miss). It has no fish, but in the spring when the snow melts, buttercups cover the southeast shore. The next (lower) lake, at 6 miles, is smaller and full of good-size brook trout. The lower lake has excellent campsites at both ends.

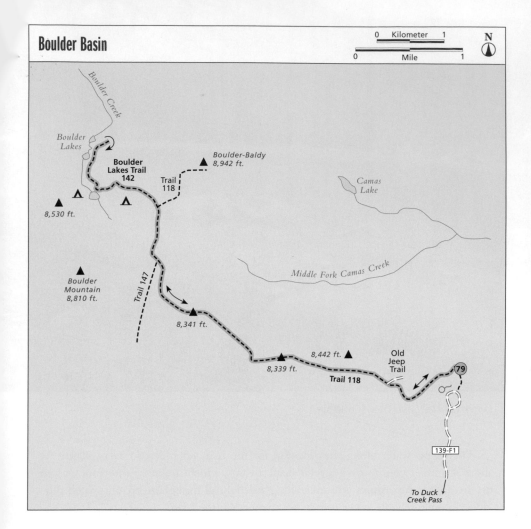

Miles and Directions

0.0 Trailhead.

1.0 Jeep trail joins main trail.

3.5 Junction with Trail 147; turn right.

5.0 Junction with Boulder Lakes Trail 142 to Boulder Lakes; turn left.

5.5 Upper Boulder Lake.

6.0 Lower Boulder Lake.

12.0 Trailhead.

Side Trips: For a spectacular view of the Big Belts, turn left at the 5-mile point and go up to Boulder–Baldy Mountain. (Originally contributed and re-hiked by the authors.)

80 Edith-Baldy Basin

A long day hike or backpacking trip into a high lake-filled basin

Start: Duck Creek Pass Trailhead, 30 miles southeast of Helena in the Big Belt Mountains
Distance: 12.0-mile out-and-back, with 20-plus-mile loop option

Difficulty: Moderate; strenuous for loop option
Maps: USGS Mount Edith and Duck Creek Pass; Helena National Forest Map

Finding the trailhead: Drive 2 miles east of Townsend on US 12 to Highway 284 and turn left, heading north for 12 miles to the Duck Creek Road turnoff. Turn right on Duck Creek Road for an additional 12 miles to the top of Duck Creek Pass. Turn right into a turnaround just after reaching the summit. The trail begins at the south side of the turnaround. Limited parking; no toilet; only undeveloped camping. GPS: N46 29.750' / W111 15.366'

The Hike

Driving along US 12 on the west side of expansive Canyon Ferry Reservoir and seeing Mount Edith and Mount Baldy in the distance, you would never guess that a spectacular lake-filled basin, accessible to all hikers, lies nestled in their northeastern shadow.

From Duck Creek Pass Trailhead, hike on Trail 151, which parallels the jeep trail on the east side for the first 3 miles, climbing steeply. Bring water because there is none for the first half of the hike.

At 3 miles, stay left on Trail 151 as it turns away from the jeep road. Trail 151 has long switchbacks down to the junction at 4.7 miles with Trail 150, which leads to Gypsy Lake. Stay right here on Trail 151 and continue until you reach a small, unnamed lake. This is not Hidden Lake. Hike around the southern shore of the small lake until you see the junction at 5.9 miles with Trail 152 to Edith Lake. Stay right again and hike about a quarter mile to Hidden Lake, which stays hidden until you almost fall into it. Retracing your steps back to the trailhead completes the 12-mile hike.

Miles and Directions

0.0 Duck Creek Pass Trailhead.
3.0 Junction with jeep road from microwave tower; turn left.
4.7 Junction with Gypsy Lake Trail 150; turn right.
5.9 Junction with Edith Lake Trail 152; turn right.
6.0 Hidden Lake.
12.0 Duck Creek Pass Trailhead.

Options: You can also hike farther to Edith Lake. Once at this lake, you can retrace your steps to Duck Creek Pass or take the longer loop option. If you're in good shape

The pygmy bitterroot, one of the rarest flowers in Montana, but found in the Edith-Baldy basin.
BILL SCHNEIDER

and knowledgeable about cross-country hiking, you can make a spectacular loop by continuing past Edith Lake and over Mount Baldy to Duck Creek Pass.

Although Edith and Baldy are rock and talus, the basin is heavily timbered. Some of the lakes in the basin don't have trails to them. You'll probably want to spend at least one night in the basin before heading home.

The loop is about 20 miles depending on how many lakes you visit, and about a third of the trip is cross-country. Although the ridge is devoid of water, the basin has plenty. This area accumulates a surprising amount of snow, so wait until at least late June (or August if you want to escape the mosquitoes).

If you're more ambitious, instead of dropping down into the basin for Hidden Lake, you can head cross-country toward the summit of Mount Baldy directly from Duck Creek Pass. All along this ridge the vistas are incredible, with the Smith River drainage to the east and Canyon Ferry Reservoir to the west. Expect to see mountain goats around the summits of Baldy and Edith. Remember, if your behavior affects the behavior of the goats, you are too close.

After leaving the top of Mount Baldy, you drop rapidly for about a quarter mile into the saddle between the two peaks, crossing Trail 152 to Edith Lake. Then

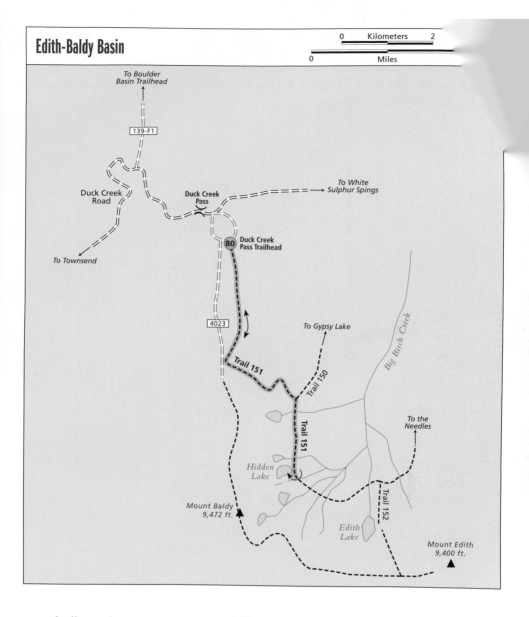

Edith-Baldy Basin

0   Kilometers   2

0   Miles

To Boulder
Basin Trailhead

139-F1

To White
Sulphur Springs

Duck Creek
Road

Duck Creek
Pass

To Townsend

80   Duck Creek
Pass Trailhead

4023

To Gypsy Lake

Big Birch Creek

Trail 151

Trail 150

To the
Needles

Trail 151

Hidden
Lake

Trail 152

Mount Baldy
9,472 ft.

Edith
Lake

Mount Edith
9,400 ft.

---

gradually work your way over several false summits to the top of Mount Edith, with Upper Baldy Lake on your left most of the way. It's 4 miles between the two summits, but it's very scenic hiking. Although it's cross-country, the terrain is easy to traverse. In addition to mountain goats, this area seems to attract unusually large numbers of golden eagles.

From the top of Mount Edith, you can see a penetrating limestone formation known as the Needles to the north and Edith Lake to the northwest. Follow a series of rock cairns toward this gorgeous, high-altitude lake.

out a mile before Edith Lake, you intersect Trail 152 again. This time, turn onto this trail (which you crossed on the way to the summit of Edith) and k your way back through the basin to Hidden Lake and then up a series of ugh switchbacks to Duck Creek Pass and your vehicle. (Originally contributed and re-hiked by the authors.)

Gallatin National Forest

81 Cottonwood Lake

A day hike or overnighter to an alpine lake in the spectacular Crazy Mountains

Start: 30 miles northeast of Livingston
Distance: 10.0-mile out-and-back
Difficulty: Strenuous

Maps: USGS Campfire Lake and Crazy Peak; Gallatin National Forest Map (North)

Finding the trailhead: Finding this trailhead can be tricky, so heads up. Take exit 340 off I-90 (6 miles northeast of Livingston) and drive 14 miles north on US 89 to Clyde Park. About a half mile past Clyde Park, turn right onto heavily used Cottonwood Bench Road (FR 198). Follow FR 198 east for 6.4 miles to the junction with Cottonwood Creek Road. Turn left (north) here, and after only half a mile, turn right (east) on Upper Cottonwood Road. Follow this road for 4.6 miles to the junction with the road to the Ibex Guard Station. Turn right (east) and go 3.1 miles to the trailhead. The road continues but has a closed gate. The road is open to the public, including ATVs and motorcycles, but not to highway vehicles. Please respect private property rights by closing the gate behind you. Ample parking; no toilet. GPS: N45 59.150' / W110 26.067'

The Hike

From the trailhead the first 2 miles of the hike are on the jeep road and are sublimely uphill along Cottonwood Creek. Since this road is closed to highway vehicles except those belonging to local residents, there is minimal vehicular traffic, which makes it a pleasant walk. The Crazies get lots of snow, so wait until late summer for this trip. Water is everywhere along this route, so you can take the filter and leave the extra water bottles behind.

After 2 miles stay left on Trail 197 where the road turns right to a cluster of private cabins. The checkerboard pattern between private and public land in the Crazy Mountains makes this development possible. The 2-mile section of road from the gate to this point is open to ATVs and motorcycles, but not thereafter.

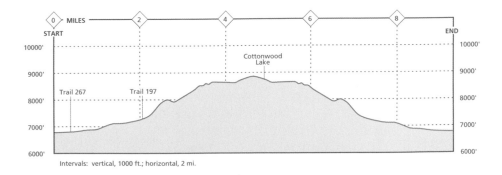

Intervals: vertical, 1000 ft.; horizontal, 2 mi.

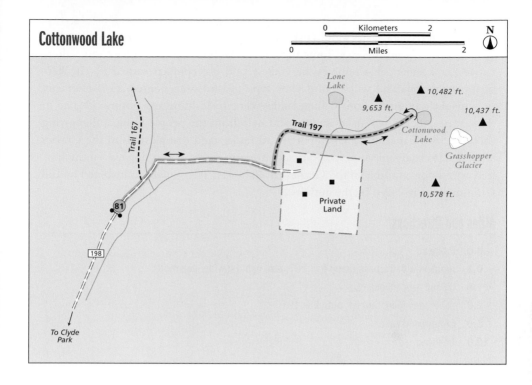

From the road the trail heads straight up for about a mile. This Category 1 hill is a real calf-stretcher that could use two or three switchbacks. It's also difficult coming down. Make sure you have your toenails clipped or they'll be black in a few days. This steep section is mostly on private land and a great example of what happens over time when people cut switchbacks. This section used to have switchbacks but enough people chose the straight up and down alternative, and this gradually became the main route. The Forest Service is currently working with the private landowners to reestablish the historic switchbacks.

After a mile the upgrade becomes gentler but continues to climb all the way to Cottonwood Lake at 5 miles. Fortunately, the scenery is so spectacular that you might not notice the steady uphill grind. The gorgeous meadows have multihued carpets of wildflowers. The trail slips away in the rocks here and there, but you can always find it again. Other sections of trail are braided, so try to use only the major route (most obvious, usually with trail markers) and let the other routes through this delicate landscape return to their natural condition.

This is one of the more popular destinations in the Crazies. The lower end of the lake has several excellent campsites, but since this is high, fragile country, be careful to have a zero-impact camp. Don't forget your stove, as firewood is scarce and should be used only in an emergency. Please don't build fire rings. The lake has a population of pan-size cutthroat trout, but use them for fun, not for dinner.

Any visit to the Crazies should make you realize that perhaps more than any place in Montana, this area deserves some type of formal protection or at least some alternative management that resolves the endless land-use conflicts caused by checkerboard ownership. This will require some type of land swap, conservation easement, or outright acquisition from willing landowners. To institute any positive change in the Crazies, the FS will need support and help from the people using and enjoying the area. In the meantime, it's important to understand that all trails in the Crazies cross private land—please respect private property rights. If you don't, even the limited access now available in the Crazies could be lost. (Originally contributed by Bill Cunningham, re-hiked by the authors.)

Miles and Directions

0.0 Trailhead.

0.3 Junction with Trespass Creek Trail 267; turn right (stay on jeep road).

1.8 Closed gate, inholding.

2.0 Leave jeep road; turn left onto Trail 197.

5.0 Cottonwood Lake.

10.0 Trailhead.

82 Crazy Mountains Crossing

A backpacking excursion through rugged mountain scenery along a trans–mountain range route

Start: Halfmoon Campground and Trailhead, 25 miles north of Big Timber

Distance: 23.0-mile shuttle

Difficulty: Strenuous

Maps: USGS Campfire Lake and Crazy Peak; Gallatin National Forest Map (North)

Finding the trailheads: Drive 11.2 miles north of Big Timber on US 191 and turn left (west) onto the well-marked Big Timber Canyon Road. Go 1.9 miles and turn right (west) at a major junction, staying on Big Timber Canyon Road. Drive 13.3 miles on this road until it ends at the trailhead and Halfmoon Campground. The trailhead is on your right just before entering the campground. You pass through a guest ranch a few miles before the end of the road. This is a public road, but there is a gate. Be sure to close it behind you. Ample parking; toilet at this trailhead; drinking water and developed camping in the campground. GPS: N46 02.500' / W110 14.450'

To leave a vehicle at the end of the hike (Cottonwood Creek Trailhead), take exit 340 off I-90 (6 miles northeast of Livingston) and drive 14 miles north on US 89 to Clyde Park. About a half mile past Clyde Park, turn right onto heavily used Cottonwood Bench Road (FR 198). Follow FR 198 east for 6.4 miles to the junction with the Cottonwood Creek Road. Turn left (north) here and after about a half mile, turn right (east) on Upper Cottonwood Road. Follow this road for 4.6 miles to the junction with the road to the Ibex Guard Station. Turn right (east) and go 3.1 miles to the trailhead. The road continues but has a closed gate. The road is open to the public, including ATVs and motorcycles, but not to highway vehicles. Please respect private property rights by closing the gate behind you. Ample parking; no toilet. GPS: N45 59.150' / W110 26.067'

The Hike

The Crazy Mountains stand majestically above the plains near Livingston and Big Timber. Severe glacial scouring has produced the enchanting valleys containing numerous high-elevation lakes. Wonderfully sculptured peaks and serrated ridges

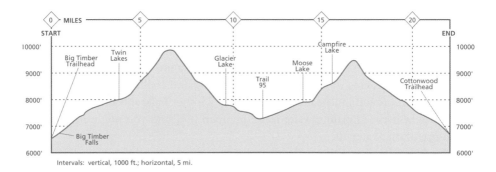

Intervals: vertical, 1000 ft.; horizontal, 5 mi.

A small mountain goat population struggles on in the Crazy Mountains. Courtesy of NPS

radiating from the core of the range rise above 11,000 feet and offer stunning views of the surrounding prairies and distant mountain ranges. This hike description is for two nights out, giving you a glimpse of how pleasant life can be in the heart of mountain goat country, the Crazy Mountains, but don't hesitate to stay longer.

Unfortunately, hiking across the Crazy Mountains means dealing with the checkerboard land situation. You'll find this hard to believe when you get there, but much of the Crazies is privately owned, and some of the private landowners do not tolerate trespassers. Be sure to take the Forest Service map and watch carefully to avoid trespassing. The FS has negotiated an easement for "foot and horse travel only" on Trail 119 from the Halfmoon Trailhead to Trespass Pass even though some of it goes through privately owned sections. But this easement does not include off-trail travel, so check the map before making any side trips. When you cross the divide above Campfire Lake, you get on Trespass Creek Trail 268, which passes through a private section after going over the pass, so please stay on the trail.

To help protect the area and help severely impacted sites recover from past heavy use, the FS has a no campfire restriction around Blue, Granite, Thunder, and Twin Lakes.

Shortly after leaving the Halfmoon Campground and Trailhead on Trail 119, drop your pack for a few minutes and check out Big Timber Falls and the cascade above it. You can hear the churning water from the main trail, and you might be surprised at the size of the waterfall.

The first 1.5 miles of this trail are on the remains of a hastily bulldozed jeep road built long ago to accommodate dredge mining for gold on private land near Twin Lakes at the head of Big Timber Canyon. Later the Forest Service closed the road to motor vehicles. Now it's gradually returning to a scenic singletrack, but you can still see scars left by the bulldozer. You can also still see some signs of mining activity above Twin Lakes, but fortunately not too much, because this place is the face of beauty. Mining it is like going to the National Gallery of Art and gouging holes out of a masterpiece.

Before you get to Twin Lakes, at the 3-mile mark, turn right (west) at the junction with Trail 118 up to Blue and Granite Lakes, which is a nice side trip if you have the time and energy. On the way to the junction, you pass over Big Timber Creek twice on two large bridges built to handle pack trains. Both bridges have natural swimming holes, which will be seductive on a hot, dusty day.

After the Blue Lake junction, the trail skirts the slopes of Granite Peak for about a mile to Lower Twin Lake, smaller and shallower than its twin about another half mile up the trail. This lake basin makes a logical first campsite. You'll find an abundance of good campsites at both lakes and along the stream between the lakes, but check carefully to make sure you're on public land.

From Upper Twin Lake the trail begins a steep, Category 1, mile-long, 2,000-foot ascent to the pass above the lake, which is the divide between the Big Timber and Sweet Grass drainages. Switchbacking across this high, open country, you'll be treated to wildflowers and cascading brooks. The stiff climb is more than compensated for by an awesome view from the top of the Big Timber Creek drainage and surrounding ridges.

From the pass you drop down about a mile into the South Fork of Sweet Grass Creek drainage and Glacier Lake, and alpine beauty fed by sheer waterfalls and a long summer snowmelt. Because of the rocky landscape, campsites are hard to find at Glacier Lake (but at least it's on public land!), so instead of staying the night, have lunch, drink some of the chilled water, watch the little icebergs float in the blue-green lake, and then move on.

From Glacier Lake the trail continues to drop sharply for about 1.5 forested miles to the South Fork of Sweet Grass Creek. Sorry, no bridge, and the crossing can be tricky early in the year, so be careful.

About a quarter mile past the creek, you pass through a series of meadows and rockslides where the trail can fade away at times. There are some choice campsites in these meadows, so you can spend the second night here, if you can find one on public land because the boundary runs near this stream. Another option would be about 2 miles down the trail where the South Fork and Middle Fork of Sweet Grass Creek merge.

At the junction with the trail coming up Sweet Grass Creek, turn left (west) and head upstream toward Moose and Campfire Lakes. It's 3 forested miles to Moose Lake, and about another mile (and a steep one) to Campfire Lake. Don't get this large lake confused with small trailside tarns in the basins near the lake. Campfire Lake is a large, irregularly shaped beauty and often reflects the surrounding peaks in its waters—and has fair fishing for rainbows too.

Campfire Lake has good campsites but is heavily used, so if you stay here, please don't make it any worse—and even make it better by reclaiming fire rings and other damage left by previous campers. Try to resist the temptation to have a campfire even though the lake's name seems to call for it.

Moose Lake might look like a logical alternative to camping at Campfire Lake, but sadly, it's all private land, as is the inlet of Campfire Lake.

From Campfire Lake you face another Category 1, mile-long, 900-foot climb up the divide between Sweet Grass Creek and Trespass Creek. From this 9,500-foot pass, the well-defined Crazy Mountain high country is at eye level. Goat trails cross the rock and snowfields that cling precipitously above the green valleys and shining lakes. On a clear day you can see the Absarokas, Castles, Bridgers, and Spanish Peaks—an inspiring view, to say the least. The lakes of the Sweet Grass drainage shine in the morning sun, and to the east the endless expanse of prairie overwhelms visitors unaccustomed to such grand vistas. It's a tough climb to get up here, but you won't regret the effort it takes. While here you can pause to reflect on the amazing fact that the Crazy Mountains are not being seriously considered for Wilderness designation.

From the divide, drop sharply down into the head of the Trespass Creek drainage. The trail winds through talus slopes and lush meadows for about 2 miles before entering the west-side forest, where it stays along the east side of Trespass Creek for 5 more miles to a jeep road built to a cluster of second homes in the heart of the Crazies on one of the private sections.

When you reach the road, turn right and walk on the road (closed to highway vehicles, but not to the public) for less than a half mile to the Cottonwood Creek Trailhead. Walking on the road might prompt you to make a call or write a letter when you get home about solving the checkerboarding problem and supporting permanent protection for the incredible Crazies.

Miles and Directions

0.0 Halfmoon Trailhead.

0.2 Big Timber Falls.

3.0 Junction with Trail 118; turn right.

3.8 Lower Twin Lake.

4.5 Upper Twin Lake.

7.0 Divide between Big Timber and Sweet Grass Creeks.

8.0 Glacier Lake.

9.5 South Fork of Sweet Grass Creek.

11.0 Middle Fork of Sweet Grass Creek and junction with Trails 122 and 123; turn left onto Trail 123.

14.0 Moose Lake.

15.5 Campfire Lake.

16.5 Divide between Sweet Grass and Trespass Creeks.

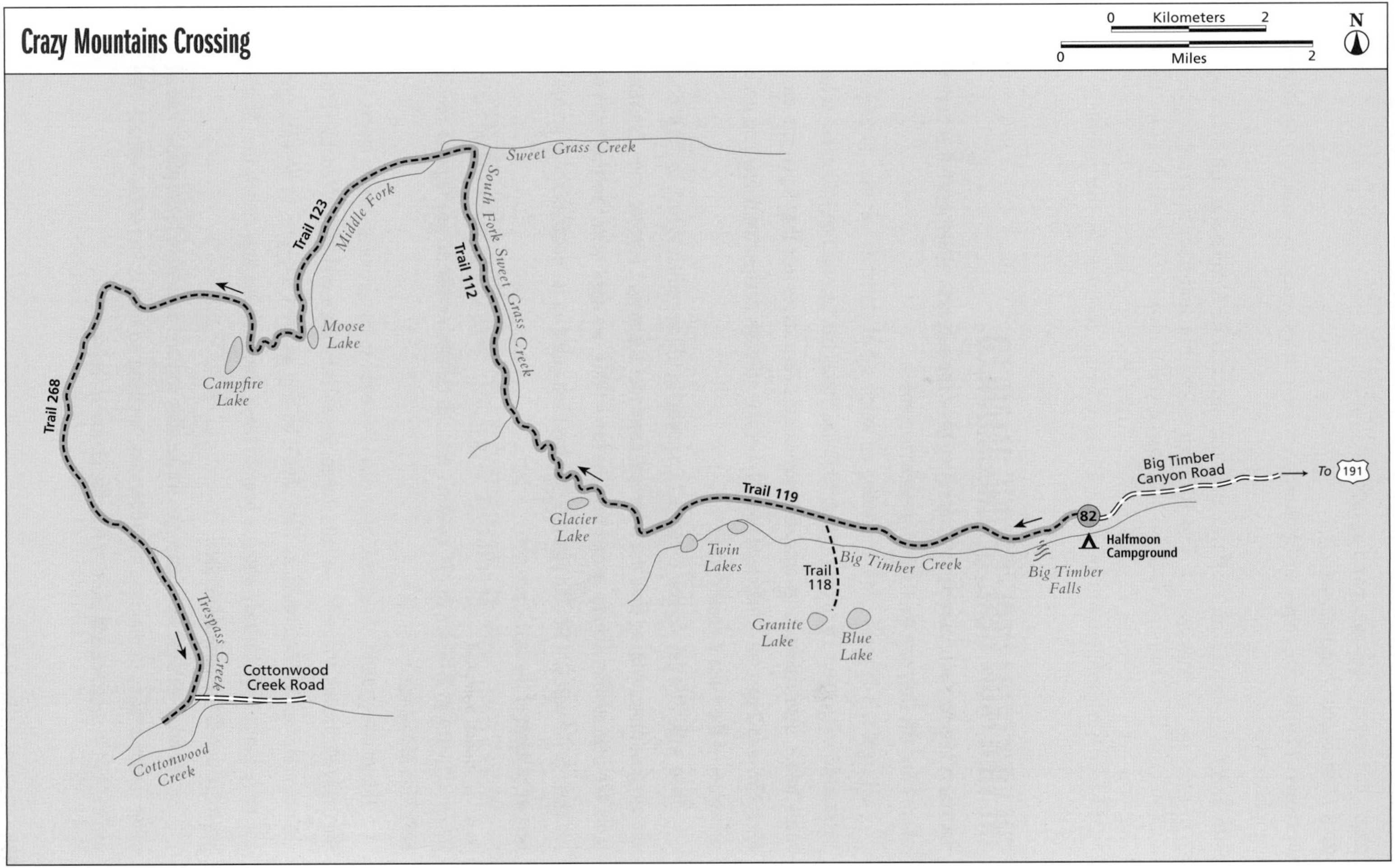

Crazy Mountains Crossing

N

Kilometers
0   2

Miles
0   2

Sweet Grass Creek

South Fork Sweet Grass Creek

Trail 112

Middle Fork

Trail 123

Moose Lake

Campfire Lake

Trail 268

Trespass Creek

Cottonwood Creek Road

Cottonwood Creek

Glacier Lake

Twin Lakes

Trail 119

Granite Lake

Blue Lake

Trail 118

Big Timber Creek

Big Timber Falls

Halfmoon Campground

82

Big Timber Canyon Road

To 191

22.5 Cottonwood Creek jeep road; turn right.

23.0 Cottonwood Creek Trailhead.

Options: This shuttle hike can be done in reverse. It's strenuous, with lots of climbing, either way.

Side Trips: It's about a mile off the main trail up to Blue Lake, steep and on switchbacks most of the way, and the Forest Service does not maintain this trail for horse use. You cross Big Timber Creek on a bridge at the bottom of the climb. From Blue Lake, you get a sweeping view of massive Crazy Peak, the highest in the range at 11,214 feet. (Originally contributed by Bruce Chesler, re-hiked by the authors.)

THE VIEW FROM HERE: GETTING BALANCED

Who hasn't heard a politician on a stump saying he or she supports wilderness but not everywhere? Instead, they say, we need a "balanced" approach.

Let's get this in perspective. Depending on which set of statistics you use, somewhere between 95 and 99 percent of the continental United States has become non-wilderness. It has roads, mines, subdivisions, clear-cuts, or impoundments. That leaves less than 5 percent—more likely closer to 2 percent—that could possibly become officially designated Wilderness under provisions of the 1964 Wilderness Act.

Then, with little debate over these facts, a politician will nonetheless rush to the podium and suggest compromising that last 2 percent down to, I suppose, 1 percent. Then, ten years later, the next politico stands up and says the same thing, we need more "balance" so now it's down to 0.5 percent. Get the picture? This has been going on for decades and is probably why we're down to the last 2 percent.

Here's a reality check for politicians: Even if every roadless acre in the United States was designated as Wilderness, we wouldn't even be remotely close to any legal or official definition of balance.

This middle-ground, "balanced" approach—this need to compromise—is why places like the Crazy Mountains, Pioneers, Gallatin Range, Snowcrest Range, and Rocky Mountain Front are not protected as Wilderness, as they should be, and as every day goes by become more and more threatened. Anybody who has been to these places knows how clearly they fit into any definition of the term *wilderness*.

So, for once, let's get as balanced as we possibly can and designate these places and all other roadless lands in Montana as Wilderness. Anything so rare is incredibly valuable. We can't afford to sacrifice any more of it to the shrine of "balance."

83 Blue Lake

A moderate overnighter to a heavily used alpine lake basin below mighty Crazy Peak in the Crazy Mountains

Start: Halfmoon Campground and Trailhead, 25 miles north of Big Timber
Distance: 8.0-mile out-and-back

Difficulty: Moderate
Maps: USGS Crazy Peak; Gallatin National Forest Map (North)

Finding the trailhead: Drive 11.2 miles north of Big Timber on US 191 and turn left (west) onto the well-marked Big Timber Canyon Road. Go 1.9 miles and turn right (west) at a major junction, staying on Big Timber Canyon Road. Drive 13.3 miles on this road until it ends at the trailhead and Halfmoon Campground. The trailhead is on your right just before entering the campground. You pass through a guest ranch a few miles before the end of the road. This is a public road, but there is a gate. Be sure to close it behind you. There is ample parking; toilet at this trailhead, plus drinking water and developed camping in the campground. GPS: N46 02.500' / W110 14.450'

The Hike

Blue Lake and four other beautiful lakes are nestled in a high basin in the shadow of mighty Crazy Peak, the highest point in the Crazy Mountains at 11,214 feet. Climbers use the lakes as base camps for an ascent of this magnificent mountain or to fish in the lakes or just relax for a few days. On weekends this area gets heavy use, but if you go during the week, you might have it to yourself.

From the trailhead, Trail 119 climbs steadily but not brutally for about 3 miles. The trail is very distinct, even double-wide in places, with some rocky sections.

About a quarter mile up the trail from the trailhead, take the spur trail to the left to see spectacular Big Timber Falls. The main trail crosses Big Timber Creek, a fairly large stream, twice, but both times on sturdy bridges. Note the great swimming holes at each bridge; you might need them on the way out on a hot, dusty day.

At Trail 118, turn left (south) and climb a fairly steep mile up to the lake basin on right-sized switchbacks most of the way. The trail ends at the short section of stream

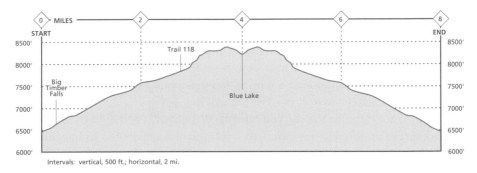

Intervals: vertical, 500 ft.; horizontal, 2 mi.

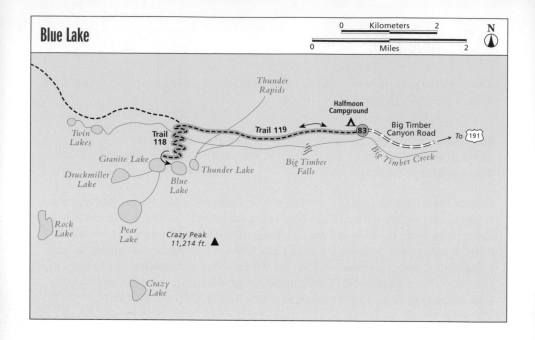

between Granite and Blue Lakes, which is actually private land, as is part of both Blue and Granite Lakes. Spend a few minutes searching for a good campsite in this area. Be sure to find one on public land, and don't pitch your tent next to another camper. To reduce resource damage, Forest Service regulations prohibit campfires in this lake basin.

The lakes have an abundance of huge whitebark pines, which you don't see often, and a few rainbow trout, which can be a challenge for a fly caster.

Miles and Directions

0.0 Halfmoon Trailhead.

0.2 Big Timber Falls.

3.0 Junction with Trail 118; turn left.

4.0 Granite and Blue Lakes.

8.0 Halfmoon Trailhead.

Side Trips: Thunder Lake (smaller than Blue and Granite Lakes but nice) and Thunder Rapids are a short jaunt along the shoreline of Blue Lake on a good social trail.

Pear and Druckmiller Lakes are more challenging, all-day trips, made more difficult by having to find a way around blocks of private land along logical routes.

Crazy Peak is probably the most common side trip, but it's only for fit, experienced peak baggers and those who want to trespass. Crazy Peak, the highest point in the Crazies, is privately owned! No, I'm not making that up.

If you have extra time the day you hike, hang your packs at the junction and take the short jaunt up to gorgeous Twin Lakes. (Originally contributed and re-hiked by the authors.)

84 Sacajawea Peak

A day trek to the top of the highest peak in the Bridger Range

Start: Fairy Lake Trailhead, 15 miles north of Bozeman

Distance: 5.0-mile out-and-back

Difficulty: Strenuous

Maps: USGS Sacajawea Peak; Gallatin National Forest Map (North)

Finding the trailhead: From Bozeman, drive 20 miles up Bridger Canyon Road (MT 86), past the Bridger Bowl Ski Area. About a mile past Battle Ridge Campground, turn left (west) and take Fairy Lake Road (FR 74) for 6 miles to the campground and trailhead. This road is passable by vehicle but a difficult route for camper trailers. Ample parking; toilet; vehicle camping at Fairy Lake Campground near the trailhead. GPS: N45 54.433' / W110 57.883'

Sacajawea Peak in the Bridger Range. JACQUELYN CORDAY

The local residents of Sacajawea Peak. JACQUELYN CORDAY

The Hike

Hundreds, if not thousands, of Bozeman-area residents have climbed Sacajawea Peak. Pack up a picnic lunch and find out why. Bring water; you won't find any along this route. Also, snow continues to cover portions of this trail until mid-July.

Find the trailhead and note the massive furrowed limestone on the east face of Sacajawea Peak just above Fairy Lake. The route, Trail 534, is a 2.5-mile, 2,000-foot,

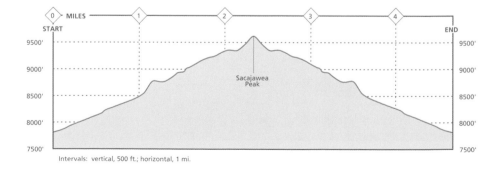

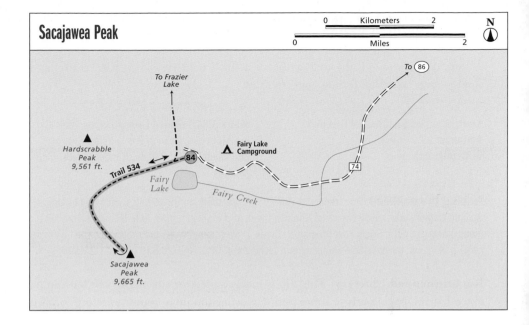

Sacajawea Peak

To Frazier Lake

To 86

Hardscrabble Peak 9,561 ft.

Trail 534

Fairy Lake Campground

84

74

Fairy Lake

Fairy Creek

Sacajawea Peak 9,665 ft.

Category H climb that goes right to the top of Sacajawea. First you climb to the saddle between Sacajawea Peak and Hardscrabble Peak, where you take the trail to the left (south) and follow its twists and turns up to the top.

When you reach the summit, you'll know why so many people go here. On a clear day you can see half the hiking areas this book describes. On a nice weekend in the summer, you'll most certainly encounter other hikers on the trail and at the summit. This isn't an opportunity for wilderness isolation and introspection, but rather a place to meet friends and neighbors who just thought they'd take a couple hours to work up a sweat and remind themselves how really swell Montana is. (Contributed by Pat Caffrey, updated by the authors.)

Miles and Directions

0.0 Trailhead.

2.5 Sacajawea Peak.

5.0 Trailhead.

85 Spanish Peaks

A long circuit through the midsection of a small wilderness area with many high alpine views, lakes, and fishing opportunities

Start: 20 miles southwest of Bozeman
Distance: 23.0-mile loop
Difficulty: Strenuous

Maps: USGS Hidden Lakes, Gallatin Peak, Garnet Mountain, Beacon Point, Willow Swamp, and Cherry Lake; Gallatin National Forest Map (South)

Finding the trailhead: From Belgrade, drive 7.5 miles south on US 191. Just before entering Gallatin Canyon, take a right (west) up Spanish Creek at a marked turnoff. After 5.2 miles, turn left (south) and go up the South Fork of Spanish Creek. Drive about 4 miles until you reach the trailhead. Large parking lot; toilet; vehicle camping; and picnic area. GPS: N45 26.849' / W111 22.599'

Recommended itinerary: This trip is nicely suited for two nights out but can be extended by making a base camp and exploring the high country for one or two additional days.
First night: Upper Falls Creek Lake or Jerome Rock Lakes
Second night: Big Brother Lake

The Hike

The Spanish Peaks is a popular hiking area—and you'll probably see some stock parties too. This route, however, skirts the most heavily used portions while still providing the same incredible scenery that has made the Spanish Peaks Wilderness nationally famous.

The Spanish Peaks could be called a pocket wilderness. It's isolated on the north edge of the sprawling Big Sky development. In the 1970s Montana wilderness advocates agreed to sacrifice Jack Creek in exchange for the designation of a segmented Lee Metcalf Wilderness. The South Fork of the Gallatin (now filled with residential and commercial development associated with Big Sky) and Jack Creek form

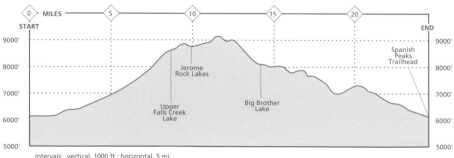

Intervals: vertical, 1000 ft.; horizontal, 5 mi.

Hiking the Spanish Peaks Wilderness. MIKE HARRELSON

a corridor of civilization between the two sections of the wilderness, the Taylor-Hilgard to the south and the Spanish Peaks to the north.

You should wait until at least early July to try this trip, preferably mid-July. Before going, you might want to call the Forest Service to check snow conditions. You want the snow line to be below 9,000 feet before taking this trip. Below 8,700 feet would make it easier to find a dry campsite and safely cross a small pass just west of Jerome Rock Lakes.

The 23-mile loop goes up the South Fork of Spanish Creek and comes back to the same trailhead through the headwaters of Camp and Cuff Creeks, using Trails 407, 413, 401, and 409 in a clockwise direction.

From the trailhead, begin hiking on South Fork of Spanish Creek Trail 407, which is well maintained (thanks to local backcountry horsemen). All major creek crossings have bridges.

At 3 miles turn left at the junction with Falls Creek Trail 410 to stay on Trail 407. At 5.5 miles Trail 407 turns off to the left and heads to Mirror Lake. Stay right on the

Enjoying the super-scenic Spanish Peaks Wilderness. JACQUELYN CORDAY

South Fork of Spanish Creek Trail 413 to Upper Falls Creek Lake. Shortly after the Mirror Lake junction, at 6 miles, you pass a junction with Trail 411 to Spanish Lakes. Again stay right, heading southwest and uphill on Trail 413.

At 8.5 miles Trail 413 junctions with Trail 412, which heads southeast to Lake Solitude, a nice side trip with lots of good campsites, great views, and fish. For now, stay right on Trail 413 for Jerome Rock Lakes. You'll pass Upper Falls Creek Lake on your right at 9 miles.

Just before Jerome Rock Lakes, at 9.3 miles, Trail 413 junctions with Falls Creek Trail 410. If you want to cut your trip short, this is a possible shortcut. From here, it's about 8 miles back to the trailhead. If you haven't had enough of the spectacular high lakes of the Spanish Peaks, however, stay left, continuing west on Trail 413 for Jerome Rock Lakes at 9.5 miles.

This first day can be strenuous, especially the big hill out of the South Fork of Spanish Creek. The second day is short and easy, though, and the third day is mostly downhill.

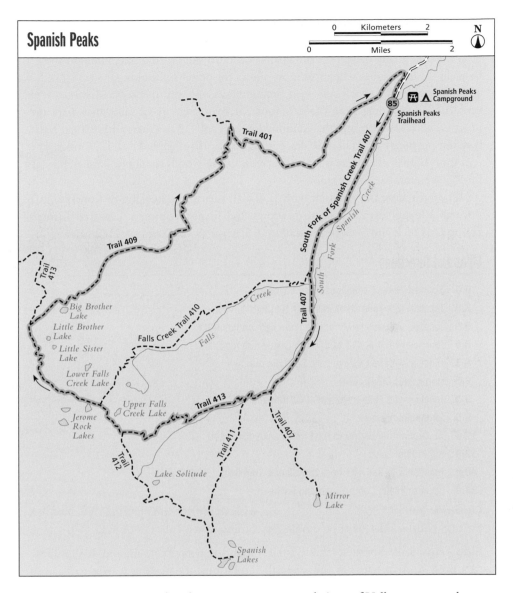

Spanish Peaks

Spanish Peaks
Campground

85

Spanish Peaks
Trailhead

Trail 401

South Fork of Spanish Creek Trail 407

Spanish Creek

Trail 409

Trail 413

South Fork

Creek

Falls Creek Trail 410

Trail 407

Big Brother
Lake

Little Brother
Lake

Little Sister
Lake

Falls

Lower Falls
Creek Lake

Upper Falls
Creek Lake

Trail 413

Jerome
Rock
Lakes

Trail 411

Trail 407

Trail
412

Lake Solitude

Mirror
Lake

Spanish
Lakes

All three Jerome Rock Lakes support smart populations of Yellowstone cutthroat trout. The lower and middle lakes have adequate campsites, but camping is marginal at the upper lake. You can find the middle lake by following the stream. Resist the temptation to build a campfire in this high-altitude area where wood is sparse and scenic. Jerome Rock Lakes is a good spot to set up a base camp to spend a day or two exploring the Spanish Peaks.

Wildflowers abound in this area, especially glacier lilies and yellow columbine. In fact, I saw fields of glacier lilies and yellow columbine, more than in well-known wildflower havens Glacier National Park and the Beartooths.

After enjoying Jerome Rock Lakes, continue northwest on Trail 413 and cross a 9,200-foot pass before Brother and Sister Lakes Basin. In June and early July, there can be some potentially dangerous snowbanks on both sides of the pass. Hike on snow-fields in the afternoon, when soft snow allows for better footholds.

When we did this trip, the next junction was not well marked and was easy to miss. After descending from the pass, look for two cairns at 12 miles that mark the junction with Trail 409 and the continuation of Trail 413 to Cherry Lake. Turn right, heading northeast on Trail 409, descending to Big Brother Lake at 12.9 miles. The trail from Big Brother Lake is a pleasant walk in the woods for about 7 miles, passing through several spacious meadows.

Upon reaching the junction with Trail 401, turn right, heading east on Trail 401 through a logged area and open meadows, and finally looping around Ted Turner's Flying D Ranch and back to the trailhead. Stay on the trail and avoid trespassing.

Miles and Directions

0.0 Spanish Peaks Campground and Trailhead.

3.0 Junction with Falls Creek Trail 410; turn left.

5.5 Junction with trail to Mirror Lake; turn right on Trail 413.

6.0 Junction with Trail 411 to Spanish Lakes; turn right.

8.5 Junction with Trail 412 to Lake Solitude; turn right.

9.0 Upper Falls Creek Lake.

9.3 Junction with Falls Creek Trail 410; turn left.

9.5 Jerome Rock Lakes.

12.0 Junction with Trail 409 to Big Brother Lake; turn right.

12.9 Big Brother Lake.

20.0 Junction with Trail 401 back to trailhead; turn right.

23.0 Spanish Peaks Campground and Trailhead.

Options: You can do this hike in reverse with about the same level of difficulty. You can also cut this hike short by 6 miles by coming down Falls Creek Trail 410.

Side Trips: Lake Solitude (about 2 miles round-trip on Trail 412 and easy) is close to a must-do side trip. For the especially ambitious, try making it over to Spanish Lakes and back for a long, strenuous day hike. (Originally contributed by Art Foran, re-hiked by the authors.)

86 Hilgard Basin

A popular backpacking trip into the southern Madison Range to a super-scenic, high-altitude, lake-filled basin; a good choice for a base camp hike

Start: Potamogeton Park Trailhead, 15 miles north of West Yellowstone

Distance: 19.0-mile out-and-back

Difficulty: Moderate

Maps: USGS Hilgard Peak and Pika Point; Gallatin National Forest Map (South)

Finding the trailhead: Drive south of Ennis on US 287 for 47.5 miles or northwest of West Yellowstone for 24.5 miles (8 miles to the junction of US 191 and US 287, continuing on US 287 toward Quake Lake) and turn north on Beaver Creek Road (FR 985). Follow Beaver Creek Road for about 4.5 miles until it ends at Potamogeton Park Trailhead. Three trails leave this trailhead; take Sentinel Creek Trail 202 on the west side of the parking area. Ample parking; toilet (with bullet holes in door when we were there!); designated dispersed camping along Beaver Creek, in addition to the developed Cabin Creek Campground on US 287 just east of the Beaver Creek turnoff. You can also stay at a Forest Service rental, the Beaver Creek Cabin, 3 miles off FR 985. GPS: N44 55.649' / W111 21.616'

The Hike

This route could be an overnighter or even a long day hike, but it would be your big loss to head back without spending at least one day exploring, climbing, and fishing in the main basin or the south basin by making this a two- or three-night base camp. Of all the Madison Range's natural wonders, the Hilgard Basin is probably the most beautiful and popular.

Three trails leave the Potamogeton Park Trailhead. You want Sentinel Creek Trail 202, on the west edge of the trailhead.

Sentinel Creek Trail 202 crosses Beaver Creek on a bridge and then climbs gradually all the way to the rim of Hilgard Basin. It really doesn't seem like you're gaining

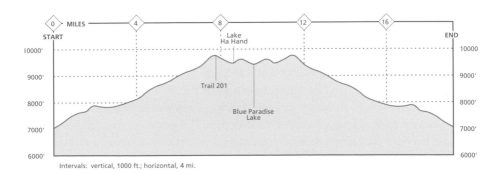

Looking south over Headquarters Pass. JACQUELYN CORDAY

2,700 feet. The sign at the trailhead says it's 8 miles to the basin, but it's a long 8 miles, all on a well-worn trail frequently used by stock parties. After a few miles, periodic feeder streams tumble down to join Sentinel Creek, so you can plan on finding water along most of the trail.

About a mile before Expedition Pass, on a high saddle, the splendor of the Hilgard Basin unfolds before you. Trail 201 turns left (south) into the basin; follow it down. At the saddle you can see Expedition Lake and several others in the foreground and Echo Peak, creating a perfect backdrop. Spend a few minutes taking in the views. Get out the map and start to make the difficult decision on which nearly perfect campsite you want. You have at least a hundred great options. They aren't officially designated but have become established through heavy use. Make sure you set up a zero-impact camp to preserve the fragile beauty for the next backpackers who follow your steps. Use your backpacking stove, leaving the area's scarce wood supply intact.

It's hard not to be thrilled at the scenery and wildness of the Hilgard Basin; Echo Peak in the background. JACQUELYN CORDAY

Hilgard Basin is very popular and gets more popular every year, and with ever-increasing use, the need for more regulation often follows. Camping is not allowed within 200 feet of any lake or 100 feet of any stream. Hilgard Basin is among the most fragile of hiking areas, so take every precaution to leave zero impact.

For peak baggers the basin acts as a base for several climbs, with 11,214-foot Echo Peak being the most popular and an easy scramble. Also in the vicinity is 11,316-foot Hilgard Peak, which is the highest and most technical peak in the Madison Range (and the highest anywhere in Montana outside the Beartooths), only for more experienced climbers.

Most of the lakes used to support trout populations, but the harsh winters have frozen out some of them. The treat here is the thrill of discovery. You never know which lake has the good fishing until you try it.

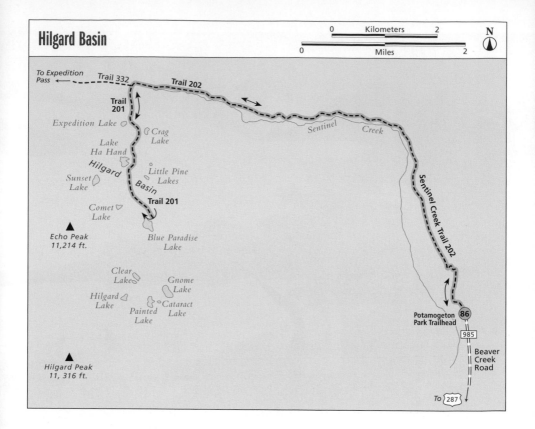

After your hike (not before it) stop into the Grizzly Bar and Grill about 10 miles north of Quake Lake for a Grizzly Burger, which may be bigger and better than the famed Grizzly Burger at the Grizzly Bar in Roscoe near the East Rosebud Trailhead.

Miles and Directions

- **0.0**   Potamogeton Park Trailhead.
- **8.0**   Junction with Trail 201; turn left.
- **8.5**   Lake Ha Hand.
- **9.5**   Blue Paradise Lake.
- **19.0**   Potamogeton Park Trailhead.

Side Trips: Hiking an extra mile into the South Hilgard Basin on a nonmaintained social trail leads you to more jewel-like lakes in the shadow of mighty Hilgard Peak, which is a must-do side trip. The nonmaintained trail leads past Blue Paradise Lake into the south basin, ending near Clear Lake. Also, you can spend an entire day just going from lake to lake in the main basin and testing out the fishing or climbing a peak or two. (Originally contributed and re-hiked by the authors.)

87 Coffin Lakes

A day hike or overnighter to a pair of high mountain lakes along the Continental Divide

Start: Watkins Creek Trailhead, 12 miles west of West Yellowstone
Distance: 10.0-mile out-and-back

Difficulty: Moderate
Maps: USGS Hebgen Dam; Gallatin National Forest Map (South)

Finding the trailhead: Drive west of West Yellowstone on US 20 for 7 miles and turn north onto FR 167 for Lonesomehurst, Cherry, and Spring Creek Campgrounds on Hebgen Lake. Drive 11.5 miles (first 1.5 miles paved), and past Spring Creek Campground on your left (west) is Watkins Creek Trailhead. Limited parking; no toilet; designated dispersed camping nearby at Hebgen Lake. GPS: N44 47.933' / W111 17.149'

The Hike

Contrary to popular belief, the Madison Range does not end with the Taylor-Hilgards but continues south across Quake Lake into the little-visited Henry's Lake Mountains (sometimes called the Lionhead Mountains, which actually refers to Lionhead Mountain, southeast of Coffin Lakes). Familiar only to a few locals, this range feature several high mountain lakes surrounded by 10,000-foot peaks.

From the trailhead, head west up the creek on Watkins Creek Trail 215 for a little over 3 miles to the junction with Coffin Lakes Trail 209. The first 2 miles go through grassy sagebrush country, beautiful but also part of a grazing allotment. Don't step in the cow pies.

Turn right onto Coffin Lakes Trail 209, which takes off up Coffin Creek for 2 more miles to Coffin Lakes, all through forested country. At 3.5 miles you reach the junction with Watkins Creek Trail 216, which veers off to the right. Stay on Coffin Lake Trail 209.

The lower lake has two or three good campsites at the lower end. It also has a good population of cutthroat trout, but the shoreline is heavily forested, so watch your backcast.

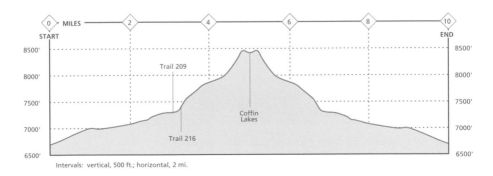

Intervals: vertical, 500 ft.; horizontal, 2 mi.

Bighorn sheep, found along many Montana trails. SHUTTERSTOCK

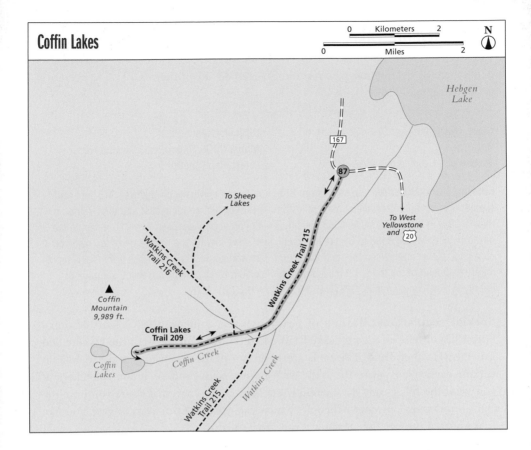

Coffin Lakes

0 Kilometers 2
0 Miles 2

N

Hebgen Lake

167

87

To Sheep Lakes

To West Yellowstone and 20

Watkins Creek Trail 216

Watkins Creek Trail 215

Coffin Mountain 9,989 ft.

Coffin Lakes Trail 209

Coffin Lakes

Coffin Creek

Watkins Creek Trail 215

Watkins Creek

Miles and Directions

0.0 Watkins Creek Trailhead.

3.0 Junction with Coffin Lakes Trail 209; turn right.

3.5 Junction with Watkins Creek Trail 216; turn left.

5.0 Coffin Lakes.

10.0 Watkins Creek Trailhead.

Side Trips: Coffin Lakes serve as a good base camp to explore the surrounding area. You can wander over to Upper Coffin Lake and scramble to the flat-topped summit of Coffin Mountain to the north. The views here of the rest of the Madison Range and the vast expanse of Yellowstone Park are stunning. Watch for mountain goats.

By climbing out of the lake basin toward the south, you can cross the Continental Divide and gaze down at the many lakes in the headwaters of Targhee Creek in Idaho, seldom visited by hikers. On the way out, you can take a 2-mile one-way jaunt over to Sheep Lakes. (Originally contributed by Ed Madej, re-hiked by the authors.)

88 Hyalite Lake

A day hike or overnighter past cascading waterfalls, 11 of them no less, to the gorgeous subalpine Hyalite Basin

Start: Hyalite Trailhead, 20 miles south of Bozeman
Distance: 11.0-mile out-and-back

Difficulty: Moderate
Maps: USGS Fridley Peak; Gallatin National Forest Map (South)

Finding the trailhead: Drive south from Bozeman by the university on Highway 345 (not well signed; also called 19th Avenue) for 7 miles before turning left, heading east and then south up Hyalite Canyon Road 62. This junction is marked with Forest Service signs. Drive 10 miles on the paved Hyalite Canyon Road to Hyalite Reservoir, then drive around the north side of the reservoir on a good gravel road. When the road forks, turn right and go past Window Rock Cabin for 2 more miles to the end of the road, 3.2 miles from the reservoir. Large parking lot; toilet; camping at nearby vehicle campgrounds. GPS: N45 26.817' / W110 57.750'

Special regulations: Because of heavy use and conflicts, the Gallatin National Forest has developed a complicated Timeshare Travel Plan for both the Hyalite and Emerald/Heather Trails. The trails are open to hiking seven days a week, but on certain days, hikers share the trails with motorcyclists and/or mountain bikers. If you want the hiker-only days, carefully check in advance to make sure you have the right—and most current—schedule, which can change from year to year. You can find updated information at www.fs.usda.gov/gallatin.

The Hike

While walking 5.5 miles south and 1,800 feet up on the well-maintained Trail 427, you pass eleven waterfalls cascading in a stair-step fashion out of a red-rocked mountain bowl. None are large, but each has its own unique character, as their names suggest: Grotto, Arch, Twin, Silken Skein, Champagne, Chasm, Shower, Devil's Slide, Apex, S'il Vous Plait, and Alpine. Each waterfall lures you onward to see the next

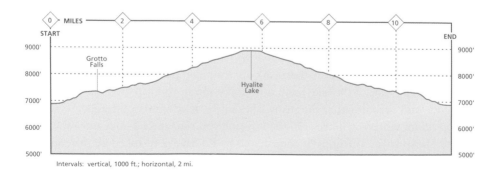

Intervals: vertical, 1000 ft.; horizontal, 2 mi.

cascade. Time on Trail 427 passes quickly, and before you know it, you're climbing out of the timber about 5 miles later into the wide bowl holding Hyalite Lake.

The Hyalite Lake Trail is justly popular with people in the Bozeman area, but most usage occurs at the lower end by day hikers who come for a short walk to see a couple of the waterfalls. By the time you reach the lake, you may have the surrounding country to yourself. The first 1.2 miles to Grotto Falls is a wheelchair-accessible trail. In some places, such as Grotto Falls, the trail doesn't go directly to the waterfall. Instead, you take short spur trails to see them.

The trail is open to mountain bikers and, regrettably, motorcycles. There aren't many places you can see motorcycles and wheelchairs on the same trail.

The lake has a few good campsites at its lower end, but they are very heavily impacted, so please have a zero-impact camp. No campfires, please.

Don't count on trout for dinner; the lake is too shallow to stay liquid in some winters. Instead, enjoy the spectacular vistas, which include Fridley Peak to the southeast and Hyalite Peak just to the southwest. A large meadow stretches around the lake and expands out to the base of Fridley Peak.

Birds seem to like the basin. On the edges of the timber, Clark's nutcrackers and gray jays flash their black-and-white patterns; Steller's jays catch the eye with their iridescent blue crests. Moreover, hummingbirds hover out in the meadow, attracted by the wildflowers. Especially abundant are paintbrush, lupine, fleabane, and four-o'clock.

In the evening you may hear or see a deer come down for a drink at the lakeshore. Spotting an occasional elk, mountain goat, or black bear is a possibility. Even grizzlies have been sighted in the vicinity, so practice all the principles of bear awareness described at the beginning of this book. Most assuredly, a few marmots will whistle at you as you explore the bowl.

Winter releases its grip on the Hyalite Basin quite late by lowland standards. Snowbanks may linger until late June, and winter can quickly return, making late September and October trips a gamble.

While enjoying your stay, try to figure out why such a stunning piece of landscape has not been made part of the wilderness preservation system.

Miles and Directions

- **0.0** Hyalite Trailhead.
- **1.2** Wheelchair-accessible spur trail to Grotto Falls.
- **5.5** Hyalite Lake.
- **11.0** Hyalite Trailhead.

Side Trips: While at Hyalite Lake, consider a couple of short but interesting side trips that begin at the outlet of the lake. One is an easy 2-mile walk to the top of Hyalite Peak (10,299 feet) for views down into Horseshoe Basin and out into the

Hyalite Lake

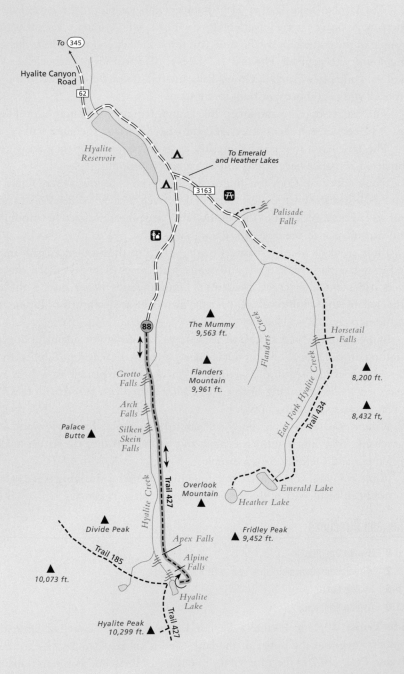

To 345

Hyalite Canyon Road

62

Hyalite Reservoir

To Emerald and Heather Lakes

3163

Palisade Falls

The Mummy 9,563 ft.

Flanders Creek

Horsetail Falls

88

Grotto Falls

Flanders Mountain 9,961 ft.

8,200 ft.

Arch Falls

East Fork Hyalite Creek

Trail 434

Palace Butte

Silken Skein Falls

8,432 ft,

Hyalite Creek

Trail 427

Overlook Mountain

Emerald Lake

Heather Lake

Divide Peak

Fridley Peak 9,452 ft.

Trail 185

Apex Falls

Alpine Falls

10,073 ft.

Hyalite Lake

Hyalite Peak 10,299 ft.

Trail 427

Yellowstone River country. The other is a 2-mile hike across a neighboring cirque and up a ridge to the Hyalite/Squaw Creek Divide. Both provide high vantage points from which to enjoy the beautiful Gallatin Range. (Originally contributed by Mike Sample, re-hiked by the authors.)

THE VIEW FROM HERE: THE MULTIUSABILITY MYTH

Multiuse routes have become popular with some public-land managers, but it almost never works out as planned. All public land users want more access, so a common agency response is taking certain routes and making them open to all, but does the so-called multiuse trail solve the problem and make everybody happy?

Hardly. It makes more people unhappy, at best.

The multiuse concept does work among nonmotorized users. Hikers, trail runners, mountain bikers, and backcountry horsemen can and almost always do peacefully and courteously share a trail. If any minor conflict arises, it's almost always quickly resolved. In this book, two excellent examples of this multiuse détente are the Stuart Peak and Mount Helena Ridge routes, both heavily used trails near cities.

Likewise, multiuse works well among some motorized users. A route can be open to ATVs, motorcycles, jeeps, and other motorized vehicles with little or no conflict. But if you put pack trains and backpackers on the same route, you have a conflict. One excellent example of this conflict is Hollow Top Lake, a route I left in this book because it's only partially on an ATV road and because it's such a great hike. In past editions of this hiking guide, however, I have had to remove routes after land managers opened them up to motorized use.

What's the answer to this dilemma? It doesn't seem too far-out to suggest that agencies label routes as nonmotorized or motorized, but never shall they merge. If hikers choose to hike on an ATV "troad," they certainly have the right to do so, but I wouldn't expect too many to do it when they have a choice of hiking a nonmotorized-only trail.

89 Emerald and Heather Lakes

A day hike or overnighter to two beautiful mountain lakes

Start: 20 miles south of Bozeman
Distance: 11.0-mile out-and-back
Difficulty: Moderate

Maps: USGS Fridley Peak; Gallatin National Forest Map (South)

Finding the trailhead: Drive south from Bozeman by the university on Highway 345 (not well signed; also called 19th Avenue) for 7 miles before turning left, heading east and then south up Hyalite Canyon Road 62. This junction is marked with Forest Service signs. Drive 19 miles on the paved Hyalite Canyon Road to Hyalite Reservoir, then drive around the north side of the reservoir on a good gravel road for 2 miles to a fork in the road. Here, turn left onto East Fork Road 3163 and continue east (past the turnout on the left for the short hike to Palisade Falls) for 2.1 miles until the road ends at the trailhead, the last mile possibly a bit rough for some vehicles. Ample parking at the trailhead; toilet with picnic area nearby; camping in nearby campgrounds. GPS: N45 27.466' / W110 55.250'

Special regulations: Because of heavy use and conflicts, the Gallatin National Forest has developed a complicated Timeshare Travel Plan for both the Hyalite and Emerald/Heather Trails. The trails are open to hiking seven days a week, but on certain days, hikers share the trails with motorcyclists and/or mountain bikers. If you want the hiker-only days, carefully check in advance to make sure you have the right—and most current—schedule, which can change from year to year. You can find updated information at www.fs.usda.gov/gallatin.

The Hike

Although somewhat rocky in places, Trail 434 to Emerald Lake is generally well maintained. Over the 5.5-mile gradual uphill pull, you emerge from the thick forest to gain increasingly expansive views of the rugged cliffs to the east. These cliffs eventually pinch in and meet the mountainous ridge from the west to form the walls of the cirque that holds Emerald and Heather Lakes and a few unnamed tarns.

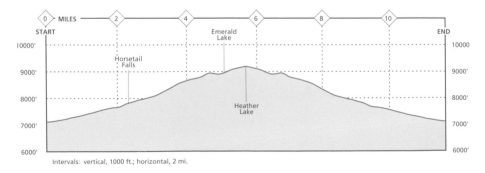

Intervals: vertical, 1000 ft.; horizontal, 2 mi.

Emerald Lake sits in a dramatic, high-altitude setting. SHUTTERSTOCK

The trail follows the East Fork of Hyalite Creek most of the way, and drinking water is readily available. Wait until July to try this hike, however, as the area remains clogged with snow through June. This route gets lots of use, and the trail is double wide much of the way. The trail is open to mountain bikes and motorcycles.

At 2.5 miles from the trailhead, the East Fork of Hyalite Creek tumbles over Horsetail Falls, a sight well worth seeing. The falls are plainly visible from the trail; the sound of falling water will be a tonic for anyone who has stayed out on the plains too long.

Perhaps the highlight of the trip is the incredible display of wildflowers. Color is everywhere. You will find glacier lily, columbine, lupine, paintbrush, alpine forget-me-not, shooting star, and many more flower species. About a half mile before the lake, you walk through a gorgeous meadow surrounded by stately whitebark pines, where the wildflower display is especially vivid.

Once at Emerald Lake, you can easily understand how it was named. It's a real jewel.

You have a wide choice of campsites in the meadows interspersed around the lake with sparse stands of subalpine timber, including lots of stately whitebark pines. They are all heavily used, however, so leave zero impact. You'll find a pit toilet at the far end of the lake.

A rough trail departs from the west side of Emerald Lake and travels about a half mile to Heather Lake, gaining 250 feet in elevation. From the trailhead to Heather Lake, Trail 434 climbs a total of about 2,000 feet, yet there are no prohibitively steep pitches.

Emerald and Heather Lakes

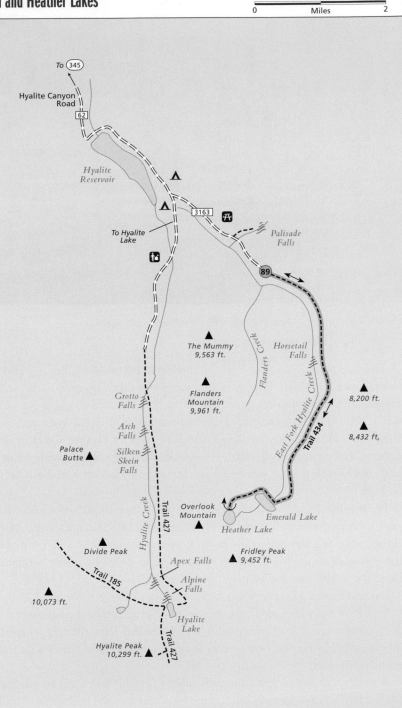

0   Kilometers   2

0   Miles   2

N

To (345)

Hyalite Canyon Road

62

Hyalite Reservoir

3163

To Hyalite Lake

Palisade Falls

The Mummy
9,563 ft.

Flanders Creek

Horsetail Falls

▲ 8,200 ft.

Grotto Falls

*Flanders Mountain
9,961 ft.*

▲ 8,432 ft,

Arch Falls

East Fork Hyalite Creek

Trail 434

Palace Butte ▲

Silken Skein Falls

Hyalite Creek

Trail 427

Overlook Mountain

Emerald Lake

Heather Lake

Divide Peak ▲

Fridley Peak
9,452 ft. ▲

Apex Falls

Trail 185

Alpine Falls

▲ 10,073 ft.

Hyalite Lake

Hyalite Peak
10,299 ft. ▲

Trail 427

Heather Lake doesn't have as many potential campsites as Emerald. The wall of the cirque falls sharply down to the shore of Heather Lake on the west side, while rock shelves and snowbanks protrude on the other shores. Both lakes offer fair fishing for pan-size trout.

These lakes are just north of Yellowstone National Park, but the chance of stumbling into a grizzly bear is remote. Nonetheless, take the standard precautions. The chances of seeing deer, black bears, elk, or mountain goats are good.

Although the trail receives above-average use, most hikers apparently have taken care not to leave signs of their passing. Please pay special attention to wilderness camping manners, however, as this is fragile, beautiful, alpine country. (Originally contributed by Mike Sample, re-hiked by the authors.)

Miles and Directions

0.0 Trailhead.
2.5 Horsetail Falls.
4.5 Emerald Lake.
5.5 Heather Lake.
11.0 Trailhead.

Emerald Lake and its clearly high water quality, the type of watershed from which we want our drinking water to originate. SHUTTERSTOCK

90 Pine Creek Lake

A day hike or overnighter to a beautiful mountain lake with attractive side trips

Start: Pine Creek Campground and Trailhead, 15 miles southeast of Livingston
Distance: 10.0-mile out-and-back
Difficulty: Moderate

Maps: USGS Mt. Cowen; Mt. Cowen and Gallatin National Forest Map (Central); Rocky Mountain Survey Mt. Cowen Area Map

Finding the trailhead: Drive south from Livingston on US 89 for 5 miles and turn left (east) onto East River Road (Highway 540). Head south for 9 miles; 0.7 mile past the cabin community of Pine Creek, turn left (east) onto paved FR 202. Go to the end of this road (2.5 miles, paved all the way), where Trail 47 starts at the far end of the campground. For an alternate route from US 89, take Pine Creek Road between mile markers 43 and 44. Ample parking; toilet; camping at the vehicle campground at the trailhead. GPS: N45 29.900' / W110 31.399'

The Hike

From the trailhead, the first mile of Trail 47 is deceptively flat. At the end of the flat stretch, you stand at the foot of beautiful Pine Creek Falls. This is far enough for some hikers who have heard about the next 4 miles. In those 4 miles the trail climbs more than 3,000 feet, a Category 1 climb. For others, however, the allure of a mountain lake held in a glacial cirque is too much to resist.

Because the trail climbs nearly 1,000 feet per mile, most people take between three and four hours to reach the lake. On the bright side, coming out takes only two hours. The steepness makes this a day trip for most hikers who don't want to lug an overnight pack up the super-steep grade.

Areas of this drainage burned in fall of 2012 during the Pine Creek fire, which started down near the community of Pine Creek. This fire burned most extremely in South Deep Creek, but burned in a more patchy manner in Pine Creek, including

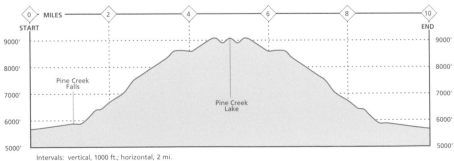

Intervals: vertical, 1000 ft.; horizontal, 2 mi.

An early summer trek into Pine Creek Lake. Mike Harrelson

parts of the Pine Creek Trail, especially between 2.5 and 4 miles. Take care to keep a heads up while hiking through a burn, as snags are unpredictable, especially in high winds.

The lake lies beneath 10,940-foot Black Mountain in an obvious glacial cirque. On the north side of the lake, the bedrock shows pronounced striations where the glacier shoved its rocky load across the granite. At the outlet a broad slab of granite impounds the lake. You'll find overly friendly ground squirrels, marmots, and pikas around the lake, and perhaps a few mountain goats, too.

The best time to visit Pine Creek Lake is between July 15 and September 30. To attempt it any earlier will mean wading through snowdrifts on the last part of the trail; in October those drifts may reappear quickly. If you prize solitude, wait until after Labor Day. Before school starts, youth camps use the trail heavily.

One of the pleasures of camping at Pine Creek Lake is the possibility of seeing alpenglow on the peaks. As the sun moves lower in the west and begins to set behind the Gallatin Range, the atmosphere deflects a portion of the color in the spectrum, leaving a pronounced reddish hue in the last few moments of sunlight. When the conditions are right and this red light bounces off the polished rock surfaces just north of the outlet, the effect is startling. With only a little poetic license, one could say it looks like the peaks are on fire.

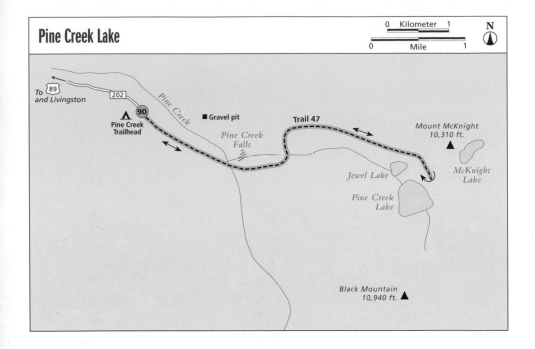

Pine Creek Lake

0   Kilometer   1

0   Mile   1

N

To 89
and Livingston

202

90

Pine Creek
Trailhead

Pine Creek

■ Gravel pit

Pine Creek
Falls

Trail 47

Mount McKnight
10,310 ft.

Jewel Lake

McKnight
Lake

Pine Creek
Lake

Black Mountain
10,940 ft. ▲

You find several campsites, most heavily impacted, close to the lake, but instead of using one of them, look for an impacted site away from the water. There are also some good sites to the southwest of the main lake, up in a little side drainage.

Pine Creek Lake has a nice population of cutthroats, but these fish see lots of flies and lures, so they can be difficult to catch.

Stock users, note that all camping with stock at Pine Creek Lake or Jewel Lake is restricted year-round. Also, the Pine Creek trail is only open to stock travel September 15 to December 2.

Miles and Directions

0.0   Pine Creek Trailhead.

0.2   Junction with George Lake Trail; turn left.

1.0   Pine Creek Falls.

5.0   Pine Creek Lake.

10.0   Pine Creek Trailhead.

Side Trips: If you have extra time, hike around to the east end of the lake and climb the divide to look into Lake McKnight and the Davis Creek drainage. There is no trail to Lake McKnight, and the country is so rough and remote that few hikers ever walk its shores. (Originally contributed by Mike Sample, re-hiked by the authors.)

91 Elbow Lake

A long day hike or backpacking trip. Mount Cowen, an incredible mass of rock and the highest point in the Absaroka Range, rises beyond Elbow Lake.

Start: East Fork of Mill Creek Trailhead, 30 miles south of Livingston
Distance: 16.0-mile out-and-back
Difficulty: Strenuous

Maps: USGS Knowles Peak, The Pyramid, and Mt. Cowen; Gallatin National Forest Map (Central); Forest Service's Absaroka-Beartooth Wilderness Map; Rocky Mountain Survey Mt. Cowen Area Map

Finding the trailhead: Drive south from Livingston on US 89 for 16 miles and turn left (east) at a well-marked turn onto Mill Creek Road. You cross the Yellowstone River after 0.8 mile. Continue driving southeast on Mill Creek Road (FR 486), which turns to gravel after 6 miles. You can cut about 2 miles off the route by taking East River Road south from Livingston and turning left on the well-signed Mill Creek Road. For the East Fork of Mill Creek Trailhead, go 9 miles from US 89 and turn left (northeast) on FR 3280, which is well signed, for 1.5 miles to the trailhead, which is located about a quarter mile before the Snowy Range Ranch. Snowbank Campground, a Forest Service vehicle campground, is on the main Mill Creek Road 1.3 miles past West Fork Road. Limited parking at the trailhead; be careful not to block the road to Snowy Range Ranch; no toilet or camping. GPS: N45 19.005' / W110 31.916'

The Hike

The rugged north Absaroka Range forms the east wall of Paradise Valley south of Livingston along the Yellowstone River. Of all these formidable peaks, the highest, 11,206-foot Mount Cowen, looms above your destination, Elbow Lake.

Leaving the trailhead on Trail 51, you stay high and skirt around the south side of the Snowy Range Ranch for a little more than a mile before crossing the East Fork of Mill Creek on a bridge to the junction with Upper Sage Creek Trail 48, which is not

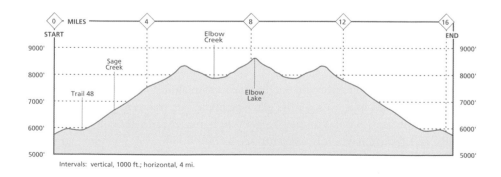

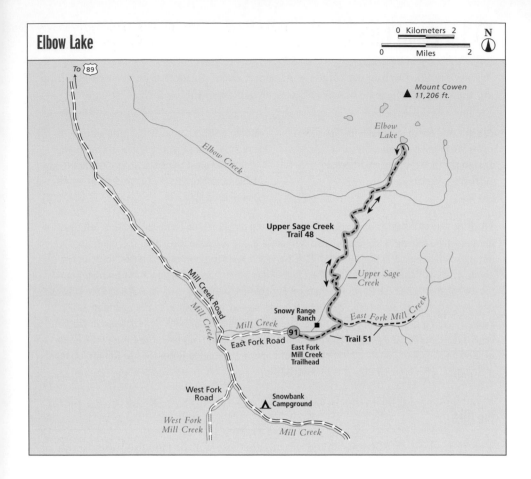

0 Kilometers 2

0   Miles   2

N

To 89

Mount Cowen
▲ 11,206 ft.

Elbow
Lake

Elbow Creek

Upper Sage Creek
Trail 48

Upper Sage
Creek

Mill Creek Road

Mill Creek

East Fork Mill Creek

Snowy Range
Ranch

Mill Creek

91

East Fork Road

Trail 51

East Fork
Mill Creek
Trailhead

West Fork
Road

Snowbank
Campground

West Fork
Mill Creek

Mill Creek

right at the bridge but about a quarter mile down the trail. Turn left and follow Trail 48 north along Sage Creek. As you cross the bridge at about 4 miles, note the major social trail coming in from the left. Ignore this and stay on the main trail.

The trail climbs steeply with no switchbacks and then crosses Sage Creek. After the creek it continues an unrelenting, Category 1 climb (with good switchbacks; i.e., not too long) across an open hillside. You probably will want to carry extra water for this stretch. Otherwise, there is plenty of water along the trail even in late August. Check with the Forest Service about snow conditions before trying an early summer trip.

Elbow Lake is 8 miles from the trailhead. You gain almost 3,500 feet of elevation, making this a tough hike even for the extra-fit hiker. The trail is in good shape most of the way. The last 1.5 miles to the lake get rough, muddy, and difficult for horses. If you hike to Elbow Lake in July, expect to see lots of wildflowers, including an ocean of balsamroot.

Start early and plan to make the entire hike to the lake in one day, as you won't find any campsites along the way. Starting early helps you get through the major climbing before the afternoon sun starts beating you down.

Elbow Lake is very scenic, with a gorgeous waterfall crashing down into the lake. Mount Cowen does lure a fair number of climbers, but don't attempt it unless you know what you're doing. Unlike most of the other peaks in the Absaroka Range, Mount Cowen is a technical climb.

You can find four or five nice sites at the lake. This lake receives surprisingly heavy use, so the campsites are quite overused; be sure to set up a zero-impact camp. You can catch some pan-size cutthroats in Elbow Lake and in Elbow Creek, but these fish see lots of artificial flies, so if you're planning on trout for dinner, take some beans and rice along as a backup plan.

Miles and Directions

0.0   East Fork of Mill Creek Trailhead.

1.2   Junction with Upper Sage Creek Trail 48; turn left.

2.7   Sage Creek.

4.0   Junction with major social trail; turn right and then left 200 yards later.

6.5   Elbow Creek.

8.0   Elbow Lake.

16.0   East Fork of Mill Creek Trailhead.

Side Trips: Explore the nearby nameless lake (no fish) to the northeast by following the stream that enters Elbow Lake's eastern side. For spectacular views of Mount Cowen, hike up the little valley on the eastern side of Cowen to the top of the ridge. Watch for mountain goats. (Originally contributed by Art Foran, re-hiked by the authors.)

92 Passage Falls

A short hike to a gorgeous waterfall

Start: Passage Falls Trailhead, 35 miles south of Livingston

Distance: 4.0-mile out-and-back

Difficulty: Easy

Maps: USGS The Pyramid; Forest Service's Absaroka-Beartooth Wilderness Map; Gallatin National Forest Map (Central); Rocky Mountain Survey Gardiner-Mt. Wallace Map

Finding the trailhead: Drive south from Livingston on US 89 for 26 miles and turn left (east) at a well-marked turn onto Mill Creek Road. You cross the Yellowstone River after 0.8 mile. Continue driving southeast on Mill Creek Road (FR 486), which turns to gravel after 6 miles. You can cut about 2 miles off the route by taking East River Road south from Livingston and turning left on the well-signed Mill Creek Road. For the Passage Falls Trailhead, continue 4 miles past West Fork Road or 2.7 miles past Snowbank Campground. It is a large trailhead with a one-way road through it and ample parking, including room for horse trailers. GPS: N45 16.466' / W110 30.083'

The Hike

This is a delightful short hike along Trail 58 to the magnificent Passage Falls, which is on Wallace Creek. The waterfall is most spectacular in the spring but worth the trip anytime. Be sure to stay on Trail 58 to the right at 1.2 miles, where the Wallace Creek Trail veers off to the left.

Trail 58 is a doubletrack except for the last 0.2 mile, where you turn left onto a singletrack for a small drop down to the waterfall. The route follows the stream until the junction with the Wallace Creek Trail. It's quite heavily traveled, so don't plan on being alone. The trail goes right down to the falls for an up-close-and-personal view.

This last section has a few steep spots, so hang onto the kids. Also, the Forest Service has signed the area asking that horses not be taken down this last short descent to the falls.

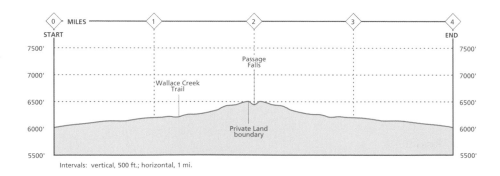

Intervals: vertical, 500 ft.; horizontal, 1 mi.

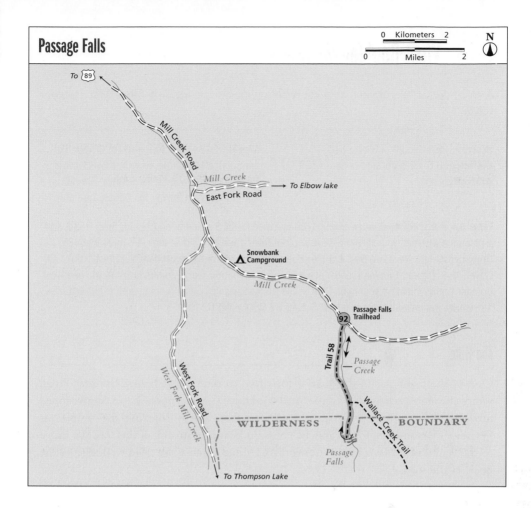

Passage Falls

0 Kilometers 2

0 Miles 2

N

To 89

Mill Creek Road

Mill Creek

To Elbow lake

East Fork Road

Snowbank
Campground

Mill Creek

Passage Falls
Trailhead

92

Trail 58

Passage
Creek

West Fork Road

West Fork Mill Creek

Wallace Creek Trail

WILDERNESS   BOUNDARY

Passage
Falls

To Thompson Lake

The waterfall is on Gallatin National Forest land but right on the edge of an inholding that's being developed for wilderness cabin sites. Be sure to respect the landowners' rights and stay on the trail.

This trail is open to mountain bikes to the falls, but not to motorized use. The 2007 Wicked-Hicks Fire burned substantial sections of this route and now provides a great example of how forests recover from fires. (Originally contributed by the authors.)

Miles and Directions

0.0 Passage Falls Trailhead.
1.2 Junction with Wallace Creek Trail; turn right.
1.8 Boundary of private property.
2.0 Passage Falls.
4.0 Passage Falls Trailhead.

93 West Boulder Meadows

A day hike or overnighter on a route following the scenic, fish-filled West Boulder River

Start: 20 miles south of Big Timber.
Distance: 6.0-miles out-and-back
Difficulty: Easy

Maps: USGS Mount Rae and Mt. Cowen; Forest Service's Absaroka-Beartooth Wilderness Map; Gallatin National Forest Map (Central); Rocky Mountain Survey Mt. Cowen Area Map

Finding the trailhead: After driving 16.5 miles south of Big Timber on Boulder River Road, half a mile past McLeod, you cross the West Boulder River. Then half a mile later, 17 miles from Big Timber, turn right (west) on West Boulder Road, which starts out as pavement but quickly turns to gravel. After 7 miles, turn left (south) at a well-signed junction. Go 7 more miles until you see West Boulder Campground on your right. Park at the trailhead, which has a parking area to the left of the vehicle campground with toilet. GPS: N45 32.250' / W110 19.083'

The Hike

One of the highlights of this hike is the drive to the trailhead. West Boulder Road winds through a scenic slice of the "real Montana"—wide-open spaces, snowcapped mountains, big valleys with rustic cattle ranches, aspens coloring the transitions between grassland and forest, and, of course, a beautiful stream all the way. We drove to the trailhead at dawn, and it looked like a video game as we tried to dodge all the deer on the road.

You can make this trip any length that suits you. It's 3 miles to West Boulder Meadows and 8 miles to the junction with Falls Creek Trail 18. The West Boulder is a great day hike, but it also makes an easy overnighter for beginning backpackers or families. The 2006 Jungle Fire burned parts of this route, starting around the wilderness boundary and up to Jungle Creek.

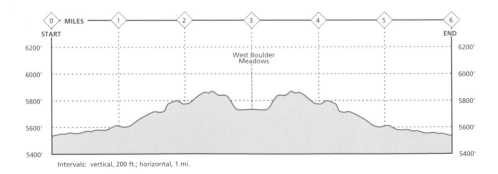

Intervals: vertical, 200 ft.; horizontal, 1 mi.

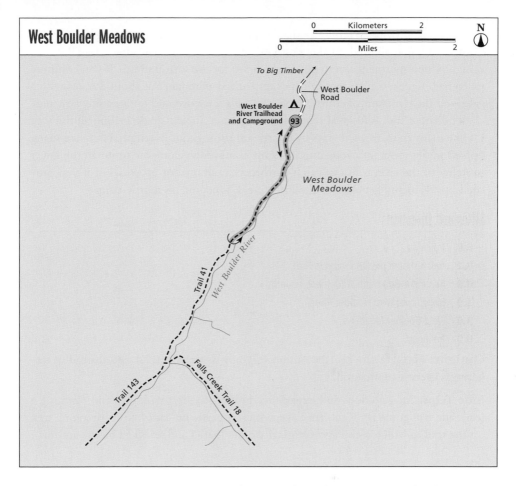

West Boulder Meadows

To Big Timber

West Boulder Road

West Boulder River Trailhead and Campground 93

West Boulder Meadows

West Boulder River

Trail 41

Trail 143

Falls Creek Trail 18

From the campground, hike up a dirt road, through an open gate, for about 100 yards. Then watch for a sign on the left and a trail heading left to the sign. Turn left here. Don't continue on the road, which goes to a private residence. This is all private land, but the landowner has been cooperative. Please show your appreciation by respecting the landowner's private-property rights.

The first part of the trail is very well constructed—raised, drained, graveled, lined with logs, a regular highway. After the bridge over the West Boulder River about a mile down the trail, you enter the Absaroka-Beartooth Wilderness, where it becomes a normal trail.

The first mile is flat, but then you climb two switchbacks and get a good view of the river. From here the trail goes through a pleasant but partially burned forest, interspersed with gorgeous mountain meadows—and large too, especially West Boulder Meadows at 3 miles. Several of the meadows have excellent campsites (be sure to pick one at least 100 feet from the river), and the river offers good fishing all the way. After West Boulder Meadows, if you decide to go farther, you can see a beautiful waterfall.

This hike provides a reminder that wilderness is multiple-use management, with livestock grazing allowed. At the west end of West Boulder Meadows, you'll see an unsightly steel-post fence, very out of character for the surroundings. If you continue on to Falls Creek, you go through another barbed-wire fence at about 5 miles with a gate over the trail. And, of course, expect to see a few cows and dodge a few cow pies.

The entire trail is in great shape, with a gradual stream-grade incline all the way. Unlike many trails, this one stays by the stream throughout its length. There are many opportunities to set up a zero-impact camp in meadows along the route. In the lower stretches of the river, you can catch cutthroats, rainbows, or browns, but if you proceed upstream and get close to the Falls Creek junction, it's mostly cutts.

Miles and Directions

0.0 Trailhead.

0.2 Trail turns off private road; turn left.

0.8 Absaroka-Beartooth Wilderness boundary.

1.0 Bridge over West Boulder River.

3.0 West Boulder Meadows.

6.0 Trailhead.

Options: This trip provides the option of going as far as you choose, instead of targeting a specific destination.

Side Trips: An ambitious and experienced hiker staying two nights and planning a long side trip could try Kaufman Lake, which is partly off-trail hiking, or a long trek up the trail to Mill Creek Pass. (Originally contributed and re-hiked by the authors.)

94 Bridge Lake

A backpacking trip to a remote, uncrowded mountain lake, one of the nicest places in the entire Wilderness Preservation System that nobody goes to

Start: Bridge Creek Trailhead, 50 miles south of Big Timber
Distance: 20.0-mile out-and-back
Difficulty: Strenuous

Maps: USGS The Needles; Gallatin National Forest Map (Central), Forest Service's Absaroka-Beartooth Wilderness Map; Rocky Mountain Survey Mt. Cowen Area Map

Finding the trailhead: On Boulder River Road south from Big Timber, drive 47 miles to the Bridge Creek Trailhead on your right (west), less than a mile past the Upsidedown Creek Trailhead, a long, bumpy drive. Limited parking; no toilet; camping at Hicks Park Campground right at the trailhead. GPS: N45 17.283' / W110 14.500'

The Hike

Only well-conditioned backpackers could make it to Bridge Lake in one day; on the other hand, it's a tad short for two days, so make your choice.

The trail starts out with a serious upgrade for about 2.5 miles, then levels out for about 5 miles until you start the last pitch up to the lake. At 2.5 miles you'll see one of the few private cabins still remaining in the wilderness. This cabin is on public land, and the Forest Service has decided to let nature gradually reclaim it instead of destroying it.

Shortly after leaving the trailhead, you cross Bridge Creek on a bridge and stay on the north side of the stream until about 2 miles before the lake. You cross several feeder streams with no bridges. At about 4 miles from the trailhead, the trail leaves the thick forest and winds through a series of scenic meadows before breaking out above timberline.

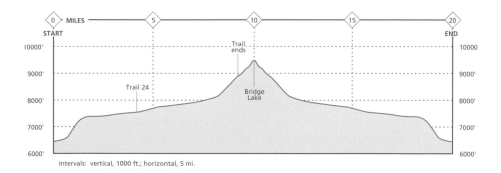

Intervals: vertical, 1000 ft.; horizontal, 5 mi.

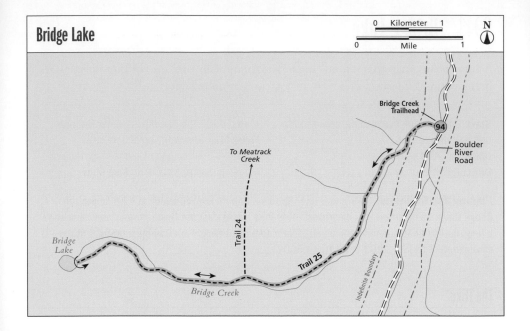

The trail is in great shape, except for the last mile, which is essentially cross-country hiking. I especially liked the "no-nonsense" switchbacks on the first climb and on the last pitch up to the lake. These switchbacks are generous curves in the trail as opposed to the near-level switchbacks that double the length of the trail. If the switchbacks on this route were like those on the Upsidedown Creek Trail, it would add 2 or 3 miles to the route.

You might think the topo map is wrong because the trail doesn't go all the way to the lake, but the map is correct. The trail ends about a mile before the lake, and you go off-trail the rest of the way. This stretch is well above timberline, though, and easy hiking, with the exception of one 50-foot stretch along the creek just before the lake. Stay on the left (south) side of Bridge Creek, even though it looks easier on the other side. It isn't. Keep your topo map out so you can see where the lake is.

If you decide to camp at Bridge Lake, look for a good campsite on the bench above the right (north) side of the lake. This search involves a little more climbing, but it's worth it. If you're wasted and can't make that last quarter mile to this campsite, you can camp on the bench just before you get to the lake, but this camping area isn't as nice. Bridge Lake is almost free of signs of past campers, so please help keep it that way. And no campfires or fire rings, please.

Bridge Lake has nice-size cutthroat trout, but they can be quite temperamental, so you could go home skunked. Don't plan on them for dinner.

Miles and Directions

0.0 Bridge Creek Trailhead.

0.5 Bridge over Bridge Creek.

2.5 Wilderness cabin.

4.0 Junction with Trail 24; turn left.

9.0 End of trail.

10.0 Bridge Lake.

20.0 Bridge Lake Trailhead.

Options: You could camp along Bridge Creek about 6 or 7 miles up the trail and take a day hike to Bridge Lake. Doing so will spare you the pain of lugging your overnight pack up the last off-trail pitch to the lake. It wouldn't be hard to find a good campsite along the creek, but it's probably not as nice as staying at the lake. (Originally contributed by the authors.)

95 Lake Plateau

A weeklong backpacking adventure to a gorgeous, lake-dotted, high-altitude plateau, plus the equally spectacular Columbine Pass, a good choice for a base camp hike

---

Start: Box Canyon Trailhead, 50 miles south of Big Timber
Distance: 34.3-mile loop with shuttle and out-and-back options
Difficulty: Strenuous

Maps: USGS Mount Douglas, Tumble Mountain, Pinnacle Mountain, and Haystack Peak; Rocky Mountain Survey Mount Douglas–Mount Wood and Cooke City–Cutoff Mountain Maps; Forest Service's Absaroka-Beartooth Wilderness Map or Gallatin National Forest Map (Central)

Finding the trailhead: Take CR 298 (locally referred to as Boulder River Road) south from Big Timber. The road doesn't take off from either of the two exits off I-90. Instead, go into Big Timber and watch for signs for CR 298 or turn south onto McLeod Street, which heads south and passes over the freeway from the middle of town between the two exits.

It's 48 miles, mostly unpaved, from Big Timber to the Box Canyon Trailhead, so make sure to top off the gas tank. It's 16 miles to the small community of McLeod and another 8 miles until the pavement ends—which means 24 miles of bumpy gravel road are still ahead. There are two major trailheads with parking areas (Upsidedown Creek and Box Canyon) providing access to the Lake Plateau and Slough Creek. Upsidedown Creek is about 1.5 miles before Box Canyon. Both trailheads are well signed. Box Canyon's parking lot can accommodate horse trailers—and does during hunting season.

A jeep road continues on to the Independence Peak area, where signs of early 1900s mining operations still remain. But almost all the trails in this region can be accessed without bumping and grinding up this very rough road. At best it is passable only with four-wheel-drive or all-terrain vehicles. GPS: N45 17.083' / W110 14.683'

Recommended itinerary: This trip works best if you get an early start from Box Canyon, but with such a long drive, it might be difficult to hit the trail early. You could camp in one of the many undeveloped campsites along the main Boulder River Road, but if you start hiking late in the day, it's probably best to spend the first night at the East Fork Boulder River. This may lengthen the trip by one day—not a bad price to pay for sleeping late. The following recommended itinerary lays out a five-day trip, starting early in the day, but you'd enjoy spending more time on the Lake Plateau.

First night: Lake Columbine
Second night: Lake Pinchot, Wounded Man Lake, Owl Lake, or other nearby lakes
Third night: Same campsite
Fourth night: Diamond or Horseshoe Lake

The Hike

Most locals consider the Boulder River the dividing line between the Beartooths to the east and the Absaroka Range to the west. Boulder River Road ends 48 miles south of Big Timber at Box Canyon Campground. In the 1970s there was a proposal to punch the road all the way through to Cooke City, splitting the Absaroka–Beartooth Wilderness into two smaller wild areas. Look at a topo map, and the feasibility of such a road becomes obvious. After a hard fight by wilderness advocates, the two spectacular mountain ranges were permanently joined into one wilderness, and the controversial road proposal was dropped.

The Boulder River is a popular place. The road is lined with dude ranches and church camps in addition to numerous summer homes. During the early hunting season in September, you'll find dozens of horse trailers parked at Box Canyon Trailhead.

The Lake Plateau region of the Beartooths is as popular as any spot in the entire wilderness. The Boulder River trailheads (Box Canyon and Upsidedown Creek) attract many backpackers. Few backcountry horsemen use Upsidedown Creek, but many hunters and outfitters use the Box Canyon Trailhead to access the Slough Creek Divide area.

The Lake Plateau is a unique and spectacular part of the Beartooths accessed by four major trails. Two of these trailheads (Box Canyon and Upsidedown Creek) originate along the Boulder River. Others leave from the West Stillwater and the main Stillwater. This variety of trails creates many options for hiking into the Lake Plateau, but the route described here is special because there aren't many opportunities like this one to see so much wild country without working out a burdensome shuttle or retracing your steps for half of the trip.

From the Box Canyon Trailhead, Trail 27 climbs gradually through timber and open parks along the East Fork Boulder River for about 3.5 miles before crossing a sturdy bridge. If you started late, you may wish to stay the first night in one of several excellent campsites located just before the bridge. This area can accommodate a large party or several parties, as long as Forest Service limits for group size aren't exceeded.

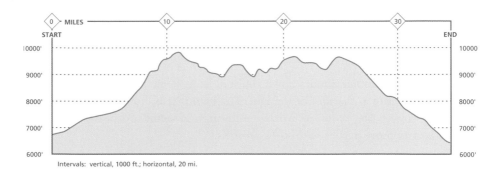

Intervals: vertical, 1000 ft.; horizontal, 20 mi.

After crossing the East Fork, the trail follows the river for about a half mile before climbing away through heavy timber. Several trout-filled pools beckon along the riverside stretch, so be prepared to fight off temptations to stop and rig up the fly-casting gear.

At 5.2 miles you reach the junction with Trail 28. Trail 27 goes straight and eventually ends up in Yellowstone National Park. Turn left here onto Trail 28. In about a quarter mile, watch for tranquil little Lake Kathleen off to the left. This is also a possible first-night campsite.

At 7.9 miles, about 2 miles beyond Lake Kathleen, the trail joins Trail 128 to Columbine Pass. Turn right (east) onto this trail, which climbs a big hill and breaks out of the forest into a subalpine panorama. From the junction it's about 1.5 miles to Lake Columbine. With an early start on the first day, this would also make a good first campsite. If it's your second day out, consider pushing on to Pentad or Jordan Lake for the second night's camp.

From Lake Columbine continue another scenic 2 miles or so up to 9,850-foot Columbine Pass. In a good snow year, snowbanks cover the trail on Columbine Pass well into July. The trail fades away twice between Lake Columbine and the pass, so watch the topo map carefully to stay on track. A few well-placed cairns make staying on the route easier.

After the Category 2 climb to Columbine Pass at the 11.1-mile point, take a break and enjoy a snack and the vistas, including 10,685-foot Pinnacle Mountain to the south. From here the trail leaves the Boulder River drainage behind and heads into the Stillwater River drainage. Hereafter, the trip leapfrogs from one lake to another for the next 14 miles.

Those who camped at Lake Columbine can make it all the way into the Lake Plateau for the next night's campsite. Otherwise, plan to pitch a tent at Pentad or Jordan Lakes. Pentad is more scenic, but Jordan offers better fishing (and suffers more from overuse). There are also several smaller lakes near Pentad: Mouse, Favonius, Sundown, and several unnamed lakes. This area has a lot of great campsites, and they won't be as crowded as Jordan Lake. Don't rush to take the first campsite. Look around for a while and you'll find a better one. It might be wise to stop at the south end of Pentad anyway, as the trail is difficult to follow because of all the tangent trails created by backcountry horsemen to various campsites. To untangle the maze, check the topo map. Trail 128 skirts the east shore of Pentad Lake, heading north.

Jordan Lake, another 2 miles down the trail from Pentad, has limited camping, with one campsite at the foot of the lake. The campsite is, however, large enough to serve a large party or several parties—although it seems too heavily impacted for use by any more parties with stock animals.

At Jordan Lake at 14.5 miles, Trail 128 meets Trail 90, coming out of the Lake Plateau and dropping east down into the Middle Fork of Wounded Man Creek. Turn left (north) here onto Trail 90, which climbs gradually 1.5 miles over Jordan Pass and drops into the Lake Plateau. This isn't much of a pass, but it's a great spot to take a few minutes to marvel at the mountainous horizons in every direction.

If you camped last at Jordan or Pentad Lake, you have lots of options for the next night out or for a base camp. The closest site is at Wounded Man Lake, but this is a busy place. The best campsite is along the North Fork of Wounded Man Creek just southwest of the lake. But consider hiking the short mile northeast from Wounded Man Lake to Lake Pinchot to stay at the crown jewel of the Lake Plateau. The third option is to turn left onto Trail 211 at the junction on the west side of Wounded Man Lake, at 18.7 miles, and stay at Owl Lake or one of the Rainbow Lakes that follow shortly thereafter. These sites offer some of the best base camps in the area because there are innumerable sights to see all within a short walk.

After a night or two on the plateau, follow Trail 211 along the west shore of Rainbow Lakes down to the junction with Trail 26 at the south end of Lower Rainbow Lake. Turn right (west) here, and spend the last night out at Diamond or Horseshoe Lake (sometimes called Upper and Lower Horseshoe Lakes). Horseshoe Lake, at 25.9 miles, is probably better because it has more campsites and leaves the shortest possible distance along Upsidedown Creek the last day—that's still about 8.5 miles to the Upsidedown Creek Trailhead, plus the 1.5 miles some lucky volunteer has to walk or try to catch a ride up to the Box Canyon Trailhead to get the vehicle. Sorry, there are no good campsites anywhere from Horseshoe Lake to Boulder River Road.

The Lake Plateau has hundreds of terrific campsites, all undesignated. Find one for your base camp, and please make it a zero-impact camp.

Anglers who want to fish the first day of the trip should camp near the East Fork Boulder River or Rainbow Creek, as most of the lakes along this route—including Lake Columbine—are barren. Burnt Gulch Lake is an exception, sporting dinner-size cutthroat trout. Cutthroats dominate the fishery along this route until the Lake Plateau is reached. Cutts are fairly easy to catch and are frequently found along rocky shorelines on the downwind sides of lakes. Anglers often fish "past the fish" by casting out into the lake.

Once the Lake Plateau is reached, you'll find a variety of fishing opportunities easily available, and Lake Pinchot would certainly make the desirable list, as would the entire Flood Creek chain of lakes.

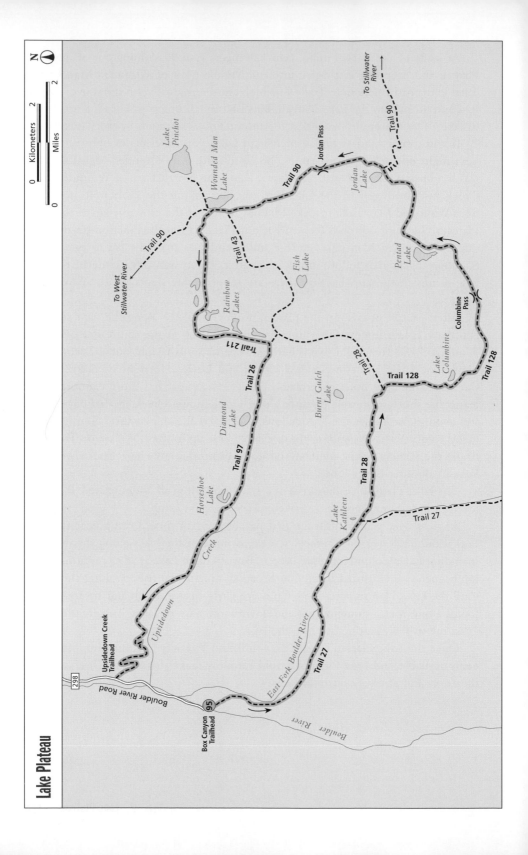

Lake Plateau

Miles and Directions

0.0   Box Canyon Trailhead.

3.5   East Fork Boulder River; cross bridge.

5.2   Junction with Trail 28; turn left.

5.4   Lake Kathleen.

7.9   Junction with Trail 128; turn right.

9.3   Lake Columbine.

11.1   Columbine Pass.

12.5   Pentad Lake.

14.5   Jordan Lake and junction with Trail 90; turn left.

15.9   Jordan Pass.

18.7   Wounded Man Lake and junction with Trail 43; turn left.

18.9   Junction with Trail 211; turn left after trip to Lake Pinchot.

19.5   Lake Pinchot.

21.0   Rainbow Lakes.

22.5   Junction with Trail 26; turn right.

25.9   Horseshoe Lake.

34.3   Upsidedown Creek Trailhead.

Options: If you can arrange transportation for a shuttle, you can hike out the West Stillwater or the main Stillwater. You might need a four-wheel-drive vehicle to get to the West Stillwater Trailhead, depending on the condition of the road. You can also make this an out-and-back trip from either the Box Canyon or the Upsidedown Creek Trailhead.

Side Trips: You could spend weeks exploring the Lake Plateau, and these are only a few of the dozens of great side trips in the area: Lake Pinchot (easy), Flood Creek Lakes (moderate), Asteroid Lake Basin (strenuous), Chalice Peak (strenuous), Lightning Lake (strenuous), Lake Diaphanous (easy), Fish Lake (easy), Barrier Lake (strenuous), Mirror Lake (moderate), Chickadee Lake (strenuous), Squeeze Lake (strenuous), Mount Douglas (strenuous), Martes Lake (moderate), Sundown Lake (moderate), Pentad and Favonius Lakes (easy), and Burnt Gulch Lake (strenuous). (Originally contributed and re-hiked by the authors.)

96 Lady of the Lake

An easy day hike or overnighter to a picturesque and accessible forested lake, a great trip for families with small children

Start: 15 miles east of Cooke City
Distance: 3.0-mile out-and-back
Difficulty: Easy

Maps: USGS Cooke City; Rocky Mountain Survey Cooke City–Cutoff Mountain Map; Forest Service's Absaroka-Beartooth Wilderness Map or Gallatin National Forest Map (Central)

Finding the trailhead: To reach the trailhead from Cooke City, drive east on US 212 for 3.2 miles to a turnoff marked with a large Forest Service sign as the Goose Lake Jeep Road, just before the Colter Campground. Turn north off US 212 and drive northeast about 2 miles up this gravel road to a cluster of old buildings. An inconspicuous trailhead on the right shoulder of the road has an old Forest Service sign for Lady of the Lake. The gravel road is passable by any vehicle, but it has some nasty water bars that could high-center a low-clearance vehicle, so go very slowly over them. You'll find limited parking and undeveloped camping sites at the trailhead and nearby. GPS: N45 2.349' / W109 53.466'

The Hike

Lady of the Lake is an ideal choice for an easy day hike or overnighter with small children. Besides being a short hike, the weather isn't as critical as it is at the higher elevations.

Set off down Trail 31. Unfortunately, you might have to get your feet wet immediately upon starting this trip. The bridge over Fisher Creek washed out years ago, and until late in the year, the stream carries too much water to ford without wading.

After Fisher Creek, the trail goes by a small inholding with a cabin, then heads down a well-maintained, forest-lined trail to Lady of the Lake. The Forest Service sign says 1 mile to the lake, but it's probably more like 1.5 miles. The trail breaks out of the trees in the large marshy meadow at the foot of the lake.

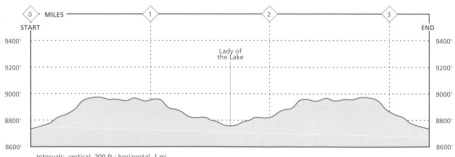

Intervals: vertical, 200 ft.; horizontal, 1 mi.

Mother moose and calf. Courtesy of NPS

Just before the lake, Trail 563 heads off to the right (south) to Chief Joseph Campground on US 212. Trail 563 also offers fairly easy access to Lady of the Lake, but the route described here is much shorter and faster. Stay to the left on Trail 31 to the lake.

The return trip involves more climbing than the way in, so allow extra time, especially if traveling with small children.

This is a heavily used area, with some major wear and tear along the trail on the west shore of the lake. The Forest Service has prohibited camping at several overused sites to allow rehabilitation. For overnighters, the best campsite is about halfway along the lake on the left just after a cut in a huge log across the trail and through a small meadow. Campfires are allowed but discouraged.

Lady of the Lake is a personal favorite place to take kids for their first wilderness camping experience. The hike is easy, and the brook trout are always willing. For those with some wilderness experience, there are four small lakes nestled in the trees to the southeast. They're a bit tough to find, but they promise solitude. Grayling are stocked in Mosquito Lake when available, while the other lakes are scheduled for stocking with cutthroats. Don't bother to fish Fisher Creek. Acid effluent from mines

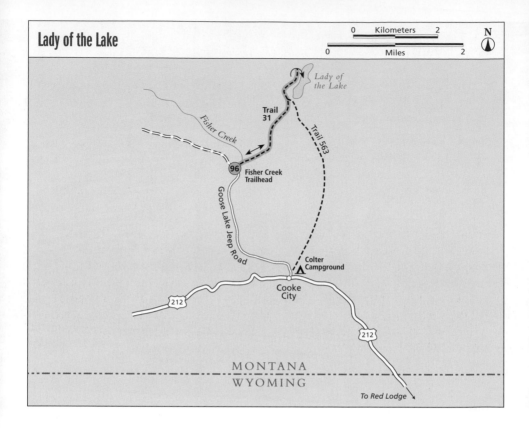

abandoned before environmental protection laws were in place keeps this stream nearly sterile.

Miles and Directions

0.0 Trailhead.
1.5 Lady of the Lake
3.0 Trailhead.

Options: You can reach Lady of the Lake by taking Trail 563 from Chief Joseph Campground. You could also use this trail to make this a shuttle trip, which means leaving a vehicle at the Colter Campground. (Contributed by the authors.)

97 Aero Lakes

A base camp backpacking adventure to the stark beauty of this high plateau area and a wide diversity of potential side trips

Start: 15 miles northeast of Cooke City
Distance: 11.4-mile out-and-back, plus side trips
Difficulty: Strenuous

Maps: USGS Cooke City, Fossil Lake, and Granite Peak; Rocky Mountain Survey Cooke City–Cutoff Mountain Map; Forest Service's Absaroka-Beartooth Wilderness Map or Gallatin National Forest Map (Central)

Finding the trailhead: To reach the trailhead from Cooke City, drive east on US 212 for 3.2 miles to a turnoff marked with a large Forest Service sign as the Goose Lake Jeep Road, just before the Colter Campground. Turn north off US 212 and drive northeast about 2 miles up this gravel road to a cluster of old buildings. An inconspicuous trailhead on the right shoulder of the road has an old Forest Service sign for Lady of the Lake. The 2 miles of road to the trailhead are passable with any vehicle, but to continue up the road past the trailhead for any reason, a high-clearance vehicle is essential. You'll find limited parking and an undeveloped campground at the trailhead. GPS: N45 2.349' / W109 53.466'

Recommended itinerary: You could hike into Aero Lakes and out the same day, but that would be a shame. Instead, plan on a long day hike to get to the lakes and spend the time to find an idyllic campsite. Then, spend two or three days exploring this incredible high country.

The Hike

This trailhead is slightly harder to locate than most others in the Beartooths, but that hasn't lessened its popularity. The area has lots to offer, and it receives heavy use both by locals and by those who travel from afar for a chance to experience this spectacular wild area.

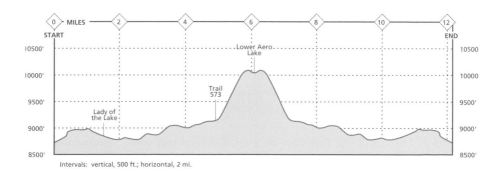

Fat brookie soon to be a high-country entrée. BILL SCHNEIDER

The trailhead lies on the eastern fringe of the section of the Beartooths that has been extensively mined, logged, and roaded. Even in the 2 miles of gravel road to the trailhead, the contrast between this area and the pristine wilderness is clearly evident. To get an early start, camp at the undeveloped campground at the trailhead.

At Aero Lakes you're many miles from the nearest machine. At night neither city lights nor smog blocks the view of the stars. Nearly one million acres of pristine land surrounds you here, more than enough for a lifetime of wandering.

At this altitude, the summer season is very short. Ice may not free the lakes until mid-July. The moist tundra tends to produce a prodigious number of mosquitoes when the wind isn't blowing, but it usually is. Bring bug dope.

The first leg of the trip down Trail 31 takes you to Lady of the Lake, an ideal choice for an easy day hike or overnighter with small children. Unfortunately, you might get wet feet immediately upon starting this trip. The bridge over Fisher Creek washed out years ago, and until late in the year, the stream carries too much water to ford without wading.

After Fisher Creek the trail goes by a small private inholding with a cabin and then heads down a well-maintained, forest-lined trail to Lady of the Lake. The Forest Service sign says 1 mile to the lake, but it's probably more like 1.5 miles.

The trail breaks out of the trees in the large marshy meadow at the foot of the lake. Just before the lake, Trail 563 heads off to the right (south) to Chief Joseph Campground on US 212. (Trail 563 also offers fairly easy access to Lady of the Lake, but the route described here is much shorter and faster.)

Once at Lady of the Lake, follow the trail along the west side of the lake. At the far end of the lake, the trail heads off to the left for about a quarter mile to a meadow on the north side of the lake, where two trails depart. The left-hand trail (Trail 31) heads northwest to Long Lake. Take the right-hand trail (Trail 573), which leads almost due north less than a half mile to the confluence of Star and Zimmer Creeks. Ford the stream here and continue north along Zimmer Creek another mile or so until you see Trail 573 switchbacking up the steep right side of the cirque. If you see a major stream coming in from the left, you have gone too far up the drainage.

The scramble up the Trail 573 switchbacks is short but steep and requires good physical conditioning. Locals call it Cardiac Hill, and for good reason. It climbs almost 900 feet in about a mile, close to a Category H on our hill rating chart.

At the top of Cardiac Hill, the trail suddenly emerges from the timber and pauses above Lower Aero Lake. Be sure to notice the dramatic contrast between the treeless plateau here and the timbered country below.

The shoreline around Lower Aero is rocky and punctuated with snowbanks. There are a number of places to camp. They all have great scenery, and the air-conditioning is always on. Those planning to stay here for two or three nights should spend some extra time searching for that five-star campsite. Drop the packs and look around for an hour or so. Don't expect to have a campfire on this treeless plateau.

To proceed to Upper Aero Lake, follow the stream that connects the two lakes. Another good camping spot is just below the outlet of the upper lake. It provides a good view of the lake and prominent Mount Villard with its spiny ridges. It also makes a good base camp for fishing both lakes and for exploring east to Rough Lake and then north up the Sky Top Lakes chain.

Although most people visit Rough Lake or Lone Elk Lake on side trips, there's also good camping there. Both are large, deep lakes similar to Aero Lakes. Sky Top Lakes might look inviting on the map, but camping is very limited in this rocky basin.

After a day or two of exploring the high country, retrace your steps down Cardiac Hill to Zimmer Creek—and then back to civilization.

There are no designated campsites in this area, but there are numerous possibilities. Please use zero-impact camping principles to preserve this fragile landscape.

Fishing is generally slow in both Upper and Lower Aero Lakes, but the rewards can be worth it. In Lower Aero the brookies grow large, and you'll also find nice-size cutthroats. Cutts can be seen trying to spawn between the lakes through most of July. Upper Aero is stocked with cutts. Fishing is tough here as the cutthroats tend to school, and they can be hard to find in a lake of this size.

Sky Top Lakes were once stocked with grayling, and these fish worked down into Rough and Lone Elk Lakes, but all seem to have disappeared, leaving just brook trout

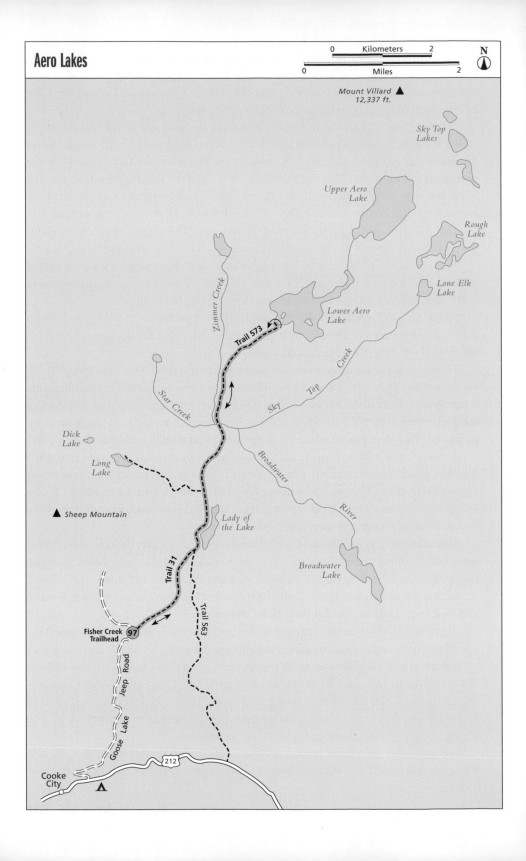

Aero Lakes

Kilometers 0 — 2
Miles 0 — 2

N

Mount Villard ▲
12,337 ft.

Sky Top
Lakes

Upper Aero
Lake

Rough
Lake

Lone Elk
Lake

Zimmer Creek

Trail 573

Lower Aero
Lake

Sky Top Creek

Star Creek

Dick
Lake

Long
Lake

Broadwater

River

▲ Sheep Mountain

Lady of
the Lake

Broadwater
Lake

Trail 31

Trail 563

Fisher Creek
Trailhead
97

Goose Lake Jeep Road

212

Cooke
City

in Lone Elk and Rough. The Sky Tops will probably be stocked once again to maintain a fishery in this chain originating on the slopes of Granite Peak.

To the east of Sky Top Creek are a number of lakes supporting mostly brook trout, although Weasel, Stash, and Surprise Lakes are stocked with cutts. For hearty souls, Recruitment Lake holds a few extremely large brookies, but the chances of getting skunked are excellent. Nevertheless, just one hefty fish from this lake would be the high point of a summer vacation.

Miles and Directions

0.0 Trailhead.
1.5 Lady of the Lake and junction with Trail 563; turn left.
2.5 Junction with Trail 31 to Long Lake; turn right.
2.8 Stream coming in from Long Lake.
3.6 Star Creek.
4.8 Start of climb to Aero Lakes on Trail 573.
5.7 Base of Lower Aero Lake.
11.4 Trailhead.

Options: This trip could turn into a long (four- or five-day) shuttle for experts only by continuing east from Aero Lakes through the "top of the world" and exiting the Beartooths at the East Rosebud or Clarks Fork Trailheads.

You could also make a loop out of your trip by exiting on an off-trail route down Sky Top Creek, but be careful on the steep upper section of the stream where it tumbles off the plateau from Lone Elk Lake. Be forewarned: This route is only for the fit, agile, and adventuresome. It requires carrying your pack cross-country over to Rough Lake (probably named for how hard it is to reach) and then down to Lone Elk Lake. From Lone Elk Lake it's a scramble down a steep route with no trail to a meadow where the stream from Splinter Lake slips into Sky Top Creek. This is a long, slow mile, and it can be hazardous, so be careful and patient. But it's also very beautiful, especially the falls where Sky Top Creek leaves Lone Elk Lake.

At the meadow there is an unofficial trail along Sky Top Creek all the way to the main trail. Follow cascading Sky Top Creek all the way until near the end, when it veers off to the left to join up with Star Creek to form the Broadwater River. The track comes out into the same meadow (where Star and Zimmer Creeks join) you passed through on the way up Zimmer Creek on Trail 573. From here, retrace your steps back to Lady of the Lake and the trailhead.

Side Trips: Possible side trips in this area include treks to Aero Lakes perimeter (moderate), Upper Aero Lake (easy), Leaky Raft Lake (easy), Rough Lake (moderate), Lone Elk Lake (moderate), Sky Top Lakes (strenuous), Zimmer Lake (strenuous), Iceberg Peak/Grasshopper Glacier (strenuous), Mount Villard (strenuous), and Glacier Peak (strenuous). (Originally contributed by Mike Sample, re-hiked by the authors.)

98 Rock Island Lake

A day hike or overnighter to an unusually large, sprawling forest-lined lake; also a good choice for a base camp

Start: Clarks Fork Trailhead, 20 miles northeast of Cooke City
Distance: 6.0-mile out-and-back
Difficulty: Easy

Maps: USGS Fossil Lake; Rocky Mountain Survey Cooke City-Cutoff Mountain Map; Forest Service's Absaroka-Beartooth Wilderness Map or Gallatin National Forest Map (Central)

Finding the trailhead: Take US 212 east from Cooke City for 3.4 miles or 58.1 miles from Red Lodge and turn north onto FR 306. Drive about a half mile to the large trailhead, which features plenty of parking, a toilet, interpretive displays, and a picnic area. GPS: N45 01.045' / W109 52.145'

The Hike

Rock Island Lake differs from many high-elevation lakes. Instead of forming a small, concise oval in a cirque, it sprawls through flat and forested terrain, seemingly branching off in every direction. You could spend an entire day just walking around it.

To get to Rock Island Lake, take Trail 3 from the trailhead. After about a half mile, the Kersey Lake Jeep Road veers off to the left. Stay on Trail 3. At 1.2 miles you reach the junction with Trail 565, which heads off to the right toward Lake Vernon. Again, keep going on Trail 3. You'll pass Kersey Lake on the left at 1.5 miles. At 2.4 miles you come to the junction with Trail 566 to Rock Island Lake. Turn right (east) here for about another half mile to the lake. The trail is well used and well maintained the entire way, with only one hill (near Kersey Lake). The 1988 fires scorched the area around Kersey Lake but missed Rock Island Lake.

Because Rock Island Lake is so easy to reach (3 miles on a near-level trail), it's a perfect choice for a family backpacking trip into the Absaroka-Beartooth Wilderness.

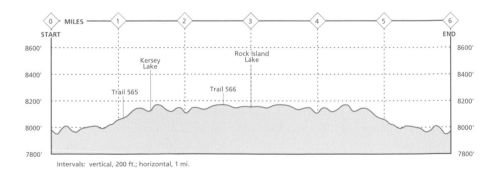

Morning mist melting off Rock Island Lake. BILL SCHNEIDER

Filterable water is readily available on the trail and at the lake, but the mosquitoes can be thick in early summer.

Those planning an overnight stay can camp at one of several excellent campsites along the west side of the lake. To get to the west side of the lake, walk past the spur trail to Rock Island Lake and continue up the main trail for about another half mile, then turn right on Trail 3. Go about a half mile and then start watching for social trails veering off toward the lake. These sites are hard to find but worth the effort, compared to camping on the east side of the lake, which is mostly rocks. There might be enough wood for a campfire, but consider using a stove for cooking. The entire area receives heavy use, and if everyone had a fire, the area would soon show signs of overuse.

This popular, productive lake has a self-sustaining population of brookies and cutthroats stocked on a three-year rotation, both of which grow fairly large. (Originally contributed and re-hiked by the authors.)

Rock Island Lake

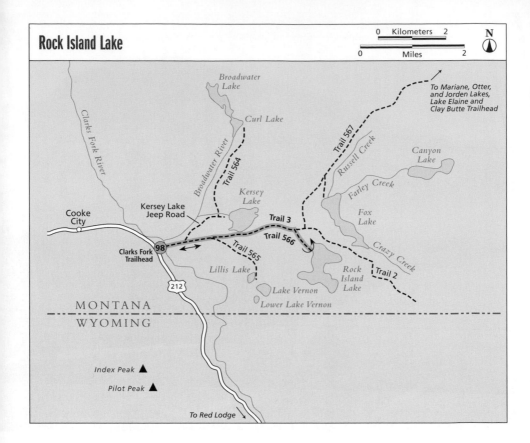

Miles and Directions

0.0 Trailhead.

0.5 Junction with Kersey Lake Jeep Road.

1.2 Junction with Trail 565 to Lake Vernon; turn left.

1.5 Kersey Lake.

2.4 Junction with Trail 566 to Rock Island Lake; turn right.

3.0 Rock Island Lake.

6.0 Trailhead.

Yellowstone National Park

99 Sky Rim

A long, strenuous, spectacular ridgeline day hike for experienced, extra-fit hikers only

Start: Dailey Creek Trailhead (WK1), 30 miles north of West Yellowstone, just south of the park boundary
Distance: 18.0-mile lollipop loop

Difficulty: Strenuous
Maps: USGS Big Horn Peak; Trails Illustrated Mammoth Hot Springs

Finding the trailhead: Drive north from West Yellowstone (Montana) or south from Bozeman on US 191 to the Dailey Creek Trailhead, between mile markers 30 and 31, 22 miles north of the US 191/US 89 junction or 0.8 mile south of the park boundary. Ample parking; toilet; no camping. GPS: N45 2.904' / W111 8.371'

The Hike

This might be my favorite hike in all of Yellowstone National Park.

For serious hikers who like to "get high" and have lots of panoramic mountain scenery, the Sky Rim loop trail is probably the best long hike in Yellowstone. It's also one of the most strenuous, but it's ideal for the well-conditioned hiker who likes to get up early and spend the entire day walking, with minimal time devoted to rest and relaxation. Besides being one of the nicest parts of the park, the far northwest corner is also the newest, added to the park in 1927.

Take more water than you normally would on a long day hike. The stretch between Upper Dailey Creek all along Sky Rim, up Big Horn Peak, and down to Black Butte Creek is a long haul without any reliable water source.

Also watch the weather closely. We had a perfect day when we hiked this route, but it was easy to see that you really don't want to be on Sky Rim in bad weather. At best it wouldn't be much fun because you couldn't see the scenery and wildlife, but more likely it would be dangerous because of slippery footing and the specter of hypothermia. If you get caught in a thunderstorm on Sky Rim, you could become a lightning rod.

August is the best time to take this hike. You stand a good chance of good weather, and you avoid hiking the ridgeline with hunters, who tend to take over the place in early September when the early big-game seasons open in Montana. Stock use is prohibited until at least July 1, later if wet conditions persist.

The first 1.8 miles up Dailey Creek starts out in the shadow of mighty Crown Butte just outside the park to the north. The well-defined trail winds through expansive open meadows broken here and there by scattered stands of trees. The scenery stays like this until about 1 mile past backcountry campsite WF2, where the trail slips

The Sky Rim Trail follows the highest ridges of the Gallatin Range. NPS, J. SCHMIDT

into the trees for the climb up to Dailey Pass. The trail is heavily rutted in spots, which makes walking difficult.

When you reach Dailey Pass, you're at a four-way junction. The faint trail to the left (not shown on some maps) follows the ridgeline and park boundary; the trail going straight heads out of the park into the Gallatin National Forest. You go right (east) and continue to climb along the ridgeline.

After a Category 1 climb up to the pass, with only a few short switchbacks near the end, it seems you should be about as high as you can get, but you aren't even close to the top. The trail follows the ridge for 0.7 mile to the Sky Rim Trail junction. Parts of this trail go along a sharply angled ridgeline, so be careful not to fall off either side. We almost missed this junction because it's natural to keep heading up the ridge. At this junction another trail heads north out of the park into the Buffalo Horn region of the Gallatin National Forest. You turn right (south).

From the Sky Rim Trail the view is fantastic. Off to the west looms the Taylor-Hilgards section of the Madison Range, with 11,316-foot Hilgard Peak; in the foreground lies expansive Dailey Creek, where you just hiked. Off to the east is the sprawling Tom Minor Basin in the shadow of Canary Bird, Ramshorn, and Twin Peaks, with a majestic backdrop of the Absaroka Range and its highest point, Mount Cowen (11,205 feet).

From here the already strenuous route gets more strenuous. The next leg of your trip, 4.4 miles along Sky Rim, goes over two more big climbs and is followed by the last pitch up to the Black Butte Creek Trail junction, one of the few Category H

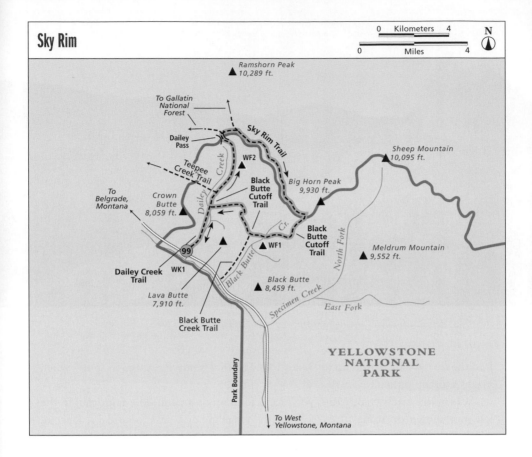

Sky Rim

Ramshorn Peak
▲ 10,289 ft.

To Gallatin
National
Forest

Dailey
Pass

Sky Rim Trail

WF2
▲

Teepee
Creek Trail

Dailey
Creek

Black
Butte
Cutoff
Trail

Big Horn Peak
9,930 ft.

Sheep Mountain
10,095 ft.
▲

To
Belgrade,
Montana

Crown
Butte
8,059 ft.
▲

Black Butte

Black
Butte
Cutoff
Trail

North Fork

Meldrum Mountain
9,552 ft.
▲

99

WF1
▲

Cr.

Dailey Creek
Trail

WK1

Black Butte
8,459 ft.
▲

Lava Butte
7,910 ft.

Specimen Creek

East Fork

Black Butte
Creek Trail

YELLOWSTONE
NATIONAL
PARK

Park Boundary

To West
Yellowstone, Montana

0   Kilometers   4

0   Miles   4

N

climbs in the park. In fact, it's probably the most precipitous section of designated trail in the park, but it isn't dangerous.

The scenery stays sensational all the way to Big Horn Peak. The trail gets faint in spots and, about 1 mile before the next junction, more or less disappears on the grassy flanks of Big Horn Peak. You won't get off the designated route as long as you don't drop off the ridgeline.

At the junction take the short out-and-back side trip to the very top of Big Horn Peak. It's hard to believe the scenery can get any better, but it actually does. This short but nerve-wracking (use caution!) side trip is definitely worth the extra effort. From the true summit of Big Horn Peak, you get a good view of the Gallatin Skyline Trail continuing over to Sheep Mountain to the south.

In addition to the mountain vistas that surround the Sky Rim, you also have a good chance of seeing elk, deer, and moose on the open slopes and along Dailey Creek. Also watch for bighorn sheep, commonly seen on Big Horn Peak. In the fall, grizzlies frequent the Gallatin Skyline area to feed on whitebark pine nuts, abundant along this high-elevation trail.

The Sky Rim Trail passes through the Gallatin Range, some of the best grizzly bear habitat left in the Lower 48. Black bears are also common in the area. Shutterstock

From here it's all downhill as you switchback down Big Horn Peak into Black Butte Creek. The trail is in better shape than the trail up Dailey Creek and along Sky Rim, so if you're behind schedule, you can make up some lost time. After about a half mile you leave the open slopes of Big Horn Peak behind and hike into a lush, unburned forest and through the Gallatin Petrified Forest.

The trail stays in the forest the rest of the way. The trail to campsite WF1 goes off to the left (south) just before the junction with the Black Butte Cutoff Trail. If you left a vehicle at the Black Butte Trailhead, you can skip the cutoff trail. If you didn't, turn right (north), go through a large meadow, and climb over a forested ridge past a patrol cabin and back into spacious Dailey Creek. At the junction with the Dailey Creek Trail, turn left (west) and retrace your steps back to the Dailey Creek Trailhead.

Miles and Directions

- **0.0** Dailey Creek Trailhead.
- **1.8** Black Butte Cutoff Trail junction; turn left.
- **2.6** Teepee Creek Trail junction; turn right.
- **3.5** Campsite WF2.
- **4.9** Dailey Pass.
- **5.6** Sky Rim Trail junction; turn right.

10.0 Black Butte Cutoff Trail junction; turn right.

13.8 Spur trail to Campsite WF1.

14.0 Black Butte Creek Trail junction; turn right.

14.6 Patrol cabin.

16.2 Dailey Creek Trail junction; turn left.

18.0 Dailey Creek Trailhead.

Options: You could start at the Black Butte Trailhead or take the route counterclockwise with the same degree of difficulty. The climbs on the counterclockwise route seem longer but more gradual as opposed to the short, steep climbs of the clockwise route. If you have two vehicles, you can skip the cutoff trail and shorten your trip by about 2 miles by leaving one vehicle at the Black Butte Trailhead (between mile markers 28 and 29 on US 191). Because of the location of the campsites, you can't really turn this into an overnighter without making it even more difficult. However, you could base camp at campsite WF1 or WF2 and make the long day hike about 2 miles shorter.

Side Trips: You would really miss something if you didn't take the short side trip (0.3 mile one way) to the top of Big Horn Peak. You can continue along the Gallatin Skyline Trail to Shelf Lake (3 miles one way), but make sure you have enough energy and daylight. You could also camp at Shelf Lake and come out at Specimen Creek, but this would be a Herculean day with an overnight pack to get to Shelf Lake from Dailey Creek along Sky Rim. (Originally contributed and re-hiked by the authors.)

100 Black Canyon of the Yellowstone

A special trip, ideal for an early season backpacking adventure, along the majestic Yellowstone River

Start: Hellroaring Trailhead (2K8), 14.3 miles east of Mammoth
Distance: 13.0-mile shuttle
Difficulty: Moderate

Maps: USGS Tower/Canyon and Tower Junction, Blacktail Deer Creek, Ash Mountain, and Gardiner; Trails Illustrated Mammoth Hot Springs

Finding the trailheads: To reach the Hellroaring Trailhead, drive 14.3 miles east from Mammoth, Wyoming, or 3.7 miles west from Tower. Pull into the Hellroaring Trailhead parking area; the actual trailhead is 0.3 mile down an unpaved service road. GPS: N44 56.882' / W110 27.167'

To reach the exit trailhead, drive east of Mammoth for 6.7 miles or west of Tower for 11.1 miles and turn into the pullout for the Blacktail Creek Trailhead on the north side of the road. Fairly large parking area (but often full); toilet; no camping. GPS: N44 57.335' / W110 35.555'

Recommended itinerary: You have many options for enjoying the Black Canyon, but I recommend an easy three-day trip with the first night at campsite 1R2 or 1R1, the second at campsite 1Y6 (3e) or 1Y8 (4e), and then up to the Blacktail Creek Trailhead on the third day.

The Hike

The Black Canyon of the Yellowstone is one of the classic backpacking trips of the Northern Rockies. It seems to offer everything a hiker might want.

This is an excellent trail with a wide choice of four- and five-star campsites. Wildlife is abundant, the fishing can be fantastic (though not in early season when the river is roaring through the canyon), and the scenery rivals almost any other hike in the park. The trail closely follows the mighty Yellowstone River most of the way.

In earlier editions of this book, this hike terminated at Gardiner, but to reach that access point, you had to cross a short stretch of private land. That private landowner has disallowed public access, so the National Park Service (NPS) has closed the Gardiner trailhead. This means, regrettably, that you can no longer add the incredible stretch of trail from Crevice Lake to Gardiner to this trip, unless you want to hike out and back from the Blacktail Creek junction.

In this edition, the hike description has been rewritten to terminate at the Blacktail Creek Trailhead instead of Gardiner. Be sure to ask about this access issue when you get your permit, though, because the NPS is trying to resolve the access problem. If they do, I recommend taking the gradual downhill route along the river to Gardiner (7.2 miles) instead of the uphill grind to the Blacktail Creek junction (3.7 miles).

The Black Canyon of the Yellowstone. NPS, JIM PEACO

After leaving the Hellroaring Trailhead, you hike through meadows and a few stands of trees down a steep hill to the suspension bridge over the Yellowstone River, going left (north) at the junction with the trail to Tower just before reaching the bridge. The suspension bridges, both this one and the one at Blacktail Creek, are highlights of the trip. Don't conjure up images of Indiana Jones movies. These are very sturdy metal bridges.

The Black Canyon of the Yellowstone above the Blacktail Bridge. NPS, Richard Lake

Shortly after crossing the bridge, you break out into the open terrain around Hellroaring Creek. When you reach the junction with the trail up Coyote Creek, go left (west).

When you get to Hellroaring Creek, be alert or you'll get on the wrong trail. Well-defined trails go up both sides of the creek to campsites. There used to be a footbridge across Hellroaring Creek (a large tributary to the Yellowstone), but high spring runoff claimed it years ago. Watch for trail markers on the west side of the creek so that you know where to ford. This ford can be dangerous in June and early July, so if it looks too adventuresome for you, hike 1.8 miles north along the creek and cross on a stock bridge, then hike 1.9 miles down the west side of the creek to the main trail.

After fording Hellroaring Creek you gradually climb over a ridge and drop into Little Cottonwood Creek and then climb another hill into Cottonwood Creek. The section of trail between Hellroaring and Cottonwood Creeks stays high above the river on mostly open hillsides. Then, just after Cottonwood Creek, it drops down to the river's edge.

Also just before Cottonwood Creek, you pass from Wyoming into Montana. If you're an angler, this doesn't matter as long as you have a park fishing license.

From Cottonwood Creek to the Blacktail Trail junction, the trail stays close to the river, offering up some spectacular scenery and plenty of pleasant resting places and fishing holes. You might notice frequent carcasses and scattered bones along this trail.

That's because this is winter range for the park's large ungulates. Each year, winter kills some animals; wolves, bears, and cougars take down a few more.

At the Blacktail Creek Trail junction, turn left (south) and then cross another sturdy suspension bridge. Right after the bridge you see the spur trail going off to the left (east) to two great backcountry campsites and a pit toilet. Take a long rest here or at Crevice Lake, if you take that short side trip—it's a steady uphill grind, about 1,000 feet total, back up to the highway.

Miles and Directions

0.0 Hellroaring Trailhead.

0.7 Junction with trail to Tower; turn right.

1.0 Suspension bridge over Yellowstone River.

1.4 Junction with trail to Coyote Creek and Buffalo Plateau; turn left.

1.8 Spur trail going north along the east side of Hellroaring Creek to campsites 2H6 and 2H8 and to the stock bridge.

1.9 Spur trail going south along the east side of Hellroaring Creek to campsites 2H4 and 2H2.

2.0 Ford Hellroaring Creek.

2.1 Spur trail going south along the west side of Hellroaring Creek to campsites 2H3 and 2H1.

2.2 Spur trail going north along the west side of Hellroaring Creek to campsite 2H5 to the stock bridge, and into Gallatin National Forest.

4.2 Little Cottonwood Creek, campsite 1R3.

5.9 Campsite 1R2.

6.0 Cottonwood Creek, campsite 1R1.

7.6 Campsite 1Y9.

8.1 Campsite 1Y7.

8.9 Campsite 1Y5.

9.1 Blacktail Creek Trail junction, trail to campsites 1Y6 and 1Y8; turn left.

9.3 Suspension bridge and spur trail to campsites 1Y6 and 1Y8.

11.2 Campsite 1A1.

12.3 Junction with Rescue Creek Trail; turn left.

12.6 Junction with Lava Creek Trail; turn left.

13.0 Blacktail Creek Trailhead.

Options: In addition to the three-day trip described here, this route makes an easy four-day trip. Stay the first night at one of the six excellent campsites along Hellroaring Creek, the second at campsite 1R2 or 1R1, and the third at campsite 1Y6 or 1Y8 (or, if you are ambitious, hike down the river to 1Y2 or 1Y1 and then back the next day) before hiking out to the highway on the fourth day. This gives you plenty of time for fishing and relaxing. If you have only two days, stay overnight at campsite 1Y9, 1Y7, or 1Y5. If you like long day hikes, this is as good as it gets. (*Note:* No wood fires are permitted at any Yellowstone/Hellroaring campsites except 2H9.)

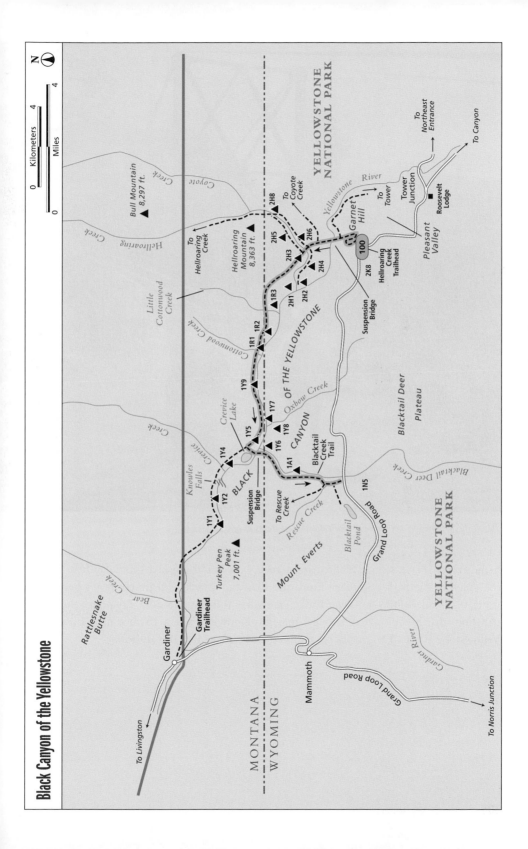

Black Canyon of the Yellowstone

A sturdy suspension bridge over the Yellowstone. MARNIE SCHNEIDER

Side Trips: If you stay at Hellroaring Creek, you might enjoy a short day hike up the creek to the park boundary. From the Blacktail Creek Trail junction, it's only a short, 0.25-mile round-trip over to Crevice Lake. You can also do a 3.6-mile round-trip from that junction over to view majestic Knowles Falls, a 15-foot drop on the Yellowstone River. (Originally contributed and re-hiked by the authors.)

101 Pebble Creek

A pleasant day hike or overnighter, mostly downhill

Start: Warm Creek Picnic Area (3K4)
Distance: 11.7-mile shuttle
Difficulty: Moderate

Maps: USGS Cutoff Mountain and Abiathar Peak; Trails Illustrated Tower/Canyon

Finding the trailheads: To reach the Warm Creek Trailhead, drive 27 miles east of Tower Junction or 1.4 miles west of the Northeast Entrance and turn into a newly constructed trailhead on the north side of the road. GPS: N45 0.314' / W110 2.037'

Leave a vehicle or arrange to be picked up at the Pebble Creek Trailhead, which is just east of the turnoff to Pebble Creek Campground, 19 miles east of Tower Junction and 9.4 miles west of the Northeast Entrance. Park at an angle in this turnout on the north side of the road just east of the Pebble Creek Bridge to leave room for more vehicles. If this small parking area is full, you can park in the stock parking lot on your right after you turn north toward Pebble Creek Campground, but please don't take the spots used by horse trailers. Limited parking; toilet; camping nearby in Pebble Creek Campground. GPS: N44 54.948' / W110 6.539'

The Hike

On most maps it looks as though the Pebble Creek Trail follows the Northeast Entrance Road, but it's actually hidden from view. In fact, you can't see the road from anywhere along the trail, which goes through spectacular meadows along a totally natural stream. It's a mostly downhill 11.7-mile hike.

The trail starts out in an ominous manner, climbing seriously for the first mile or so up to Warm Creek Pass. But once you put out the effort to get over this Category 3 hill, it's all downhill for 10.5 miles.

The trail is well defined and maintained the entire way. However, you have to ford Pebble Creek four times—each successive ford getting more difficult but all safe

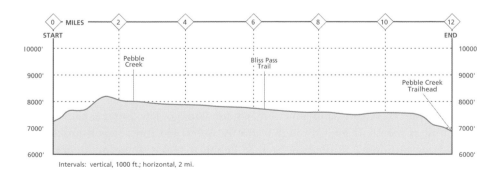

Intervals: vertical, 1000 ft.; horizontal, 2 mi.

Pebble Creek. BILL SCHNEIDER

crossings unless you go during the high runoff period in June or early July. If you see snow on the pass, that's a clue that the stream crossings will become increasingly difficult as you hike toward Pebble Creek Campground.

Once you reach Pebble Creek, follow the stream through wildflower-filled meadows (especially heavy with lupine) for another 1.8 miles to the second ford. This stretch treats the hiker to some of the best mountain scenery in Yellowstone. After this ford you enter a short stretch of burned forest broken by a few meadows. Watch for moose and elk. While hiking through upper Pebble Creek, also watch for mountain goats off to the north on the slopes of Cutoff Mountain and Mount Hornaday.

After the Bliss Pass Trail junction, where you go left (south), the trail is not quite as scenic. It goes through a mostly unburned forest, again broken by a few large meadows, all the way back to Pebble Creek Campground. Ford the stream twice more along the way. When you reach the campground, stay on the

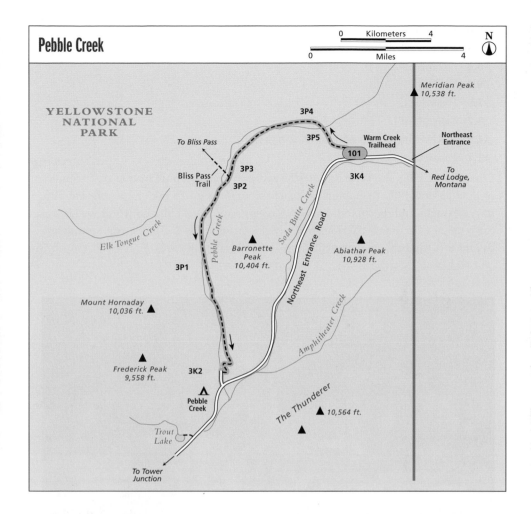

Kilometers
0   4
Miles
0   4

N

Meridian Peak
10,538 ft.

YELLOWSTONE
NATIONAL
PARK

3P4

To Bliss Pass

3P5

Warm Creek
Trailhead

Northeast
Entrance

Bliss Pass
Trail

3P3

3P2

101

To
Red Lodge,
Montana

3K4

Elk Tongue Creek

Pebble Creek

Soda Butte Creek

Northeast Entrance Road

Barronette
Peak
10,404 ft.

Abiathar Peak
10,928 ft.

3P1

Mount Hornaday
10,036 ft.

Amphitheater Creek

Frederick Peak
9,558 ft.

3K2

Pebble
Creek

The Thunderer

10,564 ft.

Trout
Lake

To Tower
Junction

official trail on the east side of the creek until you reach the trailhead on the paved highway.

Fishing in Pebble Creek doesn't match up to its famous neighbor, Slough Creek, but it can be excellent in late summer, especially in the lower stretches, where the stream is larger.

Miles and Directions

0.0   Warm Creek Picnic Area.

1.2   Top of ridge.

1.8   First ford.

2.0   Campsite 3P5.

3.1   Campsite 3P4.

3.6   Second ford.

5.0 Campsite 3P3.

5.1 Junction with Bliss Pass Trail; turn left.

5.5 Campsite 3P2.

6.3 Third ford.

7.3 Fourth ford.

8.2 Campsite 3P1.

11.6 Trail forks (right to campground, left to highway).

11.7 Pebble Creek Campground.

Options: Hiking in reverse means 10.5 miles of gradual uphill instead of 10.5 miles of gradual downhill. Beginning backpackers might want to hike into campsite 3P5, stay overnight, and return to the Warm Creek Picnic Area. This also works well if you can't arrange the shuttle. Serious hikers will consider this 11.7-mile trip a moderate day hike. (Originally contributed and re-hiked by the authors.)

After the mid-1990s reintroduction of the wolf to Yellowstone, the Big Dog not only frequents Pebble Creek, but now ranges throughout most of western and south central Montana.
SHUTTERSTOCK

Custer National Forest

102 Island Lake

A base camp hike with so much to see and do, all within reach of Island Lake

---

Start: West Rosebud Trailhead, 40 miles southwest of Billings

Distance: 12.0-mile out-and-back, plus side trips

Difficulty: Moderate with some strenuous (optional) side trips

Maps: USGS Granite Peak; Rocky Mountain Survey Cooke City–Cutoff Mountain Map; Forest Service's Absaroka-Beartooth Wilderness Map

Finding the trailhead: Drive 15 miles south from Columbus on MT 78, through Absarokee. About 2 miles past Absarokee, turn right (west) to Fishtail on CR 419. Drive through Fishtail and go west and south about 1 mile. Turn left (south) along West Rosebud Road. About 6 miles later, take another left (southeast) at the sign for West Rosebud Lake. It's another 14 miles of bumpy gravel road from this point to the trailhead. In total it's 27 miles from Absarokee and 42 miles from Columbus. The road ends and the trail begins right at the Mystic Dam Power Station. It might not seem clear exactly where the trail begins. After parking your vehicle (ample parking; toilet), walk up the road about 200 yards through the power company compound to the actual trailhead. GPS: N45 13.650' / W109 45.700'

The Hike

Most people using the West Rosebud Trailhead head up to Froze-to-Death Plateau and Granite Peak. Only a few ever go to Island Lake, even though it's quite accessible, so it provides a great opportunity to stay a few days and enjoy the many wonders of the Upper West Rosebud Valley without seeing many people. Island Lake is especially well suited for a base camp, but also makes a nice day hike or overnighter.

From the trailhead, follow West Rosebud Creek along Trail 19, where horse use is prohibited except during the fall hunting season. After crossing an overpass and a bridge over the creek, the trail follows a power line for a short way. After leaving this

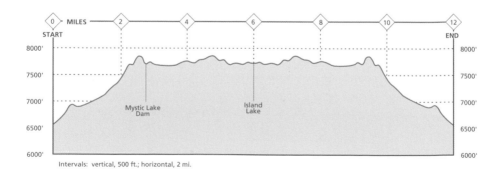

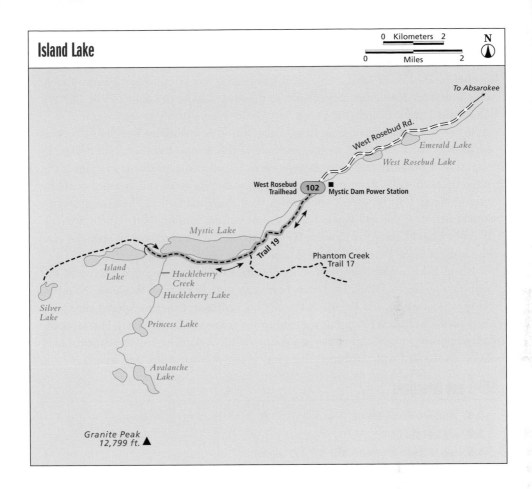

0   Kilometers   2

0   Miles   2

N

To Absarokee

West Rosebud Rd.

Emerald Lake

West Rosebud Lake

West Rosebud
Trailhead   102   ■ Mystic Dam Power Station

Mystic Lake

Trail 19

Phantom Creek
Trail 17

Island
Lake

Huckleberry
Creek

Huckleberry Lake

Silver
Lake

Princess Lake

Avalanche
Lake

Granite Peak
12,799 ft. ▲

"sign of civilization" behind, the trail switchbacks through open rock fields, offering a great view of the West Rosebud valley, including West Rosebud and Emerald Lakes.

The climb doesn't seem that steep, but by the time the trail reaches the dam at the eastern end of Mystic Lake, it has ascended 1,200 feet in 3 miles, barely a Category 3 climb.

When the trail breaks out over the ridge, it affords a great view of Mystic Dam. Mystic Lake is a natural lake, but as you'll quickly see, a dam increased its size and depth. Now, at more than 200 feet, it's the deepest lake in the Beartooths.

The sandy beach along the east shore of the lake below is perhaps the largest in the Beartooths and a great place for a break if you have the time. This is a huge lake, and a walk along its shore is the best way to appreciate it. Some people might think that the presence of the dam detracts from the wildness of the place, but the power company has done as much as possible to keep the intrusion to a minimum. In addition, the dam far predates the designation of the Absaroka-Beartooth Wilderness.

From the dam, walk along the shoreline of Mystic Lake all the way to Island Lake. At 3.5 miles Phantom Creek Trail 17 veers off to the left (east). Keep following

Trail 19 (right) as it curves along the lake. The trail is well maintained for 2.5 miles beyond the dam. Then it's another half mile or so to Island Lake at the 6-mile mark. Just before the end of Mystic Lake, at 5.7 miles, the trail crosses Huckleberry Creek, which tumbles down from several lakes in the west shadow of Granite Peak. This is a big stream, but fortunately the Forest Service has built a sturdy bridge over it.

If you're staying overnight at Island Lake, you must cross West Rosebud Creek to get to the choice campsites on the west side of the stream, and there's no bridge. In August or September, that won't be a problem. You can cross easily on a logjam at the outlet of Island Lake. Early in the year at high water, however, this crossing could be more difficult. Lots of water comes down West Rosebud Creek. The Forest Service doesn't maintain the trail beyond a point just before crossing West Rosebud Creek or above Island Lake. After crossing West Rosebud Creek, you'll find a huge flat area where many large parties could camp and still not bother each other.

Island Lake anglers will find an occasional cutthroat trout mixed in with the rainbow population. These cutthroats have migrated down from Weeluma, Nemidji, Nugget, Beckworth, and Frenco Lakes, all pure cutthroat fisheries. Silver Lake sports some nice-size hybrid trout that are hard to catch but worth the effort. Huckleberry Lake supports a healthy rainbow population, while Avalanche and the Storm Lakes above are stocked with cutthroats that grow above average in size and weight.

Miles and Directions

0.0 West Rosebud Trailhead.

3.0 Mystic Lake Dam.

3.5 Junction with Phantom Creek Trail 17; turn right.

5.7 Huckleberry Creek.

6.0 Island Lake.

12.0 West Rosebud Trailhead.

Side Trips: The unofficial trail continues beyond Island Lake to Silver Lake, which also offers another base camp opportunity. The trail to Silver Lake is muddy and brushy, and the campsites aren't as pleasant as those at Island Lake. Instead, consider visiting Silver Lake on a day trip from your Island Lake base camp. Another good side trip is up Huckleberry Creek to Princess Lake and, for the well conditioned, on to Avalanche Lake.

Two more potential side trips include a long trek to Grasshopper Glacier and a climb up to a series of lakes—Nugget, Beckworth, Frenco, Nemidji, and Weeluma— just west of Island Lake. Only those in good shape and savvy in wilderness skills should attempt these side trips. It's possible, of course, to just hang around and explore the Island Lake and Mystic Lake country for a day or two and not regret it. (Originally contributed and re-hiked by the authors.)

103 Granite Peak

A long, steep, strenuous backpack and chance to view or climb 12,799-foot Granite Peak, the highest point in Montana, but for very experienced hikers only

Start: West Rosebud Trailhead, 40 miles southwest of Billings

Distance: 21.0-mile out-and-back with shuttle option, plus the climb up Granite Peak.

Difficulty: Very strenuous

Maps: USGS Granite Peak and Alpine; Rocky Mountain Survey Cooke City-Cutoff Mountain and Alpine–Mount Maurice Maps; Forest Service's Absaroka-Beartooth Wilderness Map

Finding the trailhead: Drive 15 miles south from Columbus on MT 78, through Absarokee. About 2 miles past Absarokee, turn right (west) to Fishtail on CR 419. Drive through Fishtail and go west and south about 1 mile. Turn left (south) along West Rosebud Road. About 6 miles later, take another left (southeast) at the sign for West Rosebud Lake. It's another 14 miles of bumpy gravel road from this point to the trailhead. In total, it's 27 miles from Absarokee and 42 miles from Columbus. The road ends and the trail begins right at the Mystic Dam Power Station. It might not seem clear exactly where the trail begins. After parking your vehicle (ample parking; toilet), walk up the road about 200 yards through the power company compound to the actual trailhead. GPS: N45 13.650' / W109 45.700'

The Hike

The first leg of the Granite Peak adventure is getting up to Mystic Lake, which offers some spectacular scenery with the unusual twist of being able to observe how the Mystic Lake Power Station was built. This is a popular day hike, so don't expect to have this lake (or any other part of this hike) to yourself.

From the trailhead, follow Trail 19 along West Rosebud Creek, where horse use is prohibited except during the fall hunting season. After crossing an overpass and a bridge over the creek, the trail follows a power line for a short way. After leaving this

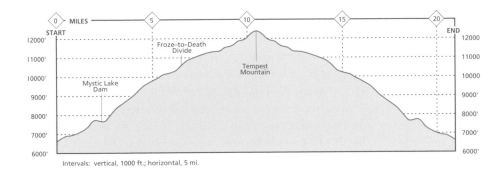

Intervals: vertical, 1000 ft.; horizontal, 5 mi.

Hiking over well-named Froze-to-Death Plateau on the way to Granite Peak. SHUTTERSTOCK

"sign of civilization" behind, the trail switchbacks through open rock fields, offering a great view of the West Rosebud valley, including West Rosebud and Emerald Lakes.

The climb doesn't seem that steep, but by the time the trail reaches the dam at the eastern end of Mystic Lake, it has ascended 1,200 feet in 3 miles, barely a Category 3 climb. When the trail finally breaks out over the ridge, it affords a great view of Mystic Dam. Mystic Lake is a natural lake, but the dam increased its size and depth. Now, at more than 200 feet, it is the deepest lake in the Beartooths.

The sandy beach along the east shore of the lake below is perhaps the largest in the Beartooths and a great place for a break if you have the time. This is a huge lake, and a walk along its shore is the best way to appreciate it. Some people might think that the presence of the dam detracts from the wildness of the place, but the power company has done as much as possible to keep the intrusion to a minimum, and it was there before the designation of the Absaroka-Beartooth Wilderness.

From the dam, walk along the shoreline for about a half mile to the 3.5-mile point and turn left (east) onto Phantom Creek Trail 17. From the lake, it's a real grinder, a Category 1 climb to the 10,140-foot saddle, partly on switchbacks. The trail takes you above Mystic Lake and gives you an incredible panoramic view of the Beartooths.

Once at the saddle, turn southwest and follow a series of cairns around the north side of Froze-to-Death Mountain. The destination is an 11,600-foot plateau on the west edge of Tempest Mountain, 1.6 miles north of Granite Peak. You can set up your base camp here.

In past years climbers have built rock shelters (rock walls about 3 feet high) on the west edge of Tempest Mountain to protect themselves from the strong winds that frequently blast the area. The Forest Service may have removed them, however, because the area is designated Wilderness, which prohibits permanent structures.

By the time you reach Tempest Mountain, you have covered more than 10 miles and gained more than 5,000 feet. You have left timberline behind many miles earlier, leaving nothing but rock, ice, and sky. No plants or grasses can survive the climate and elevation at the plateau, with the exception of a few hardy lichens.

There are some advantages to hiking and camping in such a forbidding place. The wind is so prevalent that few mosquitoes ever attempt takeoffs from ground zero. And, of course, the high altitude grants superb vistas in all directions.

Along the west edge of the plateau leading up to Tempest, the view of Granite Peak is awesome. Granite buttresses rise almost vertically from Huckleberry Creek Canyon to form a broad wall nearly a half mile wide. The north face is heavily etched with fissures running almost straight up between the buttresses. Granite Glacier clings to the center of the wall. At the top, a series of pinnacles jut from the west side up to the peak.

To those skilled in technical climbing, Granite is an easy ascent in good weather, but for those with little experience, it's challenging, if not dangerous. Probably the best advice is to go with someone who has the experience and proper equipment. Especially important is a good climbing rope for crossing several precipitous spots. The easiest approach is across the ridge that connects Granite to Tempest and then up the east side.

Check with the Forest Service for more information before attempting this climb, and get the agency's special brochure for people interested in climbing Granite Peak. In recent years not one summer has passed without mishaps and close calls, mostly due to bad judgment. One sobering concern is the extreme difficulty of rescuing an injured person from Granite, so be careful not to need it.

People have tried this hike and climb at almost all times of the year, but August and early September are best. Even then, sudden storms with subzero wind chills came come in rapidly and create an emergency. Snow can fall anytime, and the thunderstorms around Granite Peak are legendary. Be prepared with warm, wind- and waterproof clothing and preferably a shelter that will hold together in super-strong wind.

Whether or not you climb Granite, take the time to walk up to the top of Tempest. To the north and 2,000 feet below are Turgulse and Froze-to-Death Lakes. On a clear day you can see perhaps 100 miles out onto the Great Plains. And if you move a little east toward Mount Peal, you can look southwest over Granite Peak's shoulder to Mount Villard and Glacier Peak, both over 12,000 feet.

Mountain goats always looking for a handout at base camp for Granite Peak (in background).
SHUTTERSTOCK

It should be no surprise that there is little wildlife at this altitude. Nearer the saddle, where grass and a few hardy alpine plants eke out an existence, mountain goats are commonly seen. An occasional golden eagle soars through this country looking for marmots and pikas. Down closer to the trailheads, a few mule deer and black bears make their summer homes.

Camping on Froze-to-Death Plateau or Tempest Mountain is for hardy, well-prepared backpackers only. There are plenty of places to camp. The trick is keeping your tent from blowing away. This alpine area receives heavy use, so please adhere strictly to zero-impact camping ethics.

Miles and Directions

0.0 West Rosebud Trailhead.

3.0 Mystic Lake Dam.

3.5 Junction with Phantom Creek Trail 17; turn left.

6.4 Froze-to-Death Divide; turn right.

10.5 Tempest Mountain.

21.0 West Rosebud Trailhead.

Granite Peak

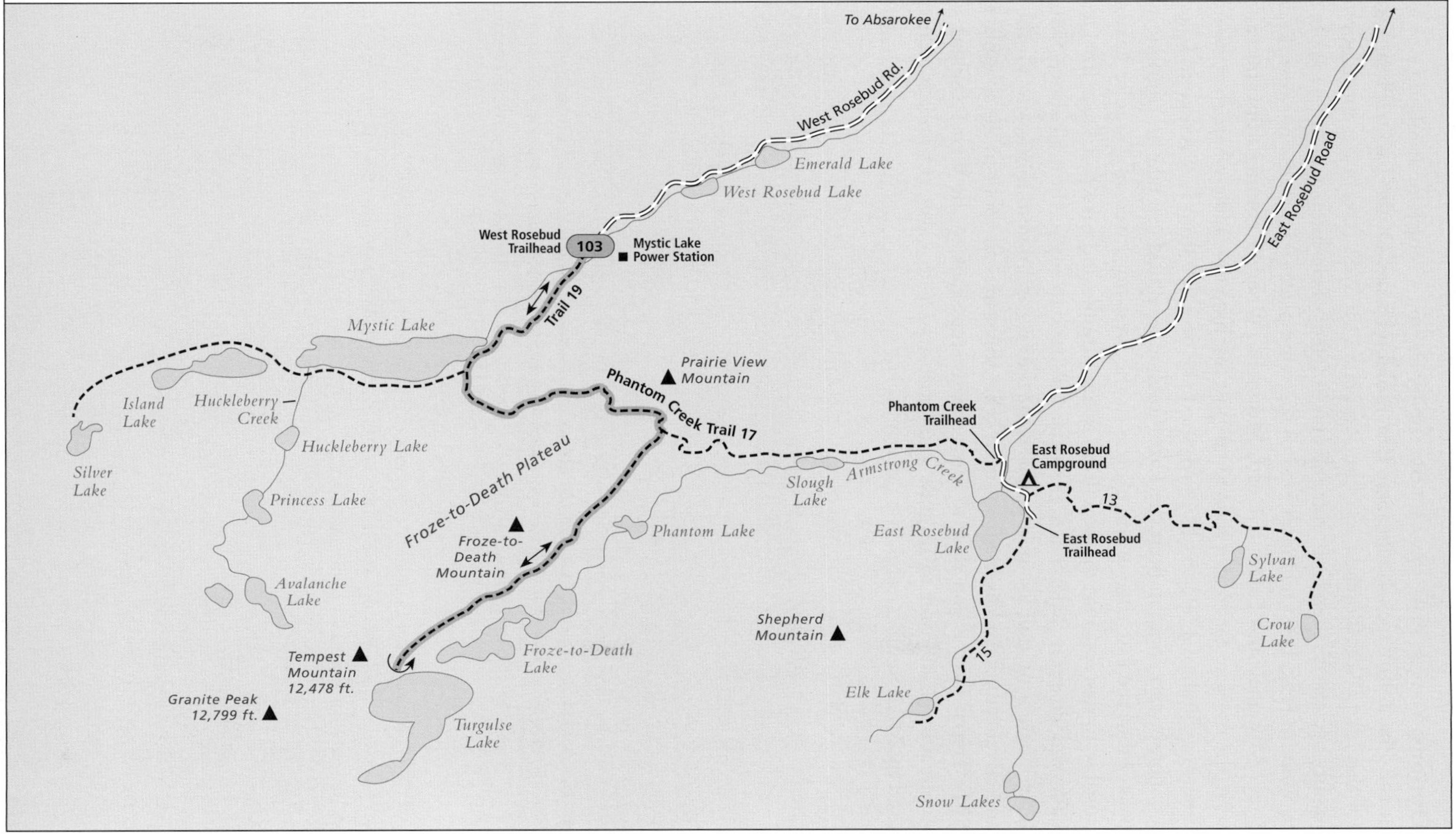

N

0 Kilometers 2

0 Miles 2

To Absarokee

West Rosebud Rd.

East Rosebud Road

Emerald Lake

West Rosebud Lake

Mystic Lake Power Station

103 West Rosebud Trailhead

Trail 19

Prairie View Mountain

Phantom Creek Trail 17

Slough Lake

Armstrong Creek

Phantom Creek Trailhead

East Rosebud Campground

East Rosebud Trailhead

13

East Rosebud Lake

Sylvan Lake

Crow Lake

Snow Lakes

15

Elk Lake

Shepherd Mountain

Phantom Lake

Froze-to-Death Plateau

Froze-to-Death Mountain

Froze-to-Death Lake

Mystic Lake

Huckleberry Creek

Huckleberry Lake

Princess Lake

Avalanche Lake

Turgulse Lake

Tempest Mountain 12,478 ft.

Granite Peak 12,799 ft.

Island Lake

Silver Lake

Options: You can make this a shuttle trip by leaving a vehicle or arranging a pickup at the Phantom Creek Trailhead at East Rosebud Lake. Of the two trailheads used for this hike (West Rosebud and East Rosebud), the West Rosebud is more popular, mainly because it's slightly shorter and cuts 400 feet of elevation gain off the approach to Granite Peak. Both trailheads lead to the same place—the saddle between Prairie View Mountain and Froze-to-Death Mountain. Whether coming from the east or west, the trails are for rugged individuals. Just reaching the saddle where the two trails meet is a climb of 3,500 feet from Mystic Lake or 3,900 from East Rosebud Lake.

Those who come in from the East Rosebud Trailhead can take an alternate way back. From the east edge of the plateau to the west-northwest of Turgulse Lake, it's possible to descend into the bowl that holds Turgulse and hike past Froze-to-Death Lake and Phantom Lake. Then cross the hill back to rejoin the trail above Slough Lake. There is no trail for most of this route, but it's an interesting way out for the fit and adventurous. And high adventure is what this trip is all about in the first place.

Side Trips: Even if you elect to retrace your steps back to the West Rosebud, you might want to dip over to Turgulse and Froze-to-Death Lakes. (Originally contributed by Mike Sample, re-hiked by the authors.)

104 Sylvan Lake

A long day hike or overnighter to one of the few easily accessible golden trout lakes in the Beartooths

Start: East Rosebud Campground, 35 miles southwest of Billings
Distance: 10.0-mile out-and-back
Difficulty: Moderate

Maps: USGS Sylvan Peak; Rocky Mountain Survey Alpine–Mount Maurice Map; Forest Service's Absaroka-Beartooth Wilderness Map

Finding the trailhead: From I-90 at Columbus, drive south 29 miles on MT 78 to Roscoe. Drive through this small ranching community, being careful not to stop at the Grizzly Bar—until the return trip, of course, when you'll be really ready for the famous Grizzly Burger. At the north end of Roscoe, the road turns to gravel and goes about 14.5 miles to the East Rosebud Trailhead. About 7 miles from Roscoe, the road crosses East Rosebud Creek and forks. Take a sharp right and continue south along the creek. The road is mostly gravel, except for a 4-mile paved section near the end. As the road swings by Alpine and around the east side of East Rosebud Lake, turn left into East Rosebud Campground to reach the trailhead for Trail 13 to Sylvan Lake and the far end of the campground. There is limited parking directly at this trailhead, but ample parking at the East Rosebud Trailhead and a full-service campground at that trailhead. GPS: N45 12.0' / W109 38.016'

The Hike

The true beauty of Sylvan Lake lies beneath the surface. There swim the gorgeous, multicolored golden trout in abundance. Biologists call the Sylvan Lake golden trout population one of the purest in the Beartooths, and they use the lake as a source of fish to plant in other lakes. However, even for the non–angler, this lake is worth the steady uphill trek.

Start up Trail 13 right from the East Rosebud Campground and gradually switchback up the steep slopes of the East Rosebud Plateau. It's 5 miles on a heavily used and well maintained trail to the lake—and almost completely uphill, but then, of

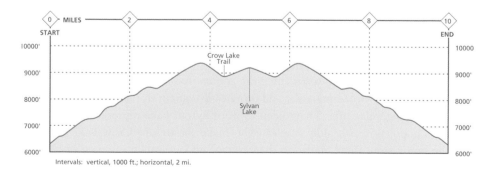

Intervals: vertical, 1000 ft.; horizontal, 2 mi.

Ptarmigan. COURTESY OF NPS

course, the return trip is all downhill. The trail is expertly designed so the climb doesn't seem so steep. The top of the ridge offers a fantastic view ("I climbed that!") of the East Rosebud drainage, including East Rosebud Lake about 2,400 feet below.

On the ridge the trail markers fade into a series of cairns for a few hundred yards, so be alert to stay on the trail. Also, don't miss the junction at 4.6 miles where a spur trail heads up to Sylvan Lake and Trail 13 continues on to Crow Lake. The junction is well marked, but inattentive hikers could end up at the wrong lake.

Sylvan Lake is more suited for day trips because of limited campsites there. The lake is at timberline, so if you do stay overnight, please refrain from building a campfire and camp at least 200 feet from the lake.

Anglers seriously intent on pursuing the golden trout of Sylvan Lake might want to spend the night. Goldens are shy and more easily caught in the morning and evening, precluding a day hike. The golden trout of Sylvan Lake reproduce readily, and the lake's population is healthy. Anglers who make the trek to Crow Lake will find that the brook trout there are larger than average and are much easier to catch than the goldens in Sylvan.

Sylvan Lake

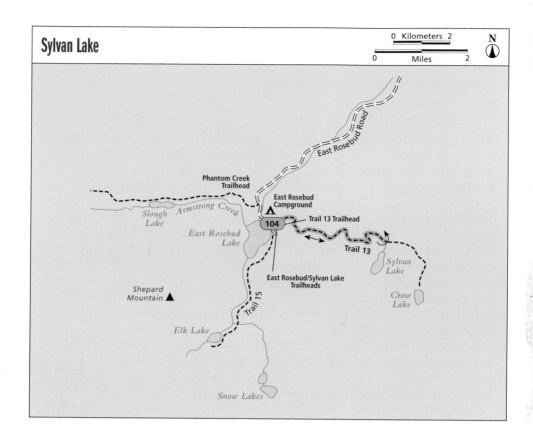

Miles and Directions

0.0   Sylvan Lake Trailhead.
4.1   Top of ridge.
4.6   Junction with trail to Crow Lake; turn right.
5.0   Sylvan Lake.
10.0   Sylvan Lake Trailhead.

Side Trips: An overnight stay at Sylvan Lake does allow time for the short side trip over to Crow Lake, which probably surpasses Sylvan Lake for beauty, at least above the surface. (Originally contributed and re-hiked by the authors.)

105 Silver Run Plateau

A long, challenging trek over an extraordinarily scenic high plateau for experienced hikers only

Start: Timberline Lake Trailhead, 10 miles southwest of Red Lodge
Distance: 14.5-mile shuttle
Difficulty: Strenuous

Maps: USGS Black Pyramid Mountain and Bare Mountain; Rocky Mountain Survey Alpine–Mount Maurice Map; Forest Service's Absaroka-Beartooth Wilderness Map

Finding the trailheads: From Red Lodge, go to the north edge of town and watch for the big sign for the Red Lodge Mountain Ski Resort; take a right (west) onto West Fork Road (also called Ski Run Road and FR 71). When the road forks at 3 miles, take the left fork, staying on the paved West Fork Road and not the gravel road continuing on up to the ski resort. The road is paved until you reach the Basin Creek Campground, where it turns into a good gravel road. Go 4 more miles and turn left (south) into the Timberline Lake Trailhead (11 miles total from Red Lodge), which has a fairly large parking lot (but too small for horse trailers) and toilet. GPS: N45 10.333' / W109 27.550'

The turnoff to Silver Run Trail 64 (the end of this hike) is marked on the south side of West Fork Road, about 2 miles past the turnoff to the ski resort. You can make it over this 2.1-mile spur road up to the trailhead in any vehicle, barely, but it gets steep and rocky in a few places, so a high-clearance vehicle is better. Limited parking; toilet. GPS: N45 8.116' / W109 21.116'

If you decide not to leave a vehicle or bicycle at the trailhead for Trail 64, you can leave it at the parking area just after crossing the West Fork of Rock Creek (ample parking and toilet), but this will add 2.1 miles to your hike because you'll have to walk down the jeep road to your vehicle.

The Hike

This is unconditionally one of the most remarkable and unusual trails in the Beartooths, or anywhere else. It doesn't feature an endless string of lakes as many Beartooth trails do, but hikers might be too busy enjoying the trip to notice. Only

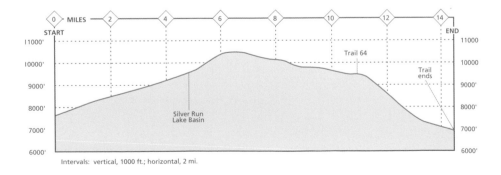

Taking a break on Silver Run Plateau. Bill Schneider

the midsection of this trail is actually within the Absaroka-Beartooth Wilderness, but the entire trip seems exceptionally wild. The 2008 Cascade Fire scorched the first few miles of this route.

Weather is always critical in the Beartooths, but good weather is essential for this hike. Double-check the weather report before leaving home, and unless you have a good forecast, delay your hike. And take an extra water bottle, as water is scarce, especially in late summer.

Another big issue on this hike is transportation; it's a problematic shuttle. Arrange to be picked up or leave a vehicle (or bicycle) at the end of the trail to get back to the vehicle at the Timberline Lake Trailhead.

For some reason that will always be a mystery to me, this route doesn't get much use. I've only hiked it twice (so far), and both times, we didn't see another hiker on the plateau. The scenic cluster of small lakes in the Silver Run Basin isn't much of a fishery, so that might be one reason for the light use. Another might be the difficulty—definitely a route for well-conditioned, experienced hikers only—so that might be the main reason. But for whatever the reason, I have to say "you don't know what you're missing," as the scenery equals or exceeds anything, anywhere in the Beartooths.

This isn't really a good backpacking route, but those backpackers who choose to spend a night or two in the Silver Run Basin won't be disappointed, because it's definitely a room with a view.

As you hike this route, you pass through four strikingly distinct environs. You start with a climb on a fairly rocky trail through a lodgepole forest, now nothing but a forest of ghostly snags, as it recovers from the massive Cascade Fire of 2008. Then, you emerge from the wildflower-carpeted burn into the postcard panorama called the Silver Run Basin, followed by 6 remarkable miles of high-altitude splendor on the Silver Run Plateau. Finally, you finish up with a steep downhill plunge through what most might consider a typical mature forest, primarily lodgepole and Douglas fir.

From the trailhead, Timberline Trail 12 ascends 3 miles through the big burn and offers a great study on how a landscape quickly recovers from a forest fire—including, for your enjoyment, a robust growth of huckleberries, raspberries, and just about every other berry. At 3 miles, turn left onto Beartrack Trail 8 and ford Timberline Creek (no bridge). Shortly after that ford and another over Silver Run Creek (again, no bridge), you emerge from the burn into the gorgeous Silver Run Basin, dotted with small lakes and all in the backdrop of mighty Silver Run Peak, which, at 12,500 feet, casts a mighty big shadow. Also, you'll find mature stands of healthy whitebark pine, which, in the era of the pine beetle, you really don't see much anymore.

You have a lot of time to relish the scenery of the Silver Run Basin as you gradually switchback up the east side of it until you step out on the unique Silver Run Plateau. Up to this point, the trail has been distinct and easy to follow, but once on the plateau, it becomes mostly a series of cairns with no visible trail. Other trails in the Beartooths have short stretches of cairns, but in this case the cairns last for about 6 miles. Fortunately, the cairns are well placed, large, and easy to see.

The Silver Run Plateau is all above 10,000 feet and affords a fresh perspective of the Beartooths. It's trackless, treeless, bugless, waterless, and peopleless—almost. There is always that determined devil, the occasional horsefly, that can follow you anywhere, defying all the laws of nature, up to 10,500 feet and many miles from the nearest horse, for a mouthful of soft meat from behind your knee. Also, the plateau actually has a few charming spring- and snowmelt-fed rivulets where you can filter water, but depending on the year and time of year, they can be dry.

Most of your off-trail trek over the plateau is above 10,000 feet, topping out at about 10,650 feet. You can see many of the highest peaks of the Beartooths on the horizon, and below you, a truly fascinating carpet of plant life such as aged willows that top out at about 10 inches in height and perhaps my favorite wildflower, the rare Arctic gentian. This is the only place I've ever seen this lovely pale-green flower.

While traveling from cairn to cairn, do a good deed and help keep them maintained. If a cairn has collapsed, take the time to rebuild it. When approaching a cairn, look for a rock or two that looks like it needs a new home, carry it the last few feet, and then use it to build up the cairn. It's the least you can do. After all, those cairns have been up there in the clouds, enduring the most severe climate in Montana, faithfully showing hikers the way for decades.

After following cairns for about 6 miles, watch for the junction with Silver Run Trail 64 at the 11-mile point. Beartrack Trail 8 continues straight into the Lake Fork

Following the cairns above the clouds on Silver Run Plateau. BILL SCHNEIDER

of Rock Creek. You turn left (north) onto Silver Run Trail 64 and head down Silver Run Creek into the West Fork of Rock Creek.

The last time I hiked this route in 2013, this junction was extremely easy to miss, so be on your toes. It was only marked (unofficially, I think, by other hikers, not the Forest Service) with two cairns beside each other and a spike of weathered wood in each—one leaning south toward Trail 8 and one leaning north to Trail 64. When you look carefully both ways, you can see cairns in both directions, your signal that you're at the junction.

After this junction, you still have another half mile or so of your fantastic journey over the Silver Run Plateau as you finally slip below 10,000 feet and then drop off the edge of the plateau.

Trail 64 drops rapidly (from 9,400 feet to 7,100 feet in less than 4 miles!) into Silver Run Creek, so steeply that doing this trip in reverse would seem unwise, to put it mildly. Stay on this trail for 3.5 miles to the trailhead, bearing right after 2 miles at the junction with Ingles Creek Trail 35. On the way down, you might see a few STOCK DRIVEWAY signs nailed on trees, which are also signs of a much different past. Decades ago the Forest Service allowed heavy sheep grazing on the Silver Run Plateau, but fortunately that grazing allotment has been abandoned, mainly because of potential damage to this fragile and unique environment. Some things do, it seems, get better with time.

Silver Run Plateau

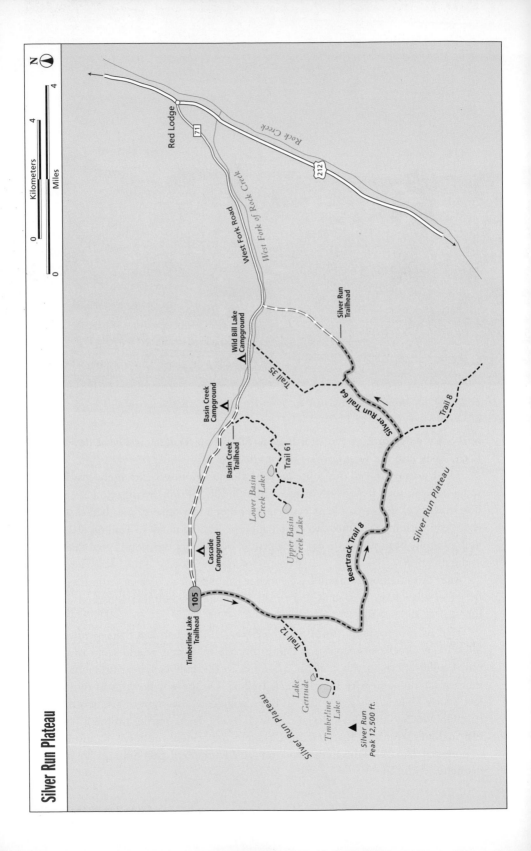

Arctic gentian, pale green, beautiful, rare, and found on the Silver Run Plateau, the only place in Montana we've seen it. BILL SCHNEIDER

Miles and Directions

0.0 Timberline Lake Trailhead.

3.0 Junction with Beartrack Trail 8; turn left.

4.4 Silver Run Lake Basin.

5.1 Trail turns into string of cairns.

11.0 Junction with Silver Run Trail 64; turn left.

13.0 Junction with Ingles Creek Trail 35; turn right.

14.5 Silver Run Trailhead.

Options: This route isn't well suited for backpacking, but if you prefer to stay overnight, you won't have trouble finding a five-star campsite in the Silver Run Basin. The basin isn't centrally located on the route, but you could stay an extra day and spend it exploring the plateau. You can also camp on the plateau, but be prepared for a dry camp and cross your fingers for two consecutive days of good weather. Wherever you camp, follow strict zero-impact practices to keep this area as pristine as it presently is. No campfires or fire rings, please.

Doing this shuttle in reverse would be possible but more difficult.

Side Trips: An exceptionally ambitious and fit hiker could take a side trip to see Timberline Lake or try a climb to the summit of Silver Run Peak. (Originally contributed and re-hiked by the authors.)

106 Glacier Lake

A short but steep hike to a rugged, alpine environment and huge, windswept lake

Start: Glacier Lake Trailhead, 15 miles south of Red Lodge

Distance: 4.0-mile out-and-back, plus side trips

Difficulty: Moderately strenuous but short

Maps: USGS Silver Run Peak; Rocky Mountain Survey Alpine–Mount Maurice and Wyoming Beartooths Maps; Forest Service's Absaroka-Beartooth Wilderness Map

Finding the trailhead: Drive south from Red Lodge on US 212 for 10.9 miles. Watch for a well-marked turnoff on the right (west) to three Forest Service campgrounds. Stay on this paved road for 0.9 mile until you cross a bridge near the entrance to Limberpine Campground. Immediately after the bridge, the pavement ends and you reach a fork in the road. For Glacier Lake, turn left (southwest). You really want a high-clearance vehicle to get to this trailhead, but you can get there slowly with any vehicle. Snow usually blocks this gravel road until at least early July. Once on the road to the Glacier Lake Trailhead, there's no chance of making a wrong turn because there are no forks or spur roads. The road crosses the state line and dips down into Wyoming for the start of your hike, but most of the trail lies in Montana. It's a long, slow, bumpy 7.6 miles to the trailhead, which is almost exactly on the Montana-Wyoming border. The small parking area is frequently full, so be careful not to take more than one space. There's a toilet and a National Weather Service precipitation gauge at the trailhead; plenty of vehicle camping at the start of the road to Glacier Lake, plus some undeveloped camping along the road, but the Forest Service has recently closed some traditional camping spots to protect water quality. GPS: N45 0.199' / W109 30.883'

The Hike

Although this route could be done as an overnighter, the Glacier Lake area seems nicely suited to a long day of exploring, fishing, photographing, and simply enjoying high-elevation majestic vistas. It's a 2-mile, mostly uphill route and the only trail in the Beartooths closed all year to horse use.

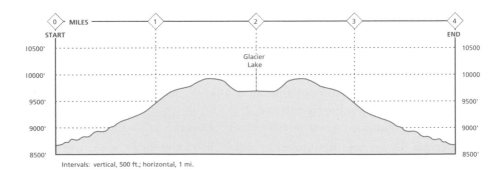

A string of tasty brook trout for dinner. BILL SCHNEIDER

The trail to Glacier Lake is short but very steep. The trailhead is at 8,680 feet and the lake is at 9,702 feet, but the route actually climbs more than the difference (1,022 feet) in the 2 miles to Glacier Lake. That's because there's a ridge in the middle that's about 800 feet higher than the lake, making the first part of the trail a Category 1 climb.

After climbing for about a half mile up Trail 3, the trail crosses Moon Creek on a bridge. After Moon Creek, the trail gets even steeper—and the higher it goes, the better the scenery. Shortly after Moon Creek, a faint, unofficial trail veers off to the north to Moon Lake and Shelf Lake. Turn left (west) and stay on what is obviously the main trail. For most of the way, the trail is rough and rock-studded, but it remains easy to follow and without hazards.

Once atop the ridge, cross some rock shelves on the way down to massive Glacier Lake. Even though the lake sits at 9,702 feet (above timberline), some large trees stand along the shoreline.

The trail reaches the lake at a small concrete dam built long ago to increase the depth of Glacier Lake. A faint trail heads off to the right and goes about halfway around the lake. After a large point jutting out into the lake, the trail degenerates into

Glacier Lake

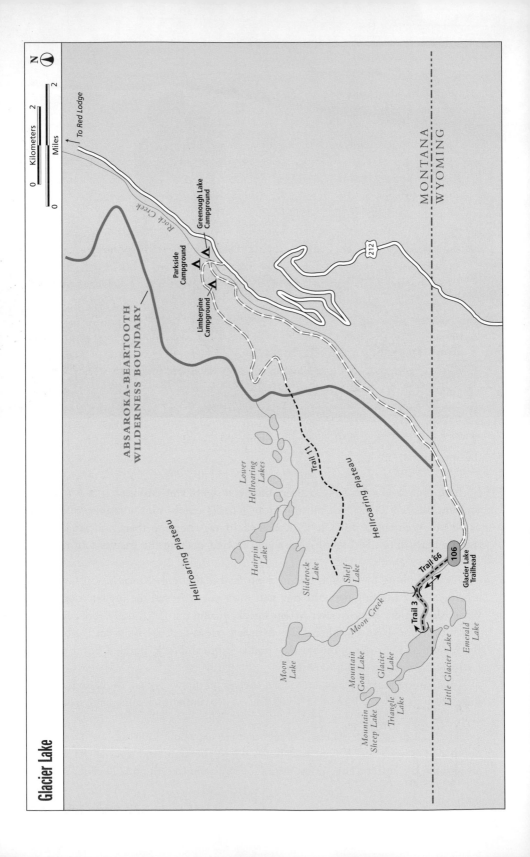

N

Kilometers
0   2

Miles
0   2

To Red Lodge

Rock Creek

ABSAROKA-BEARTOOTH
WILDERNESS BOUNDARY

Parkside Campground

Greenough Lake Campground

Limberpine Campground

212

Hellroaring Plateau

Trail 11

Lower Hellroaring Lakes

Hairpin Lake

Sliderock Lake

Shelf Lake

Hellroaring Plateau

Trail 3

Moon Creek

Moon Lake

Mountain Goat Lake

Glacier Lake

Triangle Lake

Mountain Sheep Lake

Little Glacier Lake

Emerald Lake

Trail 66

106

Glacier Lake Trailhead

MONTANA
WYOMING

a series of boulder fields and talus slopes, which makes the area great habitat for a good population of pikas.

Bearing right along the north shore of the lake affords views of Triangle Lake and access to Mountain Sheep Lake and Mountain Goat Lake at the head of the basin. Bearing left and across the dam around the south shore of the lake leads directly to Little Glacier Lake, a small jewel just barely separated from Glacier Lake. Continuing south on this trail over a small ridge treats wanderers to the sight of lovely Emerald Lake.

If you're fishing, be sure to keep track of which state you're in, and make sure you have the right license. The state line goes right through Glacier Lake. Little Glacier and Emerald Lakes are in Wyoming.

Because of topography, Glacier Lake tends to become remarkably windy during midday, so try to arrive early to catch the scenery before the winds start ripping through this valley. Emerald Lake is not quite as windy.

All of the potential campsites along the north shore of Glacier Lake are cramped and marginal at best and probably too close to the lake. For those planning to stay overnight, there are several quality campsites on the north side of Emerald Lake. The south side of the lake is spectacularly steep. This is high alpine country, so please resist the temptation to have a campfire.

Rock Creek with its ice-cold, swift-running water and high canyon walls makes spectacular scenery, but these conditions make life hard for fish. The small populations of cutthroat and brook trout concentrate in the slower water, so look for good holding places out of the current. The main fork of Rock Creek winds in and out of Wyoming and Montana, so anglers need to know which state they're in and have the appropriate license.

Glacier Lake supports cutthroat and brook trout, both of which grow to above-average size. The fish tend to school, with cutthroats working rocky shorelines, so anglers should work the shoreline as well. When water levels are high, water flows between Glacier and Little Glacier Lakes, so the fishery is the same in both. But the fish are easier to find in Little Glacier. Emerald Lake supports both cutts and brookies as well, though slightly smaller than those in Glacier. Cutts are stocked in Mountain Goat Lake and work their way down to Mountain Sheep Lake. Count on more fish in the upper lake and larger ones in the lower. Shelf Lake harbors hefty brookies, while Moon Lake grows above-average cutts.

Miles and Directions

0.0 Glacier Lake Trailhead.

0.5 Cross Moon Creek on bridge and junction with social trail to Moon Lake; turn left.

2.0 Glacier Lake.

4.0 Glacier Lake Trailhead.

Side Trips: Mountain Goat and Mountain Sheep Lakes can be reached with a reasonable effort, but Moon and Shelf Lakes are strenuous side trips. (Originally contributed and re-hiked by the authors.)

107 Martin Lake Basin

Multitudes of scenic, trout-filled lakes and a high-altitude waterfall, an excellent base camp trip with many side trips

Start: Clay Butte Trailhead, 30 miles east of Cooke City

Distance: 13.0-mile out-and-back

Difficulty: Moderate

Maps: USGS Muddy Creek, Beartooth Butte, Castle Mountain, and Silver Run Peak; Rocky Mountain Survey Wyoming Beartooths and Alpine–Mount Maurice Maps; Forest Service's Absaroka-Beartooth Wilderness Map

Finding the trailhead: The well-marked Clay Butte Road (FR 142) turns north off the Beartooth Highway 21.2 miles east of Cooke City or 40.3 miles west of Red Lodge. Any passenger car can make it up the moderately steep, well-maintained gravel road to Clay Butte Lookout, but it's not recommended for vehicles pulling trailers. The road to the trailhead turns off to the left 2 miles from the Beartooth Highway. Small parking area (way too small for its popularity); no toilet; no camping. GPS: N44 57.333' / W109 37.967'

The Hike

For those who like to spend one moderately hard day getting to a beautiful base camp and then spend several days doing scenic day trips, this is an ideal choice.

Trail 614 starts out downhill but then goes uphill after about a mile at the junction with Trail 568 to Upper Granite Lake. Turn right and stay on Trail 614. For the first 2.5 miles, the trail travels through an enormous, high-altitude meadow carpeted with wildflowers. At one point, the trail fades away into a string of cairns, so watch carefully for the next trail marker.

About a quarter mile before Native Lake, at the 2.9-mile point, Trail 614 meets Trail 619 coming from Beartooth Lake. Turn left (west) onto Trail 619. Native Lake is the beginning of a long string of lakes. It's tempting to look for campsites along the

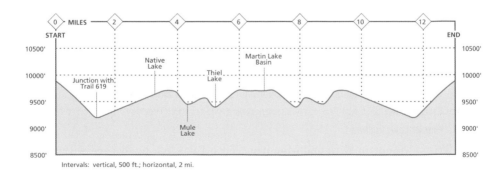

Intervals: vertical, 500 ft.; horizontal, 2 mi.

The last descent into Martin Lake Basin. BILL SCHNEIDER

way, but the best is yet to come at Martin Lake. Be prepared for short, steep climbs just before and after Mule Lake at 4.2 miles and a long, strenuous climb into the Martin Lake Basin that starts just after Thiel Lake at 4.7 miles. Be careful not to miss Thiel Lake. It's off to the left (south) at the bottom of the hill after Mule Lake, just after the trail breaks out into a lush meadow. You reach Martin Lake at 6.5 miles.

Martin Lake Basin is one of the most fascinating places in the Beartooths. Four major lakes (Martin, Wright, Spogen, and Whitcomb) are linked by a stream filled with brook trout, and there's a spectacular high-altitude waterfall between Wright and Spogen Lakes. The waterfall seems larger and more majestic here at 9,600 feet.

As is obvious from the topo map, this is lake country. Dozens of lakes lie within a day's trek from this basin. Even avid explorers could spend a week here and not see the same lake twice. Don't forget to spend one of those days simply hiking around the four lakes in the basin to fully appreciate a place that would put most national parks to shame.

You can camp almost anywhere in the basin, but the most convenient sites are around Wright and Martin Lakes. This is like a five-star hotel: Every room has a view—with free air-conditioning. You could call it nature's penthouse. Firewood,

Standing above Spogen Falls in Martin Lake Basin. BILL SCHNEIDER

however, is in short supply and essential to the extraordinary charm of this basin, so resist the temptation to have a campfire.

Most of the lakes in this area were stocked with brook trout, and the chain of lakes in Martin Lake Basin is named after the men who hauled them in. The brookies here are average for the Beartooths, with Whitcomb Lake having slightly larger fish.

For variety, Trail Lake (appropriately named) has cutthroats that are stocked but also reproduce. Head upstream from Martin Lake to reach the cutthroat hotbed found in the Cloverleaf Lakes. On the way in or out, a side trip to Swede and Hidden Lakes is worthwhile for the cutthroats found there. Goldens were once found in Hidden Lake, and a few may still remain.

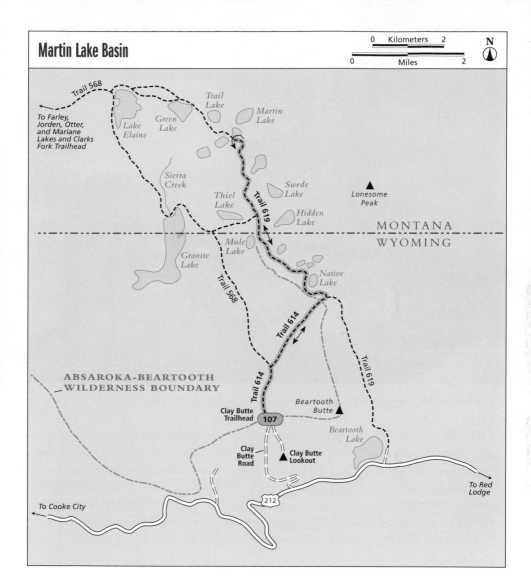

Martin Lake Basin

0   Kilometers   2

0   Miles   2

N

Trail 568

To Farley,
Jorden, Otter,
and Mariane
Lakes and Clarks
Fork Trailhead

Lake
Elaine

Green
Lake

Trail
Lake

Martin
Lake

Sierra
Creek

Thiel
Lake

Trail 619

Swede
Lake

Lonesome
Peak

Hidden
Lake

Granite
Lake

Mule
Lake

Native
Lake

MONTANA

WYOMING

Trail 568

Trail 614

Trail 619

ABSAROKA-BEARTOOTH
WILDERNESS BOUNDARY

Trail 614

Beartooth
Butte

Clay Butte
Trailhead

107

Beartooth
Lake

Clay
Butte
Road

Clay Butte
Lookout

212

To Cooke City

To Red
Lodge

Miles and Directions

- **0.0**   Clay Butte Trailhead.
- **1.2**   Junction with Trail 568 to Upper Granite Lake; turn right.
- **2.9**   Junction with Trail 619 from Beartooth Lake Trailhead; turn left.
- **3.1**   Native Lake.
- **4.2**   Mule Lake.
- **4.7**   Thiel Lake.
- **6.5**   Martin Lake Basin.
- **13.0**   Clay Butte Trailhead.

Enjoying a rare campfire while camping at Granite Lake. BILL SCHNEIDER

Options: Another reason Martin Lake is a better base camp than most is that hikers don't have to retrace the exact same route on the way out. On the return trip, from the bottom of the big hill to Thiel Lake, leave Trail 619 and follow a well-used trail that traverses the east side of Thiel Lake. This isn't an official Forest Service trail and doesn't show on the topo or national forest maps, but it's well-maintained and well-signed at the south end. In less than 1 mile, it intersects with Trail 568, which goes to Upper Granite Lake. Turn left (south) at this junction and follow this well-used trail back to the trailhead. This route still means retracing your steps the last uphill mile to the trailhead from the junction of Trails 568 and 614, but most of the trip will be new country.

You can also make a loop out of this hike by going west out of the basin, down to Green Lake, over to Lake Elaine, and then down to Granite Lake and back up to the trailhead. This is a rough trip, though, especially the off-trail section north of Green Lake.

Side Trips: From Martin Lake, hikers have a large number of choices for day trips. Here are just a few possibilities: Box Lakes (easy), Surprise Lake (easy), Mule Lake (easy), Thiel Lake (easy), Hidden Lake (moderate), Swede Lake (moderate), Cloverleaf Lakes (strenuous), Kidney Lake (easy), Marmot Lake (moderate), Trail Lake (easy), Green Lake (moderate), Sierra Creek (moderate), and around Martin Basin (moderate). (Originally contributed and re-hiked by the authors.)

108 Sundance Pass

A moderately long but not too challenging backpacking trip through spectacular mountain scenery, especially the view from Sundance Pass

Start: Lake Fork of Rock Creek Trailhead, 15 miles south of Red Lodge
Distance: 21.0-mile shuttle
Difficulty: Strenuous

Maps: USGS Black Pyramid Mountain, Silver Run Peak, and Sylvan Peak; Rocky Mountain Survey Alpine–Mount Maurice Map; Forest Service's Absaroka-Beartooth Wilderness Map.

Finding the trailheads: From Red Lodge, drive southwest for about 10 miles on US 212. Turn west at the well-marked road up the Lake Fork of Rock Creek. A short, paved road leads to a turn-around and the starting trailhead. Plenty of parking; toilet; vehicle camping in the campground. GPS: N45 4.750' / W109 24.633'

Leave a vehicle or arrange for a pickup at the trailhead at the end of the West Fork of Rock Creek Road. To find this trailhead, take West Fork of Rock Creek Road (FR 71), which leaves US 212 on the south edge of Red Lodge. Drive 2.7 miles to where the road forks. Take the left fork and drive another 11.3 miles until the road ends at the trailhead. Large parking lot; toilet; camping at several nearby campgrounds. GPS: N45 10.083' / W109 29.766'

The Hike

This well-maintained and heavily used trail is not only one of the most scenic in the Beartooths, but it's only a short drive from the Billings area, so it's very popular. You can make this hike a three-day trip, staying one night in the Lake Fork of Rock Creek and another in the West Fork of Rock Creek. Although nicely suited to a three-day/two-night trip, the route also offers many scenic side trips. Plan an extra day or two in the backcountry for exploring them.

This trail offers absolutely spectacular scenery. From Sundance Pass, for example, vistas include 12,000-foot mountains, such as 12,548-foot Whitetail Peak, and the Beartooth Plateau, a huge mass of contiguous land above 10,000 feet. Hikers are also

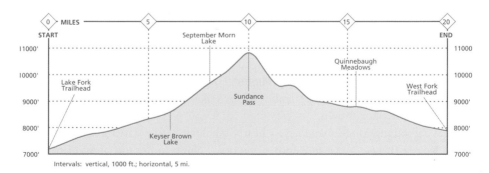

treated to views of glaciers and obvious results of glaciation, exposed Precambrian rock, and waterfalls. And watch for mountain goats, deer, golden eagles, and gyrfalcons. Goats are frequently seen from First and Second Rock Lakes.

This is a fairly difficult, 21-mile shuttle trip that starts at the Lake Fork of Rock Creek and ends on the West Fork of Rock Creek just southwest of Red Lodge. Arrange to be picked up at the trailhead at the end of the West Fork of Rock Creek Road (FR 71) or leave a vehicle there. An alternative is to have another party start at the other end of the trail, meet you up on Sundance Pass, and trade car keys.

Plan to do this trip no earlier in the year than mid-July, when the snow finally gives up Sundance Pass. This delay also avoids the peak season for mosquitoes and no-see-ums, which can be quite bad in this area, especially on the West Fork side.

The main route passes by three lakes—Keyser Brown, September Morn, and Sundance—but several others can be reached with short side trips. One of these is Lost Lake, which is about a quarter-mile climb from the main trail. This is a very heavily used lake, and it shows it. There are campsites here, but consider staying somewhere else that hasn't been trampled so much. The trail to Lost Lake leaves the main trail on the left, 5 miles from the trailhead or about 200 yards before the bridge over the Lake Fork of Rock Creek.

Another lake-bound trail departs from the main trail at 5.2 miles, immediately before the same bridge. The unofficial trail to Black Canyon Lake scrambles uphill, also to the left. Black Canyon Lake lies just below Grasshopper Glacier. The undeveloped trail to Black Canyon Lake is a rough but short hike of about 1.5 miles. Part of the route traverses rock talus with no trail, and there is a steep climb near the lake. The hike to Black Canyon is probably too tough for small children or poorly conditioned hikers. There is almost no place to camp at this high, rugged lake (no campfires allowed if you do find a spot), and it's usually very windy at Black Canyon during midday.

The main trail continues west along the Lake Fork another mile or so to Keyser Brown Lake, about 6.5 miles from the trailhead. To do this trip in three days and two nights, plan to start early and spend the first night at Keyser Brown. Although the wood supply is ample enough around Keyser Brown, this is one of the most heavily used campsites in the Beartooths. Please consider doing without a campfire.

Keyser Brown Lake is about a quarter mile to the left (southwest), so watch carefully for the spur trail to the lake. It is an official trail and signed. The lake itself comes into view from the main trail, but if you can see it, you've missed the junction and need to backtrack about 200 yards to the trail to the lake. An angler's trail leads south from the far end of Keyser Brown to First and Second Rock Lakes. This side trip involves some difficult boulder hopping. For another campsite option, continue 2 miles up the main trail to September Morn Lake, where the campsite selection is better than at Keyser Brown.

Get a good night's sleep and have a hearty breakfast before starting the second day. From Keyser Brown it's a 1,660-foot, Category 2 climb to the top of Sundance Pass at the 11.3-mile mark. The scenery is so incredible, however, that hikers might not

Whitetail Peak from the West Fork of Rock Creek. SHUTTERSTOCK

notice how much work it is getting to the top. To the north and east stretch the twin lobes of the Silver Run Plateau, rising to their apex at 12,500-foot Silver Run Peak. Directly south of the pass, 11,647-foot Mount Lockhart partially shields the pyramid of 12,548-foot Whitetail Peak.

Coming down from Sundance Pass into the West Fork won't take long. A series of switchbacks drops about 1,000 feet in about a mile to a bridge over the headwaters of the West Fork. Remember to carry extra water on this stretch—it is scarce on the pass.

Although there are campsites in a meadow about a quarter mile down the trail from the Sundance Bridge, Quinnebaugh Meadows at 16 miles is probably the best choice for the second night out. It offers plenty of excellent campsites, and there might be enough downed wood for a campfire. It's a long 9.5 miles from Keyser Brown to Quinnebaugh Meadows, but there aren't many good campsites between September Morn Lake and the meadows. Camping at the meadows leaves an easy 5 miles for the last day out. It might also allow enough time for a side trip up to Lake Mary or Dude Lake. Dude Lake is 1 mile west via a rough, steep trail from Quinnebaugh Meadows. And there's a steep but good trail from the meadows to

West Fork of Rock Creek. SHUTTERSTOCK

Lake Mary at 15.9 miles. Some people use the saddle to the north of Lake Mary as a cross-country route to Crow, Sylvan, and East Rosebud Lakes.

The final day of hiking follows the trail along the north bank of the West Fork all the way to the trailhead. Sentinel and Calamity Falls both offer good places to drop the pack and relax. The 2008 Cascade Fire heavily burned the last few miles of the route.

Both the Lake Fork and the West Fork are probably used as heavily as any wild area in Montana. Consequently, the Forest Service has rangers out enforcing several protective regulations listed at the trailhead information board. Read them carefully and then, of course, obey them. They are necessary to protect these fragile environs.

The lakes found along the Lake Fork provide some of the easiest fishing in the Beartooths. Anglers will find plenty of hungry brookies in September Morn, Keyser Brown, and First and Second Rock Lakes. Overnight campers can count on these lakes to supply dinner. Keyser Brown and Second Rock Lakes also support healthy cutthroat fisheries. For those with something other than brook trout on their mind,

Sundance Pass

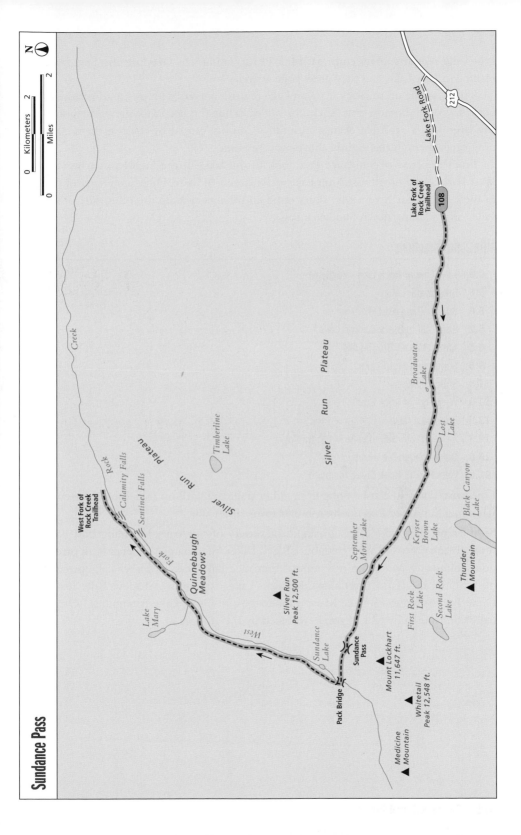

N

Kilometers
0   2

Miles
0   2

West Fork of
Rock Creek
Trailhead

Calamity Falls

Sentinel Falls

Creek

Rock

Fork

Lake
Mary

Quinnebaugh
Meadows

Silver

Run

Plateau

Timberline
Lake

Silver Run
Peak 12,500 ft.

Sundance
Lake

West

Pack Bridge

Sundance Pass

Mount Lockhart
11,647 ft.

Medicine
Mountain

Whitetail
Peak 12,548 ft.

First Rock
Lake

Second Rock
Lake

September
Morn Lake

Kryser
Broun
Lake

Thunder
Mountain

Black Canyon
Lake

Silver   Run   Plateau

Lost
Lake

Broadwater
Lake

Lake Fork of
Rock Creek
Trailhead

108

Lake Fork Road

212

Lost Lake supports a few cutthroat trout of surprising size. Grayling also have been planted in Lost Lake, and they grow large as well.

The scramble up to Black Canyon Lake rewards anglers with plenty of cutthroats near the glacial moraine that blocks the outlet. While this lake once grew exceptionally large fish, a probable change in food organisms, caused by the fish themselves, now keeps them in the slightly above-average range.

From the crest of Sundance Pass, look to the lakes in the high basin across the West Fork to the northwest. Ship Lake is the largest of these. There are plenty of fish in these waters for hikers who don't mind an off-trail trek up the other side of the valley after coming down Sundance Pass.

Miles and Directions

0.0 Lake Fork of Rock Creek Trailhead.
3.5 Broadwater Lake.
5.0 Spur trail to Lost Lake.
5.2 Spur trail to Black Canyon Lake.
6.5 Turn to Keyser Brown Lake.
8.5 September Morn Lake.
11.3 Sundance Pass.
13.0 West Fork of Rock Creek.
13.5 Sundance Lake.
15.9 Junction with trail to Lake Mary; turn right.
16.0 Quinnebaugh Meadows.
21.0 West Fork of Rock Creek Trailhead.

Options: This trip can be done from either trailhead with no noticeable difference. Climbing Sundance Pass is a lung-buster from either side.

Side Trips: This hike offers an abundant variety of side trips, including Lost Lake (easy), Black Canyon Lake (strenuous), Rock Lakes (moderate), Whitetail Peak (strenuous), Sundance Mountain (strenuous), Sundance Lake (easy), Marker Lake (strenuous), Ship Lake Basin (strenuous), Kookoo Lake (strenuous), Shadow Lake (easy), Dude Lake (strenuous), Lake Mary (moderate), and Crow Lake (strenuous). (Originally contributed by Mike Sample, re-hiked by the authors.)

THE VIEW FROM HERE: HORSE SENSE

We wouldn't have very many hiking trails if it weren't for horses. Historically the Forest Service built trails for horses, not for hikers. Now hikers have claimed these horse-packing trails as hiking trails, but believe me, they weren't built for us.

So when you step in a fresh horse apple, don't complain too loudly. The horses were there long before we were.

And when you get to a big, lush meadow and can still see the trail through it, you can also thank horses, because they keep a lot of trails—all but the most heavily hiked—distinct enough for hikers to easily follow.

But I believe that the FS should limit or prohibit horse use in most, if not all, fragile alpine areas above timberline, especially in the Beartooths. I have seen some horrific damage caused by horses in alpine areas, the type of damage a thousand backpackers couldn't do even with weeks of camping.

Plus, in the Beartooths, one of my favorite hiking areas, it's a special treat to hike off-trail to find a secluded lake or plateau to claim as my own for a night or two. But over the past few decades, horse packers have essentially constructed trails to almost all of these remote places. Two or three trips by a long pack train on the same route leaves a trail that would take nature decades to reclaim in the delicate environment above timberline.

This is a hypersensitive subject for the FS because many people in the agency use horses, both at work and recreationally, but damage to the fragile alpine areas should be the first priority. Prohibiting horse use above timberline would still leave 95 percent or more of the trails open to horses.

Next time you're talking to the FS, bring the subject up and encourage the agency to start looking at the problem.

BLM Areas

109 Humbug Spires

A unique day trek or overnighter among granite spires in a primitive area

Start: Moose Creek Trailhead, 26 miles south of Butte

Distance: 6.0-mile out-and-back

Difficulty: Moderate

Maps: USGS Butte South and Melrose; BLM Public Land States Map 33

Finding the trailhead: After driving south of Butte on I-15 for 26 miles, take Moose Creek exit 99 and head east on Moose Creek Road (FR 0101) for 3.3 miles to the Bureau of Land Management parking lot, which has a toilet and a great map on the information board. The road from the freeway is good gravel passable by any vehicle. GPS: N45 44.566' / W112 40.233'

Hiking along Moose Creek into the Humbug Spires wild area. BILL SCHNEIDER

The Wedge marks the end of the Humbug Spires Trail. BILL SCHNEIDER

The Hike

Of all the roadless country in Montana, the 11,174-acre Humbug Spires Primitive Area must rank among the most intriguing. Besides the granite protrusions for which it was named, the area has a lovely stream with small cutthroat trout and a forest of primeval Douglas fir somehow overlooked by early timber cutters.

After leaving the parking area, you cross a footbridge to the west side of Moose Creek. In the first 1.3 miles, you pass by numerous ancient trees, possibly 200 years old or older, as you closely follow Moose Creek, which is more like a babbling brook. The thick brush often hides it, but you can still hear it babbling away and setting the tone for this hike. For some reason, I had the idea this would be a hot, dry, dusty hike, but quite the opposite is true. We did it early in the morning; it was cool, humid, shady, and scenic—pretty much the ingredients for a great hike.

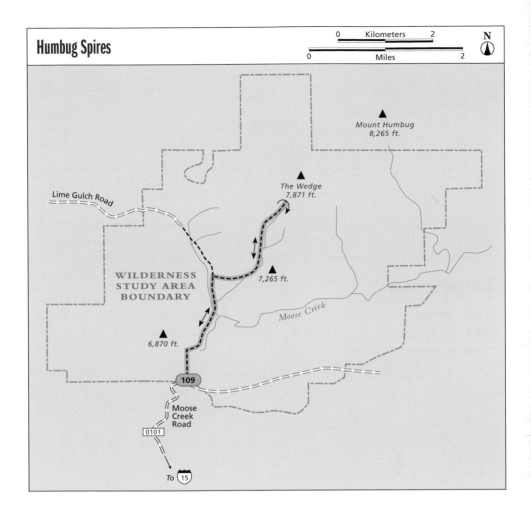

Humbug Spires

0   Kilometers   2

0   Miles   2

N

▲ Mount Humbug
8,265 ft.

▲ The Wedge
7,871 ft.

Lime Gulch Road

WILDERNESS
STUDY AREA
BOUNDARY

▲ 7,265 ft.

Moose Creek

▲ 6,870 ft.

109

Moose
Creek
Road

0101

To 15

At about the 1.5-mile mark, the trail leaves Moose Creek but follows another small, spring-fed stream for most of the route. At this point you start entering the Humbug Spires in all their majesty. Social trails, probably made by rock climbers who revere this area, lead in several directions, so—accompanied by topographic map, compass, and GPS—feel free to abandon the main trail to explore remote sections of the Humbug Spires.

If you stay on the main trail, you gradually climb (about 1,000 feet in 3 miles) through mature, unburned forest until you see an amazing formation called The Wedge protruding above the forest in the distance. You might think other formations might be The Wedge, but when you finally see it, you'll recognize it by its name. The official trail effectively ends at an old prospector's cabin at the base of The Wedge, but social trails continue deeper into the wild area.

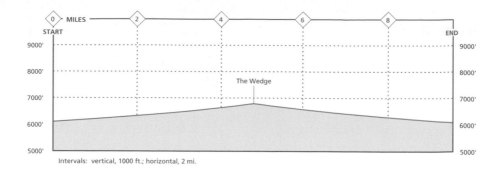

Intervals: vertical, 1000 ft.; horizontal, 2 mi.

If you camp, plan to spend the first half of your second day wandering around among the spires. You'll come home exclaiming about the beauty and uniqueness of the area. (Originally contributed by Herb B. Gloege, re-hiked by the authors.)

Miles and Directions

0.0 Trailhead.

3.0 The Wedge

6.0 Trailhead.

110 Bear Trap Canyon

A long but fairly easy day trip or overnighter along a well-known river with nationally famous trout fishing and a good chance of seeing a rattlesnake

Start: Bear Trap Recreation Area, 30 miles west of Bozeman
Distance: Up to 18.0-mile out-and-back

Difficulty: Easy to moderate, depending on how far you go
Maps: USGS Norris and Bear Trap Creek; BLM 44-Ennis

Finding the trailhead: Drive west from Bozeman on MT 84 for 30 miles (or drive 8.4 miles northeast of Norris). Immediately before you cross the Madison River (east side), watch for an unpaved road turning south and a sign for the Bear Trap Recreation Area. Drive 3.2 miles up this unpaved road to the trailhead. Large parking area; toilet; undeveloped camping along the river before reaching the trailhead. GPS: N45 36.233' / W111 34.317'

The Hike

If you're an angler, you've undoubtedly heard of the Madison River, one of the most highly acclaimed fly-fishing streams in the United States. However, you probably have not heard of a special hiking trail developed by the Bureau of Land Management along the Madison in rugged Bear Trap Canyon. If you fancy large trout, this is a 9-mile slice of heaven, but it's only for fly casters willing to walk—no motorized vehicles, mountain bikes, or horses allowed.

The Bear Trap Canyon Trail winds along the river for the entire 9 miles, gaining a mere 500 feet in elevation. In the past you could leave a vehicle at Old Madison Powerhouse at the end of the hike. For safety reasons, however, this access has been closed, making this an 18-mile trek if you want to hike all of the way. You can hike as little or as much as you like, however, tailoring your own adventure.

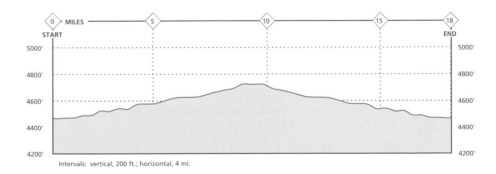

Intervals: vertical, 200 ft.; horizontal, 4 mi.

Watch out for these in Beartrap Canyon. Shutterstock

The trail starts out as a double-wide walkway and gradually becomes a singletrack as the canyon narrows. It gets brushier and rockier as you get closer to the powerhouse.

Since the trail follows the river, there's plenty of water to filter. Bring plenty of insect repellent, as the mosquitoes can be bad, especially in early summer. Many hikers (especially families) choose to stay overnight to take advantage of the early morning and late evening fishing. There are several campsites, but bring your backpacking stove, as firewood is scarce along the narrow canyon. Also, bring a garbage bag, not only for your trash but also to carry out junk left by others. The trail and campsites receive heavy use. The BLM has a three-night limit on backpacking.

Since the canyon remains free of snow most of the year, you can take the hike anytime between April and November. The heaviest use occurs when the fishing is good, especially during the famed salmonfly hatch in mid-June to early July.

The trail wanders through a spectacular canyon with sheer rock cliffs and abundant wildlife. There are lots of rattlesnakes in the area, so be alert and don't forget your snakebite kit.

In 1981 Bear Trap became one of the first BLM areas in the state to be recommended for Wilderness designation. Two years later the area became the first BLM-managed Wilderness and is a unit of the Lee Metcalf Wilderness in the Madison

Bear Trap Canyon

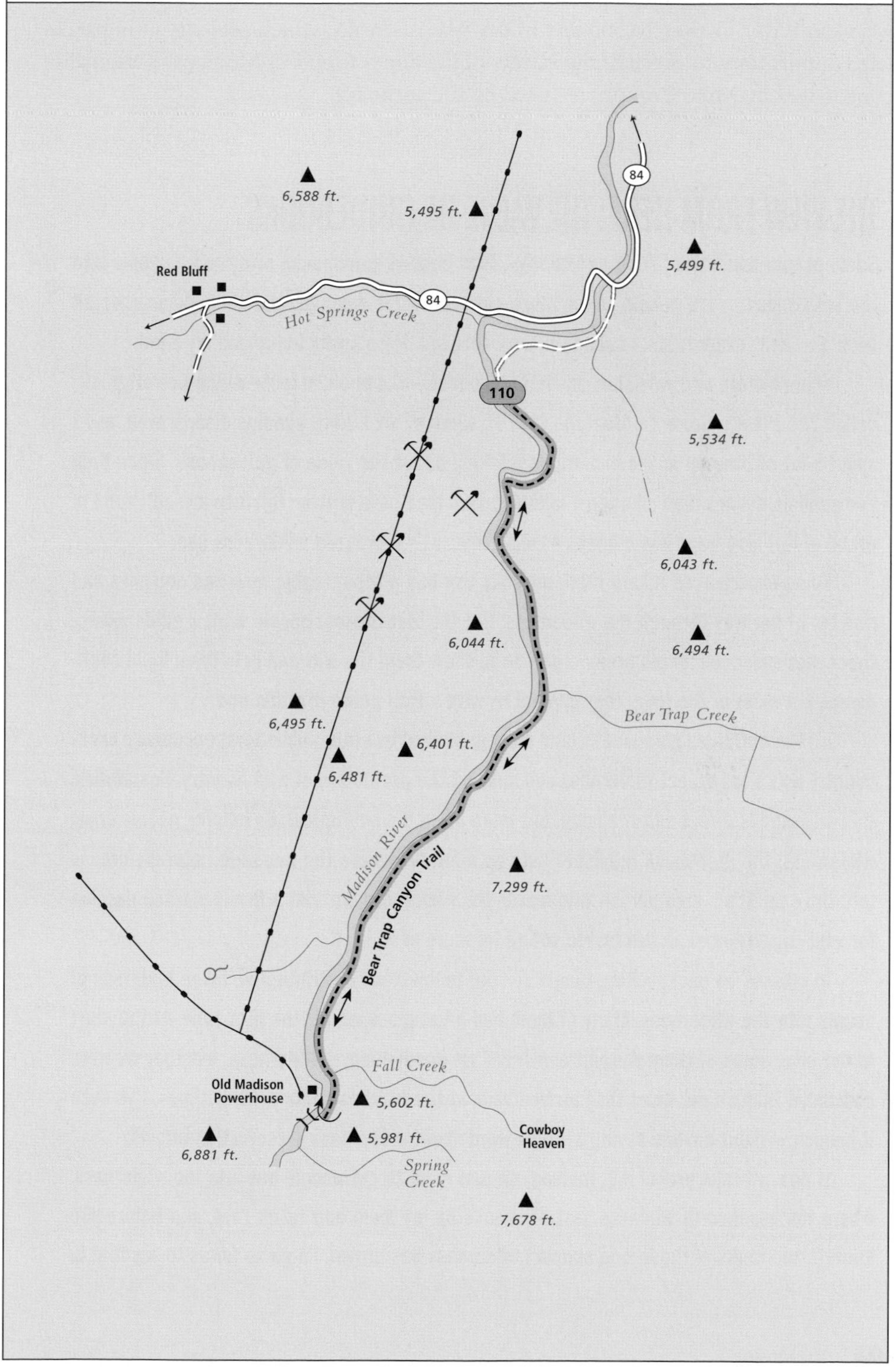

0 Kilometers 2
0 Miles 2

N

6,588 ft.

5,495 ft.

84

5,499 ft.

Red Bluff

Hot Springs Creek

84

110

5,534 ft.

6,043 ft.

6,044 ft.

6,494 ft.

6,495 ft.

Bear Trap Creek

6,401 ft.

6,481 ft.

Madison River

Bear Trap Canyon Trail

7,299 ft.

Fall Creek

Old Madison
Powerhouse

5,602 ft.

6,881 ft.

5,981 ft.

Cowboy
Heaven

Spring
Creek

7,678 ft.

Range. Bear Trap Canyon is connected to the Spanish Peaks by a strip of roadless Forest Service land called Cowboy Heaven. The elevation rises from 4,500 feet along the Madison River to over 10,500 feet in the Spanish Peaks, which presents an unparalleled opportunity to preserve the variety of life zones found in Montana. (Originally contributed by Mike Comola, re-hiked by the authors.)

THE VIEW FROM HERE: THE VALUE OF GUIDEBOOKS

Some people don't like hiking guidebooks. They believe guidebooks bring more people into the wilderness, more people cause more environmental damage, and the wildness we all seek gradually evaporates. I used to believe that too. Here's why I changed my mind.

When I wrote and published my first guidebook—this book, in fact—which was originally called *The Hiker's Guide to Montana* (1979), some of my hiking buddies disapproved, and I spent a lot of time up in the mountains thinking about the value of guidebooks. Since then I've published more than a hundred hiking guides (and have written thirteen myself), and I'm proud of it. I also hope these books have significantly increased wilderness use.

Some experienced hikers think anybody can buy a topographic map and compass and find his or her way through the wilderness. But the fact is most people want a guide. Sometimes inexperienced hikers prefer a person to show them the way and help them build confidence, but most of the time, they can get by with a trail guide like this one.

All FalconGuides guidebooks (and most published by other publishers) encourage backcountry users to respect wilderness and support the protection of wild country. Sometimes, this message is direct editorializing, but more often it's subliminal. By helping people enjoy wilderness, the guidebook publisher sets up a format where the message naturally creeps into the soul. It's a rare person who leaves the wilderness without a firmly planted passion for wild country—and an interest in voting for more of it.

In classes on backpacking taught for the Yellowstone Institute, I've taken hundreds of people into the wilderness. Many of them had a backpack on for the first time. At the start of the hike, some of them weren't convinced we needed more wilderness, but they all were convinced that we did when they arrived back at the trailhead. Many, many times, I've seen it happen without anyone saying a single word about wilderness preservation efforts.

It doesn't take preaching. Instead, we just need to get people out into the wilderness, where the essence of wildness sort of sneaks up on them and takes root, and before you know it, the ranks of those who support wilderness has grown. I'd go so far as to say that in

Miles and Directions

0.0 Bear Trap Recreation Area.

3.5 Bear Trap Creek.

9.0 Powerhouse.

18.0 Bear Trap Recreation Area.

today's political world, it's difficult to get people to support more wilderness if they haven't experienced it for themselves. I recently returned from a long backpacking trip in the Arctic National Wildlife Refuge in Alaska, which is on the menu of the oil industry. I have no doubt that if people could experience what I did on that trip, they would fervently oppose drilling in the refuge.

But what about overcrowding? Yes, it is a problem in many places and probably will eventually be one in many wilderness areas. But the answer to overcrowded, overused wilderness is not limiting use of wilderness and restrictive regulations. The answer is more wilderness. And even if we must endure more restrictions, so be it. At least we—and our children and grandchildren—will always have a wild place to enjoy, even if they can't go there every weekend. The landscape can recover from overcrowding, but if we build roads and houses there, it's gone forever.

That's why we need wilderness guidebooks, and that's why I continue to write and publish them. I believe guidebooks have done as much to build support for wilderness as pro-wilderness organizations have ever done through political and public relations efforts.

And if that isn't enough, here's another reason. All FalconGuides (and most guidebooks from other publishers) include sections on zero-impact ethics. Guidebooks provide the ideal medium for communicating this vital information.

In fifty years of hiking, I've seen dramatic changes in how hikers care for wilderness. I've seen it go from appalling to exceptional. Through the years, I've carried tons of foil and litter out of the wilderness, and I've probably destroyed more fire rings than almost anybody on earth. But nowadays, I can enjoy a weeklong trip without finding a gum wrapper or tissue. Today, almost everybody walks softly in the wilderness. And I believe the information contained in guidebooks has been partly responsible for this positive change.

Having said all that, I hope many thousands of people use this book to enjoy a fun-filled hiking vacation—and then, of course, vote for wilderness protection and encourage others to do the same.

FOR MORE INFORMATION

Kootenai National Forest

Supervisor's Office
31374 US 2
Libby, MT 59923-3022
(406) 293-6211

Cabinet and Trout Creek Ranger Districts
2693 Highway 200
Trout Creek, MT 59874
(406) 827-3533

Fortine and Murphy Lake Ranger Districts
12797 US 93 S
Fortine, MT 59918-0116
(406) 882-4451

Libby and Canoe Gulch Ranger Districts
12557 Highway 37 N
Libby, MT 59923
(406) 293-7773

Rexford and Eureka Ranger Districts
949 US 93 N
Eureka, MT 59917-9550
(406) 296-2536

Three Rivers and Troy Ranger Districts
12858 US 2
Troy, MT 59935-8750
(406) 295-4693

Lolo National Forest

Supervisor's Office
Fort Missoula Building 24
Missoula, MT 59804
(406) 329-3750

There's nothing quite like the last light on a wilderness lake. BILL SCHNEIDER

Missoula Ranger District
Fort Missoula Building 24-A
Missoula, MT 59804
(406) 329-3814

Ninemile Ranger District
20325 Remount Rd.
Huson, MT 59846
(406) 626-5201

Plains/Thompson Falls Ranger District
408 Clayton St.
Plains, MT 59859
(406) 826-3821

Seeley Lake Ranger District
3583 Highway 83
Seeley Lake, MT 59868
(406) 677-2233

Superior Ranger District
209 W. Riverside Ave.
Superior, MT 59872
(406) 822-4233

Bitteroot National Forest

Supervisor's Office
1801 N. First St.
Hamilton, MT 59840-3114
(406) 363-7100

Darby Ranger Station
712 N. Main St.
Darby, MT 59829
(406) 821-3913

Stevensville Ranger Station
88 Main St.
Stevensville, MT 59870
(406) 777-5461

Sula Ranger Station
7338 Highway 93 S
Sula, MT 59871
(406) 821-3201

West Fork Ranger Station
6735 West Fork Rd.
Darby, MT 59829
(406) 821-3269

Beaverhead-Deerlodge National Forest

Supervisor's Office
420 Barrett St.
Dillon, MT 59725-3572
(406) 683-3900

You're never too young to learn to love wilderness. MARNIE SCHNEIDER

Butte Ranger District
1820 Meadowlark Ln.
Butte, MT 59701
(406) 494-2147

Dillon Ranger District
420 Barrett St.
Dillon, MT 59725-3572
(406) 683-3900

Jefferson Ranger District
3 Whitetail Rd.
Whitehall, MT 59759
(406) 287-3223

Madison Ranger Station
5 FR 100
Ennis, MT 59729
(406) 682-4253

Pintler Ranger District
88 10-A Business Loop
Philipsburg, MT 59858
(406) 859-3211

Wisdom Ranger District
PO Box 238
Wisdom, MT 59761
(406) 689-3243

Wise River Ranger District
PO Box 100
Wise River, MT 59762
(406) 832-3178

Flathead National Forest

Forest Supervisor's Office
50 Wolfpack Way
Kalispell, MT 59901
(406) 758-5208

Hungry Horse and Glacier View Ranger Districts
10 Hungry Horse Dr.
Hungry Horse, MT 59919
(406) 387-3800

Spotted Bear Ranger District
PO Box 190310
Hungry Horse, MT 59919
(406) 387-3800 (winter)
(406) 758-5376 (summer)

Swan Lake Ranger District
200 Ranger Station Rd.
Bigfork, MT 59911
(406) 837-7500

Granite Lake in the Gallatin National Forest. BILL SCHNEIDER

Lewis and Clark National Forest

Forest Supervisor's Office
1101 15th St. N
Great Falls, MT 59403
(406) 791-7700

Judith Ranger District
109 Central Ave.
Stanford, MT 59479
(406) 566-2292

Rocky Mountain Ranger District
1102 Main Ave. NW
Choteau, MT 59422
(406) 466-5341

White Sulphur Springs Ranger District
204 W. Folsom St.
White Sulphur Springs, MT 59645
(406) 547-3361

Helena National Forest

Forest Supervisor's Office
2880 Skyway Dr.
Helena, MT 59602
(406) 449-5201

Helena Ranger District
2880 Skyway Dr.
Helena, MT 59602
(406) 449-5490

Lincoln Ranger District
1569 Highway 200
Lincoln, MT 59639
(406) 362-7000

Townsend Ranger District
415 S. Front St.
Townsend, MT 59644
(406) 266-3425

Gallatin National Forest

Forest Supervisor's Office
10E Babcock St.
PO Box 130
Bozeman, MT 59771
(406) 587-6701